Those Who Would Arouse Leviathan

A memoir of an awakening god

By

Jack Heart

Jack Heart

ACKNOWLEDGMENTS

I wish to thank Orage, Phil and especially John. - JH

ISBN: 978-1-7362880-1-6 (Paperback)
ISBN: 978-1-7362880-0-9 (ebook)
Library of Congress Number: 01945443

Cover by John Moffett.

First print edition 2021.

www.jackheart.org
jackheart@jackheart.org

All rights reserved. No part of this publication may be reproduced, distributed, or transmitted in any form or by any means, including photocopying, recording, or other electronic or mechanical methods, without the prior written permission of the publisher, except in the case of brief quotations embodied in critical reviews and certain other noncommercial uses permitted by copyright law. For permission requests, write to the publisher, addressed "Attention: info@jackheart.org,"

Copyright © 2014 Jack Heart

Forward

I wasn't really crazy till I found out I was sane. Back in New York they called me Crazy George. That was about ten years after the facts. It was around the turn of the twenty-first century when they tagged me with that. The Sopranos got a character; George Esposito named after me. I remember when the impetus for that occurred. Somewhere back in the early two thousands an old time "Good-fellow" named Capuluiso, the cousin of slain godfather Paul Castellano, died. I was good friends with his son George so even though I didn't know him with obligatory respect I attended his funeral in Brooklyn and signed the Mass card. The whole cast for the Sopranos were there, which I found tacky from the get-go. When I was invited to be introduced to them, because of that and the fact that I consider them all a walking talking racial slur to Italian Americans, I not so respectfully declined.

I remember watching the Pagans motorcycle gang and Michael Franzese on the investigative discovery channel and wondering why it wasn't me. I know Michael from way back, I know his friends, and I know his friend's friends. And they all know me. Just like I know the Pagans and was intimately acquainted with their legendary "Bubba," a man who would have scared Jesus Christ himself. Michael was the son of Sonny Franzese, a legend in his own right. A lot of these Italian dudes will play off their father's reputations, some will even tell you who their father is before they tell you who they are, but Michael wasn't like that.

It was somewhere around the turn of the twenty-first century and it was a slow night at the Café Royale, one of the New York City areas top three strip clubs at the time, along with Scores and Gallagher's. Michael had come in with his whole crew and that was about it. About a dozen of them were drinking at the bar. I was standing at the door being assaulted by a bevy of scantily clad woman. Who wasn't going to make enough money to cover the sixty-dollar house fee, who wanted to go home early, and who didn't want to work with me because my friends scared the customers away. It was one of those nights where I would be lucky to break a hundred dollars myself. I wanted to go home early.

About a half a dozen cars pull up in the parking lot and the door filled with young Hispanic men dressed to the nines. Knowing Hispanic street gangs were not allowed in the club, outside of course some OG's from the Latin Kings whom we treated like royalty to keep the rest of them out, one guy did all the talking. I told him we couldn't let MS 13 in the club, and he tells me they're not MS 13 but a rival gang at the time named neta neta. I'd heard of them and I wasn't impressed but he takes out a wad of cash that must have been about five thousand dollars. He tells me they got no guns, and they are there to spend this money. A couple of the girls were standing at the door watching this, so I went and talked it over with them. I had to let them in now. If no one made any money it would really be my fault. I told them they could come in and wanded them with the hand-held metal detector for guns, which true to their word they didn't have.

  I told them I didn't want any trouble and the first sign of it they had to leave and sat down at the bar with them. If looks could kill the looks my lone bouncer that night was shooting me from the mezzanine would have killed me on the spot. At first everything went smoothly and they were spending money faster than the barmaids could pour drinks. But they were getting loaded and dancers were trying to roll them. By then I knew what was coming. One of them gets in a heated argument with a dancer and I told them it was time to go. They weren't having it, so I grab two of them one in a headlock in each arm and start dragging them towards the door. My bouncer came flying down from the mezzanine and does the same. The rest of them start pulling out carpet razors. I stupidly didn't check them for knives.

  That was when Michael and his crew got busy. One kid James could throw kicks like Jean-Claude Van Damme. He had a body like him too and was about six foot four. The girls used to love to ogle him. He decks about a half of them with his feet. X-ACTO's were clanging all over the floor; I would pick up about a half dozen later on. When we got them outside Michael pulled his gun and saw to it that they drove off without further incident. Michael was a standup guy, and he didn't need his father. But I had seen and done things a decade before that would have turned his shock of jet-black hair white and everybody knew that about me.

  A year or two later I had to stop working in strip clubs when a drug dealer I was extorting broke my jaw. He cold cocked me when my back was turned, it was the first time I'd been knocked down by a punch in my life, at least when I wasn't falling down drunk anyway. I still got up and fought him to a draw but having my jaw wired for weeks forced me to admit I was getting old. Unfortunately, children grow up; my daughters did. One became a materialistic yuppie, a card carrying Khazarian princess. The other one followed in my ex-wife's family tradition of dedicated service in the strip club industry. When the bodies of strippers and call girls started turning up at Gilgo Beach, one or two snatched from right around the block of a club she worked at, I spent many a sleepless night.

  I had a friend, my best friend since I was eleven years old, probably the most feared assassin to ever stalk the underworld. Some of John's early work with the neighbors in a house in Amityville, the next door over from the one we both grew up in, and I suspect as one of the Son of Sam shooters, is very well known. He's dead now, so I can say it. I hadn't seen him in twenty years and from out of the blue he called my mother's phone early on a December morning in 2011. John left a long drawn out message on the machine about how a friend of mine had just committed suicide and he figured that he better call me and tell me before I heard about it on the news. It turned out to be one of my wholesalers, the biggest landscape supplier on Long Island and a major player in its real estate game. Jimmy Bissett had just purchased a twelve-million-dollar home and nobody could understand why he had just blown his brains all over his car in an east end park, right before a lunch date with his best friend. I couldn't figure out how John had known about it seemingly almost before it happened and why he had bothered calling me after all those years, on my mother's unlisted number. I'm not that sentimental and he of all people knew that.

In the ensuing days it would come out among Long Islands politically connected that the father, who had started the landscape supply business, a man I had known since I was eighteen, was being held by the police. The rumor was bodies or pieces of the bodies connected to Gilgo Beach were being dug up on the father's property. The family owned chunks of Brookhaven and the good part of Riverhead, including its famous aquarium. Newsday, Long Island's rag of a newspaper, had even printed something to the effect that the father was being questioned by police but quickly withdrew it with a disclaimer. The whole thing was covered up.

As noted on the investigative journalism show 48 Hours by the mother of Shannon Gilbert, the murdered call girl whose disappearance led to the discovery of her own and eleven other bodies around the Gilgo Beach area: Long Island is "an evil dirty place." What she said about Oak Beach applies to most of the east end: "It's isolated. It's desolate. It's a rich community. You've got doctors and cops and very very wealthy people who live there. No one's ever going to think that that's a bad dangerous area. But it is."(1) Shortly after making that statement on National TV she would be murdered by her other daughter, Shannon's sister, who is said to be insane but appeared perfectly normal in the show. Her murder effectively ended the media investigation which Shannon's mother had started into the blatant police cover up of her daughters and most likely the eleven other murders.(2)

When I called the number back a couple of days later that John had left on my mother's answering machine I started to tell him what I'd heard about the suicide, which by then was major news on Long Island. He claimed he had never heard of Jimmy Bissett and he didn't know what I was talking about. Having been through that drill before with him, I shut up immediately and never mentioned it again until now. I would find out later that the friend Jimmy Bissett was scheduled to eat lunch with was a friend of both my ex-wife Michelle and my daughter. He was a regular at the club they both worked in, if not an owner as he claimed to them. He has been very good about severing his ties with my family.

   I started thinking after that about how many people had died that John may have just found offensive and how they always seemed to be found shot dead in their own cars as if their assailant had been sitting in the car with them. There were the two guys in the Pagans motorcycle gang, the stripper that got carved up in North Amityville, the wrestler at the Crazy Clown, Sleepy Joe the drug dealer who like the wrestler worked for a mob family he didn't like, the whole thing about the Defeo's and the "Amityville Horror" when he was only fifteen and all the urban legend whispered among the Amityville locals. Even the cops were afraid of this guy. I'd seen it myself when Michelle and I went with him to the funeral of the wrestler, who was Michelle's boss at the time. I saw with my own eyes Suffolk County homicide, legendarily brutal cops with a 95% confession rate, stammering and groveling to John in the middle of the funeral parlor, while the widow tearfully begged him to help them. That was just what I had seen happen around me. He didn't advertise and never ever admitted to anything. I knew how he did it; he had done it to me, right after the two incidents with Michelle that featured me being hauled off in ambulances in the summer of eighty-nine.

   But sometimes in order to maintain ones roots in "the world of the living," as Don Henley calls this, it's necessary to compartmentalize the experiences you've had outside that world and lock them in the back of your brain in a neat little box labeled Do Not Open. That's the difference between those who remain paralyzed for life from PTSD and those who have learned how to forget and are seemingly "normal" after undergoing traumatic events.

   I had already been writing for a couple of years on Open Salon (OS) and people like John Blumenthal, one of the premier authors in America and editor of Playboy Magazine for a score of years, had told me I was good at it. I had been toying with the idea of writing a book but never of opening the little box. I was going to write about the strip club scene circa the turn of the twenty-first century at the Café Royale. There would be sex with stunningly beautiful woman and lots of funny stories about gangsters and celebrities. I figured I could make some money now that I knew how to type, which I had painstakingly taught myself to do on OS while being tutored in the art of writing by some of the best in the business. I had forgotten about the twentieth century. I had to if I wanted to live in the twenty-first. I had lived over twenty years in a world that I knew wasn't real. But as Bob Dylan said in Tangled Up in Blue: "But all the while I was alone the past was close behind…"

By the end of 2011 I drank too much, ate too much and did too many drugs. I had three or four different prescriptions just to get to sleep at night, not to mention a hip that needed replacing and at least a half dozen other old wounds that gave me trouble. I made good money doing landscaping, but after thirty years there was no more future in it for me. Quiet desperation was the best I could hope for. I had forgotten all about the little box. When John dropped back into my life with his customary homicidal greeting I began to remember. I started thinking, why not write the book? Everyone else writes a book. Why not write the book?

I went to go see him at his junk yard over by Bissett's Nursery and run the idea by him. I would never do it without his consent. His first answer was a resounding no, but when I explained to him the circumstances of our impeding old age, he lightened up. Although he still didn't think it was a good idea. I don't think he could get past the half dozen or so unsolved homicides he knew would come up; besides all that old stuff about the Amityville incident. But by the time I left, he had grudgingly consented. In the months that followed he did a complete about face and started calling me up and telling me what else to put in it; including an all-night bar fight at the Coaches Four with the notorious Pagan Vinnie Gamblers old crew. That was his idea. I had already begun with two apocalyptic brawls involving the Pagans. I thought throwing in a quaint little getting to know you fistfight was too much, but he insisted. Now I think I know why. Vinnie and his girlfriend; Gracie the top billed stripper on the circuit in the late eighties, would have prominent parts in the narrative. I didn't know that when I began the book. I had played the Fool through the whole thing. All I knew was I was giving an eyewitness account of the Babylon Working and I only knew that because Preston Nichols, the progenitor of the Montauk Projects, had clued me in years after the fact. But John knew, he had always known, probably since we were eleven years old…

After the Vietnam War, the Pagans —many of them combat veterans of Nam— had taken over Long Island's underworld, if not Long Island itself. The papers were full of their exploits. The police had at one time attempted to interfere with one of their funeral processions which were always over a hundred bikes long and guaranteed to halt traffic three towns away. Two overzealous cops pulled them over resulting in a beating for every cop on the east end of Long Island dumb enough to respond to their call for backup. I don't remember how it turned out legally for the club. I was a kid at the time, but I do remember that the two cops had to be put in the Federal Witness Protection program. Even the Hell's Angels gave the Pagans a wide birth. The Angels had a really happening clubhouse in lower Manhattan and the run of all NYC, but no Angel would dare step foot on Long Island during the seventies and eighties. It was rumored that Mick Jagger refused to use his multimillion-dollar mansion in the Hamptons, because the Pagans considered him a Hell's Angel. They had a clubhouse out in the Hamptons, but their capital buildings and the place from which they ran Long Islands thriving strip club industry were two bars; Gaslight and Bogart's right across the street from Babylon Town Hall. Various Norse occult insignias were emblazoned on the backs of their jackets, yet when I met her at the Pagans flagship clubs I didn't get it. Like I said, the Fool, but John was with me. He had arranged the whole thing, he got it. He was German, and much later when I read Miguel Serrano a few years ago I would find out what I had lived through twenty-five years ago was the religion of the Nazis...

John's been dead a couple of years now. Many of the main characters in the book have died since its completion. The last one was Gracie who died abruptly right after Peter Pan Meets Pyramid Head was published. All have died unexpectedly, some "overdoses," some for no apparent reason at all. They ranged in age from late forties to mid-fifties.

By the end of 2012, the book was done. If you believed in what's in it, and back then I still really didn't, it's the most important thing ever written. Personally, I just thought I'd written a best seller, as I'd intended from the start. Now I wanted the money. I read everything I could find on writing a query. Then I wrote a better one and sent it to all relevant publishers and literary agents in hard copy; along with a synopsis and partial manuscript, as required by individual submission policies. It cost me a few hundred dollars, but I figured after the initial expense I could sit back and sell to the highest bidder. All I got back were the self-addressed stamped envelopes requested in some submission guidelines for responses. They were stuffed with a form letter politely saying that my manuscript wasn't for them. I suspected there was something very wrong, what I'd written was an instant bestseller and I knew it. But when the post office left a note on my door to come down and pick up a piece of certified mail I was certain the worm had turned. What I got back was my partial manuscript, synopsis and query, certified mail at the publisher's expense. This is unheard of in the publishing business. The publisher would go broke in a month. Unwanted manuscripts and submissions are discarded. No one takes money out of their pocket for an unsolicited submission except the party doing the submitting. In the packet was an interoffice memo from the office of literary agent Suzanne Gluck to the legal department of the Morris Agency in reference to my manuscript, stating: "I just wanted to make sure we have a record of receiving it. Please let me know if you have any questions."

I'd used people's real names in the book but by then I knew there were problems with the book that went far deeper than liability. They'd already started working me on the internet. I was being briefed into the fact that there is no reality, and events that occur in waking moments, at least for some, more resemble The Illuminatus! Trilogy than a John Steinbeck novel. The events that we see and all the little pixels euphemistically known as people they all manifest themselves in the world around us. What is implied in the book is all true and I would find out long after writing it, when I was instructed to read master occultist Miguel Serrano by a famous Moto-Cross athlete, that it is the secret religion of the Nazis.

That would explain my relationship to Preston Nichols, the progenitor of the Montauk Project in the nineties. Before Hollywood invented The Matrix, there was the Montauk Project. It is the mother of all conspiracy theories, and the name reversed was even the original title of hit TV show Stranger Things. Among Nichols' circle of friends his story was taken so seriously that John Ford, the president of the Long Island U.F.O. Network and three of his friends were given lengthy prison sentences after being implicated in a 1996 plot to poison then Suffolk County Republican Chairman John Powell, Suffolk Legislator Fred Towle and Brookhaven Conservative Party chief Anthony Gazzola by exposing them to radium. Nichols knew things and he said far more than he wrote. One of the people he said them too was me.

I had been away for a couple of years. When I got back in 1991 I had twin two-year-old girls and a trophy wife who was a part-time mother and a full-time gangster. Money, which had always come in piles I didn't bother counting before I spent, was now hard to come by. I found myself working two jobs just to make ends meet. One of them was at a car wash by the intersection of Hempstead Turnpike and Route 109, probably the most heavily trafficked intersection on Long Island. The car wash was part of a parcel of buildings that included Total Health; a one-stop nutrition and occult store that was the hub of Long Island's thriving New Age movement. From there the most avant-garde Aquarian lectures were coordinated all over the island and New York City. Marty Myers, my mother's on again off again boyfriend until he died a few years ago, owned the whole block. He was the Jewish brains behind the "mafia" gas tax scam Michael Franzese talks about on TV.

Marty and my mother were very close friends with Dr. J. J. Hurtak the man who was covertly calling the shots, on behalf of NASA and the NSA, on the Giza plateau for the last twenty-five years of the twentieth century. I think it was through him I met Richard Hoagland; NASA's pyramids on Mars guy. When I wasn't wrestling dirt bags for a full share of the tips in the car wash I was in the store rubbing elbows with just about everybody who was anybody in the New Age movement. I think it was Deepak Chopra that I once told that he reminded me of the swami from a Frank Zappa song…

With what I'd seen and done I was hardly impressed, especially with Hurtak, his pigeon Hebrew and his "coming beings of pure light." Which he assured them all would be arriving momentarily to take over the planet and guide the human race to a new and greater destiny. They were all attending study classes on his book; The Keys of Enoch. I remember when my mother gave me a copy. I smiled and thanked her; feigned fascination, took it home and threw it in the garbage. It was a very expensive book, but it reminded me too much of my copy of Aleister Crowley's Holy Books which had nearly killed me a few years back. The covers were almost identical. Besides, it was payback for an English translation of the Gospel of Aradia that I had managed to obtain while I was away and sent home. Somehow my mother had got her hands on the extremely rare at the time witches bible while it was at my house and thrown it away; claiming it was evil.

Into this circus of the strange, seemingly, bumbled Preston Nichols. When I saw him in the store I immediately recognized him, having seen him once a few years ago in the strip clubs. Back then, as he was now, Preston was morbidly obese and dressed like he was trying to define the word nerd. Yet the night he walked into the Bogart's club is etched in my brain. He was arguing with a skinny guy about the same age as himself over rock bands. He stopped in front of me and pronounced U2 to the skinny guy like something had been decided. He was like that, what he said, in spite of a comical almost disgusting appearance and an unassuming voice, stuck in people's heads like a traumatic life-defining event. He had them snake charmed in Total Health before he walked out the door on the first day. A week later I was given his book by my mother or Marty and told I just had to read it.

First thing I noticed was Nichols story revolved around Camp Hero where my father had been stationed during the Korean War. My father was 101st Airborne; Screaming Eagles, a golden gloves semi-finalist, captain of crazy Joe Gallo's Brooklyn kiddy gang the Gremlins and about as gung-ho as John Wayne. All his friends from boot camp and he had a lot of them, had seen active combat. I had always wondered why if the army wouldn't parachute him in he hadn't swum to Korea on his own. When I asked him, he was always a little vague, but it turned out he was one of the best shots in the army. Even then if he couldn't center a bullseye at 300 yards "the scope needed adjusting." He would adjust all his friends' scopes for them when he was a hunting guide. So, what he told me, that he had been kept in Montauk to shoot for the 101st in military competitions seemed plausible.

Fleeing the Brooklyn heroin epidemic during the Vietnam War he had moved out to Long Island when I was eleven years old. I didn't like killing animals much, but fish didn't bother me in the least, so he quickly acquired a captain's license to run up to ninety-ton charter boats. I spent a lot of time as a teenager out in Montauk working on those boats. The sound of the wind whistling through outriggers and water lapping boats at dockside late at night is even now vivid in my mind. There had been a very strange incident involving the abandoned base on the fourth of July when I was turning eighteen but other than that I had never noticed anything unusual about Montauk except its physical beauty. Life itself gets no better than trolling for stripers at night in the Tournament of the Full Moon, the inky darkness pierced by the lighthouse above and water roiling with phosphorescence below.

The giant radar dish my father used to help operate was to the west of the lighthouse. My father had always been adamant that there could be no such things as flying saucers because they never picked a single UFO up on that dish during all the flying saucer hullabaloo of the early fifties. But my father had also always insisted that people made stuff up about dreams. He said he had never had a dream in his life…

In one of those funny little coincidences that aren't coincidences, I had met Michelle's grandfather about the same time I met Preston Nichols. Her father, his son, had never been right in the head and was practically a ward of the VA. He had seen something that had to do with UFO's when he was stationed in Iceland in the early sixties. By the time he blew his brains out in the late nineties because they had amputated his legs for medical reasons he swore he could see the mothership waiting for him in the night sky over Patchogue. Michelle's whole family on her father's side was military. The grandfather was the patriarch and he specialized in setting up radio towers, had one in his back yard for his ham radio. I had only gotten to meet him because stomach cancer had gotten the better of him in Southeast Asia and finally he had to come home to die. He thought his son was a blithering idiot, but he couldn't wait to see his great granddaughters. When he got stateside he immediately commissioned me to re-landscape his North Babylon home while he and his wife watched the kids for me. I winced watching three-year old's frolic on his stomach and moved to restrain the girls, but he just wouldn't have it. The man never even showed signs of pain as he sat there dying yet grinning approval at his fourth-generation progeny using his disease-racked body for a trampoline.

    Nichols had been talking a lot about microwaves and oscillating frequency's and my wife had let slip that her grandfather did a lot of top-secret work with radio signals for the military, but he didn't talk to anyone about it. At the time I knew nothing about quantum physics and even less about radio waves and frequencies so the only part of Nichols story that made any sense to me was the part about Einstein and the Philadelphia experiment. We were spending a lot of time over there, so I brought Nichols book over to his house and asked him naively whether any of the stuff in it was possible. He told me to leave the book with him so he could read it. When I saw him a day or two later the book was by his side and I asked him could any of it be true. He said nothing, he didn't have too the way he looked at me and handed me the book back like he had just touched something that he shouldn't have. He never said another word about that book. When he finally died his funeral procession closed Highway 231, the main road North and South for central Long Island and jammed it with hundreds of fire trucks and police cars. I have never seen anything like it; it was as if the president had died.

    I was always looking for explanations for what I'd seen back in eighty-nine. I'd run the gamut from aliens to Magick but had always kept Marty, my mother and Hurtak's Team Tinkerbelle at arm's length. I began paying much closer attention to Preston Nichols. When he came out with his second and third books which put Aleister Crowley at the center of it all, I knew I was being set up. Crowley was at the bottom of my rabbit hole too. Besides when I first met Nichols my ex and I lived in a place called La Bonne Vie in East Patchogue. It was an upscale apartment complex filled with mostly young married people and singles. Some of the wives there had told her they had a neat way of making fifty dollars cash for an hour's time spent listening to music in what is now the Hampton Inn in Brookhaven, about five minutes away from La Bonne Vie. All they had to do is sit in the auditorium and listen to different music as it was played over headphones and press a response button whether they liked it or not. Since she used to go up there with about a half dozen other woman from around our courtyard I never questioned it. She was always back home within an hour or two. One night she was overdue and since I didn't have the kids I took a ride up there. When I got there the auditorium was just clearing out and she was getting up to leave with her friends. Preston Nichols was sitting at the podium in the front; obviously, the man from the Brookhaven Lab giving the tests. I said nothing but when I saw him a few days later he claimed he didn't remember, and that kind of stuff was always happening with him. It was what originally inspired him to write the Montauk Projects. I never trusted him after that. The same thing was always happening to me too...

As far as I knew I had been in prison for two years, but there was something about my memories that just weren't right. When I got home the first thing I did was have sex with my trophy wife. When we finally got done we were both lying in the bed naked and drenched in sweat. She suddenly got up and started rummaging through the closet for something. She came back to the bed holding a lightweight camouflage jacket and threw it at me. I asked her "what's this?" She told me a customer who had been in the gulf war had given it to her because he had been so disgusted with the army. Curious, I examined it and could see it was full of discolored spots on the fabric where the patches and insignias had all been carefully removed as if by razor so as not to rip the jacket. I thought that was a lot of trouble to go through for a guy who was disgusted with something. So, I asked her about it. She just shrugged and said, "I don't know, maybe he didn't want anybody to know who he was, I haven't seen him in a while and I never got his name." She could do that, tell you the most outlandish lie imaginable and then never budge from that lie despite all evidence to the contrary. I didn't bother asking her anything else, I knew that would be futile, but I did keep the jacket, mostly because she hated it and hated it even more when I wore it.

Around the beginning of 1995 we moved into a condo in West Patchogue right off of Waverly Avenue. If things had been a little strange at La Bonne Vie and they were, this place made it look like Mayberry. Two years later, about a week after we moved out of the place, we sat at the bar of Kabuki, Babylon's best Sushi joint at the time. We started talking to this other young couple and when they found out we had just moved out of there they couldn't wait to relate their own experiences when they lived there. The place was three stories, with the attic supposedly off limits. But the couple was constantly disturbed by loud noises coming from their ceiling. They lived on the second floor as we did. When he went up there to investigate he found three kids growing pot up there that threatened him to keep his mouth shut. Deeply disturbed by this encounter they broke their lease and moved out.

I suspect that is an implanted memory. While living there I was attacked by globules of light in my sleep, although ultimately they were driven off. I found out from Preston Nichols that there had been a UFO crash that same night at the nearby park to the east, of course covered up by Brookhaven Lab. I went there and saw the downed trees for myself. My Rottweiler would frequently stand at the top of the stairs and growl down into the empty darkness below. I was just sitting on the couch one day when an ashtray on the cocktail table went flying across the room smashing violently in the next room. No one touched it; no one was even near it. Unmarked black helicopters periodically hovered at no more than a couple of hundred feet over the buildings, sometimes for fifteen minutes at a time. The noise was deafening but nobody ever seemed to notice or care. Guys from the Long Island Lighting Company or LILCO, practically a subsidiary of the Brookhaven Lab and Long Islands notoriously shady power suppliers at the time, prowled the grounds non-stop with hand held devices that looked to be detection meters for underground power leaks. A feeling of general uneasiness permeated the place like something wasn't right in the atmosphere; a feeling in the air itself that usually occurs as the aftermath of a very powerful electric storm.

    The courtyard was dominated by five couples, my wife and I being one of them. We were all in our early thirties and late twenties and there was an attractive woman, the same age as us that lived alone. Her I never talked too even though my kids ran in and out of her condo at will, which was encouraged by her. I was told she had a very important job with the government involving security by the other couples but with me she always kept her distance. We were the only ones with kids, and everybody partied very hard. Nobody even bothered locking their doors and we all walked in and out of each other's condos, most of the time without even knocking. It was like a commune only everybody had money, and nobody ever seemed to work much for it, if at all, including me. Of course, my wife was making a lot of money.

    There were all night keg parties in the courtyard and on sultry summer day's family outings to Cory beach in Blue Point. Preston once told me how he liked to go to Cory beach at night and test out his homemade Orgone energy weapons by shooting down UFO's…. He told me they were commonly seen at night over it, but I never saw one in the daytime which was the only time I went down there. I remember a scorching summer day we spent there that is still vivid in my mind. It was one of those days where the heat actually turned the air hazy and the bayside beach was packed with young married couples accompanied by their rug rats and dragging along anything that would float. As we passed by the concession there was a very strange looking older man by the tables who was talking real loud to no one in particular. You could hear him all the way down by the beach as he gave an historical recount of all

Those Who Would Arouse Leviathan

Americas presidential administrations since Kennedy, finally concluding that HW Bush was the only one that was any good and how HW was the greatest American who ever lived. At the time I agreed with him. I think everybody on that beach did. Couples were making love right in the water with their kids building sand castles on the beach. It was like something right out of Woodstock. Michelle and I waded out to chest deep water and went at it next to a very attractive blond and her husband doing the same thing a few feet away. I think we all climaxed at the same time, but nobody ever spoke a word to anybody but their own spouse. The act itself was almost mechanical but intensely pleasurable.

We had two neighbors named Joe. One was married to a girl who was partially paralyzed from cerebral palsy. He was a military man who had been shot in the head during a training exercise, leaving him with a golf ball sized crater in his skull and a full disability pension. One night we were all sitting around drinking beer, neither military Joe nor his wife did cocaine. We were watching TV as the biggest forest fire Long Island had ever seen engulfed the Pine Barrens around the Brookhaven Lab, threatening to take out the lab itself. Miles upon miles of scrub pine were burning out of control and every fireman available on Long Island & in New York City was already there. The local news stations were asking for volunteers among able-bodied men and we guessed we were their guys since neither one of us had to work. Daybreak we headed east on Sunrise highway both wearing our camouflage jackets. On the 20-mile drive I saw sections of pine bordering the highway suddenly just burst into flames a hundred feet high. The radio was explaining that this was because the pines were so dry that when an ember hit them they were like kindling but I have never seen anything like it before or since.

Somehow and I really don't remember, we ended up in the middle of a very large open field with the woods burning around it. Smoke made it impossible to see much further than a hundred feet. Above us was a blue and white helicopter which I at first took to be a police helicopter but it was too big. It looked to be one of those luxury models. It wasn't moving and just hovered about five hundred feet above us, the backwash from its propeller clearing my field of vision to it. A white Bronco driven by a very hard looking man about the same age as us pulled up from out of the haze and the guy, with an exasperated look on his face, starts talking to me like he knows me. He gestures with his chin up at the helicopter and says, "that's Pataki up there in the helicopter." Then he drove off looking disgusted. George Pataki was the governor of New York at the time. A figure emerged from out of the swirling smoke wearing what looked to be a long flowing kimono like they wore in ancient China. He was oriental and looked to be a hundred years old. He got to about forty or fifty feet away and our eyes met briefly. I could see in his eyes a look of disappointment like I had betrayed him. Then he looked down again. The helicopter was still overhead, and the smoke abruptly lifted so I could see for a couple of hundred yards. At the outer perimeter of my field of vision about half a dozen more figures, also wearing flowing gowns were slowly making their way toward the oriental Methuselah in front of me. The helicopter took off and so did Joe and I making are way back to the car which must have been a mile away. I don't recall us ever having done any work or even how we knew where the car was, but it all seemed normal. On the drive back we never even discussed the oriental people dressed up like they were from the eighteenth century. When I did finally think about it when I got home I told myself a Chinese restaurant must have been caught in the fire. Even though I knew there were no Chinese restaurants in the middle of the Pine Barrens…

    It all came to an abrupt ending in the summer of ninety-six. It was the weekend, and it was my birthday. We were with Joe and his wife Laurie. We had taken their camping trailer out on the beach at Smiths Point. Laurie's Joe was friends with the government security lady. He had the keys to her condo, which he spent a lot of time in when she was away. He was very different from military Joe and although he wasn't a big man; right beneath his warm and friendly veneer there was something menacing about him, much like myself at the time but with Joe there was an undertone of malice. He was the only one who would answer me back. One night in the courtyard round about the second or third keg I was accusing them all of being aliens, haranguing all of them for being strange, Michelle too. None of it was unusual. I didn't keep my mouth shut about what I saw and heard; leastways not to the perpetrators. As if he had been waiting for it Joe says to me "you're always accusing everybody else of being an alien. Haven't you figured it out yet? You're the alien." Then military Joe immediately jumps to my defense denying for everything he's worth that I'm an alien and aggressively admonishing Joe for saying such a thing to me. There were about a dozen other people out there listening to this bizarre exchange intently. Afterward no one said a thing for the rest of the night.

    Joe and Laurie had a three-foot Iguana that had the run of their place and Michelle, and I had a three-foot Savannah Monitor named Gizmo that I had bought as a hatchling before I went away in 1990. Gizmo lived under the couch; usually. Joe and Laurie also shared our appetite for cocaine and sex which both were very much fueling the two-day party at Smiths Point that July weekend. The night on the beach was

Those Who Would Arouse Leviathan

one of the strangest of the many strange nights I have known. But to quote Jim Morrison from Strange Days:

> *"Strange days have found us*
> *And through their strange hours*
> *We linger alone*
> *Bodies confused*
> *Memories misused*
> *As we run from the day*
> *To a strange night of stone"*

    Around sundown a couple of unmarked black helicopters passed over, going from west to east along the surf line, which was about half the length of a football field down from the camper. No sooner had I remarked to Joe about how low they were flying than another appears in the west heading east along the beach no higher than a couple of hundred feet. Joe stepped out from the camper and walked down a ways toward the beach, so his silhouette was clear in the light of the setting sun and started signaling toward it like he was hailing a cab. By then I could see it was a brand-new Apache gunship painted gun medal black with no markings. It veered up the beach straight at us and settled over our camper so close that the sand from its prop wash was stinging my face. All the while Joe was acting like it was a joke. He continued to signal the pilot who if he could roll down the window was by now close enough to spit on him. After about thirty seconds of this the gunship rose to about four hundred feet and took off to the east.

    I don't remember it getting dark, but I was probably in the camper doing something obscene with Michelle. When we came out there was a firework display on the bay side of the island and a lot of boats had come in close on the ocean side to watch. The barrier beach is less than a thousand feet wide at Smiths Point, so they had front row seats, along with us and everybody else who had a camper on the beach. About a quarter mile offshore, all lit up, was a boat that was close to three hundred foot long. It dwarfed the eighty to hundred- and twenty-foot party boats that were out there. The water is no more than twenty to twenty-five feet deep where it was. I have never seen a boat that size that close to a Long Island beach. I could not see what kind of boat it was. But it was there and then it was gone, I didn't see it coming in or going back out. When the display was over, we went inside the camper. When we came back out there was nobody, not a single soul on the beach and the campers around us looked eerily deserted; in fact, they looked like the tombstones in a graveyard. The darkness seemed perceptibly tinged with a blue haze and the beach shimmered with a pale white glow. The only sound was the sound of the surf. All the boats were gone except for the three hundred-footer. It was now a good three miles off the beach where it would stay for the rest of the night. It was the only other sign of life that night except for the light display that was taking place high in the eastern sky over the ocean. There were so many lights coming and going it could only have been a military exercise, but Joe started insisting they were UFO's.

He wrapped himself in a beach blanket to look like an Old Testament prophet. He already had the long staff which he had carved from a piece of bamboo earlier. He climbed to the top of the highest dune, about thirty feet and began a sermon about how if we wanted to leave all we had to do is want them too and they would come and get us. Uncannily, one of the lights broke off as if on cue and started heading towards us. It seemed like it took forever to get to us and as it did the light on it grew brighter and brighter. When it finally got close enough to see it turned out to be a helicopter with a search light. Joe still standing on the sand dune in his Jeremiah outfit solemnly pronounced that one of us didn't want to see it so that's why we all saw it as a helicopter. If everyone had really wanted to see it then it would have remained a UFO, which was really what it was. Everyone laughed uneasily.

There was nobody around, not one of the thousands of people camped out at Smith's Point beach that night was to be seen, not a soul and we knew there weren't going to be any either. Feeling sensual in a very dark kind of way, Michelle and I went over the dunes to explore the bay side of the island, among other things. I don't remember when we took our cloths off, but I remember skinny dipping in the bay. When we came out we sat on a blanket she had set up on a dune. Suddenly, I felt what I thought was a hypodermic needle being pushed into my shoulder. I swatted at it and saw her do the same to her arm. After it happened a couple of more times to each of us I did end up mashing what appeared to be a very large mosquito on my forearm, but she and I were just looking at each other. I lived on the water all my life and I've been bitten by thousands, if not hundreds of thousands of mosquitoes, never like this. We grabbed up our stuff and ran full speed back to the camper not bothering to put our cloths back on. When we broke into the path between the dunes that led to the camper, I stopped short and so did she. Right in front of us was a ditch big enough to bury the camper in. It wouldn't be there in the morning but that night we had to go around it to get back. We both saw it, nearly ran right into it.

Somehow I had pulled my shorts on by the time we found Joe and Laurie detaching their Bronco from the camper. Joe was making a

Those Who Would Arouse Leviathan

joke out of it and saying he wanted to take a ride down to the inlet to see if there were any people left in this world, but he was really going and wanted us to come. Michelle suddenly became panic stricken, insisting that I should go but she had to stay there. As we drove the mile or so east down the deserted surf line to Moriches inlet I rode in the front with Joe while Laurie sat in the back. I can't recall whether the light show in the eastern sky was still going on, but I remember seeing the lights of the inlet reflected on its black water. I don't remember anything after that till daybreak, when I was tending a bonfire in front of the camper and trying to make out what kind of boat the three-hundred-foot enigma still out there was. I never was able to identify that boat, even in light of morning. A few nights later, Michelle and I were bouncing around the bars on Park Avenue in Babylon with my cousin and his fiancé when we first heard the news. TWA Flight 800 out of Kennedy Airport, scheduled to stop in Paris and Rome, had just gone down about a dozen miles off the beach east of Moriches Inlet. Two hundred and thirty people were killed including a bunch of teenage girls who were going to see Paris for their summer vacation. The plane had gone down exactly where we had seen the light show a few nights before.

    I was horrified. I actually moved out of the condo and back into my old room at my mothers. When Michelle came over with the kids I didn't say what I suspected. I just told her I couldn't live with the drug dealing and nonstop partying anymore. She stayed that night and early in the morning there was a knock at the door. When she answered it was the police and they had a warrant for her arrest. My sister came in my room and told me. When I went out to the living room to ask questions; I too was arrested. When they took us to booking in Yaphank in the Southwest corner of Brookhaven Township, there were about eighty people in handcuffs. I knew them all and almost all of them were involved with Long Islands strip club industry. It was one of the biggest narcotics investigations ever in Suffolk County and our phones had been tapped for years. It may have made the front page for the day but just like all the other news on Long Island that summer it would be brushed aside by the Flight 800 investigation in the days that followed. The cops, many of them in black hoods to cover their faces, weren't even talking about their big bust, except for maybe the asses on some of the strippers they now had in handcuffs. All they were talking about was Flight 800. I knew I had nothing to do with their drug ring, in fact I hadn't even known it existed. They didn't even know what they were charging me with, I wasn't worried. They certainly didn't have me on a wiretap, I never sold any coke. Because of what I had seen on the beach days before Flight 800 went down I listened intently to their chatter.

The consensus among the cops was it had been terrorists and it was being covered up to avoid an international incident. Many of them had been the first responders out of Yaphank; the precinct that covers Smiths Point and Moriches Inlet. I heard them saying that a speed boat had come in from offshore and picked up something at Moriches Inlet then made its way back offshore in a hurry and shot the plane down with a hand-held anti-aircraft missile from about seven miles off the beach. They had it all on radar. The speed boat then simply vanished from the radar screen. The cops were speculating that it may have been picked up by a submarine. They had been told not to talk about it by the FBI but a couple of them seemed to be going out of their way to talk about it, in front of me.

Michelle had been charged with two high felonies and she had been bailed out the same day by her father. I was charged with purchasing forty dollars' worth of cocaine on the phone; an E felony only to a cop with a vivid imagination and a district attorney fresh out of law school. It would eventually be plea bargained down to a fifty-dollar fine, but in the meantime nobody bailed me out and I had to spend the weekend in the Riverhead correctional facility. It all got just too weird when they put me on the tier with John Ford; the guy who had tried to poison Suffolk County's political bosses with radium. When I found out who he was, I told him I knew Preston Nichols and he looked like I had just kicked him in the nuts. His whole body sagged, and he turned a "whiter shade of pale" as they say in the song. He said nothing to me for the rest of the weekend. Indeed, he would not come out of his cell after that. I was bailed out Monday morning by my sister.

I was troubled a day later when I attended a lecture above Total Health. I didn't even know who was giving it I just needed to get away. It was a small crowd, maybe two or three dozen people. The classrooms above Total Health didn't fit much more. Preston Nichols just strolling into one as he did that night was pretty much the equivalent of Paul McCartney popping into the local pub. People like Nichols, Hurtak and Hoagland were booked in the lecture hall around the corner where they would lecture to over a hundred people. But nobody had seen him in a while, and everybody wanted to know what he'd been up too so the podium was immediately yielded to him. He was wearing a cast on his arm and began with a yarn about how they had tried to assassinate him with a pulse beam weapon causing him to crash his car. He seamlessly shifted to the fire, all the while looking at me while he was talking about it; saying much of the underground beneath the Brookhaven lab had been taken out in a military action by the United States which had declared war on the rest of the world. After the lecture, I pulled him aside and told him what had happened. It was the first time I ever really talked to him in private. He told me that he had always suspected that I was part of the Montauk Projects and that he thought he knew me, but it was useless to try to remember what you had done on another timeline because the laws of physics made it impossible. After that, we started to talk in earnest.

He started to come around Total Health far more often after that. Above the classrooms on the third floor were offices that we would hang out in. One-night Michelle was up there with us while he and I discussed what really could only be described as a paranormal storm. With Amityville, what I had seen in East Islip twelve years earlier in 1983, what I had taken part in eighty-nine and now flight 800 and the great fire of ninety-six I pretty much had figured out by then that I was in the eye. I asked him, the guy who claimed he was shooting down UFO's off Cory Beach at night, whether he thought there was anything we could do about it. He starts talking about some Orgone machine he had built based on the orgasmic energy concepts of Wilhelm Reich and looking at my wife and I like this is what he had been waiting for. Then he says, "you two can close the portals with it but I will have to be in the room to operate it while you have sex." She suddenly sprang out of her chair at him screaming in his face "you fat fucking pervert!" Then she bolted out the door, down three flights of stairs and out into the middle of traffic where I had to chase her and carry her back to the sidewalk.

Considering whom my wife was it was a completely over the top reaction. She was a second-generation strip club entrepreneur. Her mother had started as a barmaid in a Babylon strip club and ended up owning her own club in Miami. I had seen Michelle manufacture cups of urine in the bathroom and sell them to patrons for a hundred dollars to be greedily consumed at the bar. Her response was particularly inappropriate since she and I had been practicing sexual Magick since the first time we slept together. Michelle was also by her own admission, at the very least, a second-generation Witch, not a Wiccan either.

During that year alone in the Condo we had opened up portals repeatedly, paranormal phenomena so real I had ejaculated blood. Another time the condo shook so bad we had to call up my mother to come get the girls out of there. It went on for hours; like a train shakes a subway platform but without the noise except for the rattling of household items. When my mother got there, we sat on the couch for a while and watched the cat chase weasel like shadows around the room. My mother who had never seen anything like it before saw that neither Michelle nor I was alarmed, other than me wanting my daughters out of there. She kept asking me whether the source of the disturbance was me or the house. I didn't answer her.

Michelle and I had opened a portal one night which illuminated the far side of the darkened room in a deep purple hue. We were both overcome with ecstasy in its presence and I wanted to go into it and see what was on the other side. But Michelle ran in the bathroom, turned on the light and started gauging her arms with a nail file so that I had to physically stop her. Afterward she claimed to remember only the part about opening the purple portal and the intense euphoria emanating from it. But her arms were scarred for weeks.

Many times, I had stopped Michelle from dragging various characters into our bedroom. The fact that Preston Nichols had even brought something like that up to us, of all people, was enough to sell me on the idea of trying it but for reasons that became apparent only much later, years after I had written the book, Michelle wanted no part of it.

John would die suddenly and later in 2016 at Jacksonville the woman I was staying with from the DoD, Ingo Swans successor in the military application of remote viewing, would insinuate that the leader of the Gilgo Beach serial killer cult had collapsed and died in his driveway. She accused him of being a stupid brute but she and her friends were yet to be put in their place and besides, I had often thought the same thing about her. The murdered call girl Shannon Gilbert's Asian driver had taunted her while she was on the phone with police and cowering behind a couch sobbing that they were going to kill her. He asked her if she had ever watched Fear and Loathing in Las Vegas. The movie is based on a book by Hunter Thompson. It references the harvesting of Adrenochrome from dead babies and its use as an agent to contact interdimensional entities. It's all right there on the twenty plus minute long 911 recording, a confession from right out of the mouth of their paid coolie as to just how far elitism has been carried in the twenty-first century. But maybe that's why the police are withholding the recording. Long Island is an evil dirty place. "It's desolate. It's a rich community. You've got doctors and cops and very very wealthy people who live there. No one's ever going to think that it is a bad dangerous area. But it is..."

John had been urging me before he died to self-publish. John Blumenthal told me the same thing. He told me that with the effect the internet has had on the publishing industry that was now the best way to go, you retain all the rights. That's what he had just done with his latest novel Three and a Half Virgins. But I wasn't a famous writer like him, and I had no intention of peddling my own book. I started writing on the internet and my first serious piece; Behind the Bush: Aleister Crowley, Yeats, the Anti-Christ & Armageddon, went viral. By the end of the summer of 2013 assorted gremlins and spooks had begun to tumble of

Those Who Would Arouse Leviathan

every window I opened on the internet. From the things I saw them doing, manipulating Facebook like it was some kind of video game and indeed the internet itself, they were professionals of the highest caliber. As time went on they showed me other things, things calculated to let me know they were masters of this reality and the news was just stuff they invented to give the "Untermensch their daily dose of opium." What is in the book is their bible and they are not about to let their farm animals read it. They have dogged me for seven years now, but I am one of the two main characters in the book and I say there are plenty of Dogs left out in the yard to take it and run with it. As Jim Morrison said "Calling on the Dogs, calling on the Gods…"

The Kingdom / מלכות

I made all this up. This couldn't possibly have really happened. Jack Heart is not even my real name.
"Need I add that, as the book itself demonstrates beyond all doubt, all persons and incidents are purely the figment of a disordered imagination?" – Aleister Crowley, Moonchild, London, 1929.

CHAPTER 1

Bobby's cheeks puckered to his face where nicotine stained buck teeth protruded prominently on a head that leaned forward like a burden his neck couldn't quite tolerate. His pale blue eyes seemed to leer into space as he grinned at me while Marlena momentarily distracted the two young deputy sheriffs. He pressed a spent 5.56 shell casing into my mangled hand and spoke in a hushed tone. "I was up there. There's dried blood all over the place. It looked like a slaughterhouse." He beamed with pride as he recounted violating a police crime scene. "The supers not supposed to let anyone up there, but I told him Marlena was your sister and we had to pick up some things for you." Bobby's black leather jacket was adorned with Nazi insignias, satanic icons, and bullets suspended from chains. On the left shoulder written in white magic marker was the slogan 'DEATH BEFORE DISHONER'. We never told him that he had spelled dishonor wrong and I don't think the rest of his friends could read.

It was hard to imagine anyone following Bobby. But they did. There was about seven or eight of them. Like Bobby they all rode Harleys. A few had been Pagans who defected when the power in the topless bars had shifted into my hands. There was also Tommy a big clean-cut Irish kid who was not a biker. Tommy's passion was hockey. He had been Bobby's best friend since childhood. Tommy was by far the toughest. He had a right hook that could drop a mule.

Bobby was indispensable to me in maintaining order in the clubs. He was close to six feet tall, in his early twenty's, and only about a hundred and forty pounds but he had a pair of solid brass balls. I had once seen him draw a bead with my AR15 on a 'made man' because Bobby felt the guy had been spending too much time talking to Marlena in the clubs. Bobby had every intention of pulling the trigger if I hadn't stopped him. The man was pulling onto Sunrise Highway and he drove off that night never knowing how close he had come to encountering a fusillade of bullets as he left. Bobby's father had spent years in Vietnam working for the CIA and he had taught Bobby all about guns. I had to repress my laughter as I lay there chained and broken in my hospital bed thinking about how Phil and I had labeled Bobby's motorcycle gang the Cretins. The Cretins motorcycle gang was our answer to the Pagans motorcycle gang who had proceeded and been displaced by me as the mob's muscle in Long Islands topless bars. The Pagans had their own president whom they always deferred to with the reverence reserved to that office. Bobby was now the acting president of the Cretins. The president of the Pagans thought he didn't have to take orders from anyone which is why the Pagans fell from power. Bobby was much smarter. He realized that his only reason for existence was to serve me and I took my orders from Richey Capri. Some people, including Richey's father, felt that I also took orders from the Devil. Those that knew me better thought I was the Devil. But those that knew me best knew the Devil was just a friend of mine.

    Bobby whispered and sneered in the same breath. "The supers really scared. I heard you dumped a thirty-round clip in there. I wonder if they found all the bullets. I know they didn't find all the casings." I took the casing in my right hand, the one where the caste extended from my elbow to the middle of my fingers. Only three of the fingers were functional. I awkwardly placed it on the table next to me with the tray of half eaten food and overflowing ashtrays. Bobby looked at me quizzically which made him resemble a lab rat investigating its cage. His sparse blond facial hairs could have passed for whiskers. His whispering became conspiratorial "there was an exorcism up there that's why the supers so scared." I was thinking to myself that this supers always been too friendly for his own good. When he had put Michelle's name on the lease with mine without consulting me, I had contemplated shooting him for a while. I remembered seeing him before I passed out. He had been on the grounds when I jumped out the second story window. But my memories were a confabulation of pain mingled with the lingering aftertaste of cocaine, blood, and sex.

    The cops were enchanted with Marlena's gothic beauty. She was about five foot six and a couple of years older than Bobby. Her raven colored hair was almost as long as Michelle's, flowing like a river of darkness to her ample ass. Her milk white skin was smooth and unblemished like a child's. Brick red lipstick accentuated a pearl white smile cultivated by some North Shore dentist, a product of her affluent upbringing. Her eyes were blackened with makeup to match her tight black sweater that fell to the same length as her hair over black tights that were tucked in at the knees to black Italian leather riding boots.

Bobby continued in his conspiring whisper. "The people that own the apartment are Chinese or some shit. The neighbors told me they had these three Buddhist monks up there all decked out in feathers and robes waving magic wands." I interrupted him "In Moonchild Crowley said the way of the Tao is the most potent form of Magick." He looked at me again with his quizzical lab rat face "what were you doing up there? Marlena always said Michelle and you had charged the entire apartment with some kind of sex energy. She got as horny as an ally cat in heat just sitting around that place." I answered him a bit curtly "Why Bobby? Do you know anything about Crowley besides what people like Janet and I told you when we were drunk?" I suppressed a laugh as I imagined trying to explain Chaldean, Gematria, and Temurah to a guy who adorned himself with the slogan death before dishoner. It's too bad Janet wasn't around but Michelle had long since run her off. She was a dancer that had been part of my entourage before Michelle became its queen. Janet was a dedicated Wiccan and she had good reason to be afraid of Michelle.

My mind wandered as Bobby continued. I was thinking of all the nights I had slept with Janet on her big waterbed. I had never had sex with her. She was one of the smartest girls I have ever met. She understood the roots of what we did went back since the days before Egypt and she was well versed in both the Golden Bough and the Golden Dawn. Janet once wanted to do a ritual 'sky clad', which is naked, with me and some of her coven. I declined knowing it would not end in copulation because Janet was convinced, she was not allowed to have sex with me. I never like to start what I don't finish so I had to keep my clothes on, especially in bed, because Janet didn't. She had a lithe muscular body with perfectly proportioned breasts and ass. Her thin platinum blond hair was cut in a Dutch boy haircut that accentuated her androgynous erotic appearance. This was the late eighties when dancers were still paid a minimum of seventeen dollars an hour plus tips. The agency had to be careful who they sent to certain clubs. If the girl was not of the highest quality her car might get burned in the parking lot or the agent could get hassled when he came to get his envelope. At least that was before Phil beat the agent; Savage, almost to death in front of Richey's club in Nassau County. Now we were the agency for both Nassau and Suffolk Counties.

Janet and I would spend days scouring lower Manhattan for books and ingredients for incense and potions. Sometimes we would take Bobby and Marlena in tow, sometimes girls from her coven. Janet was able to make all kinds of concoctions from Kava Kava tea on up to stuff that would produce a mildly hallucinogenic state but nothing close to the effects of an incense Michelle had made after she had accompanied Janet and I for the first time to lower Manhattan. Michelle had a long list that she had gotten from her mother. In order to fill it to her satisfaction she made us take her to every place we knew of in the city and showed us some we didn't know. That night I did not go home with Janet. I went home with Michelle and had a different kind of sex, so different that once I had it I could never go back to what most men think is sex. There is reproductive sex between biological organisms which every animal and most humans live their life in pursuit of. Then there is intercourse with the unseen, opening one's self up to the darkest corridors of erotica. That was the last time I ever saw Janet. She stopped dancing at the clubs after that night.

Bobby straightened his posture and started talking in his customarily mocking tone. "One of your bullets went through a water pipe. The whole first floor was flooded out and had to be evacuated, so much for their leases." Bobby hated everything that was not wearing either leather or expensive perfume. "What were you shooting at? I hear you just missed that cunt downstairs husband by an inch." "Yea" I said. "Bartle's thinks he is going to get attempted murder on that one." "Did you fuck her?" He asked. He was probably referring to her impromptu topless sunbathing sessions where we had watched her from my kitchen window casually sprawled out on her belly on a lawn chair. Her top was off and her legs spread invitingly with her bikini bottom tight against her glistening crotch. "No" I said. "If I fucked that bitch, I would have to package it as payback for the super putting Michelle's name on the lease. Michelle would find out. She has ways of finding things out that you don't even want to know about Bobby. Besides I don't fuck with married woman. See? That turned out to be a really good policy. If I was having sex with her Bartle would actually have a case."

I grimaced in pain. There is no pain like the throbbing of shattered bone mingled with the acute burning sensation of butchered ligaments. I had smashed the window of my apartment with the still smoking AR15 and thrown it to the ground outside. When I thought about it I decided to get as far away from the scene as possible. The cops were going to come into that apartment and up those stairs shooting regardless of whether they found the gun outside or not. I pulled on a pair of jeans and started to go down the darkened stairway, but I saw movement in the shadows and Michelle was taunting me about it waiting on the stairs for me. I went to the broken window and jumped from the second floor. I landed on my feet and felt my right ankle pop. Something else gave in the bottom of my left foot. But I knew if I wanted to live I had to get as far away from the gun as possible. Since I was wearing only jeans they might not shoot if they figured I wasn't armed.

    I started to run and with each step my right ankle became looser till it was flopping around like an untied sneaker. I ran into the super at the next building. He was standing there as if nothing had happened. He ushered me into an unfurnished apartment in back of him and told me to stay in there. When I checked the door, I found he had locked it somehow from the outside. Or at least I thought he had. The whole thing smelled like some kind of set up. All the shades were drawn, and he had been casually standing outside talking to a madman who just opened up with an assault rifle. I took a running dive through the window. I was certain that apartment would be my coffin if I waited for the cops to come through the door. I ran for the six-foot cyclone fence at the end of the property and remember almost clearing it with one leap in spite of my ankle which was now wobbling like a loose shower slipper every time I came down on it. I remember the top of the fence spearing a hole through my ass as I landed on it. Then everything went black. I woke up in the emergency room.

    The glass had severed four or five arteries on my arms and torso and many of the ligaments that attach the fingers to the forearm on both arms. My right ankle was so badly compounded that the doctors told me I would never walk again without a cane. The arch in my left foot was also cracked and the doctors told me a cracked arch never heals completely. I had castes on all four of my limbs and over each of the castes was a manacle that was chained to the bed. Apparently, law enforcement still considered me to be a very dangerous man, at least what was left of me. I wondered if I really had to, could I get up out of the bed. Pain is an insidious and creeping thing. It never confronts the warrior during the heat of battle. Pain waits silently in ambush for the quiet moments after. It was now washing over me like some great wave rising up out of a disturbed sea. Every four hours the nurses administered morphine which would envelope me in a warm womb that I was methodically torn from with each tick of the clock. Always before it became intolerable another syringe bearing angel in white appeared to begin the cycle all over again.

My orthopedic surgeon: Dr. Arvan, was a contrite and sadistic yuppie who considered it his civic obligation to keep me in as much pain as possible. I had paid out of my own pocket to have Dr. Levine, who was my family doctor and also a resident at Good Samaritan Hospital where I was being held, increase my dosage of morphine to twice what Arvan had been giving me. It was almost noon and Arvan was due through the door at any moment now fresh from 'an early nine.' He would arrive with a flourish of self-importance like the leading act in a night club. He would be wearing some outlandish golfing outfit like his pale-yellow pants, black and red checkered sweater vest, topped with a matching yellow and black checkered cap. He would talk to me with his customary disapproving distain. I looked at Bobby who was always good for cold cocking whomever I told him to with a pair of brass knuckles he kept in the right pocket of his black leather Cretins jacket. "Hey Bobby" I whispered "you got your brass knuckles?" I imagined Bobby knocking Arvan out, right from underneath his checkered cap. The mental image made me smile and grimace at the same time.

Bobby sniffled like a rat trying to locate cheese. "What?" "Never mind" I answered. "Didn't your daddy ever tell you to never fully load a thirty-round clip for any kind of an M 16. That's why they used twenty round straight clips in Vietnam. Anything more than twenty-eight rounds and you're pretty much guaranteed to jam the fucking thing on the first shot. I always load twenty-seven. If you can't do the job with that just slap in another one. It ain't like you got to fuck with it by wedging the clips forward like on an AK." "AK's can take a full forty round banana clip" he answered smugly. "Yea" I said "and they are strictly spray and pray for anything out further than a hundred yards. They're never going to find all those bullets anyway. That clip was loaded with hollow points. They shattered on impact. Where did all that blood come from? I don't remember bleeding till I started going through the windows. In fact, Michelle was acting like she was hit, and I knew she wasn't because there was no blood." He gave me another quizzical rat look and said "she was covered with blood when she was interviewed on TV. Margret said she can't understand how anybody could look so hot all covered with blood." Margret was Richey Capri's bisexual lover who managed the Rainforest in Nassau County. She had been seduced by Michelle at first sight, most people were.

Marlena had the deputy's engrossed in conversation. For once it was really like Miami Vice for those guys. Bobby looked over disapprovingly. Bobby was chronically jealous. He had reason to be. On the exterior Marlena was far too much woman for him. That is if you did not know that she was bipolar and given to manic depression and violent outbursts when deprived of her Klonopin, which she sometimes was when I overindulged with her prescription. I watched as the cop's eyes took turns wandering from her face to her breasts that strained tauntingly against her sweater when she laughed. Bobby also noticed and had assumed his familiar posture with his hands on his hips glowering from Marlena to the cops who were seated in chairs at the foot of my bed. The rest of the girls at the clubs had given Bobby the nickname 'watchdog' and Marlena could no longer dance in the clubs anymore. She had stopped anyway a couple of days before I had assigned her to Bobby. Even her waitressing had gotten ridiculous with him cold cocking a customer a night with those brass knuckles. I had to tell him to stay out of the clubs when she was working. It was better that way for both of them. Without him around she had no problems clearing five hundred dollars a night. With the Pagans gone everybody in the strip club business was making money. Back then I always made sure my people got the lions share even if it sometimes meant pointing a loaded forty-four magnum at Richey.

I wasn't telling Bobby anything. I haven't told anyone anything until now. In all truth on that Labor Day morning of 1989 Michelle and I were just doing the same thing we had always been doing. We have been here now for over a hundred years. You were just too busy paying homage to us by killing each other to see us. In 1987 shortly after my twenty-eighth birthday a group named Guns & Roses revived a sound that had been dormant for at least a decade. The sound had originally been given to Robert Johnson half a century ago and passed around amongst musicians till it reached its widest distribution toward the end of the Vietnam War. Guns and Roses came from out of nowhere and ended up going nowhere. But for a few years they would be "more popular than Jesus." The album they released was titled Appetite for Destruction. Immediately after its release that album would provide a soundtrack for the next two years of my life. "Welcome to the Jungle."

CHAPTER 2

Like waves on a beach we can only recede. That's what it means to be born, to be cut, and to bleed. It wasn't always like that, or maybe it was. My earliest memories were of being surrounded by machinery and a constant deep mechanical humming rose and fell like the breath of fitful sleep. Maybe it was the 'mother ship' or the 'Montauk underground' like Preston Nichols author of the Montauk Project would later claim but I am inclined to believe it was the post-natal care room at Maimonides Medical Center in Brooklyn where I was born to a well to do family. I grew up in Brooklyn. My father had a Fur business on Twenty-Seventh Street and Seventh Avenue in Manhattan. The city bought him and his partners out when they built the Fashion Institute of Technology.

From grades one to five I attended the finest Catholic school in NYC. Every couple of weeks the nuns wrote the names of the thirty or so kids in my class on a scrap of paper. They would put them in a jar and draw one. That child got a statue of Jesus, Mary, Joseph, or one of the archangels. I would always win. It got so I was no longer allowed to participate in most of the drawings because it was a foregone conclusion that I would win. My room looked like a miniature cathedral with no more room for statuary. Later I would break all the statues in a hormone fueled fit of rage. But that wasn't till after I was 'baptized' and I'm getting to that.

The nuns started looking at me very strangely. They used to rub me for luck. I was told that I should pray for an end to human suffering and the Biafran and Vietnam wars. Every night I did so dutifully. I was such an ardent believer that I wanted to do battle for the Lord against his enemy's so I demanded an audience with Satan so that I could confront him. I guess I never really believed he would show up because when he did, right there in my mother's kitchen, I was horrified. It was for a fleeting second, but it was very real. He did not have horns and a pitchfork like I expected. He was a hulking humanoid figure that looked like he was made out of glowing molten rock.

Like most little kids I loved baseball. My team was the Mets, at the time the worst team that ever played the game. Around the end of the sixties I started changing my praying habits. The Vietnam and Biafran Wars were still raging and now there was also starvation in Bangladesh, but an end to those calamities is not what I wanted. What I really wanted was for the Mets to win the World Series. I became insistent with God. Children can be so petulant. The year was 1969. That year the Mets suddenly went from being the worst team that ever played the game to winning the World Series. It is still considered the most inexplicable event that ever occurred in sports and the sixty-nine Mets are known to this day as the Miracle Mets.

My life began to change after that. Once when I was learning to ride a bicycle an unseen force seemed to seize control and propel the bike a half a block down the sidewalk of East Second Street with me frozen onto it and unable to jump off. Just as the bike hit the curb to Fort Hamilton Parkway something seemed to snatch me off. I landed unscathed on the sidewalk and the bicycle crossed two lanes on the parkway between traffic and suddenly made a U turn and headed right back to me jumping the curve where it fell gently right next to me.

I began to dread going to bed. There was scratching from inside my pillow, taping on the walls, and I would awake at night to see apparitions at the foot of my bed. One time there was a dwarf hooded in a long dark cloak dancing what I now know is called widdershins. I was frozen with terror and it lasted for quite some time till I summoned the nerve to leap from the bed and dash past it and into my parent's room. I refused to sleep in that room for some time after that and would sneak into my sister's bed in the next room as soon as my parents were asleep.

My Weimaraner, who normally followed me everywhere, had to be dragged into my room by my father with his claws digging into the ground. He would spend the night trying to sneak out whenever he thought I was asleep. He was never there when I woke up. One morning I awoke to find myself on the floor with a broken collar bone. I was in a caste for months. On another night my youngest sister was crying out incessantly for permission from my parents to get up and get a glass of water. She heard a man's voice reply from my room telling her to get up and get her glass of water.

It all ended when I dreamed of a dark and menacing whirlwind. It was a tornado about the size of a man in the confines of my parent's room. I knew instinctually, even in my dream, that it was the swirling heart of evil itself. It was sucking up everything in the room and everything it consumed became a part of it. When I was the only thing left in the room its malevolence focused on me. I could feel it irresistibly pulling me towards it. Then I woke up. I was in a state of panic. I went downstairs to tell my mother. She was in the kitchen preparing breakfast. As I forced myself to speak there was a sudden pounding that seemed to echo through the entire house. I think I actually screamed that it was coming for me, but it turned out to be my little sister tumbling down the stairs. She had overheard me from upstairs and wanted to know who or what it was that had told her to get that glass of water. The haunting of my childhood ceased after that. In fact I completely forgot about it, or at least I pushed it to the back of my mind where it could be dismissed as the overactive imagination of a child.

My teenage years were filled with marijuana, fishing, pursuing girls, and fitful sleep, but there were aberrations. My parents had moved the family to Amity Harbor, Long island, in the summer of 1970. I met John in the sixth grade. I had made friends with some of the older kids in the neighborhood who also attended Catholic school at St Martin's in Amityville, but I had no friends in my own grade. Johnny Vento, one of my older friends, noticed I was despondent and moping around the school yard shortly after school began. He decided I needed a friend and took me by the arm and dragged me around the corner of the schoolyard. It was there I first formally met John. He was pummeling our sixth-grade classmate Howie Sullivan, whom I had already found out was a wiseass, like a drunk beats his wife. It was a classic schoolyard brawl. The entire sixth, seventh, and eighth grade, whose lunch period it was, gathered in a circle around them. Sullivan kept getting up and John kept knocking him down with round house rights to the jaw. Sullivan finally got tired of letting John use his face for a punching bag and gave up. Vento dragged me over to John who was now being treated by the rest of the kids as the triumphant villain in a WWF wrestling extravaganza. Vento explained to John above the din of the rest the kids screaming for John's head, that I needed a friend and he didn't have any. We ended up spending just about every day of the next five years together till we were both thrown out of St John's High school when the auditorium burned down right before the Easter play.

I was 'baptized' in the summer of my twelfth birthday. All of our spare time was spent on the Great South Bay in boats in the summer and out on the ice in the winter. It was a week or so before July thirteenth, my birthday. John and I had made one of our numerous exploratory forays to the islands between Fire Island and the mainland. They were choked with six-foot-tall razor-sharp marsh grass but the larger island had a football field sized circular clearing in the center. I was fascinated with herpetology at the time and in the clearing, I found what I now know was an Indian Star Tortoise. The tortoise, which has spectacular yellow sunbursts covering its carapace, is native only to the semi-arid grasslands of India. I didn't know then what it was except that it was a tortoise and that it wasn't a box turtle which I had been finding since I was five years old in Brooklyn. I was stunned to discover a tortoise on the salty marshlands of the bay where the only reptilian fauna were the

Those Who Would Arouse Leviathan

Diamondback terrapins that were all over the place. Delighted with my find John and I raced back to the boat to bring it home for identification and observation in a terrarium.

The boat was anchored about a hundred feet out on the flats which were about knee to waste deep depending on the tide. I started wading towards it, tortoise in hand, and I stepped in a hole or at least what I first thought was a hole. I didn't panic. I didn't want to let go of the tortoise. I felt for the ledge, but it was as if the bay had come inland to engulf me. I was suddenly in deep water, deep water all around me. I started inhaling seawater as I kept going under. My feet frantically sought the ledge I had dropped from. I knew those flats like the back of my hand from crabbing them and I knew there was no deep-water channel running through them. Even though I knew how to swim I panicked. John swam over and tried to help me, but I had lost it. I started trying to climb on top of him, flaying away at him. I remember him telling me he would swim for the boat which had by now somehow broken from its mooring and seemed to be skimming along the surface into the deep water of the far away State Channel. Every time I went down, I would come back up fighting for my life. I remember the shimmering sun on the other side of the translucent surface. It seemed to be pulling me back up through depths that were impossible for the bay let alone the shallow flats between the islands. Each time I went under I would claw my way back through the unnaturally clear water to the life-giving air. I went down over and over again, and I knew I was going to die but I didn't. My foot finally found the bottom where my head was above water and John got back with a life preserver. It seemed like I had gone down a hundred times and when he dragged me to the shore and pumped my chest, I just kept vomiting an endless flood of red tinged water. I thought one of my lungs had exploded.

When we got back to my house my parents rushed me to the hospital where I checked out no worse for the wear and tear. The doctor couldn't explain why the water I had vomited up at the islands was red and said it had to have been my imagination. Later I was getting the prescribed bed rest and John came to visit me. He brought me a tape and said "listen to this. The lead singer died today. You're really gonna like this." The album was The Doors, Soft Parade. When I started listening to the cassette, I was immediately struck by the singers haunting deep baritone voice that seemed so familiar to me. We had been studying poetry in school and I had already read much of Walt Whitman, along with some of Longfellow, Emerson, and Sandberg. I was hardly impressed but when I listened to the words of Soft Parade, I knew I was listening to genius of supernatural proportions. They say a picture paints a thousand words, but the words of the singer Jim Morrison painted a thousand pictures. When I got to the song Wishful Sinful, I was dumbfounded. He seemed to be describing what had just happened to me. He sung about seeing the sun shining deep beneath the water, about loving to hear the wind cry but being unable to escape the blue magical rising of the sea. He seemed to be singing to some other entity, an entity that was right back where he came from, an entity that he loved and longed to join by some mysterious rites of the water. Later I found out Morrison believed, or at least he said, he was possessed by the spirit of a Dine Shaman who was killed in a traffic accident he had witnessed when he was a young boy. The Dine speaking people in America's Southwest believe a tortoise can be used to transport a soul.

I would also find out later that Morison was found dead in the bathtub of his hotel room in France supposedly of a heroin overdose, but he did not take heroin. The bath was filled with strange reddish tinged water and nobody that knew him, outside of his girlfriend Pamela, saw the body to identify it. His manager went to Europe but never actually looked in the closed coffin to make sure Morrison was in it.

Morrison had another song on another album, Waiting for The Sun. That song was titled Yes, The River Knows. In the song Morrison says he's going but he needs a little time before keeping his promise to drown himself in mystic heated wine. He talks about breathing under the water of a river that flows endlessly through time.

CHAPTER 3

John lived the next door over from the "Amityville Horror House" on Ocean Avenue. We attended Catholic school with the Defeo's, the people who were slaughtered there. Allison was in the grade below us and Dawn the grade ahead. My earliest recollections of Butchy were of him taking pot shots from the boathouse at us with his twenty-two rifle as we motored Johns boat up the canal. The bullets would plink right into the water as he shot all around the boat we were in. Butchy was what everyone called Ronald Defeo the man convicted of murdering his whole family. John would turn the boat around and rush home. From his room in the attic which overlooked Defeo's boathouse he would hastily empty his own twenty-two rifle into the boathouse in retaliation. It wasn't that they really hated each other. Sometimes they would even hang out together. They shared a mutual friend named Bobby Kelsky. I had been in the Defeo house on more than one occasion myself with John. I remember one time being over there. We couldn't have been out of St. Martins Grade School yet. In the kitchen Mrs. Defeo was heating up TV dinners for the two little boys and Allison whom John was sweet on. The mother asked us if we wanted a TV dinner.

This was all just good clean fun on Ocean Avenue. When we were thirteen years old we would tie cinder blocks to John's mother's terrier and throw them in the water while the dog frantically clawed on the algae covered boat slip with every muscle in its body pulled taught as a bow string. When we got tired of that we would fill balloons with an unlit acetylene torch and chase the dog around the property igniting the balloons with firecrackers. Somehow that dog died of old age, a condition Johns later dogs would never see.

One time we convinced Billy Smith to come out on the boat with us to the islands. Billy Smith was the toughest kid in Amityville in our age group, but he was a little slow in the head. John said we were going to shoot birds with a high-powered CO2 rifle he had just bought but when we got to the islands, he told Smith to run shooting him point blank in the chest for emphasis. We spent the rest of the day happily hunting Smith in the tall grass. When he finally got a hold of John, he beat the hell out of him. But Smith had to later be taken to the hospital to have four pellets that were imbedded in his flesh removed.

John was almost fifteen and I was fourteen when the Defeo family was massacred. We were in the ninth grade of Saint John's High School in West Islip. John stopped attending school for a while and the rumor was that he had come under police suspicion for giving an erroneous statement that he heard the dog barking late on the night of the killings. None of the other neighbors had heard any barking dogs. John was never implicated, and he never talked about it but afterward following High School he was attacked by an acid crazed hippie that was a friend of Butchy. The guy bit a hole in Johns hand while screaming that John was responsible for those murders and that he was the living incarnation of Satan.

Catholic school came to an end the same year of the murders when the school auditorium burned down. Somebody smoking cigarettes underneath the stage had accidentally ignited a fire. When the custodians attempted to put the fire out they found all of the fire extinguishers were empty because we had used them up horsing around. All of the kids that hung out underneath the stage were asked not to come back the following year. I, along with my friend Kenny from the tenth grade, went to Copiague High School. John went to Amityville HS. We didn't see each other much for the next three years but we hooked up again right after graduation. Back then everyone was dealing drugs.

Kenny by then had become a major Quaalude dealer sometimes bringing thirty thousand at a time into Queens. I was attending Community College only because I was making good money there selling Kenny's Quaaludes. John called me one day and one thing led to another and we were once again best friends. Until then I thought I was the strongest man alive, at least in the arms. John and I had a curling contest almost immediately, two fifty-pound Dan Laurie plates on a straight bar. I got about twenty strict and John kept going to thirty-two with his left arm lagging behind his right. I became furious but everybody there said he had kept his back straight. We put two more fifty-pound plates on the bar. I got it up three times, jerking it. John proceeded to do it ten times; doing four plates in the same fashion he had done two plates. As Kenny and I drove home I was still seething and remarked to him "I can't believe he out curled me, nobody's ever even come close to doing that before. He was cheating. His left arm was dragging way behind." Kenny answered "yea but his back was straight you were jerking them. What do you want he has you by forty pounds and four inch's?"

I thought about it. John had developed into two hundred and twenty pounds of six-foot four wasp waist muscle. He looked like a Teutonic war God with his very German face and long brown hair pulled back into a ponytail. If you grabbed him it was like seizing hold of one of the old hulking steel outboard engines, he wrestled all day at the makeshift repair shop he had set up at his grandfather's house. He had shoulders like John Wayne with arms like the trunks of midsized trees. His biceps weren't defined like my own, but they were bigger, noticeably bigger, and mine were seventeen inch's when I wasn't lifting.

CHAPTER 4

In the period right after high school we would have parties at Johns parent's home. His mother and father would frequently be gone for a week at a time on cruises to Watch Hill in their boat. It was at these party's that I became aware that evil is a conscious presence with its own agenda, a disembodied intelligence separate from the incarnate beings through which it manifests itself. To let it into you, to surrender to it with complete abandon, to let it take you where it will, is a primordial pleasure that nothing in this world has to offer. I remember floating through a drug induced haze and feeling a smug sensation of approval as people and events streamed passed me in a blasphemous parade. Someone was violently fucking Johns golden haired little sister's friend in the dingy on the back lawn. Her shrieking was drowned out by Frank Zappa singing: It Can't Happen Here, through no less than a dozen oversized speakers. I didn't understand exactly what it all meant back then but it all seemed so right. The song and the music were a disjointed and seemingly confused acid trip, synchronized with the hallucinogens I had ingested. Zappa kept repeating "I remember tutu" and incoherently describing the quintessential suburban family that has no worries in the world because "it can't happen here." Zappa shouts out to Kansas, Minnesota, and Washington DC, derisively assuring them that it can't happen here, not in the suburbs; "But." Jim was shirtless, flexing his huge muscles in the full-length mirror propped up on the floor of the weight room that John had set up in the adjacent attic. He was bellowing like an animal with a weird light illuminating his Nazi blue eyes. Frank Zappa continued ranting mockingly from the stereo accompanied by John now singing along as he laughed hysterically. John was still laughing when he looked at me with an eerie red light illuminating his face as he sang along with Zappa. "Plastic folks, you know / It won't happen here / You're safe, mama (No no no) / You're safe, baby / (No no no) / You just cook a tv dinner (No no no) / And you make it / Bop bop bop (No no no) / Oh, we're gonna get a tv dinner and cook it up (No no no no no no no!) / Oh, get a tv dinner and cook it up / Cook it up / Oh, and it won't happen here / Who could imagine / That they would freak out in the suburbs! (No no no no no no no no no no / Man you guys are really safe / Everything's cool)." John was hysterical now gesturing next door as he mimed "They had a swimming pool."

    Eric and I were in John's room doing shots while Cathy, John's golden haired little sister, and her friends desperately entertained us with their teenage innocence hanging in the balance. John brandishing a very large knife was no longer singing. He was crawling out onto the roof to pursue long haired freak Willie C who was screaming "nobody dissects the C!" Luckily for Willie besides being a drug addict with rotten teeth he was also a roofer.

    One night a couple of guys and I were partying up in John's

room with a big bag of Quaaludes. We would crush a Quaalude and mix it with some pot then stuff the whole thing into a regular pipe bowl and suck it down in one huge bong hit. When you let the smoke out you would drop the bong and almost lose control of your bodily functions. John had been out clamming on the bay that day and dredged up an old rusty revolver that he was enthralled with because he said it was probably a murder weapon. He had a brand new 357 magnum which he took out for comparison. He was drinking a forty-ounce bottle of Colt 45 and he put a little in a glass. He took the bottle of rubbing alcohol that we used to clean the bong and poured an overflowing shot which he then poured into the glass with the beer. He looked at us and laughed his cartoon villain laugh as he guzzled down the whole concoction. He repeated the procedure three more times till he could no longer talk. Anyone else would have died or at least went into a coma but he put a bullet in the 357 and nonchalantly spun the chamber. He then put the gun to his head and pulled the trigger. We were shocked and nobody made a move to disarm him. He spun the chamber again and suddenly pointed the gun at me and pulled the trigger. I leapt to my feet and in one motion grabbed the old rusty revolver from the table and pistol whipped him on the side of his head opening a long bloody gash and causing him to drop the 357. Bleeding, he started laughing as if nothing had happened.

    Around the time of these celebrations of murder and mayhem John 'ripped a drug dealer off' for a huge quantity of synthetic mescaline. Nobody but John knew who the drug dealer was. Whoever they were they weren't from around by us. I don't know how much he actually had but we were all making a fortune selling it at half price. For 'recreational' purposes we would put twenty or thirty of the little yellow pills in a shot glass and down them with a beer. It seemed like we had an inexhaustible supply and it went on for weeks. One night I was home sleeping when I was awakened by my father in the early hours of the morning. John was on the phone. When I answered he was incoherent and rambling on about how he had killed them all. He said, "at first I was just playing with my sword." He had a Samurai sword. "But then I wanted to cut her head off and when I tried the blood spurted all over me. It felt so warm and good I just had to keep going. I killed them all. The blood is all over the house you have to come over and help me clean it up." I hung up on him but Phil, never one for squeamishness when it came to a homicide, received the same phone call shortly after me. He went over there, and I found out from him the next day what had happened.

    Johns phone call to Phil was the same as the one I got, with John not saying who, what, where, or when, only "come over you have to help me clean it up. I killed them all. The blood is all over." On his way over Phil was certain that he was going to find Johns family in the same condition that the Defeo's had been found. But when Phil got there, he found out Johns parents and sister were away on the boat. John had taken a massive dose of mescaline and slaughtered his vixen pit bull along with her whole litter chasing them around the house with the Samurai sword and decapitating them.

John had despised Defeo senior ever since his father and Defeo had nearly come to blows on the front lawn. Afterwards John had always referred to Defeo as 'that fat loudmouth Guiney.' The Indians believed that you could send someone straight to hell by burying them face down. All of the dead Defeo's were found face down.

In a lot of the spectacular murders that have spawned supernatural folk lore like Jack the Ripper, The Zodiac, and The Amityville Horror, five innocent victims die. In Amityville there were six but according to Butchy; Dawn, his sister was one of his accomplices. Somebody probably also should have checked out why David Berkowitz was singing "Stacy was a whore" at his trial. Did the 'Son of Sam' know Stacy Moskowitz? Were the rest of those killed by the Son of Sam just collateral damage? Investigators seem to remain oblivious that the oldest book of the Qabalah might contain a clue. The Sepher Yetzirah, or the Book of Formation, is the foundation of occidental occultism. In it there is a passage called five over five: "and as there are in man five fingers; over against five, so over them is established a covenant of strength."

Eliphas Levi, whom Aleister Crowley believed he was in his last incarnation, wrote about five over five. Levi took great pains to write cryptically so that only other adepts could understand him and as with all that is arcane in the Qabalah the passage five over five can only be explained when the proper Gematria, Temurah or Notarikon are applied to it. Temurah and Notarikon are techniques for the permutation of the Hebrew alphabet in sacred scripture. Gematria assigns a number to each of the twenty-two Hebrew letters. When the sum of words is the same, they are interchangeable and can be used to describe each other. In his sprawling autobiography Crowley talks about a member of the English royal family that was one of his followers and hopelessly addicted to cocaine and alcohol. He mentions how this man kept in his room a strong box filled with five bloody pieces of petticoats that were a macabre souvenir of some ritual the aristocrat had performed.

Later when John got out of Attica, he would introduce me to Aleister Crowley. John had somehow acquired a whole box filled with rare books. In the abbreviated two years he had spent in Attica John had become an expert on secrets which most men spend their lives in search of just trying to get a peek behind the veil. He had also become the heavyweight champion of Attica and had his sentence cut short by a powerful politician on the stipulation that he would fight Larry Holmes. John reneged on that arrangement when he got out telling me "it's not the same when you hit guys and instead of going down, they hit you back." A bum named Gerry Cooney from Long Island fought Holmes for his title shortly after so I guess the politician found a man. Cooney lasted thirteen rounds with Holmes. I don't believe he would have lasted three with John.

John had done the time on a biker rap that he took for the Pagans. He had been hanging around with some guy named Moriarty who was the clubs 'sergeant at arms.' They needed gas so John took it. When the filling station attendant objected John knocked him out. Moriarty took five dollars from the unconscious guy's pocket. When they were pulled over later by the police, they found a sawed off shotgun John always carried in his boot. He took the whole rap for the robbery. I couldn't understand why John was hanging out with them that night. He had a blood feud going with them from the previous year.

When John was still in jail I had tracked Moriarty down to a strip club in West Islip named Stonehenge. I had my father's big silver hunting knife and I had every intention of gutting him with it. When Moriarty came over to me as I was carving my name in the table there was about twenty other Pagans in the bar with him, all of them wearing colors. I was with my friend from Norway; Egil who couldn't fight his way out of a wet paper bag. Moriarty said something like I hear you've been looking for me and I just leered at him as I continued to carve my name in the table. I took the cigarette out of my mouth, locking eyes with him, and pressed it to the top of the hand holding the knife. I don't know how long I had it on there, but it burned a small crater that took months to heal. The smell of burning flesh wafted through the bar as I laughed hysterically at the look on his face. I was taking acid and I didn't feel a thing. He looked like he was going to be sick. Nothing happened. I am not capable of committing unprovoked murder and he was not doing anything to provoke me. We finished our drinks and left the now silent bar.

CHAPTER 5

Johns war with the Pagans had started when they tried to assassinate his friend Big Dave in Philadelphia. Known as the Bubba, Big Dave was a Pagan, who was one of the most decorated soldiers coming out of the Vietnam War. John told me he had done six tours there. John said he had met Dave when they worked the door together at a disco in Levittown named Feathers. Big Dave also had mob connections and acted as the go between for the mob and the Pagans. At the time the Pagans ran APP Talent Agency. The agency supplied all the stripers for Nassau and Suffolk Counties from a list of a hundred and fifty girls. Each strip club put ten dollars in an envelope for each girl that worked an eight-hour shift for them. The envelope was picked up at the end of the week. The gang members also extorted both the girls and the bar owners. The mob got a cut of everything. This went on in every strip club on Long Island. I don't know why but one of the Pagans emptied a 357 magnum into big Dave's stomach in Philadelphia. He lived but he would never be the same again dying a few years later with most of his intestines removed.

One night shortly after big Dave was shot; John and I decided we needed hundred-pound plates. We had to go into Dan Laurie's in Brooklyn to get them. Besides the hundred-pound plates John purchased matching five-pound gold anodized wrist bracelets for practicing punching. They had the word power engraved into them in large letters. John put them on while he was still inside of Dan Laurie's and we drove back to his parent's house on Long Island. All the way back John was laughing his patented cartoon fiend laugh. He kept smashing the bracelets together screaming "power!" Upstairs he put a brand new hundred-pound plate on each end of a Z curl bar and started doing triceps kicks still wearing his Power Bracelets. There was a heavy bag suspended from the center beam in the attic gym. John started doing spinning back fists against it with the bracelets. He jumped and whirled focusing his maximum acceleration on the point where the bracelet smashed into the bag. With each blow the hundred- and twenty-pound bag was being lifted almost to the center beam supporting it. All the while he kept laughing like the mad villain in an old cartoon. Till this day I have never seen anybody hit a heavy bag with that kind of force. The effect was as if somebody was driving a small car into it.

As we exited the house to the driveway, he executed a perfect spinning crescent kick that went whizzing over my head like an errant rifle shot. We drove down to the strip in Amityville to the Pass Time pub where Butchy had announced to the world that his family had been murdered some five years ago. We did a few shots there and ambled down to the Copper Fox about a half block away. There we did a few more. All that night Johns face had been animated with a satanic grin that seemed to illuminate the area around him. John a couple of other people from the Copper Fox and I walked across the street to one of Long Island's first gyms, Future Man. There were two forty-five-pound plates on each side of an Olympic bar on a bench. Some Arnold Schwarzenegger types were taking turns bench pressing sets of ten with it. John ripped it off the bench and with his back straight, still wearing his power bracelets, and lagging left hand method, proceeded to curl it a dozen times as everybody in the gym counted off. Even as he was curling the inhuman weight John was laughing his cartoon villain laugh.

    With that they decided to go to Crawdaddy's on the corner of 110 and Montauk highway. I knew this was all going somewhere I didn't want to go at the time, so I went home. People still talk about what happened that night. I wasn't there so all I can tell you is what they say. John had gotten a ride from a few of his 'Amity-villain' groupies up 110 to a bar where the Pagans were giving one of their founding members a birthday party. It was a combination birthday party and going away party for Charlie Brown who was dying of cancer. John had walked into a bar full of them still laughing hysterically like he had just tied the movie heroine to the railroad tracks. He had made his way to Charlie Browns guest of honor barstool and in a matter of fact fashion back fisted him twenty feet across the bar. With that all hell broke loose with some of the witness's saying John had taken on as many as fifty Pagans and got the better of them until the fight was broken up by a contingent of riot gear clad police from Suffolk County.

    After that the Pagans put out a contract on John which according to the Amityville police called for him to be beat to death in a public place. John went into hiding and they started showing up in force at all the bars on Montauk Highway that we frequented. John suddenly started acquiring military weapons. I have never figured out from where nor did he ever tell me. He had a WWII belt fed machine gun complete with green and red tracer rounds every three loads to complement the assault rifles which he had stashed all over his parents' house. He had carefully choreographed a scene in his head where they would pull into his driveway with their bikes and he would open up with the machine gun from his room above wiping out most of them. He would finish off the survivors with the rifles and assorted knives he had laying all over the place. The police knew about all this except the machine gun and had the house under twenty-four-hour surveillance. We would do bongs up there and every time John thought he heard a bike out would come the belts of ammo and the gun. The Amityville cops would knock on his door and taunt him by telling him which bars the Pagans had been in looking for him the night before. One cop told him "I wouldn't want to be you with a gang of two hundred- and fifty-pound known killers dogging my trail."

John did not stay in hiding long. He disappeared for about a week and everybody thought the Pagans had got him. By then I knew better. When he reappeared he was sunburned all over. He told me he had been watching the Pagans clubhouse in the Hamptons from the dunes surrounding it. He had laid motionless up in those dunes for almost a week straight and drawn a bead on each and every one of them through the scope of his Mauser sniper rifle as they came and went. Upon his return John immediately got to work in his grandfather's garage welding various gears and rods together to make weapons. There was the royal crowner, a huge gear welded in the middle to a two-foot steel rod. There was the poker and jabber which was a pry bar cut down to about two feet and sharpened to a point at the cut end. He would demonstrate their usages for anyone who asked. The poker and jabber was a classic he would hold it in the middle with his left hand and rotate it as he shot out long lethal jabs repeating like a mantra 'you poke and you jab, you poke and you jab'.

We all hung out over at Egil's house. His father had been the eldest son so when Egil's grandfather in Norway passed away Egil's father inherited the family farm and fortune. He went back to Norway leaving Egil, his brother Geir, and sister Vigdis, with a ten-room house on the water that was all paid up. I had moved right into the master bedroom. The place was party central. John came over one night uncharacteristically frantic. He said "their all on the Amityville strip right now and they have the Tuilliga brothers and their whole dojo with them. Tom, Jim, and Eric's brothers are already there. The rest of my Amity-villains are on the way. Let's go settle this once and for all." There was about ten of us at Egil's including Eric who was one of the toughest people I have ever met. His brothers were supposed to be even tougher; Eric was the youngest. His father had been one of the most decorated hero's in the Pacific theater during WWII and raised his four boys alone in his own image. Stevie was the third ranked wrestler in the nation at

145 pounds and Joe was just a complete lunatic. It was said he was the most dangerous of them all. Eric at 145 pounds could almost keep up on the curls with John and me. He had never lost a fight in his life. Everyone called him Mad Dog because right out of High School he had taken on the supposedly toughest man in Amityville, a two-hundred-and-fifty-pound body builder and martial arts 'expert'; Kenny Styler. When Eric got through with him Styler had to be taken to the hospital where the doctors thought he had been attacked by a rabid dog.

The Pagans were mostly middle-aged fat men and they were no match for the crew John had assembled but they did not become the second most powerful and richest bike gang on the East Coast by being stupid. They knew that too. Tom Tuilliga had recently graced the cover of Muscle and Fitness magazine. He had just won the Mr. America contest. Inside the magazine there was a ten-page article and photo spread telling the reader that Tuilliga had combined the precepts of body building and martial arts making him a guru of fitness and the most dangerous man alive in hand to hand combat. His brother was just as big, and they had a whole contingent of tough guys from the North Massapequa-Farmingdale area which they trained. The Pagans had ingratiated themselves by giving Tom and his brother bikes and wining and dining them, all the while probably questioning their ability to take on John and his crew. A showdown between them and us was inevitable and now it would happen.

We all piled onto the back of Eric's flatbed truck. John was clutching his poker and jabber sporting his Sunday go to meeting satanic grin. When we pulled up to the Amityville strip it looked like some kind of a bazaar was going on. Maybe a hundred bikes lined the south side of Montauk highway from the Copper Fox to 110, a distance of about two hundred yards. Men were milling all over the street many wearing Pagans emblazoned cut off dungaree jackets. Eric did not hesitate for even a second. He floored the big international flatbed slamming it into the people and bikes in front of the Copper Fox. Everything went flying like well struck bowling pins, a tangled mass of flesh, bone, and polished steal, hurtled through the air towards an abrupt stop on the concrete and blacktop. We bailed off the back of the truck like angry hornets in all directions. From the corner of my eye I saw men streaming from the Copper Fox.

I had been involved in riots between Blacks and Whites at Copiague High School, but I have never seen anything quite like this. It was a flaying mass of humanity, swinging bottles, sticks, bricks, and chunks of concrete torn from the sidewalk. I saw Eric's truck wheel hopping in reverse, running over more bikes as a bunch of leather clad men clung to the running boards and open door trying to drag him from the driver's seat. The truck came to a halt atop a mangled bike, as I made my way through the melee in an effort to help him. They had him trapped in the truck and were punching away at him. I started bailing them off of the truck kicking and punching at them till Eric was able to hop down and begin to savage his assailants like a cornered panther. His brothers and their friends got there and together they began to badly mall his attackers. Eric bit a man that he had pinned to the ground right in the face. I started looking for John.

Nassau, Suffolk, and Amityville police cars, sirens screaming, pulled up to the edge of the maelstrom which encompassed the area where the bikes were parked. As the cops got out, they locked their guns in the trunks of their cars and donned nightsticks and riot helmets before they joined the fray. Everyone was screaming, yelling and cursing, as they tried to kill or maim the guy next to them. I saw two sets of legs sticking out of the hedges adjacent to the Chapter 2. I recognized Johns Ostrich skinned boots and ran over dodging bottles and bricks. When I got there John was on top. I went to separate them. I could not tell who was winning. When I grabbed his shoulders, John turned to look at me and it was then I could see both of their faces. Tom Tuilliga's face was a bloody mass of ground flesh and John had been chewing his ear off, literally. I will never forget the look on Johns face. It was a look of pure ecstasy and he screamed his villain laugh "ha ha haaa!" He went back to pummeling Tuilliga and I walked away, a bit troubled. Violence is not supposed to be something you enjoy but I was finding out quickly that it was even better than sex.

The police started getting the upper hand. The whole thing had lasted about a half hour. By now there were at least a hundred cops. Eric's truck was gone. There were about a half dozen mangled bikes lying where it had been. The Pagans and some cops were trying to hold a guy in leather down who was convulsing like a squirrel that had just been run over. The brawling had thinned out now with many of the participants to hurt to continue. In the center of Montauk Highway about twenty Pagans were making a last stand back to back in a circle surrounded by about fifty people. The Pagans were bloodied and gored. Their cloths were in tatters. Many people had taken colors that night. Eric would later use three or four jackets to decorate the walls of the basement at his father's house.

The bikers held the crowd off swinging chains and pipes. Tom a hulking third generation German dock builder from Amityville was in a frenzy. I saw that night what the ancient monks had seen when they coined the phrase "God save us from the fury of the Norseman." His face was glowing red above his beard, he was completely berserk screaming as he charged into the center of them. He was impervious to the blows raining down on him from the pipes and chains. With each blow he struck another biker was launched like a bloody projectile. Bikers would get up dazed and reform their circle. This was repeated a couple of more times till the cops got even that side show under control.

The cops had gotten everyone separated with the bikers on one side of Montauk Highway and us on the other, them in between. I melted back into my own crowd and made my way back to Egil's where I found Eric and a bunch of other people. Eric's brothers had ushered him out of there fearing he had killed someone, perhaps more than one, but nothing ever came of it. The cops had known this was coming for weeks. They were probably just happy it was over, and nobody actually did get killed. The Pagans by their own bragging were outlaws. I guess they just had to take their lumps when they got them.

Foundation / יסוד

CHAPTER 6

John was beside himself the next day. He had lost his poker and jabber in the melee. Eric ridiculed him, mimicking him "you poke, and you jab, you poke, and you jab." We were now drinking for free in all the clubs on the Amityville strip. Many of my nights were spent working the door at the OBI South, the hottest club on Long Island. The OBI was a sprawling old beach house situated at the mouth of Fire Island inlet with a long dock that accommodated hundreds of people extending over the water. On a Sunday it was the place to be if you were young and from the West end of the Island. It drew massive crowds and was owned by an eccentric New England aristocrat named Bob Matheson who would eventually run for Suffolk County legislator with a media campaign that would have been over the top even by present day standards. Matheson was on local TV and radio every five minutes railing about corruption in

Suffolk County. He would continue to campaign even after he lost bombarding everybody with the slogan "get out of NY State before it's too late."

Matheson was born with more money than he knew what to do with and the bar was his personnel kingdom. Geir and his friend Phil O'Sullivan had gotten jobs there as bar backs and always bragged about how hard they worked and how much money they made. One night I decided to give it a try myself. The work was just as they said. More often than not they would have four guys carrying three cases at a time up the basement stairs all night in an effort to keep the legions of bartenders stocked. Beers were flying out of there faster than we could bring them. On a good night you would walk out with close to 300$ in tips after the bartenders gave you your cut. Matheson had so many bartenders he didn't need bouncers so only his friend Hank worked the door.

Not long after I started working there a professional creep attempted to steal Bobs Mercedes. It was daybreak and everybody had long since left except for me and a few other bar backs that were closing. I ended up tackling the guy in the parking lot and holding him down for about an hour till the State Troopers, who hated Matheson, finally decided to show up. The OBI was right on top of the marshlands and on that still morning mosquitoes were swarming like dust clouds. Unable to even swat at them I was literally eaten alive keeping this guy pinned. Every couple of minutes Matheson would yell from the doorway with his thick New England accent 'Hold him, hold him, don't let him get away, the cops are on their way.'

I never had to carry another case again after that. I would stand at the front door with Hank or mill around the floor honing clumsy pickup lines. At the end of the night I still got a full cut of the tips. I wouldn't get out of there till about seven in the morning. A lot of the time I would drive over the Robert Moses Causeway and go to sleep serenaded by the breaking waves of the Atlantic and the shrill cries of gulls. The beach was deserted in the morning, but I always spread my blanket where I was sure to awaken to the heavy aroma of suntan oil in a forest of deeply tanned limbs. You could just about smell the sex oozing from the almost naked bodies of nubile young girls.

It was the summer of my nineteenth birthday, and I was the lone bouncer in the hottest club east of the city. Some nights were slow and my only job was to keep the huge central fire place of the bar stoked with wood while Matheson lounged with his trophy girlfriend telling me with his New England drawl "you got class, you got class." The fringe benefits of the job were innumerable, but it was on a night when things were a little slow, they reached their full potential. There may have been only a hundred people in the bar, but they all agreed the sexiest looking girl they had ever seen was tearing up the dance floor. Every guy in the bar was riveted. She had flowing long red hair and an exotic looking face. She looked in her mid-twenties and was clad in a tight-fitting brown leather motorcycle suit that showed off endowments that other girls dream about having. She looked like she had been air brushed. I must have been what she was looking for because she followed me home on her bike that night and went down on me in my car at Amity Harbor beach.

It was twilight a couple of days later when I showed up at her door in a Midtown Manhattan high-rise. She had a green mud mask on her face and was wearing nothing but a bathrobe. She washed off the mask and let her robe drop to the floor. Her leather riding outfit had not been lying. She still looked airbrushed when she was nude. Her only flaw was a pubic hair growing out of one her nipples. I wondered why she didn't cut it, but I guess that's Europeans. She was French Algerian, the idle and resentful spawn of rich refuges. We did it so many different ways and in so many positions that it was nine in the morning before our imaginations and our bodies gave out. She told me her family had lost all their property but kept all their money and that she would never have to work. I told her my favorite author was Albert Camus. He was at the time. We had breakfast at Tiffany's where it was twenty dollars for eggs.

On off nights I hit the clubs in Manhattan and Long Beach. Sometimes I hung out locally in the Amityville-Copiague area. Being in the neighborhood bars was like being a prince in a nocturnal kingdom. There were more bars in that area than anywhere else in the world at that time. The next town east: Lindenhurst, was in the Guinness Book of Records at that time for the town having the most bars per person in the world.

I remember one-night John, Jim, and I walked into Crawdaddy's one of the larger clubs in the area. John was shoveling coke in his nose in the back room used by security. Jim and I were leering at the crowd on the dance floor and doing shot after shot at the bar, slamming the empty shot glass's down and demanding more. The doormen and bouncers were desperate to rid themselves and their hapless patrons of our menacing presence. They directed us to this girl on the dance floor who they had to keep stopping from taking her clothes off. Delighted, we shepherded her out of the club to the more intimate Chapter 2 next door. The Chapter 2 had about thirty or forty people in it. I think it was a Friday night. The men in the bar immediately realized what was about to happen and made a mad dash to lock the female patrons in the back room. In the crowded confines of the bar they had to watch sullenly as John and Jim had repetitive violent and loud sex with Rosy on the pool table.

John paced around the bar his fingers embedded in Rosie's crotch waving her aloft naked with one arm, his evil villain laugh reverberating through his captive audience. Jim was pounding her so hard from a standing position the pool table was moving across the floor. All the while Jim kept snarling "c'mon Rosy, c'mon Rosy". There were about a dozen girls in that bar. They must have suffocated crammed into the tiny back room because it went on for hours till we wandered off leaving the naked Rosy prostrate on the pool table. Her pubic hair glistened with Jim's saliva and semen under the overhead lights.

Eric was more reclusive than the rest of us. His face was a bit misshapen and his body although small was freakishly muscled. His Popeye forearms were overlaid with veins the size of steel cables. Combined with his oversized tendons it gave him a somewhat Neanderthal and rigid appearance. Eric was self-conscious and stayed home in his basement most of the time which served as a clubhouse for us. We told him about Rosy who had now morphed into 'Rosie the Riveter.' Eric went back and found her the next night, once again taking her clothes off in Crawdaddy's. He whisked her off in his International and disappeared for two days. After that Jim and John would ask him constantly where his girlfriend Rosie the Riveter was.

Eric finally did decide one night that he would go out drinking, but he did not want a drinking buddy who talked too much. He broke into a Funeral Parlor in Copiague and almost succeeded in getting a corpse through the window. Asked what he was going to do with the corpse. Eric would tell you he was going to bring it into the Copper Fox and buy it a drink.

Eric was not the only one who kept strange company. Jim had made himself the bouncer of the Copper Fox, his favorite hangout. Jim was what Hitler's conception of the Aryan superman looked like. His fierce blue eyes stared out menacingly from beneath his close cut platinum blond hair. Standing at about six foot he had a tremendous chest and legs like telephone poles. These attributes had won him a football scholarship to Penn State. He drank his way out of Penn State within a year and was hanging out with us. One night Jim took a huge shit in the urinal of the bar. He picked it up and placed it on the bar and made the bartender serve it shots, which he drunk along with his own.

A few days after Jim had bonded with his new friend John and I paid him a visit. As we sat up at the bar guys started filing through the front door. All of them were wearing either leather pants or chaps which was odd because we had not heard any bikes pull up. There was between twenty or thirty of them and at the end of the procession in walked the Tuilliga brothers. Tom Tuilliga was wearing a pair of buckskin chaps and had grown his hair long, I guess in an effort to hide his mangled ear which matched his now mangled nose. Tuilliga wouldn't be doing any more magazine covers and it was obvious he was out for payback. They all settled into the back of the bar around the booths talking loudly and screaming war hoops. These guys were in as good a shape as we were and we were badly outnumbered, even John was a bit tentative. Jim had not been a big factor at the first fight, and he was out for glory. He strode into the middle of them like he was goose stepping for the Führer and screamed back at one of them "you scream like a woman!"

    The guy took a round house swing at Jim which was a big mistake since Jim was just as fast as he was muscular and knew how to keep his punch's short and crisp. Jim laid him out with a straight right before the looping roundhouse completed its arc. They all tried to get Jim at once and in the narrow confines of the bar the pool table forced them to come straight at him single file. He nailed about five guys with a flurry of lethal rights and lefts as be backed towards us past the pool table where the bar opened up a bit. That was where John met him, right where he had enough room to use the spinning back fists and crescent kicks which he practiced day and night. I have seen many bar fights in my life but I never saw anything quite like this. The first guy John nailed was Tom Tuilliga when he came from the other side of the pool table. John did this with a spinning back fist that looked like it could have been choreographed for the Spandau Ballet. Tuilliga was picked up off his feet and sent sprawling a good ten feet through the air smashing against the wall with a resounding thud. Tuilliga's brother was right behind him and caught a crescent kick that practically ended his night right on the spot. It was as if somebody had set a class five tornado loose in the middle of the bar as everything that came within Johns perimeter was met with an assortment of kicks and punches and sent hurling in all directions. These guys were all trained fighters so most of them were able to get up and come right back at him. Jim settled in at his back hitting anything that came within his range. I tried to join them, but Jim connected on me with a solid right. I was the only thing that withstood that punch without going down and I heard Jim apologizing to me over the din of the brawl.

    It seemed to go on forever. When it looked like John and Jim would be overwhelmed by sheer force of numbers, I turned the pool table over on their attackers, and we backed our way to the front of the bar. By now the Copper Fox had filled with Amity-villains from the surrounding bars. The bar was divided with Johns supporters at the front of the bar and the Tuilliga's at the back. Everybody squared off in a temporary lull due to the breathlessness of the participants. Intermission was broken by one of the old time Amityville tough guys walking up to Tom Tuilliga and telling him "now you got a beef with me." Tuilliga knocked him out with one devastating right. With that somebody went behind the bar and started emptying out the coolers and handing out bottles of beer and liquor which were being hurled at the Tuilliga's and company. They returned fire with the contents of the unrefrigerated cases in the back of the bar and everybody was using chairs and tables as shields and projectiles. The air in the bar became thick with flying objects accompanied by a cacophony of smashing glass.

    The front lines of each crew were where people were becoming bloody messes so John, Jim, and I, hung out in the rear tossing an occasional bottle. Somebody handed Jim a bottle of Wild Turkey and Jim said, "no, no don't throw this!" It was put back behind the bar. The police never even showed up. I guess somebody down at headquarters was tired of this shit. The fight only ended when there was nothing left to break or smash and most of the participants were covered with blood. Tuilliga's crew skated out the back door with him being the last to leave. He turned and made a little speech "hey look this was the best bar fight I was ever in. Nobody got killed and it was fun. Nobody should press charges and let's just forget about it." That was the last I ever saw of Tom Tuilliga. He never joined the Pagans and I guess he wizened up. Never fight another man's battles if he is not going to even be there.

    The bar looked like a bomb had gone off in the middle of it. There was not a stick of furniture left. The pool table was upside down and all the stools had their legs torn off to be used as clubs. Broken bottles covered the floor, submerged in their own spilled contents. The mirrors were busted behind the bar and not one beer remained in the coolers. The only thing left undamaged was the one bottle of Wild Turkey that Jim had stashed. He popped the cork off and took a long swig handing it to John and I. Jim surveyed the damage and said, "at least I saved the bar."

    John became proactive after that. When he heard the Pagans were recruiting another rough crew from a bar called the Coaches Four on the west side of Massapequa, he became the doorman there and took Bobby Kelsky along with him. This crew was a little different. Some of them were much older. One of them; Cliffy had done twenty years upstate. He had bigger biceps than even Kenny Styler who was the most muscular man I'd seen till then. They were led by Vinnie Gambler who would go on to become one of the most powerful Pagans. John immediately banned them all from their own bar and spent the next few weeks enforcing his edict. John and Kelsky throttled them every night but these guys never gave up. They were like the Michael Myers of bar room brawling.

Kelsky couldn't show one night and John asked Eric and me to come down and help him 'keep the peace.' I wasn't doing anything that night and since Eric's relationships with both Rosie the Riveter and the cadaver had failed neither was he. Why pass up free drinks and a hundred dollars out of the draw at the end of the night? When we got there the place was packed with a crowd from Massapequa's wealthy South Shore area probably because John had gotten rid of all the assholes from North Massapequa, the poor part of town. John was sitting still as a cigar store Indian on his stool in front of the door, staring at it with the intensity of a soldier on watch at the front line. Eric never passed up an opportunity to goof on John and from our vantage point at the bar he remarked to me "look at him. Who would pay him to scare their customers? He's the idiot son of his idiot father."

A hulking giant of a man appeared through the door and had a brief conversation with John then left. John came over to us and said "get ready that was Cliffy. He pretends to be my friend. They want to come in again. I told him no way." A little guy came through the door and without warning John pounced on him pinning him in the foyer and raining down punches to his head. John threw him out through the front door like he was tossing out a bag of garbage and that's when it all began. Outside there were five more of them and John carried his attack to them on the sidewalk. Eric, right behind him, grabbed one by the face with his patented pliers like grip and wrestled him to the ground, gouging and biting him at the same time. You did not want to fight Eric, nobody did. I immediately decked one and chased another one two blocks where I gave him a beating too. When I got back John and Eric had beaten the other four to a bloody mess and a couple of them were lying on the sidewalk not moving. When we got back inside I asked John what it was about those guys "do they enjoy getting beat up?" John answered "they'll be back. They always come back no matter how bad you beat them up." Then he went back to his stool staring at the door.

They were back in less than an hour with ten more guys. In fact, they came back again and again that night led by a fat slovenly looking guy who would gesticulate and curse loudly in front of the bar actually jumping up and down in a rage. Eric took to calling him the lively fat man. Each time we would dutifully go outside and beat the shit out of them. These guys had no idea how to fight and were human punching bags to the last man. We fought them four or five times over a span of five hours. The only injury any of us received was John jammed his thumb badly upper cutting one of them. John was convinced that this was excellent 'training' for us but Eric in his salt of the earth way prevailed on him "these guys are drinking in the woods and doing who the fuck knows what else. It's only a matter of time till one of them go's home and gets a gun. What the fuck are you even doing over here? This is their neighborhood bar. Why don't you just leave them alone? They ain't bothering us!" John finally listened to reason, probably only because his thumb was swollen like a sausage. He closed the bar for the night, grabbing a hand full of money out of the draws and dividing it amongst us. We never went back there again, and I heard somebody killed the lively fat man a few years later. When I took over the strip clubs I would become friends with Vinnie Gambler. He was probably the only Pagan I ever took a liking to.

CHAPTER 7

The summer of my nineteenth birthday, 1978, was the quintessential endless summer. It was the summer I would spend my last week in Montauk. My father had gotten his charter boat license shortly after moving to Long Island. My mother, upwardly mobile in her new career as a landscape designer, introduced him to Stanly Lipkin and Gil Hollenbeck, heirs to Broadway Maintenance, the company that had the contract to put up all the light poles for Lilco, Long Islands power company. These guys were second generation idle rich and had matching Bertram sport fishermen docked at my father's house. One of them had a father with a sixty-four-foot yacht docked at the Star Island Yacht Club in Montauk. My father also had his own boat an old wooden Ulrichsen. Till then my summers were spent mating on these boats and running them back and forth from Montauk to Amity Harbor.

I had watched the waters off of Long Island rapidly deteriorate under the emerging weight of globalism. Montauk was once a terminal for most of the pelagic game fish in the Atlantic. Three miles off the beach you could hardly drop a feather lure back forty or fifty feet from the boat without drawing a strike within minutes. Twelve miles off the beach there were shoals of giant Bluefin Tuna. All this ended in the late seventies when the government allowed Russian factory ships to within the twelve-mile limit to fish American waters clean. There was strenuous objection in the charter boat and local commercial fishing industry to increase America's coastal boundaries to two hundred miles, which was what most other countries had at that time. Captains were running their boats through Russian long lines and firing on the factory ships with their rifles. There were frenzied meetings and nonstop lobbying but all to no avail. By 1978 the waters off of Montauk and all the rest of Long Island were devoid of fish. Like everything else in America some elitists had cut a deal and fuck the working man's livelihood and fuck the food supply too.

The Tournament of the Full Moon in late October was an annual rite of passage for me. I spent my nights trolling the riffs for Stripers under a moon that was a luminous pit in the black sky. I would watch entranced as phosphors danced in the wake of the boat until the spell was broken by the resounding scream of wire line being pulled from a bent rods clicking drag. Days were spent milling around the docks and being regaled by stories of two-ton Great White Sharks courtesy of Frank Mundus the model for the character Captain Quint in the movie Jaws. When Mundus retired to Hawaii one of my father's closest friends; Russ Grandenetti, took over the captainship of his boat the Cricket II. Mundus was a latter-day pirate who could kill a case of beer in two hours by himself and take a charter out in Gale force winds to pull stripers from twenty foot breakers in the Shagwong riff off the Montauk lighthouse. I would sometimes take the long walk from Keelers Marina to the lighthouse to watch him do it when all the other boats in Montauk were dockside due to inclement weather

That summer I also had been able to find my first regular sexual partner that met my aesthetic criteria. Marie was a year younger than me. She was a platinum blond beauty with upturned breasts and legs right up to her neck. She had a French pedigree that was attested to by her mother who only spoke French. I was chipping heroin at the time and engaging in marathon sex with Marie, the byproduct of spending every day since puberty masturbating half a dozen times a day. There was no way I wanted to go fish the Bluefin Tuna Tournament in Montauk, but my father and his friends insisted remarking on my relationship with Marie 'absence makes the heart grow fonder.'

It didn't. It just made me horny. We trolled for three days without even a single takedown from the outriggers. I was getting a really great tan, which Marie would love, but I was also getting really bored. I knew just how to remedy the situation. When time for the second day of the tournament gave out we were pulling into port. I made it a point to take off my shirt and go up on the bow leaning on the bow rails I struck my best demigod pose as we passed the dockside bar and restaurant; Grossmans, a watering hole for rich Manhattanites out for a weekend excursion via the Long Island railroad to Montauk. I could almost hear the aging debutantes go silent as we motored past. I was truly a magnificent specimen and I knew it. When we got back to port I hosed the boat down and went to Grossmans. There was no need to shower we were using artificial lures and there wasn't a Bluefin tuna

Those Who Would Arouse Leviathan

within a hundred miles of Montauk, besides the sun on my skin all day affected me very strangely back then. I would turn a deep crimson red like an American Indian and my skin would emit an intoxicating scent that I could smell myself.

I seated myself at a booth on the dock and ordered a drink. When the waiter came back he pointed to another booth and told me the woman over there would like to pay for it. I gestured for them to come over and they did. Two thirty something female predators from Manhattan, one was pretty hot too. I was shy but she sure wasn't. She bought me drinks and a lobster dinner. She told me when she saw me up on that boat she knew she just had to have me. I had never heard a woman talk this way before. She told me I was the most beautiful man she had ever seen 'the very embodiment of the flower of youth.' I took them on a drunken tour through Montauk that night while she begged me to drive them back to Manhattan where we could go skinny dipping in her penthouse pool. I had to decline. I could not disappoint my father that way and we ended up going at it on the lawn of the open gazebo in the middle of town. In the distance Lynyrd Skynyrd's Free Bird wafted from one of the bars.

The next day I had a huge hickey on my neck which amused my father and his friends to no end. I wondered how I would explain it to Marie as we spent another futile day trolling under the broiling sun. I kept hearing the lyrics to that song in my head. It was a soulful goodbye to what had been and an exhortation to move on to what will be. Up until then I had taken it for granted that I would be a charter boat captain like my father and all his friends. It was what I had been raised to do, but there was no more fish in these waters, and I would have to find another place in the world.

At the time there was nothing sinister about Montauk. Preston Nichols had not yet written the Montauk Projects nor had I come into contact with him and his sidekick; Al Bielek, at least that I can recall. During the course of my life I would get to know him only too well. What I can tell you about Montauk during the time period this part of the story takes place is that my father had been stationed in Camp Hero in Montauk for the Korean War. And there was one very strange incident that took place two years before the summer I have just recounted, when I had just graduated High School.

We had all just started hanging out together again. By then Kenny and I had Tommy and Egil as constant companions and John had Eric. There were girls of course, for some. Kenny always had a steady girlfriend and Tommy was the blond-haired heart throb of Copiague High School, but we wanted to have a 'men's' extravaganza to Hotdog Beach in the Hamptons for the fourth of July. Kenny had a big bag of fireworks left over from what he couldn't sell by the fourth and John had just gotten a two-pound brick of some really fine hash. We packed all the 'contraband' into Eric's old station wagon and left at sunset on July third. On the way there John became insistent that we should go shoot the fireworks off at the old military base in Montauk. Nobody had ever been there and nobody else wanted to go. It was forty miles out of the way, but John said there would be too many cops at Hotdog Beach, and we would get him busted for the two pounds of hash he had taken along. John threatened to take his hash and go home so we were left with little choice. That hash could be converted to girls at Hotdog Beach and it wasn't the fourth yet anyway so we gave in.

    We pulled off to the side of the road at the base and had to walk about a quarter mile through the woods to get to the beach below. No sooner had we started walking than John, who was leading the way, starts making hand signals like he's GI Joe. Suddenly I was blinded by a bright light and when I managed to focus my eyes there was a cop with a big flashlight in one hand and an even bigger gun in the other pointed straight at me. He says, "alright tell your friend to come out with his hands up." I was only seventeen at the time and nobody as of yet had ever pointed a loaded pistol at me. Eric was by now hiding in the bush right in front of me so I said, "Eric come out it's a cop and he's waving a gun around." Eric complied and the cop starts telling us this was private property and he could arrest us for being on it. I wanted to ask him if it was standard operating procedure to shoot teenagers for trespassing in Montauk but there was something I was even more curious about. I asked him how he had known we were there, and he tells me, still aiming his gun at us, he had gotten a call. We hadn't been there for even a minute and there was not a soul around. Then he tells us we have to get out of Montauk, or he would arrest us and proceeds to follow us about twenty miles all the way to South Hampton. We had two pounds of hash in the car so needless to say it was a very tense drive.

    We went back to Eric's basement all the way in Amityville, on the other side of the county, to ditch the hash and await Johns inevitable, or so we thought, phone call. It was about midnight by the time we got back, and we sat around till noon smoking Johns hash and waiting for him to call. He never did. Eric called Johns mother and told her what had happened. She begged him to take her car and go look for him. Halfway between Hotdog Beach and Montauk we spot the four of them looking worn and bedraggled walking towards Hotdog Beach. When we asked them why they didn't call all they could say is there were no phones. The town of Montauk was maybe a mile or two from the base. Like I said I used to walk to the lighthouse all the time and it's even further from town than the base. All of them were very evasive about what they had done when we left, only saying they had stayed the night on the beach and gotten a ride to almost where we found them. John said he had seen the cop and that's why he was signaling but he was a good hundred feet in front of us and the cop was behind us. Their story never did make any sense. They couldn't even tell us who had given them a ride and why they had been dropped off in the middle of nowhere.

      Eric and I had taken some of Johns hash along for company, so we all headed back to Hotdog beach. It wasn't long before a carload of girls pulls up next to us hooting and hollering. They gestured for us to follow them and we did to a rundown house somewhere in the Hamptons. There were four of them and I guess they were a year or two older than us and they all looked like they had been around. When we went in the house one of them told us her name was Maid Marion and we should be quiet, or we would wake her grandmother up who was sleeping in the next room. It was three in the afternoon. We hung out and smoked hash with them for the rest of the day. Granny never woke up and the door to her room remained shut. Everybody got laid except for Eric and I. That wouldn't have been so unusual for the time, except for Egil. Egil? He talked about Maid Marion for the next couple of years till he went back to Norway to join his father.

      I would not believe anything Preston Nichols says except that he is from East Islip but he would tell anyone who would listen that the Montauk experiments, whose objective was not only to bend time but create super soldiers, were carried out by Nazi's who had been merged with American intelligence during 'Operation Paperclip.' They were led by John Von Neumann a Hungarian Jew who had come over during the thirties. Von Neumann was the greatest mathematician on this side of Bernhard Riemann and he did so much top secret work for the government that when he was dying of pancreatic cancer in the fifty's he was kept under twenty four hour military guard to keep him from talking while he was on pain medication.

      John's grandfather spoke with a thick German accent and ever since we were kids I used to tease John that I knew his grandfather was a war criminal and I was going to turn him over to the Jews. John would get really flustered which is why I did it. He would insist his grandfather wasn't even German he was Hungarian. Well he sure as hell looked like a German to me. In fact, one could easily imagine that sweet little old man exchanging his rose pruners for a dental drill and merrily drilling away at a prisoner saying 'you vill tell me vhat you know.'

CHAPTER 8

When summer finally ended I tried to return to school but unless you have some clear objective school is no place for a man at nineteen years old. A friend of mine from school was dealing Hydro. Back then it was called Maui Blue and an assortment of other names culled from High Times Magazine. He said he could get coke, so I gave it a try and laid out seven hundred dollars for a quarter ounce. I had tried it a couple of times before with John and never felt anything, but this was the good stuff. My long love affair with cocaine began.

Besides its ability to switch sexual stimulation into overdrive cocaine also opens doorways to other worlds and was used extensively by the priesthoods of our forgotten past. The Smithsonian would prefer to keep it a secret but in rigorous scientific studies conducted by German scientist's in the early nineties nine Egyptian mummies dated from between 1070 B.C. to 395 A.D. have tested positive for both nicotine and cocaine. Both substances are only found in the new world and according to the standard version of history should not be in any corpse from Egypt dated prior to 1492. These mummies were sequestered in the vaults of the Munich museum and locked away from any further scientific inquiry "on grounds of religious respect."

Boredom was beginning to intercede between Marie and me by then. When I did some coke with her in my car at Amity Harbor beach I tried showing her some of the things I had on my mind in pornographic magazines. She became upset and made me drop her off at Mo's Place, a bar up the block. I later heard she told all the other girls in town that I was a pervert.

John had taken up with some twenty something local pig from Amityville. He had gotten his own little love cottage on the north side of Lindenhurst. Her name was Sharon and he even had his own song at the time it was all over the radio; My Sharona by the Knack. It was a smash hit which was incomprehensible to me at the time. The lyrics were just a string of idiotic cooing baby talk with a dubious dance beat by an unknown group. John was never much of a poet and the only dancing he ever did was when he was laying people out in the streets so in retrospect the song was entirely appropriate to him. The girl was a dedicated whore. She had already fucked everybody in Amityville, and she was just getting started. John wallowed in his own self-pity over her and began taking heroin on a far more regular basis. In between he terrorized everybody she fucked behind his back, which was everybody she met.

Around that time Big Dave came back to Long Island. His reappearance was heralded by the execution style murders of four Pagans and their associates on the east end by a couple of Italian kids. The local rag for Long Island; Newsday, said it was some kind of robbery of a jewelry store the Pagans owned but I knew better. One day I went over John's house and he told me to come in. Seated on the couch with some scrawny blond who was covered with Tattoo's was a bearded man at least three inches taller than John. I was introduced to Big Dave and his girl Cat dancer. Right away Dave starts questioning me about this guy I knew from school, Glen. Glen ran APP Talent Agency for the Pagans. He was bisexual and had more money than he could use. He was attending Community College because he was bored. He latched on to me like a barnacle either because of the way I looked or because he knew who my friends were. If he knew who my friends were he didn't know well enough to shut up. One night at a party over at his mansion in Nesconset he starts telling me something to the effect that Big Dave got what he had coming, and he better not come back, or the Pagans would finish the job. Of course, I told John the next day.

Now Dave wanted to know exactly what Glen had said. Dave was probably the scariest man I have ever seen, six foot seven with shoulders as wide as Johns. When he looked at you his eyes looked like portals to hell. He had spent six tours in the bush killing gooks for Uncle Sam and who knows how many men he had killed for the Mob, the Pagans, and only the Devil knew who or what else. I probably should have told him exactly what Glen said but the way I looked at it I had already told John and fulfilled any obligation I had towards my group. I am nobody's 'bitch.' He kept asking me and I kept telling him "I don't carry tales about what another man said to me." John looked really perplexed. I don't think he ever expected a reaction like this, and he kept saying "just tell him!"

When the tension had reached an absolute crescendo suddenly there was a ring at the doorbell. Anxious to get out of Dave's face I answered it. It was two detectives with a warrant for John's arrest. It seems John had imbedded his truck in the house of Sharon's latest penus du jour. Apparently nobody was home so John just left the truck sticking halfway into the living room. When the police arrived, they found a cache of military weapons in the truck's cab including John's trusty belt fed machine gun. The detectives had a warrant for his arrest. I told them "he don't live here no more I do." They wanted to come in to search the house for him, but I blocked the doorway and told them they weren't coming in without a search warrant. The stocky looking cop says, "how about we just walk right through you?" I tell him "you can try." He looked like he was getting ready to do exactly that when I see his eyes diverted over my shoulder. I turn around and there was Dave looming in back of me. The cop starts stammering "Da Da Dave we didn't know you were back in town. Oh. Is John a friend of yours? We didn't know that." Then he tells Dave the whole story of why they are looking for John. All the while the cop was speaking Dave never uttered a word. Finally, he says "I haven't seen him." The cop continues with his pandering, handing Dave his card "well this is no big deal. If you see John just tell him when he gets a chance to come down to the stationhouse and we can straighten this whole thing out." They left and we all had a laugh "this is no big deal."

Dave and I never hung out after that. John always said that Dave respected me, but he didn't like me because I should have just told him. He died a year or two later. The Pagan had shot him over a dozen times with a 22 and a 357 in the gut. The doctors had to remove over 'thirty feet of his intestines.' Glen disappeared after that and so did a few more people. Later I would find out that Glen's disappearance was the result of Vinnie Gambler dangling him headfirst out the second-floor window of APP talent Agency. That was when Savage took over the agency.

CHAPTER 9

Marlena caught site of Bobby's battle posture out of the corner of her eye. As she had been conditioned to do she ended her conversation in mid-sentence. She turned towards me and sauntered away from the now smirking cops. She stood over me and began to caress my face with her hand that was as soft as rose petals. Her nails were long and manicured with tiny suns and moons stenciled on them. The smell of her perfume was intoxicating. She cooed "oh you poor thing." Past the dark blur that was her I saw the smirks of the cops evaporate as they settled in to watch their favorite TV show; Alf, the sarcastic cat eating alien marooned on earth. All the cops loved this show. In fact, my two favorite deputy sheriffs, a middle-aged man and woman, would discuss it endlessly. Stuffed animal aliens, if they only knew what I knew they would be cleaning their guns.

Marlena seated herself in the lone chair beside my bed. Bobby stood stoically, if he had nothing else besides his balls he had the chivalric code. I wondered how he could even stand at all. He was wearing his cowboy boots that seemed to continue for inches beyond his toes, tapering to an impossible point. The toes on the boots were turned up and tipped with silver, giving the overall effect of a man wearing rockets on his feet. Phil and I joked behind his back that if only the boots were tipped with tiny bells and he had a matching hat his court jester uniform would be complete.

Marlena abruptly blurted out "has Michelle been up to see you?"

I answered "Wolf just got the restriction on her lifted. She'll be here. When SCPD was sitting on me she was sneaking by the door and having the nurses deliver notes to me for her." Bobby chimed in "how come she wasn't allowed to see you anyway?" "Because she's my codefendant" I answered. "She's taking the rap for the forty-four Magnum I always carried. Actually, it is really her gun. I couldn't believe it when she pulled that thing on Red for teasing her cat. I knew then something was moving the pieces. The Ruger Blackhawk has been my favorite handgun since I started reading Soldier of Fortune. Oh yea, lots of stunningly beautiful five foot two women carry around a single action forty-four Magnum with an eight-inch barrel in their pocketbook."

I gestured for Bobby and Marlena to move closer noticing that the cops were engrossed in Alf, these cops didn't care anyway. "She had that gun the night of Doxies party. It was in the car and she stuffed it in her pocketbook and wanted to take it into the party. She took off with it because I wouldn't let her into the club with the gun. She wanted to shoot Dianne. She would have too. She told me when she left that night she just rode around for a while and pulled over in Valley Stream. Three Niggers' come walking by the car and one asks her what time it was. She pulls the thing and takes a pot shot at them. Can you imagine? I guess Homey knew what time it was then."

I continued "Wolf says Bartle's is really leaning on her to say that pistol is mine. Who knows maybe he has a body on it. Ain't mine and who knows where that pistol comes from? Wolf doesn't care anyway. He guarantees she will get a fifty dollar fine. If he can get Phil sixteen days for cutting a head off and taking it by limo in a hatbox to Manhattan she doesn't have any worries. Wolf will just make it go away like he did all those headlines about this and like he did to the fucking Suffolk County Police Department."

SCPD had guarded me in my first few days in custody. No one was allowed to see me, and they had four cops in the room at all times. An old acquaintance of mine; Charlie Bartle's, was heading up the investigation and had personally installed his own pack of loyal hyena's to bed down next to me. One of the hyenas had explained to me that Bartle's had been promoted and I had been talking about how I had broken his arm at The Block for the last couple of years. Now it was time for pay back.

One cop was constantly calling him, always making it a point to say "gotta call Charlie" before getting up and leaving the room. Another one was a pimply faced sadist who timed my pain medication to make sure the nurses didn't come early with it. He had gotten in an argument with one because she was trying to give me a shot fifteen minutes early.

Then there was Charlie's intelligence operative, who looked more like an undercover child molester. He kept telling me I was going away for life unless I told them all about Richey Capri. I kept telling him "all I know about Richey is that he has been sleeping with your wife."

I will never forget when Wolf walked into the hospital room brandishing his papers like Van Helsing confronting Dracula with a crucifix. There were two Deputy Sheriff's behind him. "Out!" Wolf said in a loud commanding voice as he pushed the papers in the child molester type cops face. "Get out now!" The child molester cop looked at the papers and nodded to the rest of them and they grudgingly got up and filed out the door. Wolf followed the last one out and stared down the hall as they left.

As the picture of him embracing Ronald Reagan in his office attested to Wolf was about as high a powered lawyer as there was on the East Coast. Wolf told me that the Suffolk County Sheriff's Department would now take over guard duty and that they were civilized. He was right they were. He then told me that I wasn't going anywhere anyway and that when the time came he would get the bail down to a couple of thousand dollars. I could only nod in grateful awe when he told me I would have to do two to four years because I had a prior conviction for a violent felony but he could hold off sentencing for at least a year. These guys made their own laws.

At that point my most attractive nurse entered. She was waving a syringe full of dreams so I told Bobby and Marlena they would have to go. I don't remember her name, but she had long dark hair with a body like a dancer coupled with a wholesome disposition. I remember when she told me she was getting married in a month. I congratulated her and told her "just make sure he is one of your own kind." This troubled her and for the rest of my stay at the hospital she never passed up a chance to ask me to explain what I meant. Poor girl, I do not explain myself.

Bobby and Marlena left and I watched the nurse as she pulled the cap off the needle, flicking the dropper with her finger. She drained the air bubble, gently pushing the plunger till the precious liquid dribbled down. I rolled onto my side and she pulled my sweats down. There was a pin prick in my right buttock and the smell of alcohol as she cleaned the injection site. A warm hazy feeling enveloped my head and chest working its way down my spine as she pulled my sweatpants back up and I rolled over. I lit up a Marlboro with my good fingers.

CHAPTER 10

Morphine, I had my brief affair with its sister heroin years ago.

Those Who Would Arouse Leviathan

After Big Dave had died it seemed everyone was on heroin. John had become really bad. His arms and hands swelled till he looked like a balloon man at a children's party. I was up to twelve bags a day, a hundred and twenty dollars. Nobody ever will say it like the New York City street poet Jimmy Carroll: "need the angel whose touch don't miss when the blood runs through the dropper like a thick red kiss." There is a supernatural ritual seeing the blood bloom like a rose in the dropper. You pull back on the plunger and feel the anticipation of the warm numbness spreading through the loins. You push the plunger and the orgasm of bliss spreads with each beat of the heart.

We were going into the city and buying bundles and ounces in Harlem and the South Bronx, bringing them back to Long Island to sell. That kept us in heroin. I had a Ford Fiesta Turbo that had the biggest four-cylinder engine I have ever seen fitted in sideways under the hood. You could make it take off down the road wheel hopping and it burned rubber in every gear. It was the fastest thing I have ever seen with a twelve-inch wheel base.

One day John and I decided to chip in on an ounce. The day had begun early in the afternoon when he picked me up in his truck. The floor of the truck was covered with pistols. He hands me what looks like a miniature cylinder that was just big enough to hold five or six blanks with a one-inch barrel and a little tiny trigger. He doesn't say anything just gives me his satanic idiot laugh. He pulls up to the stop sign to talk to Johnny Vento, the kid who had introduced us in the sixth grade. I'm thinking it's a toy and laughing like an idiot myself. I point it at Vento with every intention of pulling the little trigger and scaring the shit out of him and John starts screaming "no, no!" as he grabs my hand. Turned out it was a real gun which John demonstrated by emptying it into a 50-gallon drum of fuel at Egil's from five feet away. As he was firing we all ran down the block fearing the drum would explode. All of the little 22's bounced harmlessly off the drum. Later John just said, "I knew nothing was going to happen."

John, Egil, Tommy, and I piled into my Fiesta and we took off for Harlem to buy an ounce. Egil drove. Before Egil's father went back to Norway he had been the head mechanic at Porsche & Audi in Amityville and the whole family treated driving like an art form. Egil always wanted to drive my car and show me what it could do. He said, "it is the fastest stock four cylinder ever made." He wasn't about to pass up an opportunity to be the getaway driver in a trip like this. John armed everybody. An ounce of pure heroin then cut up into a lot of ten-dollar bags. You and your friends could get high for days and you could still make money. The problem was finding the stuff pure.

Harlem back then was filled with abandoned buildings and piles of rubble that once were buildings. The rubbish piles took up whole blocks. When we got in we drove around the neighborhood a bit. Black stretch Cadillac's were pulling up to some of the abandoned buildings and Italian guys in suits would go in making deliveries. The secret was going into the building as soon as the Italian guy comes out before anyone's had time to touch the stuff. We pick a building and John and I go in. Two black guys in the doorway demand five dollars for admission. John doesn't say a word and without even showing them he's armed knocks them both out cold. We run up six flights of stairs and walk into the apartment with the guy who had the dope. We quickly struck a deal for an ounce. After shooting a little to make sure it was good we left.

When we got back out on the street we get in the car and Egil started to pull onto the avenue. All of a sudden a half dozen unmarked cars pull in front of us, breaks screeching. A White guy in a tea shirt jumps out holding a badge and says, "alright boys it's all over get out of the car." Yea right, Egil throws the car in reverse and go's wheel hoping as he fishtails around them backwards. We took off the wrong way down the avenue at a hundred miles an hour swerving in and out of oncoming cars. John and I were screaming for Egil to take a side block, but he just kept going. No man who valued his life was ever going to follow us. Finally, Egil turns down a side road filled with abandoned buildings. We ditch all the guns and the drugs out the windows as we go screaming down the street. The cops pick us up at another intersection and Egil starts to pull over. Suddenly John remembers the gun in his boot. He yells at Egil to "take off!"

By this time, we had at least a dozen squad cars behind us, sirens blaring. Suddenly Egil veers the car right into a three-story high pile of rubble. It was mostly bricks. Somehow he picks his way up and over it. He comes out on the street on the other side. John finally ditched the last gun which was good because the cops picked us up again at the intersection. When we finally pull over John jumps out and punches a cop in the face, don't ask me why. All the cops start swinging at us and each other with magnum flashlights and Walkie-talkies. Some of the cops were uniformed and some from a mayor's task force. They didn't know each other. Once the fight was over amongst themselves, they arrested us. These guys had a sense of humor and fair play.

A Black cop was showing one of his friends how he subdued the hulking John who had stopped fighting as soon as he hit the first cop. It was as if John knew he would start a riot and was entertaining himself. Demonstrating with his Walkie-talkie the cop says, "aye hit him with dis and I's kicked him like dis!" His gun fell out clanging on the floor when he demonstrated his kicking technique. Everyone from the station house dived for cover. All the cops had a laugh about it including the one who dropped his gun. We told them we didn't know who they were, and we were just trying to score. It was plausible since they didn't know who they were. The precinct was like a carnival. Cops were coming from other precincts just to meet Egil. I thought they were going to ask him for his autograph. They all said they had never seen anybody drive a car like that. "But you can't get away from a radio" they kept telling us.

They ended up fingerprinting us and giving us all full body cavity searches. After that they let us go giving Egil a bunch of tickets and trying to scare us with stories of what happens to white kids like us who come into Harlem trying to score drugs. That made us laugh later on, at least those of us that knew we were the spawn of the Devils own nightmare.

Egil beat the tickets by going to Norway and Eric moved in with Vigdis eventually marrying her and ruining the perfect party house. After Harlem I quit heroin cold turkey, crawling up my bedroom walls for a few days then walking away clean from it. John kept doing it till he went to jail.

Victory / נצח

CHAPTER 11

The American dream ended with the eighties. We awoke cold and naked in an economy car, dreams slowly fading like an old needle scar. At least that's something like the line in a poem I wrote around then in my youthful exuberance. I had gone to Florida with an old friend; Mike Guccione, who had moved to Merit Island when we were fourteen years old. He had bought a house in Melbourne and was undergoing a painful divorce. While I was staying in Melbourne a girl told me it was the place of Jim Morrison's birth. I hung out on the beaches and bars of A1A where I wrote poetry and shot up houses and cocaine. It ended with Mike's father and uncle driving me to the airport and asking me to never return again or 'there would be a contract out on me and the FBI would be told whose bullets they had dug out of a wall in West Palm Beach.' It seems I was a one-man crime wave. Not that they found that so disreputable. They were mobsters themselves, but they wanted their sons following them not me.

When I got back, I went into the construction business with my mother who was by now a renowned landscape designer. I bought a couple of pickup trucks and managed to get an almost brand new 1700 International box truck from a rental place with a bank loan. It was bright yellow, and Eric cut the box off in one day with a torch working all night. The next day he made panels for it and I was now in business. Some of the construction contracts I was working on for my mother required two foremen and two ten-man crews. I paid my men a hundred dollars a day. The foreman made a hundred and fifty plus incentives. The only criteria I had for my employees were that they had the strength of an ox and the temperament of a wolf. I sometimes had up to eight different parole and probation officers calling me to check up on their charges.

The dawning of each new day heralded endeavors which could only be compared to gladiatorial training under the relentless summer sun, the work only ended with the exhausted suns inevitable surrender to the cool breezes of the evening. Like some unseen hand dusk caressed the salty residue of sweat encasing sinewy muscles. An aphrodisiac of red blood pumping through strong veins mingled with the neon promises of the night. The whole atmosphere was charged with sexual anticipation.

I would drink beers and casually fling the empties from the cab into the rusty eight-foot bed in the back of my pickup truck. When the cacophony of their rolling around became too much it was time to toss them into the trash receptacles of the nearest convenient park. I do not seem to recall the carnage and trails of mangled body's left as roadside victims of the villainous drunken drivers that the modern media has somehow turned into beasts of mythical proportions. Once upon a time in America not that long ago the sight of a squad car did not invoke fear in the hearts of every American who was not a Stepford citizen. Police officers actually drove drunks' home and would never dream of drawing their gun unless you had drawn yours first. There was no arbitrary test decided by a three inch plastic tube that could make the absurd statement that a drooling senile old woman was a better driver than the reigning NASCAR champion if the racecar driver had recently drank a couple of beers.

When I first graduated High School, we would build huge bon fires on the beach and gather by the hundreds in Tanner Park overlooking the bay. We smoked our pot and pursued our teenage love affairs. They were looking for the Son of Sam in the city, but this was Long Island. If the cops came around, they gave us a knowing smile and told us to behave ourselves. I loved my country because I was free before freedom was just a word in a Janis Joplin song. I remember when the Iranians took hostages and burned our flag in the street. I would have gladly gone to Iran and killed every one of those bug-eyed bastards. By the time the eighties were over I would have handed them a match.

CHAPTER 12

A few years later I was calling myself an outlaw but perhaps a knight errant would have been more appropriate although the whole chivalric thing does ring pretty corny in the twenty first century. From the time I was old enough to talk I knew there could be no higher aspiration for a man than to be a poet warrior. If you have not slept with the most beautiful women you have ever seen, if you have ever backed out of some critical moral dilemma for fear of personal injury, if you have never prevailed against overwhelming odds to see your enemy driven before you, then it is my contention that your life and all your material possessions are less impressive to the Gods than some homeless war veteran, who has done some of those things, that you leave laying in the street.

The cops all knew me and not because of John. I wrecked my first bar by myself when I was about twenty-one years old. Mo's place, every working-class neighborhood used to have at least one place just like it 'oh don't fuck with that guy! He'll kill you!' You know; the place where testosterone is as plentiful as the beer. The owner was a muscle-bound aficionado of blow dryers named Harry Defrance. Harry liked to snort cocaine with underage girls in the backroom. The bouncer was some rotund little man with a third-degree black belt. Joe Scarione was making a fortune with his karate school and he had everybody in Copiague convinced that he was the second coming of Bruce Lee. To me it just looked like he had swallowed Bruce Lee.

I knew there would be trouble that night. I had been in there early drinking with some pretty rough characters, among them Dave Lamante president of the Long Island chapter of the Pagans, his brother; Ronnie, and another guy that Suffolk county homicide later dubbed Lurch. Back then he was just Phil, a guy I had known for years. After work we would all meet at the combination Dojo and gym in Phil's basement which was kindly donated by the Amityville Police Department when they had made a procedural error and tried to arrest Phil in my yard out of their jurisdiction. When the legal wrangling was over, they had to pay me twenty five thousand dollars and meticulously observe the order of protection the judge had issued on my behalf.

Phil had the same eyes I had seen on sharks during the years of my youth as a fishermen. They stared straight out from under his long brown hair, uncaring, unflinching, and unfeeling. At six foot two and two hundred- and forty-pounds Phil just may have been the strongest man alive, although he didn't advertise. He would just look up the record and break it in the gym we had set up in his basement. I had seen him squat with over twelve hundred pounds. The bar bearing the weight of six one-hundred-pound plates on each side would reverberate like a guitar string plucked while it was stretched to its breaking point. He would eat a giant raw steak and just start slapping hundred-pound plates on a homemade Squat Rack welded by Eric. There were bent bars strewn all over his basement. The bars would invariably bend like a U around his massive shoulders. He could do sets of ten lateral pull downs with five hundred pounds.

The Pagans were courting Phil hard. At the time they had just given him a vintage Harley-Davidson Café Racer and were sitting in Mo's Place buying us shots of Wild Turkey. Phil had been Big Dave's personnel chauffer during the last year of his life and just knowing Big Dave, whom the Pagans called the Bubba, had a religious significance with the Pagans. It turned out to be a lot of shots since Dave Lamante seemed to have this strange idea that he could out drink me. I knew that even though Dave was a lot older than me there was nothing he could do better than me. I made no attempt to hide my distain for him and his bicycle club. I knew what John had done to them.

It seemed like every time we did a shot another one of Kevin McCauley's crew filed into the bar. They were all making money stealing cars for the local Mafioso. McCauley was their leader and I will have to admit a better-looking specimen of a young man I have never seen in my over fifty years of existence. Six-foot-tall with a body like Adonis capped by long wavy brown hair and that perfect square jaw that only a select few of Irish descent are blessed with. He could fight too. I had watched him spar on the beach and he was as good with his feet as any other man I've ever seen.

In retrospect I guess Kevin and I were rivals but at the time I was completely naive to stuff like that. When Kevin's girlfriend propositioned me the night before she was to leave for army boot camp I sure as hell wasn't turning her down. This girl was the proverbial blond beauty, that all American girl that most guys only get to dream about. We spent the night in the cab of my pickup truck overlooking Amityville beach. In between making sweat soaked love she told me how unhappy she was with Kevin and her life in general. How she was joining the army just to get away from him. It was the next day now. The girl was already gone, and Kevin thought he was entitled to some payback.

Dave gave up after only about ten shots. We walked outside with Joe Scarione who assured Dave that he would let nothing happen to me while he was working. Dave claimed he had a date with two girls at Something Else the Pagan watering hole a couple of blocks east on Montauk Highway. He left Phil with strict instructions to come and get him at the slightest sign of trouble and he would bring the whole club. With that we slowly sauntered back into Mo's Place. The roaring sounds of bikes faded into the night. I knew full well I was pretty much on my own in this one.

    Phil had a big bag of Quaaludes on him and when we took our seats at the bar I told him to give me one. Phil being the stupid Polock that he was took two. I had a beer and reveled in the Wild Turkey buzz already coursing through my veins. Soon it would combine with the Quaalude and unleash the Demon that shares my body. All the while McCauley's boys were filing in, gathering around the pool table in the back. I didn't count them, but the number was definitely between ten and twenty. By the time McCauley made his grand entrance the Quaalude had done its job well. I know when the Demon is free. It's like being a passenger in a car. I am no longer driving the vehicle and everything, even my memories of events, are in a red haze.

    McCauley strode to the back in quick purposeful movements and began playing pool with himself never looking at the balls just staring malevolently at me. I turned around to see Phil's face down on the bar in a puddle of his own drool. It wasn't Phil's fault. Alcohol and barbiturates do not affect me the way they affect others, if anything they demonically stimulate me. I am the real-life Dr Jeckel and Mr. Hyde.

    It was Hyde that walked up to the pool table and asked McCauley whether he was there to fight or play pool. McCauley let out this animal scream and sprung over the pool table swinging the cue stick at me in the same motion but Hyde see's everything coming at him in slow motion and he has superhuman strength. Hyde stepped into McCauley's leap and wrapped his arm around McCauley's snapping it with the ease of which a man would snap a piece of dried kindling. McCauley was still screaming but now it was in pain as he lay on the ground and Hyde purposefully set about breaking his other arm oblivious to the blows being rained down upon him by McCauley's friends. When Hyde was done with McCauley, he turned on the insects that had been attacking him. Three of them went to the hospital with bruised hearts from heart punches. They all had severe facial contusions, but Hyde was nowhere near through. He ripped the payphone off the wall and proceeded to beat anyone who was dumb enough to still be standing with it. Because Mo's place also needed to be punished, he went behind the bar and used the pay phone to smash every bottle of liquor in that bar. Then he kicked out the plate glass windows and explained to the cowering Joe Scarione that it was now his turn. To the little fat man's credit, he did manage to land a kick to my back. That was the only mark I got on me that night, but he also slept for a long time after Hyde hit him with a right-hand counter punch. In fact, Hyde finally decided to leave and go home because he thought he might have killed him.

    The police, the ambulances, and the Pagans, all responded at about the same time. I was home sleeping like Lon Chaney Jr. The two cops who moonlighted for my mother building outdoor decks told me that when the police got there, they just assumed the Pagans were responsible. When the indignant owner of Mo's showed up and refused to stop shouting they resculptured his hair with their nightsticks and charged him with removing his own payphone since 'it would have required premeditation and the use of a machine to pull the two through bolts out of the concrete.' I was never charged with assaulting anyone. Back then, before Bernie Goetz, you could not be charged with assaulting a professional criminal.

    This was not to be the last time I did the cops a favor. My foreman was a Black guy named Steve Husbands. We were up at a place in Amityville that was called The Block in the eighties. At the time it was probably the worst area in the country. The Five Percent Nation of Islam was just taking hold and they had laid claim to the pool hall on the northern corner as their clubhouse. Crack had not yet been invented but these were the same fledgling gangstas that would go on to become the Supreme team of Rap folklore. If you take the express train; Amityville to Jamaica is about a twenty-minute ride on the Long Island Railroad. There were more people from Jamaica than from Amityville hanging out at the block and there were always hundreds of people milling around at all hours of the day and night.

    Steve was making over a thousand dollars cash a week working for me at the time and in Black culture back then that entitled him to the finest girl. Her name was Candy. And believe me she was. One of the Five Percenters was upset that Steve had taken his Candy. Steve's brother: Michael, was a renowned martial artist whom Chuck Norris refused to fight and Steve himself was a nationally ranked hundred- and sixty-pound wrestler so it wasn't much of a fight. Steve proceeded to beat him like the proverbial red headed stepchild, and I sat in the cab of my 1700 International laughing, but it soon turned deadly serious. The rest of the Five Percenters came swarming out of the pool hall and engaged the outnumbered Rasta's who had been cheering Steve on since he was Jamaican.

    Predictably in the wild melee that ensued I lost it. The next thing I remember was Steve driving my truck as I was making a perfect shot with my 300 Savage rifle, skipping a six-inch chunk of black top right into the back of a fleeing Five Percenter. The whole corner of the pool hall was collapsed. It turned out that I had sent the big flatbed wheel hopping in its lowest reverse gear right through the front window. Then I went home and got the rifle and had Steve drive while I took pot shots at their feet as they scurried for cover. I remembered none of it. Needless to say, I had serious anger management issues but again back then you could not be arrested for assaulting a professional criminal. The police force was not yet a paramilitary unit and since my truck had my name and telephone number prominently displayed on both sides, I attributed their lack of retribution as a display of their gratitude to me for doing their dirty work for them. That pool hall would remain boarded up and a reinforced monument to Hyde. Eric welded my tail lift back together and nobody from that side of town would ever fuck with me again. This was to be my undoing when later I would develop a crack problem.

CHAPTER 13

The chains pulled taught around the casts and jerked me back down into the hospital bed as if I had been levitating in my sleep. I was drenched in sweat and for a moment I did not know who or where I was. The combined restraints of my injuries and the manacles had frozen my body to the bed and I felt a claustrophobic panic beginning to overwhelm me. I forced myself to concentrate and evaluate my situation. My memories suddenly came flooding back as if some great spigot had opened a subterranean torrent of distorted images and swirling sorrow.

I had been dreaming. I was in Aleister Crowley's Boleskine House overlooking Loch Ness. There was a cavernous opening in a wall. It looked like some kind of vault. Within the vault was a gateway which was guarded by a male and a female child. The children were about twelve years old and of oriental descent. They were both wearing flowing silk robes and they did not speak but somehow I knew that Crowley had used them to carry out the instructions given in S.L. MacGregor Mather's translation of the Sacred Magic of Abramelin the Mage. Crowley had secured the house by the lake and undergone all the purification rituals prescribed in the manuscript. At the moment when the ritual is supposed to culminate with the appearance of an Angel who will transmit, through a prepubescent child, the sublime revelations that can transform a man into a God Crowley added his own little twist to the ritual. He slit the throat of each of the children and opted to forgo the ungainly intermediary's in favor of the knowledge being delivered directly to him. The children now stood as eternal sentinels to the portal he had opened up. They gestured for me to enter into the portal and when I did, I saw that Crowley had unleashed three great demons into the world. Two of the dark Gods had already insinuated themselves into the collective soul but the third still lurked on the bottom of the lake. I saw them in their unimaginable vastness and all the corruption they had brought upon the earth, now reeking with filth. Suddenly I realized that they were aware of my presence as was the one that was dormant on the bottom of the lake. The one on the bottom of the lake was the most powerful and maybe because I could not see it the most sinister. It rose up to meet me and I was griped with fear. I took flight over an endless roiling sea hurtling faster and faster through the grey and angry sky. The terror at my heels took the form of construction dumpsters and I could hear them clanging together as they pursued me. I flew faster and faster till my momentum hurled me across the dreams event horizon and I crashed down into the hospital bed.

    The evening's shadows had begun to encroach in the corners of the hospital room. I must have been sleeping for hours because the deputy sheriffs were already on the night shift. The deputy the other ones called 'Deputy Droop along' behind his back sat in the corner enveloped by his own ten-gallon hat. His emaciated chicken body barely filling out his child sized uniform and the oversized gun in his holster threatened to drag him over if he stood up. He never spoke to me in more than one- or two-word sentences and only when he had to. The other deputy looked at me with concern that may have bordered on empathy. He said "are you alright? I've wrung for the nurse." She came in and tried to feed me some of the food from the cold uneaten tray next to me. I declined and told her I had just had a vivid nightmare that was more like a hallucination. She explained to me that my Dr. had prescribed Halcion for me to sleep at night and it was notorious for its hallucinatory side effects. I made my obligatory request for pain medication and she complied returning in a few minutes with a syringe that was dripping with dreams. She told me that she would hold off on my nightly mega dose of Halcion till my Dr. could be consulted. This was the nurse who had faced down the pimply faced SCPD cop who was monitoring my pain medication. She looked like she was just over the edge of forty and made hard as granite from years of gluing soldiers back together in Vietnam. She made it obvious she knew more about traumatic wounds than any of the doctors. I would see her again much later when I got sick in Wyoming the medium for Attica. That's the way this swirling madness is, faces and events are swept in and out of my awareness repetitively. What I think and do becomes songs and pop culture and what is pop culture and songs become what I think and do. I do not know if I am the reflection or the image. There is an occult school of thought which adheres to the belief that God must uphold his creation, every second of every hour, in eternal vigilance. If ever God should be distracted or lose concentration, then his entire creation would cease to exist. God would need a filing system, like the library's Dewey Decimal System, to perform this seemingly impossible task. Somehow, I seem to have accessed that system.

    Way back when I was the angelic little boy collecting Roman Catholic icons the nuns had made us do a reading comprehension test on a paragraph, they gave us to read. The paragraph was about a man who had entered a church in a state of delirium. He was flaying his arms through the church's stain glass windows and cutting himself up like a holiday roast. He screamed incoherently about being pursued by demons and Hecate herself whom he had summoned in a Black Magic ceremony. The paragraph ended with him bleeding out as a mutilated mass of flesh, still murmuring about Hecate when the police and the priests arrived. The nuns had been apologetic afterwards and explained to us that the state required the tests and they had no choice in the format. They told us that Hecate was the Goddess of Witchcraft and that she is Dianna the Moon Goddess in the most malevolent of her three forms. It had always stuck in my mind as something that had no place in a ten-year old's Catholic education. Now I had enacted the very same nightmare.

    I was at the height of my earning power when I rented a house in Wheatley Heights with Steve. Wheatley Heights served as a buffer between affluent White Dix Hills and Long Island's largest ghetto, Wyandanch. The houses unfurnished rooms would host parties where I would dump out bags of coke on my bureau and the rocks would bounce off its polished surface while I watched the girls crawl around the floor, with their ass's straining upwards, trying to find them. That was the closest I would get to intercourse then. I would go out with different girls but as Ozzy Osbourne said in Paranoid: "nothing seems to satisfy." My mind was a labyrinth of disembodied pornographic images. It was all about hedonism then and I was in a constant state of arousal, but I did not know yet for what let alone how I could possibly get it.

    My mother had landed a contract to landscape the parish of Maria Regina in Farmingdale. It was almost a hundred thousand square feet of sod and over a hundred trees along with all the bushes, plants, and masonry work. I had open sores on my knees from laying sod all day. The house in Wheatley Heights was on a dead end with acres of sprawling lawn bordered by woods on two sides. I would park my trucks in the back and start partying before I even got in the shower. There was the Ritz in Manhattan and Malibu's in Island Park. The hottest new spot on Long Island was Spies right over in Farmingdale. If all else failed there was always Mo's place and the Amityville strip. Bob Matheson had long since heeded his own advice and left town taking with him the seashore innocence of Long Island embodied by the OBI South. Jim, who was my other foreman, would sometimes not make it to his car in the front of my house. I would find him instructing the local Black kids on how to guzzle a forty of Colt in the vacant lot adjoining the property. Steve was running an after-hour ticket scalping agency out of the house and supplying coke to celebrities.

    Kenny who had always been good at dealing drugs had traded in his Quaalude connection for some Columbians who were processing paste right in New Jersey. The Coke was made with ether. It was the finest fish scale that ever hit the streets. You could smell an open bag from across the room. The phone kept ringing incessantly up in my room one night. I shared the phone line with Steve, but he wasn't answering. It was four in the morning, so I picked it up and curtly asked "who's this?" A jovial voice answered "its Joe. Is Steve there?" Losing my patience, I said "Joe who?" "Joe from Aerosmith." he replied. It turned out it was Joe Perry. He wanted an ounce of that rocket fuel he had been hearing about and he needed it delivered "to L'Amour East tomorrow night before the show." Kenny got all excited about meeting Joe Perry and decided to deliver it himself. I went with him figuring I would get to hang out with the great guitarist in the famous club. When we got there at the appointed time, we went to a steel door on the side and knocked. A Black guy who was about six foot six and four hundred pounds answered and ushered us in. He brought us to a bathroom with a couple of sinks and stalls and told us to wait there he would go get Joe. A few minutes later Joe came back with him and eagerly forked over twelve hundred dollars for an eight-hundred-dollar ounce. He started greedily shoveling it in his nose. I tried to warn him that it was stronger than what he was used to, but my words went unheeded. Abruptly he scurried into a stall and closed the door behind him. The sniffing sounds continued but there were no other signs of Joe. After about ten minutes we asked the bodyguard if Joe was okay. With a look of disgust on his face he started addressing the stall "Joe, Joe. Joe!" We heard a whispering sound and the bodyguard put his ear to the stall. They carried on a conversation in hushed tones that were inaudible to us even though we were only a few feet away. After a while the bodyguard came back to us rolling his eyes "now he thinks you guys are cops. You don't know. I go through this with him every other night. I gotta have him on the stage in ten minutes. Could you guys just leave so I can get him out of there?"

    Negron was always over the house in Wheatley Heights. He was a frenetic Puerto Rican who was Steve's partner with his side businesses.

He would sometimes work with us on the truck. One day on the way home he pulls out with some Angel Dust. I smoked it with them and had what can only be described as a psychotic episode that lasted for about a week. Ronald Reagan was reasserting the empires global might and had invaded the island paradise of Grenada off the coast of Venezuela. All over the TV American soldiers were waging war on Cuban soldiers in a showdown that had been twenty-five years in the making. Probably out of a combination of the chemicals and envy I began to believe I was there and that Negron and his brother, who was in reality a Repo man from Queens who sold ground up crystal methamphetamine as cocaine on the side, were some kind of Cuban intelligence operatives. I saw the day to day construction tasks as incursions to kill the Cubans. I hid my break from reality from everyone around me but I remember the intense exhilaration I felt during that time. It was from the bowels of my body beyond my rational minds reach.

  The envy may have been the result of a flirtation I had with joining the army a few years before. There was a recruiting office right next to the APP talent agency and I figured I would hear what the guy had to say. He ended up getting me to take a bunch of tests and then he called me for months. He told me that I had scored extremely high on the tests and that I could be whatever I wanted to be in the army. I told him that what I wanted to be was in a war and that since Vietnam was over there wasn't any chance the army could give me what I want. When Grenada came I was making too much money to reconsider the recruiters offer and even if I did by the time I was ready to be deployed it would be over anyway.

  In the morning I would awaken to the sounds of birds outside the window. Sometimes I had not slept at all and would just put on a pair of sunglass's and jump in the truck to drive the five miles to the church. I would have Modern Love blasting on the radio. It was being played on every station all day every day. I had seen the concert live from the second row of Madison Square Garden when Bowie had done the tour. Again, I was living in the Lyrics of a rock and roll song. The theme of the song was getting to the church on time. The church promoted the party and suspends belief in everything else including God, man, and love. The song was right. At the time I didn't believe in anything I could not see. I had no religion beyond my own hedonism and love was just another word for lust. Soon I would see things that no man should ever see but for then I was becoming uncomfortably aware that I was following some script that was woven into the tapestry of the collective conscious. There are templates to which everything that exists must conform. Over and over again we play out the same dramas. It's always the same situations but in different settings. Some dramas are set in bar rooms, some in offices, and some on as grandiose a stage as the Trojan War. C J Jung called them archetypes. Fredrick Nietzsche called it the eternal recurrence. When Nietzsche saw it clearly it drove him mad.

John had long been released from prison when I got the house. His story was he wasn't going back. He had taken up with a girl named Meryl and he couldn't marry her soon enough. I don't remember why but I was saving a very expensive bottle of twelve-year-old Wild Turkey. I ended up drinking it in my room with Jim and John. When we came down Steve was outside with a bunch of people having a barbeque. Jim went into his Aryan demolition mode and chased Steve around the house for a couple of laps before John and I got Jim into the car and out of there. I was getting weary of Jim's vendetta against Steve. Jim was running one of my crews and Steve the other. I couldn't have them both together even when we worked. Jim's crew would work on one side of the parish and Steve's crew the other. Jim was almost certain to attack Steve on sight with robotic redundancy. Steve was usually fast enough to give him the slip but a few months earlier Jim had wedged him up against a truck with his fingers dug deeply into Steve's mouth and eye sockets. Jim was trying to get enough leverage to break his neck when I hit him with a cross body block to break it up. Jim was incredulous with me, later saying "what were you doing I finally got the nigger in the mask?" The mask was what Jim called griping the human face like a bowling ball. Steve for his part also blamed me. He was tired of living like Inspector Clouseau in the Pink Panther under constant threat of attack from a murderous version of a Cato who looked more like the poster boy from the SS. I was at my ropes end with both of them but what was I going to do? They were both my friends and they both needed the job. Besides they were both very good at getting the maximum amount of work out of my other employees.

The whole thing started years ago on a sultry summer night not long after John made his peace with the Pagans. John had found an abandoned barnacle encrusted forty-five-foot yacht floating around the flats of the Great South Bay. He towed the old wooden relic back to his parent's dock and immediately installed two bilge pumps that looked like they belonged on a battleship. John would need to keep the seawater out since he then outfitted the hulk with the thousands of dollars in stereo equipment, he had appropriated from various nightclubs he and Big Dave had worked at. All night we would blast Frank Zappa from the boat serenading the tourists who were milling around Ocean Ave sometimes in the hundreds. That night when John, Jim, and I, pulled into the driveway there was an unusually large crowd on Ocean Avenue. We were tired of playing them It Can't Happen Here, I guess because they didn't get it. We were debating on whether we should play Zappa's Live from the Fillmore East or just throw on his Wonderful Wino song. We elected to go with Live From the Fillmore East wherein Howard Kaylan and Mark Volman of the Turtles provide the vocals to a song about their dick which is a monster, a reamer right into the heart, a Harley that needs to be kicked to start. It's all done to the tune of a combination of Frank Zappa's peerless guitar work and the Turtles pop smash hit Happy Together.

We grabbed some supply's from the boat, a few bottles of Colt and a three foot bong with a bag full of fine Columbian that had been run through a box screen to enable us to inhale a whole regular pipe bowl in one hit. We turned the sound system up full blast and went amongst the crowd. We were just getting warmed up when we finished the forty's and atomized them in the middle of Ocean Ave. The spectators, some from clear across the country, weren't seeing no ghosts just a glimpse of the contempt that feeds the malevolence of the hell that so fascinated them. I would think that it was more than they ever could have hoped for on their pilgrimage to see the Amityville Horror. John was doing his best satanic laugh as he milled around the crowd incinerating enough pot to roll three joints in each hit, he took out of the huge bong. The tourists loved it unfortunately Johns father didn't. He came running out of the house screaming at John "this is your problem!" He snatched the bong out of Johns hand and smashed it in the street. The supposedly unbreakable PVC pipe fragments were almost as small as the remaining shards of glass from the Colt bottles we had just smashed.

It was live theater at its finest when John's father stormed back into the house. I am sure nobody from Kansas had ever seen anything like it and there just happened to have been four of the most beautiful woman I have ever seen shining like polished silver among the unkempt hordes that were our audience. They were from Kansas and said they were cheerleaders for the Kansas City Chiefs. They had been up in New England on vacation and decided they just had to see the Amityville Horror House. We invited them to party with us on Johns "yacht" in the back and they were only too eager to comply. We ended up going skinny dipping and swimming into the Defoe's boathouse with them. That was as far as they were going but they had their story for the folks back home and we had ours. John wasn't satisfied with ours. So, when an old high school friend of mine named Millie came around later looking for drugs John got a bit frisky with her. She seemed like she was enjoying it to me, so I wasn't saying anything. About an hour after she left a storm of bottles pelted the boat and an army of Mo's place denizens attempted to come on board. John sent a couple of them flying overboard with spinning back fists and they ended up fleeing back to their cars, but Jim had caught a quart bottle right in the face landing him in the hospital for weeks. There must have been about twenty or thirty guys there and I knew all of them and they were all throwing bottles because there wasn't any five of them that could stand in with one of us. But Jim blamed Steve because he was the easiest to remember since he was the only Black guy there. They all tried to apologize when they realized I wasn't going to let a friend get raped. Seems Millie had neglected to even say I was there. They even went to the hospital to see Jim trying to apologize but that only made it worse because it was easier for Jim to memorize Steve's face.

CHAPTER 14

Kenny's sisters had come of age along with the punk rock scene on Long Island. They had always been nuisances when we were younger, and Kenny would be forced to stay home to babysit them. But now they were bombshells dressed in tattered skintight animal prints showing off more curves than the Interborough Parkway. There were five of them in an extended family. Paige was the oldest sister at eighteen spending every summer day on the beach working on her deep bronze tan. Her best friends were Edna, Genie and Gabriella who preferred to be called Goby. Edna was a blond that was too fast for her own good and she would die of AIDs a few years later. Genie looked like a California surfer girl and she liked to hang out up in Edna's room with her playing with Chinese throwing stars and dirty needles. Goby was by far the most beautiful, a first-generation German immigrant with a long slinky body that drove me out of my mind. I pursued her relentlessly, but she seemed immune to my charms which made me want her even more. She fucked everybody in town but me. One night I had followed her into a local bar in Copiague and she was with some thirty something drug dealer. I went nuts and started throwing chairs through the windows. The two of them skirted around me and out the back door retreating to the drug dealer's house while I beat the hell out of the hapless bouncer and bartender. When I was done laying waste to the place I went and got my big truck and tried to back it through the front door of the drug dealer's house but I couldn't get it under the tree in the front. The cops ended up coming along with my mother and my mother's carpenter cops. The cops decided I was too drunk to drive the truck and it simply wasn't feasible for me to kill somebody right in front of them. They drove me up to Pathmark to collect Phil who worked the nightshift there. He came down and disengaged the truck from the tree and got it safely back in the lot. It was up to Zappa to make the music that would mock me. He cut a song soon after; Goblin Girl, a song about a weird girl whose specialty was oral sex.

    The fifth one was Dawn, Kenny's younger sister, at sixteen she was Victoria's Secrets version of Kenny. Dawn had Kenny's green eyes and dark hair with breasts that strained tauntingly against the skintight shirts she wore. She had more street smarts than the other four combined. The girls were like my private harem. I took them all over with me. I wasn't having sex with them, but everybody thought I was. One night a drunk at Mo's place had the audacity to ask me what it was like having five girls like that at my sexual disposal. I just sneered at him. It was still early in the eighties, but I knew then people were already basing their perceptions of reality from the twisted images coming out of Hollywood.

    It all seemed monotonous like rain every night. I can still see the neon reflected in the puddles outside of Mo's Place. Steve broke up with Candy and took up with some twenty something White girl named Debbie who lived over the gas station across the street from Mo's Place. Steve had what I call the OJ Simpson syndrome. That's when a Black guy ignores the most beautiful Black woman in favor of the first available White slut. It almost always ends in disaster for the brother and it would for Steve too. Debbie soon became fast friends with Kenny's sisters and crew and her apartment became our private after hour's club. One night I took one too many Tuinals and passed out there. When I came to the girls wanted to go across the street and drink. I was walking around the bar and everybody was laughing at me. Somebody told me to go in the bathroom and look in the mirror. The girls had painted my face to look like the androgynous gender confused singer Boy George. I'll be dammed if I didn't look just as good as Mick Jagger ever did. I left it like that. Another time the bar was closing so I pulled my pickup out with the green light in order to park it at the gas station. There was an explosion right at my side and the truck went tumbling over and over like it was in a spin cycle at the laundry mat. Some guy had run the light at sixty miles an hour and broadsided me. The upside-down truck was still spinning like a top and I could hear the girls screaming and crying as I waited for it to stop. When it did, I kicked out the front window and climbed out without a scratch on me. It wasn't human and I knew it. At this point I did not know whether I was a man or a God. Maybe I had drowned long ago and this was just all one drawn out final dream.

    Things were happening that should only happen in a dream. In my last year of college, I had attended the Seldon campus of Suffolk County Community College. I couldn't stand it anymore. I was embarrassed to be there. I envied the guys whom a generation before me had Vietnam as an option to this cultural absurdity. I remember that campus crowded with White kids, some Black, all with pretentions of being bourgeois. Get married, procreate, get a job, there's nothing else for you here boys and girls. Or maybe just take a long swim away from the beach and see if you can make it back like Albert Camus character in the The Stranger. These people were all going to spend their next fifty years living a lie. The main campus had a two-level lounge with a central stairway and there were always hundreds of 'students' milling about. Between class's I would find a place in an out of the way corner and sprawl out on the floor like a soldier at rest, blasting my Walkman as I tried to become invisible. There were two girls there and the social life seemed to revolve around them. They were like they just stepped out of the Rolling Stones song Nineteenth Nervous Breakdown. I would blast it on my Walkman as I observed them from afar. They were trying so hard to be the center of the crowd clomping up and down the stairs in the heavy high heeled shoes that were the style then and talking as loud as possible trying to draw attention. In their own way they seemed a little pathetic, but they were both strikingly beautiful. The tall one's name was Julie Anne and she was the Dragon Princess of Shirley, Long Island's trailer park capital. Most guys were too afraid to even talk to her if they weren't spoken to first. Her family was mob royalty. Her eyes were big brown pools that a man could drown in and her long slender body sleek and perfect. Her little Puerto Rican side kick was named Sonia and she was just as stunning in a more sexually provocative kind of way. I had once watched Sonia doing lateral pull downs in the campus gym. She was wearing an open backed shirt and you could see all the perfectly striated muscles in her back ripple as she strained against the weights doing countless reps. At the time I was invisible, but I fantasized about a ménage a trois with both of them.

    I had never forgotten these girls. Years later I would still sometimes drive the twenty extra miles out east to the beach at Smiths Point hoping I would run into them. Every time I got around Mastic and Shirley, I could almost smell the sticky sweet aroma of the dangerous perfume that was Julie Anne's aura wafting through the dilapidated gas stations and boarded up buildings of those shit hole towns. Kenny started doing business with a forty something year old guy named Rick from out in Seldon. Rick had mob connections which was how he knew about Kenny and his rocket fuel cocaine. I didn't know anything about Julie Anne except what I just said but I smelled her all over Rick. We partied a few times over Kenny's and Rick became enamored with me as many people often do. Rick invited me to come over for a big barbecue he was having at his house in Seldon. I was sitting in the backyard drinking beers with about thirty other people when she walked through the picket gate still comporting herself like royalty. The strangest part of the whole thing was I wasn't in the least bit surprised. There was about a half a million people living on that part of the island at the time and at least half of them thought they were mobsters like Rick. She was still with the same guy she was with back in college and she still looked entirely like to much woman for him. I guess I wasn't as invisible as I thought I was back in school because she remembered me. She had been with that guy for about five years and it took about a month of Rick carrying messages back and forth between us until I got her to consent to meet with me at her sister in laws house. She told me her boyfriend wouldn't go near the place and I told her about my fantasy back in school involving her and Sonia. She told me Sonia would be there too.

    I may have been convinced of my own invulnerability, but I was no fool. I wasn't going alone. I could not take Phil he would scare even these girls, so I had to get John away from Meryl for an evening. I did this with promises of cocaine and Penthouse center folds. John had seen Marie. As a matter of fact he had begged us to have sex on his bed in his house in Lindenhurst so he could watch. Too bad for him I wasn't so inclined back then, but he knew I wasn't fooling around when I mentioned the caliber of the woman. When we got there, I met her sister in-law for the first time. She was as hard a looking woman as I have ever seen, around thirty-five years old and completely spent. She immediately starts showing me these framed aerial photos of her house hanging in the hallway. The photos were courtesy of the FBI. Seemed Julie Anne's brother had been running a storage facility for dead Guido's in his backyard. When the FBI had raided the house a few months back they had found no less than six of them stuffed into barrels right next to his barbecue. I had heard about this on the news, but I had never put the two together. You would have thought she would have mentioned a little thing like that in our previous months' worth of conversations. Rick never had either. Of course, John thought it was really cool and made himself right at home settling into the Italian silk sofa with his ostrich skin cowboy boots up on the coffee table.

    I began appraising the situation in my head. Julie Anne was putting her cards right on the table. She wasn't looking for a sexual escapade that night. If she had to she would. But what she wanted was a relationship. She was done and she knew it. The whole mafia princess thing was over. No more designer cloths and fancy cars, no more exaggerated respect and the soft lies that she so wanted to hear. Her whole world was over, and her current boyfriend was never going to get it back for her. He was afraid to even go near her brother's house. She had probably been playing me all along that's why it had all been so easy. Rick was her talent scout and I was invited to that party with the specific intention of her meeting me. It was all the better that she knew me from her glory days in school when I was invisible. Wow, all this shit was going on in my mind all night as we did line after line of Kenny's finest. Sonia got there and it seemed like she just did what she was told. John had her on her stomach sprawled across the silk couch with her shirt off. He was massaging that perfectly arched back of hers and lecturing her about Wilhelm Reich and Orgone energy. She would have blown him if he asked her because that was what Julie Anne wanted. Julie Anne and her sister in-law talked casually about the murders and how stupid it was of her brother to have those body's in the backyard like that. At one-point Julie Anne even laughingly suggested that somebody should kill her boyfriend so that she would be free to go out with me. By daybreak my head was spinning. I can't say I wasn't intrigued with the whole thing. I was attracted to her like I was never attracted to any other girl before. She was a Sicilian pedigree and she wasn't going to be taking any shorts. I knew enough to know that if I had sex with her that night or on any other night, she would have her hooks in me and my life, as I knew it, essentially would be over. I needed time to think this whole thing over, so I made my goodbyes and John grudgingly unhanded Sonia. John was pushing three hundred pounds now. The Teutonic War God body was gone for good and he was never going to have another opportunity like that. When we got in the car, he said "what are you doing we had them." I said "you had her naked for two hours on the couch. Were you waiting for my permission? Wilhelm Reich? You think these girls want to know about Wilhelm Reich? All they want to know is what we can do for them." We didn't say anything else to each other for the rest of the ride home. I think he knew what I was thinking. He always does.

CHAPTER 15

I started dwelling on Julie Anne too much and became morose. Rick was still acting as the messenger between the two of us and one day I was over his house. I was partying coke in his room with him, his wife, and a few other people. All of a sudden Rick starts shouting to his twelve-year-old daughter that she should come in the room. When she did Rick cut her out a line and told her it was cocaine. He told her that her and her friends would be doing it soon and that when they did they should always get it from him. He made her snort the line and told her "daddy always has only pure coke. You never know what other people are going to try and give you." His wife chimed in "always get it from Daddy dear." I had seen many strange and appalling things, even by then, but this made my stomach retch. I asked Rick to give me an ounce I would give it back to him after I saw Kenny. Then I immediately left making some excuse about being somewhere else.

    I don't know whether it was that night or a few nights later but I was at my parent's house. I had a handful purple Xanax from the bottle of ten thousand that a nurse at the Veterans Hospital in Kings Park procured for Steve every month. My parents were gone. They were on a cruise through the Caribbean in a seventy-foot boat my father was captaining for my mother's boss; Lenard Tower. My father would come home a few weeks later with stories of being tailed at night by mysterious lights and standing guard with a rifle while everyone else slept. After my mother and father had come home "Mr. Tower" would lose the boat when he was struck by a submerged object off the coast of Puerto Rico. The boat was hit so hard that it sunk in seconds and his wife had to swim underwater to untie the lifeboat. At the time I was worrying that my parents were on a cruise through the Bermuda Triangle, but I was feeling good anyway. It was the first time in a long time that I had. I was on the bulkhead with the boats when John pulled up with Meryl. We laughed like we used to and did Xanax and coke which were spread all over the kitchen table. We ended up in my room on my old bed. Meryl must have been pushing two hundred pounds and John three. I don't know if they wanted to have sex, but we didn't, to my relief, just laid there laughing and joking. Rick had been calling me all day wanting his cocaine. I had been telling him all day that I was coming over to give it to him. John and Meryl left but I wasn't' alone long when Steve came over with a curvaceous blond named Lea that he said was a new waitress at Spies. She had a California tan and a California body, and she was doing up all the lines on my kitchen table. Steve gives me a look like we were both going to do her. It was just one of those nights.

    Rick called me again asking for his coke and something inside of me snapped. I told him I was coming over just as soon as I loaded my semi-automatic shotgun. When I got off the phone, I took the shotgun from the closet of my old room and loaded it in front of Steve and the waitress. I was waiting for Steve to leave so I could go to Seldon and kill Rick and his wife. But Steve knew that and refused to go. While Steve and the waitress were in the kitchen doing lines, I placed the gun, unseen by them, under the couch in the living room. The couch was in front of a bay window overlooking the street. I wasn't sure if Rick knew where my parents lived and if he tried a drive by I intended on making him pay. Rick called again and I told him I had a moral obligation to rid the world of both him and his wife and hung up. About an hour passed by with me keeping a wary eye out the bay window and Steve and his new waitress cavorting in the kitchen and bedroom. Steve came out to the living room to get me and took a look outside for himself. He said he thought he saw something outside and before I could say a word, he was outside the door saying, "before you just start shooting let me check this out." Steve took two steps before he was engulfed in a sea of swarming blue uniforms. They continued past him through the front door with their guns drawn and pointed at me. There was at least a dozen of them. They ran into the bedroom and right to my closet door like they knew where I kept the shotgun. When they found nothing in the closet they demanded to know where the shotgun was, specifically saying shotgun. By now they had already been in the kitchen and seen the piles of coke and Xanax on the table. I told them that it would be inadmissible in court since they did not have any warrant. Undaunted they continued to demand that I turn over the shotgun. I relented and pointed under the couch. A cop reached under and pulled out the gun nonchalantly unloading it and spraying shells all over the living room. I asked them how they knew I had it and they said a neighbor had overheard me and called them. Could be. That neighbor did live in the house across from my old room, but the houses are not so close in Amity Harbor that you can hear what the neighbors are saying next door. The cops left without further ado leaving me with my unloaded shotgun and all the drugs on the table. By now I figured the girl had to be an undercover cop, but they just left her there with us. I was looking at her oversized belt buckle figuring I was speaking into a mike. Steve couldn't have called them no matter how worried he was about me. The police had already gunned down his youngest brother execution style in front of the local Speedy Mart. Steve continued seeing the girl for the next couple of weeks and nothing else happened. Once when both of them were in his room over at the house in Wheatley Heights Negron had dumped out the contents of her pocketbook looking if we could find anything that would tie her in with the police. There was nothing.

    The whole incident had severed my link with Julie Anne. We never saw or spoke to each other again after that. I have no doubts she would have forced me to live out the lie and I would not be telling you the story which I am about to tell you now.

    After the contract with Maria Regina Church was completed the house in Wheatley Heights became too expensive to keep around just for the sake of partying. I moved back in at my parent's house. By then my father was dying of cancer and nobody had ever told me what to do there anyway. I continued hanging out at Mo's place with my entourage of prototype twenty-first century "holes." One night I was mixing pharmaceuticals and hallucinogens with the girls in Debbie's apartment. I remember Edna's bare foot running up and down my leg under Debbie's kitchen table. When I woke up it was morning and Debbie and I were naked in the bed with Genie snoring on the floor covered by a blanket. I made the mistake of telling Steve which led to a couple of fist fights between us and a generally otherwise amicable parting of the ways.

Majesty / הוד

CHAPTER 16

Nietzsche once said, "if you gaze long enough into an abyss, the abyss will gaze back into you." I don't recall gazing into any abyss. I hadn't even read a book since high school let alone anything by the master philosopher. Nevertheless, there was an abyss dead ahead, a yawning black hole with a singularity at the center that would rend to pieces every notion by which man desperately clings to his contrived perception of reality.

It was in the tail end of June, one of those endless summer days that make life worth living. I pulled my big flatbed truck onto Sunrise Highway and slipped it into high gear. Behind me the sun was dropping like a great red fireball into an ethereal sea streaked with pastel pinks and ominous purples. I lit up a cigar sized joint and felt the air whipping through the trucks open windows. My flesh tingled with its cool caress. I had been working outside all day with my shirt off turning my complexion glowing crimson bronze with a hint of a stinging sensation. I could feel the muscles rippling beneath my skin. They were still pumped from the day's exertion. It was a confirmation of my own virility every time they strained against the black fishnet shirt I was wearing. I was heading east to Kenny's new house he had rented with his wife Patty, his five-year-old son, and his recently born baby. I got off the highway at Carlton Avenue in East Islip heading south and made a left before the railroad tracks turning into an enclave with streets named after long dead presidents. The houses were worn and run down, not as bad as Mastic and Shirley but they had long since lost their suburban charm. I made a right and another left around a sump onto a road that ran parallel to the railroad tracks and I rumbled past Kenny's house. The lights were on and I saw Joey Beranek's car in the driveway along with a beat-up white van I didn't recognize. It was a two-family home and Kenny had the portion toward the street and the train tracks. I went about a half a block down to the cul-de-sac and made a U-turn in its aborted circle. I looked over my right shoulder at a vacant lot that stretched about the length of a football field before turning into woods and thickly tangled underbrush. The woods fish hooked from the tracks around the lot and continued through the backyards of the houses terminating at the corner with the fenced in thirty-foot-deep sump. Stagnant water submerged the bottom. The lot itself looked as if it was being used as an improvised dump by the Long Island Railroad. There were four and five-foot-high mounds of dirt, covered by weeds, and piled at impossibly steep angles as if they were built by some subterranean insect engineer. Towards the center there were charred debris strewn about in a haphazard fashion as if somebody had been burning something and then tried to put the fire out. Minus the burnt wood the overall effect was like a miniaturized version of an abandoned Mesoamerican city reclaimed by encroaching jungle.

    I parked the truck in front of Kenny's house and leapt the three feet from its cab to the street. I walked around the front of the truck and up the entrance to the two-car driveway towards the house. Pausing I took one long hit from the last of the joint and flicked it into the street watching its burning embers scatter into the evening breeze. I studied the van trying to figure out who it belonged to and I noticed through the closed windows that the front of its cab was partitioned from the back by a jet-black curtain. The borders of the curtain seemed to emit a faint glow that was illuminating the cab, but I couldn't be sure because of the overhead street light that had just come on. The glow seemed to flicker as if someone was burning a candle in the back. The van was motionless which was kind of creepy because I was sure it was occupied. I cleared my lungs of the pot and inhaled deeply seeking the reassurance of tasting the sweet summer air. There was nothing, no fragrant lilies and fresh cut grass, no sounds of children laughing and playing on the edge of evening. I listened more intently and noticed there were no chirping crickets or sounds of anything else except the far-off forlorn whistle of a train. It was as if I had stepped into some coterminous world where what I was seeing didn't really exist but was only the residual impression of the world I had left behind. I was startled by the long whistle of a train thundering by on the tracks not fifty feet away. I had never heard it coming.

    Regaining my composure, I barged through the unlocked front door without knocking. Kenny had been my best friend since we were thrown out of Catholic school together. I was the only one, including his brother and sisters that was allowed in his closet at his parents' house when he wasn't home. I remember opening that door and having bags of Quaaludes swallow me up in a pharmaceutical avalanche. Joey and Kenny were seated on the couch at the far side of the room. In front of them was a table supporting a small mountain of coke. Kenny immediately began cutting me a line and Joey said "where have you been? I haven't seen you in Mo's Place for a while." I answered him like it was a chore "Steve and I got a divorce and I'm tired of you people trying to get me to get you coke at all hours of the night. As a matter of fact, I just gave Dawn a bag of coke to sell in the bar. But I guess you haven't seen her, or you wouldn't be here." I looked at Kenny grinning and said "woops there goes another ounce. You told me to give it to her." "I know" he said. "She's my problem. She's my sister. I want her to make money but then she doesn't give me mine. She's about to get cut off." I replied "you better not do that. I ain't acting as a drug liaison anymore, I'm a landscaper, besides" I gestured at Joey "these junkies are mainlining it in Al's van in the parking lot of Mo's." Joey denied it of course but everyone knew.

    Joey started to fidget on the couch. His slightly goofy face was accessorized by string straight platinum blond hair and buck teeth, all supported on a pear-shaped body. The goofy face contorted to a look of confusion as he glanced at his watch. "Ten O'clock" he said. "How is it Ten O'clock? I got here at about eight thirty. It doesn't even feel like I have been here a half hour. That stuff must be even better than I thought it was." I was incredulous. I asked him "What time did you say it was?" I didn't wait for an answer. I was probably already up on the running board of my truck by the time he gave it. I turned on the lights and looked at the dashboard clock; sure, enough it was Ten O'clock. It was just getting dark when I got there. I was at Kenny's no more than two or three minutes by my calculations. I walked back in and as I passed the van I saw it was now rocking rhythmically back and forth. When I came back in I wasn't saying anything about the time. I looked at Kenny still seated on the couch and said, "what's with that van in the driveway it looks like someone's going at it in there?" He flashed me that knowing white smile emphasized by his twinkling green eyes and said "my new neighbor the dyke and her girlfriend. They're not allowed to do it in the house, so they do it out there almost every night." I said "you think they would mind if I watch?" He laughed and said "you don't want no part of that. They're both fat disgusting pigs. That is one strange family. The mother seems like she's their prisoner and the family's run by the sixteen-year-old son who looks like he just crawled out from underneath a rock and smells like it too. They all call him Chief. Never heard them call him anything else. Then there's the little one he's the weirdest one of them all. He's supposedly a deaf mute and you only see him at night. I don't think he even lives there. Every night the fat dyke goes out and picks him up. He must live close by. She's never gone more than five or ten minutes. Funny I never see her leaving to drop him off. He's only about twelve years old. I don't know what a kid that age is even doing out that late."

A grin crossed my face. I figured he had to be putting me on, sure when we were little he used to like to set things on fire and watch them burn but he never told lies nor did he exaggerate. I said, "what the fuck are you trying to tell me you are sharing a house with the Adams family?" He told me "you ain't even heard half of it yet. The kids in this neighborhood are like a cult or something, like we used to set fire to things when we were kids these kids crawl through the walls of these houses and watch the people inside them. And that Chief character next door seems to be their leader." This sounded like a case of cocaine paranoia, but Kenny was practically immune to cocaine. He could do a huge line eat a ham sandwich and go to bed five minutes later. Besides Kenny didn't do all that much coke, not every day, not even every week. Like I have already said Kenny was good at dealing drugs. "That's crazy" I scowled at him. He answered indignantly "I've seen it myself and all the people in this neighborhood know about it. A few days after we moved in I was walking my dog down at the lot on the end and this guy comes out and starts talking to me. He said that burnt wood over there is from when these kids burned down their own clubhouse while they were inside it. One of them got third degree burns all over his legs. That's the kid that lives next door to me, Billy. The fire department had to pull him out of there. Then he tells me that a couple of days ago he's sitting there watching TV in his living room when the ceiling caves in and three kids come raining down between him and the TV. They just got up and walked out. When he called the cops, the cops told him there was nothing they could do about it, since he couldn't identify who the kids were." He was starting to get my attention when I asked, "He didn't know them?" As if he knew what he was implying he took a deep breath and said, "He said it was a couple of boys and a girl but it was like the police didn't want to know about it." "The kids must have come through the attic." I said. "You can't crawl through a ceiling, unless you happen to be rodent or something." "No." He said. "I asked him that too. He said it was in the living room on the first floor. He can't figure it out either."

I didn't know what to make of what he was saying, and I really didn't believe much of it. It was secondhand information. I would have just told him to cut me another line but at that moment I was plunging into the abyss. Kenny, Joey, and I, all looked at the ceiling above the couch where they were sitting simultaneously. Kenny stood up triumphantly and Joey terrified. I was already standing. I will not sit on a couch with its back to the window and that was the only other couch in the room. Across the ceiling a dragging sound began from the wall by the stairs. The sound was heading toward the far side of the house, the windowless side facing the railroad tracks. It was distinct, halting, and deliberate, no auditory hallucination, besides we all heard it. "The bastards been listening to us." Kenny said. "I knew it! The other day he was watching Patty take a bath. I heard him behind the medicine cabinet." I couldn't believe what I was seeing and hearing. Joey said he had to go now. His pasty white complexion was a vivid red. The noise continued slowly, inexorably, across the ceiling towards the windowless wall adjacent to the train tracks. Against that wall Kenny had his seven-foot-tall entertainment system. On top of the entertainment system, out of reach of little Kenny is where he kept his coke. I waited till I heard Joey's car pull away. I looked up at the ceiling and said "alright you little fuck. Are you testing to see if this is a game? Well your about to find out right now." I went back out to the truck. By then the van had stopped rocking. I returned with my Gerber Guardian II knife. The thing had about a ten-inch double edged blade that was sharp enough to shave with. I could whip it overhand like a Nolan Ryan fastball and stick an insect fifteen feet away. I said "this will go right through that plasterboard ceiling. Now what are you going to do?" The noise continued moving toward the wall and the cocaine. I looked at Kenny and said "alright you have joists running about every sixteen inch's off center across that whole ceiling. They support the floor above and this ceiling is just the facing for them. Nothing could crawl that way. Maybe a rat that has gnawed holes through about a dozen two-inch-thick joists. But that's no rat. It's too loud and too deliberate to be any kind of an animal." Kenny and I both agreed that Chief had to have made some alterations on the joists prior to Kenny moving in and was somehow pushing and dragging things through the holes he had made from his own side of the house, or somewhere outside, or both.

    At about that time Patty came down from little Kenny's room upstairs right above us. As her name implied she was very Irish looking. With blond hair and piercing blue eyes she was a bit heavy set but had a good sturdy body. I had always thought Kenny could have done better but Kenny wasn't drawn to the kind of woman I was. Kenny asked her if she had heard anything upstairs. She said she hadn't, and little Kenny was asleep. "What are you doing with that knife?" She asked me. She had never liked me. I think Rick had been her friend originally. Kenny told her what was going on and she looked at us both disbelievingly. The noise which was now between the far end of the couch and the entertainment center suddenly bolted to its right parallel to the joists and right towards the bay window. It made something like a whooshing sound silencing abruptly when it got to the wall. Patty heard it and she became insistent on moving the coke to their bedroom upstairs. When she came back down she was skeptical about the whole thing again.

Kenny and I were not. I tucked the knife into the sheath in my pants and we went outside. There was about an eight-foot overhang above a single step wooden porch shared for the entrances of both residents. Kenny's side of the overhang ended about where his bay window began. The overhang had a sloped roof like the rest of the house and there was clearance for people inside it along its whole length, which was about twenty feet. Kenny went over to between his door and the neighbors and looked up at the hole where the light fixture for the front entrance should have been. "There was a light on here yesterday." He said. "I know it was on all night." I went over and looked up at the hole. The porch was dark, and the hole was darker. I said "Chief are you up there? You think this is funny Chief? It would be really funny if I had a nail gun in the truck. What kind of chief are you? Are you an Indian chief? Do you have other little Indians up there with you? Do you have any idea what kind of insects are up there with you in the dark; wasps, hornets, spiders, who the fuck knows what else. No wonder you smell like shit." When we went back inside Patty was upstairs.

Probably for the first time in my life I was intrigued by one of its events. This was the phantasm that had stalked me from my crib, the unnamed darkness that lurked on the periphery of my dreams. This was not just a fleeting glimpse or a random shadow that would quickly become a faded memory. This was an event that was being witnessed by others, an event that could be scrutinized. This was my raison d'être, my reason for existence, the part in me that I had by now thoroughly convinced myself didn't exist. What had happened at Kenny's that night could not be explained with rationalizations. But artificial me, the disguise that I was so comfortable wearing for both the rest of the world and for myself, could never admit that, at least not yet and never publicly until now.

I had put Kenny to work investigating everybody in the neighborhood. In school we had called Kenny the Mayor because he was friends with everybody. That's how he had made his current Columbian connection. The guy had gone to Copiague High school with both of us. I remembered him, vaguely. The guy was just some no English-speaking immigrant that hid in the corner afraid of both the Black kids and the White kids. His only memory now of high school was Kenny was his only friend. And Kenny was cleaning up on that memory. The guy wouldn't sell to anybody else on Long Island.

It was the first really hot spell of the year when I pulled in front

Those Who Would Arouse Leviathan

of Kenny's about a week later. I had just finished my first big job of the season but even with a pocket full of cash the Maria Regina job seemed like a thousand years ago. My landscaping business was slow again and whatever I had Jim could handle even if he had drunk two quarts of Wild Turkey the night before. I immediately got out and walked over to the soffit on the overhang by Kenny's bay window. I climbed up on the railing around the porch and pushed against the soffit. It was secured solidly and the cedar shingles adjacent to it above the window looked like they had never been moved. I jumped down onto the porch to take a look at the hole for the light fixture. Before I did I looked across the lawn at the neighboring house. Sprawled out on an easy chair in the brilliant light of noon was a young girl basking in the sun. She was wearing a bikini and looked to be about sixteen years old. She could have been the coal miner's daughter splayed out as the sacrificial virgin in some titillating Hollywood B movie. She was a real cracker beauty and it just didn't seem right that she could lay there like that on her back with her legs spread in such an inviting fashion. Her crotch pointed right at me.

    When I went through the door Kenny was on the couch in his usual place by the entrance to the kitchen. I said, "Who's the girl?" He gave me his little sly smile and said "that's Kim Jackson. She's the people next doors daughter. Would you believe she is only twelve years old?" I deadpanned "no." He continued "She also has really bad asthma and isn't allowed out of the house. Since I have been here the ambulances have been here at least three times for her. She could just get an attack and die at any moment. That's the first time I have ever seen her hanging out outside." Jokingly I said, "maybe she knew I was coming." He wrinkled his nose a little and said "naw. That's jailbait" like I didn't know that already. Suddenly remembering I said, "I forgot to look at the Chiefs peek hole." He said "go out there. You're going to freak out." When I went outside the light fixture was back in place. Kenny came outside and said "the next day it was just back on there, like it was nobody's business. I even asked the little creep next door. He says the landlord was fucking with it." We both looked over at the girl. She seemed like she was oblivious to us. Her head was thrown back, and her eyes were closed. But she was only about forty feet away and almost naked in a very sexually suggestive pose. I kind of doubted that she was unaware of our presence. I looked at where the bikini bottom pulled taught against her crotch. I could see the area around it was wet.

    We went back inside, and I thought I heard Kim's mother over the background noise of the TV screaming for her to get inside. I asked Kenny if he had found out anything new. He said, "plenty and you got to hear what happened the other day." I was already hooked. I had to know what was going on there. "What?" I asked him. He paused and took a deep breath. "It was about four o'clock in the morning and me and Patty were sleeping when all of a sudden this screeching starts from over in the woods. It sounded like a monkey or some kind of giant parrot. It was loud enough to wake the dead. It must have been up in a tree somewhere back there." He pointed between the lot and his house and continued talking. "The cops got here fast, and they were all over the place. People were all out in their backyards in their pajamas and bathrobes. The cops cordoned off the area from here down to the lot and told everybody there was a dangerous animal loose in the woods and everybody had to get in their houses. I saw these other guys through the kitchen window. They looked like fireman. They were carrying ladders through the yards. They must of went up in the tree and got it because it shut up pretty abruptly. Then everybody just picked up their barricades and left. No one said a word about what it was." I said, "your fathers the bay constable you can't find out?" He said "I asked him. He said the cops don't know what it was either. Some kind of federal animal control agency came in and got it. "That would be Plum Island." I said. "It's off of Montauk. That's where the government does its Dr Frankenstein routine on animals for the whole country. That's about sixty miles and a short boat ride away. Kind of out of their jurisdiction weren't they?" He just looked at me and said, "It didn't take them that long to get here, seemed like they were just right around the corner."

    I asked him if he had talked to any of the neighbors. He said "yea all of them. Their all really scared but their all insisting that's it's just these kids. Apparently Chief over there" he gestured to the ceiling above him "is the leader of his own little satanic cult. Kim's father next door caught him leaving all the shades on his window across from Kim's wide open in the middle of the night while he did this weird little naked dance around candles." I found myself wondering about the whole neighborhoods apathetic reaction to being surreptitiously cast in a real-life version of Children of the Corn and said "and he didn't kill the kid or at least call the police?" "He went over there." Kenny said. "He spoke with the mother and she said she would make him stop. He says it hasn't happened again. He's watching." I was smirking when I said "yea I see he's got it all under control" referring to his almost naked daughter posed like a thanksgiving turkey right outside the front door. Kenny continued. "I been talking to the kid next door on the other side; Billy, the kid that burned his legs. He's about fourteen. He's already told me that this kid Chief," he again gestured to Chiefs now customary place in the ceiling, "worships the devil and so do his sister and brother, that all the kids in the neighborhood were afraid of them. Because Chief did bad things to people, and he hinted that Chief was responsible for his legs." I asked, "What do you mean?" He answered "well when he said that shit he looked down at his leg real coyly. But the kids a little con man. I trust him about as far as I can throw him. He wants me to take him fishing at Heckscher State Park next week. I'll get more out of him then." "We can take him shark fishing." I said "Or how about I just get Phil and John down here to give them a little parental guidance. I don't care what these kids are doing. It doesn't sound like those federal people pulled no kid out of that tree."

We went outside to look around the neighborhood. The first thing I noticed was a wire extending from Chiefs room upstairs over the roof and down around the other side of the house running into the basement. It looked like the wire for a TV. Around the back many of the people had recently installed fences. Some were still in the process of building them. Kenny now had a six-foot stockade separating his yard from the woods. It was connected with the fences of the neighbors on each side. I asked him "who put that up?" He said. "I did yesterday. My lats are killing me from digging holes all day. I don't know how you guys do it every day." I sarcastically said "well its Chief's backyard too. Why didn't he help you? Isn't he afraid the beast of East Islip will return?"

I looked across at Kim's window. She was no longer outside. But her father was, and he was looking up there too. Raked across the aluminum siding directly under her window were what looked to be claw marks. They were also on the siding beside the window but were much less pronounced. The spread between the gashes were about a half a foot each but they were made in uniform groupings of four like a giant hand or paw had been clawing underneath Kim's second floor window. Kenny also saw them and followed by me walked over to Kim's father saying "what the hell? How long have those been there?" The father said "I don't know. I just saw them. He must be trying to climb through her window with a ladder. I better call the police" He looked to me like he was more than just a little spooked. I couldn't resist chiming in. "Kenny and I used to do work for Joe Altieri. That's the guy who does all the guarantee painting work for Al-Can and All-Site on Long Island. They do all the aluminum siding on the East Coast. We ran six-man ladder crews spraying sometimes two houses a day every day for a year. Those marks weren't made by no ladder. Those look like claw marks to me. Maybe a twenty-foot grizzly bear" I said smirking. The guy just looked at me, turned around and walked inside. He looked like he was going to throw up.

We went around the other side of the house to examine Chief's wiring job. As we came around the far side the wire started jumping in two-foot leaps and slapping against the house as if someone on the other side of the roof was whipping it back and forth. When we ran around to Chiefs window the wire was motionless running straight out his window and over the house. The same way it had been before. When we went around to the side where the wire ran into the basement it started to jump around again. It could not have been being moved from the basement since someone had drilled a hole right through the foundation, run the wire through, and sealed it with tar. We must have tried three or four times, but we could not catch Chief moving the wire from the window of his room. That wire looked like it never had budged from the place where we had first seen it drawn taunt out the window and over the roof. I looked at Kenny and said "come on now Kenny he's playing with us, got us chasing around his little wire like cats after a ball of string. This kids going to have to get dealt with." Kenny said "oh yea real good idea. With all the shit I got laying around the house." Resignedly I said "Well lets go inside and do some lines and drink a few beers. It's too hot out here maybe we can catch him later when its dark." Kenny agreed and said, "let me just show you this before the garbage men get here." We went out by the garbage pales in the street and he pointed triumphantly. There was a clear plastic bag with assorted nastiness in it along with what looked to be about a half dozen empty cans of Raid wasp spray. I said "I guess he never thought of that before. I need a line."

    Patty had taken the kids to the pool at Heckscher State Park. Sometime during the day, I had taken some Xanax and fell asleep on the couch. When I awoke the baby was crying and Patty was banging pots and pans around in the kitchen. Kenny was upstairs with the baby which was probably why it was crying. It was almost dark. There was a knock at the door and when I answered Chucky, Dawn, and a couple of girls I didn't know were out there. Chucky, along with our friend Tommy, had been the Copiague high school heart throb. He had moved to Mount Sinai and nobody had seen him since. Dawn pushed passed me snickering "what the fuck did you do to that faggot Joey? He says he will never come here again. He thinks the place is haunted. What a little bitch. Now I have to come here all the time? I don't even have a car." She screamed up the stairs "Kenny you have to get me a car!" I told Chucky and the other girls to come in and went back to the couch. Kenny came down and sat next to me telling Patty to go upstairs and take care of the kids. Dawn flopped into the loveseat by the window with her white high heeled marsh mellow shoes on the upholstery. There was no other seats left so Chucky and the other girls stood. We made small talk about Chuckey's new life in Mount Sinai which is where the other two girls were from. Eventually Chucky asked Kenny for a quantity of coke which Kenny dutifully pulled down from the top of the entertainment center. He had put it back up there after deciding Chief wasn't after his coke. Kenny and Dawn went outside to have a few words and the girls sat down in Dawns now unoccupied loveseat. Chucky continued to stand making small talk with me when the dragging sound started again right above his head. Chucky was astonished as were the girls who were with him. They got up and huddled close to him as he stared up in amazement at the ceiling. I went to the door and told Kenny he better come in. We went through the whole story with Chucky. All the while Dawn was telling her brother he should get Patty and the kids out of there and let me start blasting the ceiling. During that time the dragging sound continued off and on. Chucky looked like he wanted to stay and help us investigate the mystery, but Kenny had given Dawn some coke to sell and she kept saying she had to get out of there.

    We all went out into the darkness together walking Chucky to his car. He kept saying "nobody could crawl through that ceiling. That's what I do in Mount Sinai. I build houses. What the fuck was that?" Dawn screamed loud enough for the whole neighborhood to hear her "don't worry they'll figure it out. They figure everything out. That's why they're the only guys with any money from Copiague. The little faggots in this neighborhood are in a lot of trouble!" As Chucky walked out in the street to get in his car two bottles came flying from out of nowhere. They just missed his head and smashed in the street. I broke into a run yelling over my shoulder "I think they came from over the tracks!" The three of us clambered over the embankment. When we got to the other side we heard the sound of running footsteps on pavement, but we couldn't see anybody even though the view up and down the street was unimpeded. A voice came from the direction of the footsteps saying we will get so and so on them "He's in the army." And another voice answered him as it faded into the darkness with the footsteps "yea we'll get the army. The armies on our side." Chucky left. After that I never saw him again. Even as she was getting in the car Dawn kept telling me I should go and get John and Phil. I was beginning to think she was right, but I kept telling myself these are kids.

    As Kenny and I walked back to the house together I said to him "they must have ditched behind one of those houses on the other side of the tracks, some of them must live over there. We gotta figure out which house it is." He looked at me disbelievingly and with little enthusiasm said "yea." Exasperated I said "what the fuck do you think its ghosts. There ain't no such thing as ghosts. Those were flesh and blood kids that just threw flesh and blood bottles at Chucky." He said, "what the fuck were they talking about, the army?" I didn't answer him. I had no answer. As I took the step back up to the porch I looked at Kenny's front door. Somebody had splashed a can of used coffee grinds all over it. It looked like it was piled four inches thick on the welcome mat but then I quickly realized the whole mass was a writhing colony of ants. The ants had already covered Kenny's door. Not wanting any of them to get in the house we went around to the back door. It was covered with ants in the same manner as the front door. I said, "the little fuck emptied some of those ant colony's you can grow in a fish tank on your doors while we were chasing the other ones over the tracks." He didn't say anything as he jumped gingerly over the ants to get in the house. I took my car up to the store and purchased two cans of Raid. When I came back I put an end to the ant plague. Patty swept up shovels full of dead ants for what seemed like hours complaining all the while "you didn't have to kill them they would have went away on their own."

  Later on, that night Hal came over in his Ferrari. Hal was a mid-twenty's rich Jew from Dix hills whose father owned a chain of jewelry stores. I liked Hal so I ended up leaving with him and picking up three girls driving around Copiague at six o'clock in the morning. Even more luckily these girls were in their own car because the Ferrari only had two seats. We made plans with them to go back to Hals pool house. I figured I would need a deluxe bag of coke for the occasion, so I called Kenny from a pay phone. He didn't answer even though I kept it ringing for a long time. Kenny always answered his phone. We had to go back to East Islip to pick up my car anyway, so we had the girls follow us back there. When we arrived, I banged on all his doors and windows with a great deal of persistence and for an extended length of time. I disappointedly came to the conclusion that the day's events really had frightened him, and he had taken Patty and the kids to a motel. I wasn't doing another twenty-four hours in any pool house with these girls unless I was really high, so I ended up going to Jim's and crashing out there Hal was on his own.

  When I woke up I called Kenny again. There was no ring or any other kind of a preliminary. There was a dial tone and as soon as I dialed his number I could hear the familiar sounds of Patty banging pots and pans around in the kitchen with the water running. I listened for a while and I heard a distant baby crying but no one talking. I wasn't more than fifteen minutes away, so I went to his house. When I got there Kenny was outside with little Kenny and Patty was in the kitchen. I checked the phone in the kitchen, and it was firmly on the hook. I asked if the baby had been downstairs, if little Kenny had been inside, or if Patty had been using the phone. She said "no." Kenny said "I've been home for two days and nobodies been calling me." He couldn't understand why he couldn't hear me banging on the doors and under his bedroom window. He said, "the baby's up by six, every morning." I said "I just called your phone and listened to everything that was going on in your house while it was still on the hook." "What do you mean?" He asked. I explained to him what had happened. I said "I think you're under some kind of surveillance Kenny. Sounds to me like it's some kind of technology that hasn't made the TV yet, probably never will. I guess I accidentally tapped into it when I dialed your number."

Kenny took it real serious. Instinctually Kenny was one of the smartest guys I have ever met, maybe the smartest. He stopped dealing coke and took a vacation in Atlantic City with his Columbian connection. He was gone for about a week and he left Patty with his stash. I went over there one day to see how she was doing, and she told me she had pulled a bag off the top of the entertainment system and dumped it all over. She said all she could get back out of the carpet was about an ounce of rock and she might as well do it. She and I took a ride over her friend's house; the kids were over her parents. Patty and her girlfriend started dropping rocks in ammonia turning it into a nasty tasting form of free base. They made me smoke it with them probably to insure that I didn't tell Kenny because she wasn't allowed to base. Two girls practically forcing me to smoke cocaine with them was sexually titillating so I went along with it. It was just a mind game at the time. Nothing happened. It was my best friend's wife. It was the first time I had ever tried base and I ended up being convinced that it was a waste of perfectly good coke.

When Kenny got back from Atlantic City his father confirmed my suspicions. Kenny was on law enforcements radar. He closed shop and started making arrangements to move the family to Florida when he was done living out his security in East Islip. Kenny and I started doing a lot more coke. He had a lot left and my season was really slow that year. The both of us became obsessed with finding out exactly what was going on in East Islip. By then John was, for the first and only time in his life, happily married. I got him to come over Kenny's by promising him a bag of coke that he could take home and do with Meryl. When he did come over, wearing his ostrich skin boots just for the occasion, nothing happened. John went on and on lecturing me that night. "See. You should know much more than I do. You have a way higher IQ than I do. You like to read books and I hate to read books. But I read a lot of books when I was in jail and I took them home for you to read. You have never even looked at them. They're still sitting up in a box in my old room at my mothers. You can't see the nose in front of your face. You're like some stupid Guiney gangster in a bar." I don't remember much else about that night except John left early with his bag of coke and I consented to take a look at the books.

He came over my mother's house a few days later with the box full of hardcover books, some quite old. He got my attention immediately when he said "you better read these. Your right there is something going on over there. When I left Kenny's, I stopped at that big club over on the corner. I don't even know why I stopped. I have never been in there before. When I walked through the door there was a guy standing there with these two big muscle-bound dudes who were afraid to even ask me for the cover. I go to push past them, and this guy starts talking to me like he knows me calling me by my first name. "Hey John. John I been waiting for you." He hung out with me all night. Turns out he was the owner and he kept giving me free drinks. He was talking about some really crazy shit. Saying he was with the Mafia and the CIA, that they were the same thing and that they had been watching me for a real long time now and they wanted me to work with them. I don't know anything about anybody crawling through walls, but this guy was clearly waiting for me at the door and he knew all about me." I just looked at him and wondered whether he had consented to work with them or not. But as I have intimated before in this story there is a formality between me and John that should not exist between two guys who have known each other as long as we both had. I observed protocol and started looking through the books.

There was this huge blue book; The Golden Dawn by Israel Regardie. It was full of symbols and rituals. There was Practical Magick by Aleister Crowley containing the same symbols and rituals and two volumes by Godfrey Higgins about Masonic lore. There was a thin white book called The Holy Books by Aleister Crowley that John said was the most important. He snatched it from my grasp and started reading passages like some Jurassic Age Shakespearean actor having an orgasm during recital. From what I could gather from the obscure symbolism that I did not understand yet Crowley was saying that he had killed the old God, or at least he was going too and that he would be the new one. There were also other books including two more by Israel Regardie, The Middle Pillar and the Garden of Pomegranates. John explained to me that Regardie was the only man that wrote books about him that ever really knew Crowley, having been his personnel secretary. The Garden of Pomegranates would be the first book I would end up reading but not yet. I already believed in demigods. In fact, I was already fully convinced that John and I were just such entities but praetor-human intelligences had thus far been beyond my range of experiences. My father hadn't taught me much about philosophy and religion, but he had taught me to believe nothing of what I heard and only half of what I see. I was going with that for now. I still do.

A reconnaissance of the area Kenny had moved to revealed that beyond the vacant lot and burned out fort, about a quarter mile down the tracks, was the Great River Train Station, a major hub for the Long Island Rail Road's south shore line. East of the train station was Heckscher State Park and miles of virgin woodland. There was nothing unusual about the area geographically except that it was a bit more rural than the majority of Long Island's South Shore. Carlton Avenue had some clubs and some bars and a lot of dilapidated stores. The area Kenny's house was in was between Montauk Highway and Sunrise Highway. It was strictly White working class.

I took a look at Chief and his menagerie of a family. Chief himself skulked about. You would see him coming and going, sometimes with his family, sometimes alone, but never laughing or joking. He looked like a young version of Charles Manson without the beard but the same long dark hair and wild staring eyes. Sometimes I would pass him on the porch. When I glowered at him he would look down to avert my eyes. He always smelled like rotten eggs and the scent would linger long after he had passed. One of the neighbors had told Kenny that they had seen him climbing out of a man hole of the neighborhoods partially constructed sewers. The sister was a fat dyke just as Kenny had said. She was about eighteen. She had dark hair, a bad complexion, and the IQ of a door knob. The little brother as predicted only appeared after dark. He was an undersized twelve, skinny and frail, pale white with closely cropped dark hair. He either could not or would not talk. Billy had told us that when he played with the other kids he would communicate by whistling to them. You could hear whistling outside at all hours of the night. When questioned about the kid's nocturnal habits Billy was evasive saying something about his father, whom the kid lived with, working at night. The mother didn't look like anyone in her family she was bleach blond, well kept, and about mid forty's.

Billy lived in the single-family house next door on the side towards the lot. He was about fourteen years old and shared the house with his mother. He was as disingenuous as anyone that age could be. He spent all day practicing in his backyard with a bow and arrow. He would seek me or Kenny out and talk to us for hours. Somehow you knew he wasn't really saying anything. Whenever he was questioned about the strange goings on in the neighborhood he would always intimate that it was Chief without coming right out and saying so. Flanking the other side towards the sump was the single-family home that was the residence of Kim and her family. I rarely, if ever, talked to Kim. Her father looked like he was about to have a nervous breakdown. I figured seeing her speaking to me would push him right over the edge.

One day Kenny and I were over by the sump with the dog and I spotted a two-foot-long greenish brown snake in the sand by the fence. As I have said I have had a lifelong love affair with herpetology so knowing there are no venomous snakes on Long Island I immediately grabbed my prize to examine it. I was a little surprised when it spread a cobra like hood and hissed at me. It was a Hog Nosed Snake, the only one I have ever seen on Long Island. Although they are harmless they do a perfect imitation of a cobra, hood and all, to scare away predators. If that doesn't work they will keel over and play dead excreting a noxious foul-smelling fluid all over themselves. I was going to keep it and put it in a fish tank at home but when I saw the fat dyke's window was open on the van I couldn't resist. Grinning like an idiot I threw it in the van. The next day when Billy saw me he couldn't wait to tell me that the girls had found it and had nearly had apoplexy. They had to get Chief to remove it from the van for them. Billy assured me that Chief said 'that was a really good one.'

I needed to turn up the heat a little which I did by inserting Phil into the situation. Phil came up with the same solution he did for everything. He told a mortified Kenny that he would make Chief disappear. Kenny said "you can't do things like that around here. First of all, I don't do shit like that. Second of all the police are watching this place. And third of all these are just kids." Phil started hanging around the house. He told us "you guys are just doing too much coke. Nobody could walk around inside walls and even if they could nobody would be stupid enough to play around over here. Give me a few ounces of coke and there will be no kids left in this neighborhood. I have to see this to believe it." Patty said, "I already told them that." Pointing to me she continued "nothing ever happens when he's not here. The few things I have seen seem to all revolve around him. It's as if he is the source of everything." Kenny chimed in "he hasn't been over for the past couple of days and the knick-knacks on the entertainment center have been moving around. I marked where they are, and I have been watching them. They are moving around!" Phil said "you're probably just playing your stereo to loud. Or it's the vibrations of the trains going by. What do you think its ghosts? There are no ghosts or believe me I would have seen a few by now. Do you think Chief can make himself invisible? I can't believe somebody like you is even saying shit like this. Eric already went over this whole house and he said none of the shit you're talking about is possible. The guys a master carpenter. He builds high-rises in the city!"

Phil was right. I had brought Eric over to check out the house and he had checked the attic and the basement, to Patty's incessant objections. Eric had pronounced the house secret passage free. But he told me something else on the side that I never have told anybody. "Watch Patty. Whatever is going on there she's involved." Kenny had a native intelligence that he couldn't articulate with his limited command of language, but Eric had something else. Eric was half animal. The biting incidents, the oversized tendons and blood veins coiling around his arms were not the only manifestations of that fact. He was as sentient as any cat or dog. If Eric said something was going to happen it almost always did. Everybody knew this about him.

    That day we watched the knick-knacks for hours. A glass figurine slowly but surely moved about six inch's during the course of the day. Its movements were so slow they were beyond the realm of human perception, only about an inch an hour, but after six hours the figurine had moved six inches. Phil insisted it was the rumbling of the trains passing by every hour or so that moved them, but he was being obstinate. The figurine was steadily moving which Kenny proved to him by placing another knick-knack next to it. In an hour the figurines had about an inch clearance between them even though no trains had come, no music was playing, and the entertainment center was perfectly level. Patty kept coming in the room and saying to me "it's you. It's you." But she would not explain herself. It had rained torrentially during the course of the day and outside a brick chimney stack ran from the basement to about three feet above the ledge of the roof. Around dusk, very loud and very clearly, a suction sound could be heard coming from the stack as if something was scaling it outside making its way to the roof using suction cups. When we went outside there was nothing. Phil quipped "it must be Batman. Good I always wanted to kick his ass." Looking at me he said, "you take Robin."

    It was after dark when we again heard the suction sound coming from the chimney stack outside. We all ran outside at the same time practically getting jammed in the doorway together. The sound of running footsteps were coming from over by the sump and Kenny and Phil took off in hot pursuit. I ran around the side of the house to see if anybody was by the chimney. I didn't see anybody, so I started toward the street to catch up with Kenny and Phil. I had the overwhelming sensation of being watched and I hadn't checked the roof anyway so when I got out into the street where I would have a clear view of it I stopped running and turned around. There on the roof with its long legs spread for balance and one arm extended to brace itself against the top of the chimney was the essence of my nightmares. It was not human. That was plain enough. It was at least seven feet tall with membranous bat wings semi folded into its back. It had no head only two dinner plate sized glowing red eyes that seemed to grow right out of its shoulders. Its eyes did not stare but rather burned themselves right into me and for a long time afterwards I would see them in reflections at night and in my dreams. Years later I would read John Keels descriptions of what was called the Mothman but at the time I had never even imagined that something like that could exist, at least in my waking hours. After what seemed like forever suspended in time with our gazes locked in what could only have been an ephemeral embrace I broke free and took off down the block after Kenny and Phil. When I got to the corner Phil was climbing over the fence out of the sump saying, "there's no one down there unless you think their hiding underwater." Kenny looked at me and said "did you see anything around the house?" Staring into space I said "no."

    I had never had a hallucination before even though I had taken massive dosages of hallucinogens trying to induce one in myself. I had always figured if I could just have a hallucination the mysteries of my childhood would be solved. Sometimes it had appeared as if the patterns on walls, rocks, and plants, were some kind of ancient and universal written language but there is a big difference between a delusion and an illusion. Once I took about twenty hits of John's mescaline and stared all night into the water from the docks at the Venice. After a few hours the reflections of lights from the surrounding buildings seemed to dance like burning cities on the waves of the bay. But as far as seeing pink elephants or even spontaneously seeing visions I had never come close. What I had seen was real and it wasn't something any 'sane' person would see so I kept my mouth shut. When we got back to the house Patty was waiting for us in the doorway. I was silent the rest of the night and we sat in the living room doing lines. Patty kept asking me "did you see something outside?" Phil said "there's nothing out there but a couple of kids fucking around. Believe me." But Patty was mocking and insistent "no. Look at him. He's all white. He looks like he's seen a ghost. You kept looking out there. What did you think you were going to do if you ever actually found what you were looking for? Turns out all you could do is run away from it. Why bother looking for something if you're just going to run away when you find it?" I didn't answer her, but Kenny angrily did "what the fuck are you talking about Patty? I think you're doing too much shit lately. There ain't nothing but a few ounces left and I'm selling the rest to Bates tomorrow for whatever I can get for it. That's it! Party's over for everyone!"

    There was a ringing in my ears all that night and the impression of children's laughter right beyond the threshold of perception. When I went in the kitchen for a beer Patty had hung a wicker basket of burnished glass stones over the kitchen counter. Two of them were red like giant ruby's and caught the stove light reflecting like a pair of eyes in the rain splattered window over the sink. They seemed to be reminding me that I would never be alone again. I had listened to the song Easy Ride by the Doors since John had dragged me out of the water now I knew. Eyes like burning glass. "The mask", the veneer of the lie, had been ripped from the face of the liar. I could see him clearly now, as clearly as he could see me.

We kept shoveling coke up our noses and we kept hearing footsteps running around outside the windows. Every time we heard a noise Phil would respond by bursting out the doors in a futile attempt to catch the noises source. Around daybreak Kenny, Phil, and I snuck out the front door and made a mad dash to the railroad track embankment slipping and sliding over its rocky gradient. On the other side of the tracks we waited. As the first rays of daylight lifted the veil of darkness from Kenny's house we watched in amazement. Billy was running around the house in circles pausing occasionally under the windows. His body was hunched over as he ran like a marathon runner almost out of gas. Phil looked at us victoriously saying "should I go slap the shit out of the ghost now?" We crossed the tracks and stood watching as the kid darted first one way then another around the house. Although we were less than a hundred feet away, standing right there in the open, it was as if he could not see us. After no less than a dozen laps he ran around the back and didn't come back. When we looked he was nowhere to be found. He had pitched a tent in the fenced enclosure of his backyard. We watched the tent for a while waiting for him to come out. Finally, Kenny said "you guys better go home. That kids fourteen years old. I'll handle it."

I saw Kenny a few days later but I already knew all I would ever need to know. Kenny said "I caught up to him a few hours later. He says he was looking for Chief they were camping out and playing tag. He seemed to be shocked that I had seen him. He didn't know what to say. Then when I seen Chief he said he doesn't know what the kid is talking about. He used to hang out with Billy, but they don't even talk to each other anymore. All I know is I never seen him hanging out with Billy and their both too old to be playing tag." I said, "well Kenny there's a lot of things you haven't seen, you and everybody else in this world." He asked me again if I had seen something that night and again I told him "no."

I told myself that it must have been one of the kids wearing a costume. That Patty was in on it with them and they all must have been pilfering Kenny's coke all along. That would explain their strange behavior. The noises in the ceiling continued and by the time Kenny left for Florida they had spread to the rest of the house. I kept trying to set traps for Patty by getting her out of the house and telling Kenny to look here and look there. He never found anything, and I never outright told him that I suspected his wife of anything. One morning right before they left I went over there with Eric's shotgun and told her to bring the kids to her parents I was going to settle it that day. She had a screaming fit telling me "everything that is happening here is all because of you. I really don't think you should even be around my kids. You have no idea what you are. Thank God we are moving to Florida."

    Around midnight Kenny and I took a ride to the seven eleven over on Connetquot Ave by Heckscher State Park. As we pulled back onto the side roads we saw three young girls walking and noticed one of them was Kim. I pulled up to them and Kenny said, "what are you doing out this late?" She laughed at him and looked at me and said "there's been some changes. I decided to take you up on your offer." She showed me the back of her hand and on it was carved a bloody cross. I said "what the fuck are you talking about? I never made you any offer. This is the first time I have ever even talked to you. Are you high on something?" She laughed again and said, "I drunk some wine." Then she said "oh yes you did. And I like it." We pulled away as she continued to laugh, and I said to Kenny "what the fuck was that about?" He said "I have no idea. And as far as I know she's not even allowed out of the house, let alone this late and this far."

    About a month or two later Kenny called me from Florida and told me to read the paper. The big story in Newsday that day was a fourteen-year-old boy had been arrested in East Islip and charged with over forty counts of sexual assault. Turns out innocent little Billy had been sodomizing all the other little boys and girls in the neighborhood. A neighbor had called Kenny in Florida. The neighbor had also told Kenny that the reason Chief had tried to burn Billy alive in the clubhouse was to put a stop to his reign of terror. By now I believed none of it. Plato wrote that men were hairless apes who sit frozen in place in a cave with their back to a fire and watch shadows on the wall cast by the procession of reality that passes between their backs and the fire. If one of the apes was ever dragged from the cave and forced to watch the spectacle from a hole in the ceiling above they could never go back to sit with the other apes and endure their bestial chatter.

Beauty / תפארת

CHAPTER 17

    I awoke to a breakfast of hard-boiled eggs and morphine. My favorite deputy sheriffs were at the foot of the bed discussing last night's episode of Alf. I listened to their conversation for a while. Alf liked to eat cats. He wanted to move to Alaska and leave law enforcement behind forever. Her husband was resentful that she was more of a man than him. It was causing marital distress. I knew I would be seeing Michelle that day. I could feel the darkness in which she moved closing in. I was blowing smoke rings at the ceiling watching them rise and dissipate, wondering if the souls of the dead departed in the same manner. She came walking through the door like the titillating suspect in a Hollywood murder mystery. She had on a white blouse and those skintight black diving pants that showed off an ass that was just too perfect to be human. There were diamonds on her fingers and diamonds on her ears. Her hair fell in wanton abandonment almost to her knees like storm clouds framing a dark angel's face. Electric blue stiletto heels showcased her tiny feet. She was no more than five foot two, without the heels, but everyone always knew when she was there. The male deputy sheriff's jaw dropped, and the female deputy looked at her with grudging awe. Michelle came toward me like an erotic king cobra approaching its prey. Her venom was pure sexual bliss. I was reminded of the line from Celebration of the Lizard "I can't live through each slow century of her moving." She kissed me like she was trying to drain the soul from my body.

    "Lick" she said. "Oh, my Lickster!" Those were her baby talk nicknames for me. It wasn't because of my talent for cuningless, which was considerable; it had started off from a TV commercial: "in the center of it all is the Milford Plaza." She used to say I was the center of it all. Then she started calling me her Chicken. Then I became the Milford Chicken. Through some mysterious transubstantiation via Kentucky Fried Chickens slogan "finger lickin good" I became Lickster. The last time I had seen her she had told me Lilith had come for me, but she wouldn't remember any of it. She never did. Lilith was just using her body, the highest complement the Demon Queen could pay to any Daughter of the Owl. Michelle's lineage stretched back, via her mother as it must, to when the prophet Isaiah shared the earth with that ancient order dedicated to the Queen of Demons. We made small talk and she told me how the super had let her keep the parrots there while she found somewhere to stay. I wondered how her familiar a vicious Amazon parrot she called Tony had liked the visit from the Taoist monks. She told me Wolf had told her that Bartle's was a circus clown and that he didn't care if there were five body's on that gun. All she was paying was a fifty-dollar fine. In the meantime, she and our cat, a very expensive Himalayan named Beijing, had moved temporarily into my old room at my parents. My mother had always liked her. Even my oldest sister who was already a famous environmentalist, a cross between Euell Gibbons, Rachel Carson, and Reinhard Heydrich, liked Michelle. Everybody liked Michelle. She had a way of ingratiating every woman she met and seducing every man. After a while she left, and I watched her ass moving as inexorably as Foucault's Pendulum as she walked out the door. By then it was time for another shot of morphine and more waking dreams.

  My parents lived in one of the biggest homes in the waterfront community of Amity Harbor, between Amityville and Copiague. It was sprawling ranch, the last house on the right where Coolidge Ave ended at the canal. The house was situated on a raised mound of earth that was knit together by four great maples that ran in a row along Coolidge Avenue. The property was in the shape of an L joining a smaller section along; Jefferson Avenue, a small private road that ran parallel to the canal. Jefferson Avenue separated the house from its hundred and eighty feet of bulk headed canal. A half-grown Lebanese cedar grew on the lawn between the house and Jefferson Avenue. The house itself was no more than sixty or seventy feet from the water.

  Hurricane Gloria was billed as the biggest storm that would strike Long Island since 'the big one' came through in the thirty's. It had reached category four status on the open Atlantic. Most of Amity Harbor was low lying beach so it was evacuated but my father had three boats valued at close to a half million dollars tied along his dock. All the boats on the canal, which anyone planed on keeping, were cross tied in preparation for the storm. Cross tying involves loosely tying them on one side then from across the canal pulling them to the center and tying them on that side too, leaving enough slack for the storm surge. This was a tricky proposition for my father since he had three boats all over thirty feet. If too much slack was left in the ropes the boats would slam into each other. So, all the boats were secured towards my father's side of the canal and somebody had to stay to let out slack during the surge. Somebody was me. At the time I had just turned twenty-six. My idea of exercise was popping a Quaalude and swimming from field two at Robert Moses to Kismet, about five miles, in the breakers. I had my big flatbed parked at the highest point of land right by the house and my 08S Stihl chainsaw. That model is like a Harley engine driving a chainsaw blade. If I had to I could cut my way out. Coolidge Ave halfway to the Montauk Highway was canopied by sixty to seventy-foot-high maples. I also had an AR15, for looters, that I had recently purchased from Edelman's gun shop on a trip there with John.

I had no apprehensions as I awaited the storm. I must have been the only human being within that mile distance from Montauk Highway to the bay. It's funny. I had nightmares about floods and giant waves all through my childhood. Either I had watched too much Flipper, or it was some racial memory left over from the last time God had arbitrarily drowned the human race. But by then I had outgrown fear, all fear. By the time Gloria hit Long Island it was recorded as a category two but Gloria shredded the instrumentation for Islip Macarthur Airport. Its known Gloria scored a direct hit on Amity Harbor then skirted the coast again making landfall sixty miles east at Quogue where it was recorded as a category two. Gloria ended up taking out practically every maple in the canopy over Coolidge Avenue, ripping them up in root balls as big as the houses.

I smoked a joint and stood on the dock as the wind built to a crescendo. I have heard many descriptions, but I think the noise of a thousand trains rushing by is appropriate. When it reached its peak, you could scream at the top of your lungs and not hear a thing but that angry wind. I watched the thirty-foot Lebanese Cedar, legendary for its strength, strain horizontally as it battled for its life. I watched a sixty-foot maple tear up a forty-foot section of the front lawn as it collapsed in the street with a crackling thud that was swept away by the wind. Shingles were flying all over the place and the overhead wiring came down in mass as electricity danced up and down Jefferson Avenue. It was low tide so when the surge toped the dock it had already come up a good three feet in a few minutes. I began giving the boats slack at the far corner of Coolidge and Jefferson, the point furthest from the house. Frenzied sparks flew from downed wires on a transformer not forty feet away. The sound of it exploding punctuated the wind. By the time I reached the last cleat the water was between my navel and chest and I had to work submerged holding my breath. When my task was completed I turned to wade back across Jefferson Avenue to the house, now the only one in sight above the waterline. It was then I was startled. Two dark objects appeared at the limits of visibility, one in the east, one in the west. They seemed to be suspended motionless for a few seconds. Then with unbelievable speed they converged between me and the house. They hovered thirty feet in front of me and thirty feet above me. They were shaped like funnels not more than twenty feet long and ten feet wide at the top. They were pitch black, their darkness rotating like miniature tornados as they remained suspended above me side by side seemingly immune to the wind. I got the distinct impression that they had intelligence and they were looking at me. I stared back in amazement. They emitted a shrieking that could be heard even above the wind. After a few seconds they took off in the directions in which they had come at a speed that made them appear as blurs. Their screaming sound faded in the wind as they disappeared into sheets of driving rain.

    When Vigdis and Geirs father finally remembered that he had a house in America he sold it. Vigdis and Eric moved to a place in Lindenhurst. One day shortly after Kenny had moved to Florida I was hanging out with them drinking and moaning about Julie Anne. On the way home I swung left onto Montauk Highway and hit the gas to take the short ride to Copiague. I was in the right-hand lane and going pretty fast, about eighty. I went to swing over to the left to pass a slow-moving car in front of me and another car occupied by four old people who looked like they had just come from a bingo game came out of nowhere to block my access to the left lane. They were doing eighty too. The speed limit was forty on Montauk Highway and nobody did eighty, except me, let alone four geriatric patients. I looked over at their faces and they were grinning malevolently at me. I jammed on the breaks to go in back of them and they jammed on theirs. Still going faster than the almost stopped car in front of me I figured maybe I could go up on the shoulder and pass it on the right. I slammed into a telephone pole at about forty miles an hour. The old people came to a stop a little in front of me, I figured to help me, but the two on my side rolled down their windows in unison and screamed "fuck you" as they laughed hysterically. They accelerated away and gave me a departing finger out the window. The steering wheel was bent straight up and was now flush with the dash board. I hadn't been wearing a seat belt, I never do, and my legs had hooked around it preventing me from being vaulted through the windshield. I was furious. I wanted to kill them. They had just deliberately tried to kill me. I jumped out of the car to run after them figuring maybe I could commandeer a car and catch them at a light. I felt my thigh bone push right through the cheek of my ass. It had been pulled clean out of the socket. I collapsed under the weight of my own body.

    I lay on Montauk highway bent like a pretzel and writhing in agony. When the police came one of them kept begging me to pass out until I got to the hospital where they would give me morphine. When they finally did get me to Brunswick Hospital in Amityville it took four shots till the pain finally subsided. I was there for two weeks. Vigdis was an assistant nurse there so she was delegated as my personal nurse. Jim came up every day after work. All of the rest of the nurses knew Jim.

Those Who Would Arouse Leviathan

When he wasn't their patient he was sending them patients. My room was pretty much off limits to any medical personnel that frowned upon their charges doing bongs in their hospital bed. Sometimes there would be ten people in my room and constant traffic in and out at all hours. John only came up to see me once, in the middle of the night, looking very shady in a black leather jacket that would have fit a Tyrannosaurus Rex. He was evasive and said he needed to have a talk with me when I got out of the hospital. I left after two weeks still in a full body cast. I just couldn't take it anymore I needed a beer which Vigdis and her coworkers weren't letting me have because of my pain medication. Don't ever let anybody bullshit you. After morphine, which Brunswick wasn't giving me because I told them of my past heroin addiction, alcohol is the best pain medication.

True to his word John came over the very same day I got out. He looked in disgust at his books still in the cardboard box in the corner of my room. He said "you ain't read any of these yet have you? I don't think you understand. You have to read them. You don't have a choice. I went as far as I could with this. I can't learn to read Hebrew. Without knowing Hebrew, you can't really know what Crowley did. Crowley knew Hebrew, Chaldean Hebrew, better than anybody who ever lived. You shouldn't be in that bed or in that cast. You should have too much power for that. They know who you are now. They will kill you if you try to walk away. Why don't you just start with the Masonic Big Book?" The Big Book is what Free Masons call The Secret teachings of all Ages by Manly P. Hall. "I don't have that one. You will have to buy it. Hall is a thirty-third-degree Mason. Only they really knew what Crowley was talking about. The kings and queens of Europe, the financial tycoons of America, don't worship God and Jesus. They worship Crowley. He's their God. The guy who invented the Blitzkrieg studied at the feet of Crowley. Everything the Nazi's believed is based on the teachings of Crowley. They don't want regular people to know but it's true. Why would you share power with your livestock anyway? Read Anacalypsis by Godfrey Higgins. That's those two blue books in there." He gestured to the box as he continued speaking. "He was also a thirty-third-degree Mason. Do you know how much those books are worth?" John had collected all kinds of things in the fifteen years I knew him. He had once shown me a first edition of Lewis Carroll's Alice in Wonderland when we were about thirteen years old. Even then I knew the book was priceless. I had always wondered where he had gotten it. As if to answer my question he went on "all my family are Masons. My uncle and my grandfather are very high-ranking Masons. Start by reading Godfrey Higgins and Manley Hall. Then learn the Hebrew. You can't do anything else right now anyway. The next time I come here I want to see everything in this room floating around like in Poltergeist!" With that he left without even saying goodbye.

I found Higgins very hard reading, so I sent my mother on a mission to purchase the 'The Big Book.' It set me back four hundred dollars, but it was well worth it. Hall is a erudite and accomplished writer. Everything that one needed to know to exorcise the lies that are inculcated into man and woman with every word they speak was contained in that book. In the section about Pythagoras Hall attributes this saying to him through the writings of Iamblichus: "Having departed from your house, turn not back, for the furies will be your attendants." Once one has peeked behind the veil of Isis they must love what they see in single minded dedication. Isis is like all other woman. She will not suffer those who scorn her. I would find that out the hard way.

CHAPTER 18

Reaganomics had already infected the country. With it came crack cocaine for the nation's urban poor and working class. I made more money than most catering to the whims of the few who prospered from the Voodoo economics but my friends, except for John, were the "poor and infamous" as Phil called himself. I started frequenting a house just south of the Block occupied by a brother and sister; Jonathan and Renee, about the same age as me. Jonathan and Renee were poor and black. The Block was now featuring the largest chunk of freebase that could be had in the NY area for the smallest amount of money. Twenty dollars would buy more than a gram of rock. If you took it to Lafayette and Hunts Point in the Bronx you could make a hundred dollars. I knew plenty of guys who were. It seemed like freebase had been legalized at the Block. The police were almost completely absent, and the surrounding neighborhood lay in ruins. Those that remained untouched by the madness never left the safety of their own homes. My whole construction crew would smoke at Jonathon's house and we would leave jobs undone for days while I crashed out there. It got so my mother was afraid to go get paid for fear that she would have to pay me.

One day Renee, a couple of miscellaneous black guys and I were indulging in our depraved habit in the back bedroom. 'Rasta Joe' burst through the door with a shotgun. I threw Renee on the bed behind me. I looked in his eyes and saw he wasn't going to shoot if I did not force the issue. After all I had been on his side five years ago at the pool hall. Besides rushing a shotgun at anything less than a few inches is suicide. Rasta Joe backed out of the room snarling at Renee to tell her brother

Those Who Would Arouse Leviathan

"somebody's got to pay." Gradually I got to know everybody in the neighborhood even Rasta Joe who was a nice guy when he wasn't leveling a shotgun at you.

Pi and his family lived in a two-story home with a finished basement across the street. There were two brand new cars in the driveway and the home was immaculately furnished. Everybody in the neighborhood knew the family had nice things. Pi had worked hard all his life to acquire them and his wife was still a registered nurse. Eventually the whole family would succumb to crack addiction with his wife holding out the longest until one day her car stopped leaving for work in the morning. I will never forget the day Pi and I were in the basement when he started bellowing up the stairs at his son "what did you do with daddy's pipe?" I was partying one day with Pi's nephew; Andre, in a room he rented in Pi's house. Andre was a really tough Black guy about the same age as me. He looked at me and suddenly got introspective. He said "I know you ain't no cop, but I'll tell you this somebody's watching you. Some Nigger from the city was hot on Renee and he was really jealous of you. Crackheads told me he was laying for you outside in the bushes with a gun. Somebody jumped him and knocked him out, threw him in a car. Nobody's seen that Nigger since." I never even asked Andre whether the guy who jumped my would-be assailant was Black or White. I just figured I got lucky. The guy had already done someone dirty and payback came at an opportune time for me.

When I was 14 years old I had been in a work program where urban kids were given summer jobs by the state cleaning out local parks. Kenny's brother and I were the only white kids in that program. Kenny's father had used his position as the bay constable to pull some strings and get us in there. I became close friends with a girl named Tracy Bowen. Tracy's family had been heavily involved with the local commerce and had burnt the house to the ground one night while cooking shit up. Tracy now lived in a trailer next to the burnt-out shell of the house. Her bodyguard Clyde was her constant companion. Clyde looked like a giant black fire hydrant and had a similar personality. Tracy needed a bodyguard because the bottom of the trailer was paved with stacks of twenty-dollar bills. I am not exaggerating. There looked to be at least a million in twenty's strewn carelessly around that trailer at all times. Sometimes I would get high with my childhood friend, but it always made me really nervous being around all that cash in that neighborhood. I do not care how tough either Clyde or I were.

Nietzsche's most famous maxim is "what does not kill me makes me stronger." Freebase cocaine did not kill me. It became inevitable that

I would give it up. When I did kick the habit, I was angry. I had sat in a front row seat and watched sorrow and human misery be distributed in a highly addictive and smokable form. At the time I was naive and blamed the Suffolk County Police Department. I was streetwise enough to know that cocaine could not be sold that cheap, illegally, for a profit. I knew it was coming in at the Chinese restaurant at the south corner of the Block and I thought I knew who was bringing it there. I contacted Geraldo Rivera through one of my mother's clients; Dr Frank Fields, who was the Science Editor for WABC, the network Rivera was working for at the time. Having grown up in Babylon, the neighborhood adjacent to the Block, Rivera took an immediate interest in the story. After confirming that there was an open air drug market in the middle of suburbia Geraldo set me up with his brother; Craig. In those days they were a team. Craig did all the field work, principally the filming and Geraldo took care of the production and presentation.

I took Craig into Jonathon and Renee's house where we placed a duffel bag rigged with a camera in a prominent position on the dresser. One of the crackheads became fixated with the duffel bag and started asking questions about it and Craig's abstinence. Craig started stammering an answer that he had to keep an eye on the bag, but I put an end to the whole matter by telling the crackhead that if he were going to smoke and get paranoid he would have to leave. We stayed for hours and when we finally left Craig talked incessantly about all the great footage he had and how none of it would have been possible without me. Craig asked me to go for dinner and drinks, but I declined. I was there to do a job not socialize.

Craig spent days filming the Block and the Chinese restaurant with a film crew hidden in a van in the parking lot of the Social Services center across the street. He was very excited about the footage he had acquired of the police ignoring blatant transactions as they sat in a squad car next to his camera crew across the street. He had also caught some of the mysterious comings and goings at the Chinese restaurant. The restaurant was frequented by two or three middle aged Black men who seemed incapable of dressing without finishing off their ensemble with some off-white raincoats they had purchased from central casting of the Pink Panther. One of them had a large birthmark on his face that made it impossible for him to go unnoticed. We figured the raincoats had to be from a precinct in the city which had worked a deal out with Suffolk County PD.

Craig seemed to think we had the story of the year. He said that this would be a one hour special but when the show finally aired it was less than fifteen minutes and used none of the footage I had got them and never even mentioned the Block. I was told that's just the way the TV news business is. The studio made the final decision on what would be aired. The next time I saw Geraldo it was on TV as I watched along with the rest of America and he failed to produce the 'hidden treasure of Al Capone.' He made a fool out of himself and the station which had relentlessly promoted the one hour special before it aired. By then I was already charged with second degree assault on a police officer. My life would never be the same again. I remember how much I enjoyed watching Geraldo tarnish his career forever on national TV. At the time I did not know that he had been fired from his job at ABC over his criticism for their refusal to air investigative journalism that was critical of the government. I just knew that I needed to get my teeth capped.

When the show had not aired I had not been disappointed. I picked at least half of my labor up from the Block every morning. I had enjoyed living in Suffolk County and still did some work there even though most of my jobs were in Nassau County. I continued living my life as if nothing had happened because nothing had. I pulled into the Block one day and I was stopped by Suffolk County PD. Two cops about thirty-five years old each got out of the squad car and I got out of my International truck. The two of them belligerently asked what I was doing there, and one climbed into my truck and started fumbling around. I really had no answer for them. I was there every day frequently mingling in the crowd. It was as if I had showed up for work and was suddenly asked what I was doing there. One of them began poking me with his nightstick. He poked me quite a few times before I decided to disarm him, wrenching the club from his grip and tossing it away. His partner came around behind me and grabbed me in a chokehold with his nightstick. I grabbed the club and used his grip on it to whirl him over my back at the same time dislodging the stick and taking possession of it, which I dutifully tossed away. I was well aware that they could shoot me. All the while more cops and people were arriving. The crowd was becoming openly hostile witnessing the police assault one of the few reliable employers in the area. They had to be forcibly restrained by the arriving cops. Suddenly a guy comes running out of the crowd and starts throwing powder puff punch's at me. It was none other than birthmark still wearing his raincoat.

I brushed him aside and looked around. I thought about letting Hyde loose, but I knew it could only end in my death, so I let them handcuff me. The two cops I had disarmed took me in their squad car and as we pulled out of the parking lot the passenger cop said take the long way and with that turned around and proceeded to knock almost every one of my front teeth out. He struck me viscously as many times as he could and with as much force as he could generate with the nightstick within the cramped quarters of the car. Every time he smashed me in the face I would sneer fuck you and spit blood and teeth at him. When we finally did arrive at the station house I figured the commanding officer would want to know how my face got like that but instead I was taken to his office and the door was shut behind us. He mocked me as the beating continued all night hidden from view of the other cops.

The three of them were all laughing at me with the commanding officer saying "you're supposed to be such a tough guy. I never seen no tough guys cry before." I don't know why but I just sneered "someday somebody's going to break into your house and beat your son the same way you're beating me." I saw his face drop and his ruddy red complexion go pale. He looked like a suddenly staggered prize fighter. Weeks later he would make repeated teary calls to my mother asking how I had known. It turned out that was exactly what had happened years ago. Four men in ski masks had broken into his home and beat his son into a coma. He was now a vegetable. I heard he quit the force shortly after my beating. By then he was a mental case.

I was bailed out the next day. When the case went in front of the Grand Jury I chose to testify. By now my regular lawyer; Sidney Chase, had been disbarred for accepting stolen merchandise for his services. Chase had sued the Amityville Police for me, and he had sued a lot of other cops during the course of his career. I guess they got tired of him and set him up; at least that's what I heard. He was steering all his clients to a legal lightweight named Bruce Torino. I believe it was under Bruce's advice that I did not mention Geraldo Rivera at the grand jury hearing. In retrospect Bruce was probably Sidney's brother-in-law.

The two cops showed up looking only slightly less gay than Don Johnson in Miami Vice. Charlie Bartle, the one that had done most of the clubbing, was even wearing Topsiders with no socks along with some kind of theatrical plastic caste. Many of the people in the grand jury were Black and made it obvious that they did not believe either the cops or the heavy hitter District Attorney who was assigned to prosecute me. They were deadlocked for hours which I was told is very rare at a Grand Jury hearing. But she did finally get the indictment.

The Reagan administration was perhaps the most corrupt in American history. Gary Webb chronicled the drug dealing in his 1996 expose book; Dark Alliance. The CIA was trading guns for cocaine with the contras in Nicaragua and bringing the coke into America for distribution as crack cocaine in America's cities. In response to Webb's book Reagan's successor Bush senior appointed an Inspector General to the CIA. The newly minted Inspector General Frederick Hitz issued two reports in 1998 containing devastating admissions about the CIA's knowledge and protection of contras known to be active in the cocaine trade. In Volume Two, published on Oct. 8, 1998 Hitz identified more than 50 contras and contra-related entities implicated in the drug trade. He also detailed how the Reagan administration had protected these drug operations and frustrated federal investigations throughout the 1980s. The reports were ignored by the media in favor of by now President Bill Clinton's sex life. Webb ended up committing suicide by shooting himself twice in the head.

When the case started out I had four witnesses, but they all folded one by one under police pressure. I remember the day it became apparent I would have to plead guilty to a felony. My men were working about a mile from the courthouse and I refused a ride with my lawyer because I was so disgusted with him. I did not know where the job was. I only had directions. I walked there in the brilliant sunlight of midday summer. When I got to the house Richard Capri was standing in his driveway and I was to begin my two decade's long association with this strip club impresario. When Richey died in 2008 he left enough money to buy John Gotti ten times over. I know because I was one of the people involved in the legal battle over that money. Henceforth I was to be a professional and if I busted anybody up I got paid for it and got paid very well. My affiliation with Richey now gave me a license to do whatever I pleased in Suffolk County and a cop like Bartle couldn't do a thing about it. Bartle would find that out a couple of years later.

CHAPTER 19

Richey was a dead ringer for actor Chazz Palminteri in the movie; Bronx Tale, right down to his balding head and his conversation. Again, art was imitating life just a little too closely to be dismissed as coincidence or some vaguely defined word like synchronicity. He talked frenetically as he walked aimlessly about the grounds of his property. There were three or four Pagans, wearing their colors, washing the windows on the front of his house. Richey wanted to make the top half of his home into a tropical jungle. The second story of his house off the Long Island Expressway in Brentwood was just one big room separated by a hanging partition. On one side was the standard bachelor's pad of the well to do Wall Street yuppie but when you walked through the partition there was a large open area with several skylights on a raised ceiling. My job was to furnish the skylight room with a fishpond and waterfall, then adorn it with every oversized houseplant known to man. I would procure the house plants through my younger sister, the one who didn't resemble Reynard Heydrich. She was an executive of Flower Time Nursery the major retailer for garden and plant supply's in New York at the time.

    Richey let loose with a meandering stream of consciousness about his theories on Plato, Nietzsche, Machiavelli and gangsters. I looked down on the ground and there was a two-inch-thick wad of brand new hundred-dollar bills wrapped in a rubber band. I picked it up and said, "I think you dropped something." Barely acknowledging it he stuffed it carelessly in the front pocket of his sweats. Later I would find out that Richey knew where every dime he ever made was located. He must have been testing me. I asked him about the Pagans washing his windows and he told me "yea, they came with the strip clubs I bought. They do everything I want for me but having them around is a real pain in the ass. They are constantly extorting the girls and making my father's life miserable at the clubs. That's when they're not scaring the shit out of my customer's. I could make twice as much money by getting rid of them. I hear you know some guys that would be just the right people for that job."

    I knew what I was getting into but as I saw it with a felony assault on a police officer on my record life in these here United States was going to be no bed of roses anyway. To be surrounded by exotic naked women and fresh one hundred-dollar bills sounded like a very acceptable consolation. I told him "Jimmy Lyn's going to be in prison for the rest of his life and Miss Iris went back to Puerto Rico now that they busted Mad Mario for the 'Easter Sunday Massacre' in the city. Lurch is definitely available, but he is facing quite a bit of time himself. He has to take his case to trial. It's going on two years now." Richey said "tell him not to worry about that. I can take care of it. Bring him by here tomorrow to meet me."

    By 1988 everybody but his mother, John and I referred to Phil as Lurch behind his back, even his sister. Phil was a pathological sadist and by then rumored to be a brutal killer. In the underworld you could scare people, like parents scared their children with the bogey man, just by mentioning Phil's name. He had managed to fly under the radar on Long Island by confining his handy work to the Bronx where he would prowl around sometimes only in sneakers and shorts exposing the hideous scars on his chest. He had gotten them from scalding water in a childhood accident. Crowds of Latinos and Blacks would scatter like cockroaches when the lights were turned on at the sight of Phil stalking down the streets of the Bronx.

    Occasionally I would drive Phil from Long Island to the intersection of Lafayette Avenue and Hunts Point Avenue in the Bronx.

Those Who Would Arouse Leviathan

This was Phil's play pen, the very asshole of the earth, the South Bronx circa late eighties. Buildings were crumbling to the ground everywhere you looked. One street was blocked off once because 30 guys were having it out with baseball bats and pistols, not a cop car for miles. 'King David' had a place in a corner store where you could go in and order any kind of gun you liked. He would have it for you the next day. This looked to be the only store open on that block. Each dilapidated building that still had floors contained its own community of desperados.

The many people stuck there still trying to earn a living commuted to work through a landscape of drug addicts and prostitutes. Other people made their living preying on everyone else around them. These were Phil's friends, his homeboys. He was known in all the buildings. We would hang out at King David's store for hours. Crack was everywhere. White boys drove in from Jersey looking to score day and night. Unable to resist the temptation of using my white skin as a lure I participated in more than a few robberies'. When the White boys came back with guns looking for that White guy who had robbed them I was treated to a grand tour of the subterranean city below the streets. All of the buildings seemed to be connected from below by abandoned subway tunnels. Phil and I would sometimes spend days wandering from building to building through the tunnels, smoking endless chunks of cocaine, guided through the subterranean corridors by an entourage of prostitutes and small-time players.

Phil was an enforcer for a woman named 'Miss Iris' who was 'head of the Puerto Rican Mafia' and owned a string of topless bars on Rosedale Ave. What a setup she had. You would go in those bars and get coke right over the bar and snort it out in the open like it was legal. The cash registers at the bar were equipped with red flashing lights and when they went off you knew to put your drugs away because the police were coming in for their pay off. Two or three detectives would walk in and go in the back room with the manager. When they left the lights would stop flashing and everyone would go back to what they were doing.

Phil's specialty was said to be 'flying lessons' off the roofs of buildings for those who were recalcitrant in their gambling and drug debts. His crew was all Black. Snoopy was the Jamaican kick boxing champion. King David was a Rasta man whose specialty was procuring guns. Mad Mario killed ten people on Easter Sunday in a tenement apartment leaving only a blood-soaked baby crawling around the carnage. Larry Davis, the legendary black gun fighter who shot it out with a swat team and won, was rumored to be part of it, although I never met him.

Phil had swatted Snoopy like a fly when Snoopy tried to protest that Phil had stolen his girlfriend, a Black prostitute from the Bronx. Phil's latissimus dorsi were so overgrown that the upper half of his arms actually rested on them with the lower half dangling down. His pot belly led me to call him Clyde after the orangutan in Every Which Way But Loose, the seemingly rip-off movie of Johns exploits made by Clint Eastwood. In retrospect Clyde probably was playing Phil in the movie.

    Phil also did work for the Gambino crime family which is how he met Miss Iris. He had hijacked an Este Lauder truck and Miss Iris and her friends simply loved buying hundred- and twenty-dollar bottles of White Linen perfume at the forty-dollar price we were selling them at. I had once went over Phil's house and found him mechanically beating a man over the head with a five-pound chunk of hash. When he was done he put the hash in his house and casually left the man in a pool of blood lying on the front lawn. He got in the car and remarked to me "the Gambino's gave me some hash and wanted their money, that guy was here to collect. I hope I didn't kill him; my mother will find him in the morning and be pissed."

    Phil liked hurting people to the point where he would become sexually aroused by it. I had met Phil when he was sixteen years old. He was a year or two younger than me. Back then Phil was friends with Geir and Phil O'Sullivan who were also a year or two younger than me. I was over Egil, Vigdis, and Geir's house, before their parents had left for Norway, sitting around watching TV with Egil, Geir, O'Sullivan and Danky. Danky was half Black and half White. He had grown up with Geir and O'Sullivan. He had come in to visit them from where he had moved in the Bronx. Everyone was mellowing out smoking pot when in through the door comes Phil wearing his uniform of cut off sweatpants with no underwear, no shirt, and dirty size thirteen sneakers. "Hey Danky" he says in his monotone nasal voice "you moved to Greenpoint over by my cousin. I heard the Nigger's there are pretty tough. Sometimes I go in and visit him and we hunt them down at night. I stabbed one just a few weeks ago. I like to go Nigger hunting in the Bronx. Hu hu hu." Danky makes a big mistake and answers him "yea, White people can't even come into my neighborhood. They will just fuck them up on sight!" Phil looks at him and says "Why? What are you a Nigger now? What you don't like White people no more?"

    Phil was huge even then. He grabbed Danky in a headlock and began to leisurely punch him in the back of the head. It looked like an agitated gorilla playing with a rag doll. He called Danky every racial epithet in the book saying, "you leave a White boy and you come back a Nigger wanting to talk shit to me." Thus, began a three-hour marathon torture session of Danky. Nobody interceded. They probably should have but they didn't. I usually laugh at shit like that, but I found this disgusting. You could see Phil had an erection through his shorts as he beat and stabbed Danky all over with a little two-inch folding knife. It went on for hours. Phil never released him from the headlock even as he reclined on the couch watching TV with Danky's gurgling head clutched to his chest. When he decided Danky "is getting blood all over Geir's house" he hog tied him and suspended him upside down from a rope on the dock dangling him in the water "to wash off the blood." When Egil finally protested and said his mother would be home soon Phil reluctantly left the half dead Danky hog tied in the garage. Egil, Geir, and I drove the kid back to the Bronx that evening in a long silent ride. It looked like he had been run over by a car, repeatedly. I thought he should have been brought to a hospital. But we dropped him off on a side street at his own insistence. I think he just wanted to get away from us as fast as possible. We never saw Danky again.

CHAPTER 20

In the mid-eighties the Great South Bay of Long Island was no longer a source of income for the generational family's that had fished its waters for two hundred years. In the early seventies you could almost walk across the clam boats plying its waters from Massapequa to the Robert Moses Bridge. Anyone, if they worked hard enough with a rake or thongs, could pull two hundred dollars a day or more from the muck below its ten feet of water. Many thousands did from wooden flat-bottomed skiffs, open boats crudely built at eighteen to twenty-two feet long. The plywood box around the center console where the controls were located was the boats only concession to the elements. Every canal in working class areas was full of them. By the time I graduated Copiague High School in 1977 the Great South Bay fisheries had collapsed. Seventeen percent of my graduating class joined the armed forces right out of high school setting a national record at the time.

The sewers had come to southwestern Suffolk County. 'Progress' works out well for the rich and the poor, not so well for the working man whose job it usually takes. The construction of the "Southwest Sewer District" was rift with scandals. Rigged bids and contracts doled out to the nonexistent companies of political cronies insured an environmental disaster. A processing and pumping station was built on Bergen point in Lindenhurst and an outlet pipe was run through the bay and over Gilgo Beach three miles out into the ocean. The pipe leaked like a sieve. The South Bays clams were no longer harvestable because of pollution levels in the bay and an economic catastrophe ensued along its shores. The area of Lindenhurst by Venetian Shores was particularly hard hit because almost all its residents were clam diggers. Nobody who lived down there wanted to be anything but what their father and grandfather had been before them. Every day the sun would rise over Bergen Point looming on just the other side of the canal. On it stood the great temple; Southwest Sewer District # 3 - Bergen Point Wastewater Treatment Plant, a vast sewage treatment complex, a shrine to the Gods of money and the political corruption bought and sold. The cronies actually had the nerve to build their golf course right next to it. I did not fail to see the irony of the whole thing.

The area by Venetian Beach became an open-air marijuana market. Cars from all over Long Island would pull around the bend in front of its gates and be greeted by a throng of surfer type teenagers. Blond haired girls would cut in front of blue-eyed boys at the windows of cars. Everybody had bags of weed to sell. I looked at these kids as an unlimited supply of labor for my landscape business. Jimmy Lyn and a couple of nefarious characters from the Pagans named Jenson and Evers looked at them as an unlimited supply of retail drug dealers.

I christened this spawn of the displaced bay men; Bay Rats. The best of the bunch were Rickey Verity, known as Whitehead for his shock of long platinum blond hair, and Charlie Murray who was his dark-haired counterpart and partner in crime. Both these kids were like matching bookends, six feet of lithe teenage American muscle. They would prowl Venetian shores on their skateboards. Dispensing bags of weed like some earthbound Silver Surfers. I immediately took a liking to both of them. Charlie Murray became my foreman when Jim wasn't working but Whitehead had his own thing out on the bay. His father had died on it, rumored to have been murdered in a turf war over the still lucrative scungilli pot lines. Whitehead was one of the last bay men. At eighteen years old he eked out a living for his whole family netting shiners for bait, spearing eels, and setting out Scungilli pots, in between pedaling bags of weed on the shoreline.

Jenson and Evers had 'The Club.' Jimmy Lyn had Phil. Houses got shot up, mostly by Phil. A guy named Duffy who hung out with Lyn got stabbed up at his construction job and stuffed in a plastic garbage bag before he was thrown into a ditch that was being dug. He was left to die, but Duffy didn't die. He was found by his coworkers and rushed to the hospital. The doctors still thought he wouldn't live. I remember being in the waiting room with Lyn and Phil. Lyn who was the quintessential black Irishman and born criminal was crying. Phil told him "don't worry Jimmy he'll live. He'll live because he wants to smoke crack again." Phil and I left while Lyn maintained vigil at the hospital. On the way-out Phil snickered to me "boo hoo they stuffed my Duffy in a Tuffy."

A few days later Phil was drawing a bead with a rifle when Jensen's mother answered the doorbell I had just wrung. I pushed the rifle up in the air knowing full well Phil had every intention of shooting her. When they found out Phil was hunting them down both Jenson and Evers turned themselves in and confessed to 'stuffing Duffy in the Tuffy.' They asked for police protection for their families. Once a kid named Berry had owed Lyn for a couple of pounds and no one could catch this kid. He was fast and he kept running away. One day Lyn screech's up to him in his car and Phil gets out. Berry runs away. Without bothering to chase him Phil yells out after him "You may run faster than me Berry, but your mother can't." Phil goes over Berry's parent's house, rings the doorbell and when Berry's father answers Phil drags him outside beats the shit out of him and throws him down a flight of concrete porch steps. Berry paid up the very next day.

Money was flying all over the place and Lyn and Phil were robbing drug dealers from Jackson heights to Lindenhurst. One-time Lyn sold someone a pound of pot in his kitchen and as soon as the guy handed Lyn the money Duffy burst through the front door grabs the pot and runs out the back door. If we didn't know you you were getting stuck up, sometimes even if we did. Lyn thought he was the second coming of Jesse James. He even favored a black powder Colt Dragoon to the assortment of semi-automatics he had laying around his house. Suffolk County Police Department was afraid of us. One time they pulled John, Phil, Lyn, and I, over by the beach. The car was full of guns and we all got out. The cop took one look at us and told us to go.

Another time down at the American Venice Bridge White Head and Charlie set this guy up to buy a couple of pounds. The guy gives them the money they give him the pot and Phil and I pull up. Phil immediately starts pounding the shit out of the guy who had the pot and I go chasing Whitehead down the street. He makes me run about a mile and Whitehead could run like a deer. Then like the kid he was he stops and starts laughing hysterically as he hands me the money. Phil pulls up in the car. He has the pot and there's blood all over him. Whitehead and I get in and we go find Charlie. Phil explains "you have to give them a really good beating, so they don't ever think of trying to come back." I wondered if he had an erection. Venice Bridge was right by the block Phil lived on, but nobody was going to ever come after Phil. He wanted them to.

We go pick up Lyn who had supplied the pot and decide to go to some shit restaurant named Blue Lagoon to split the money which was a few thousand dollars. As we pass the First Precinct on the way there Phil sees a cop getting out of his car. Phil swerves up on the lawn like he's going to run the cop over and keeps going back onto the road and to the restaurant. The cop follows us to the restaurant parking lot and Phil gets out, still full of blood, and says "look, I got no license, no insurance, and no registration; if you want to talk to me I will be inside eating with my friends. I'm not in a good mood." The cop says nothing as Phil stalks away. Nobody ever came in the restaurant.

Lyn rented a house in the American Venice around the block from Phil. The inside was furnished with piles of fur coats, dirty designer clothes, and children's toys. Three semi naked, all under six, blond girls played with miniature electric cars, almost as expensive as real ones at the time. Lyn's wife was an ex call girl soon to be cheap trick crack hole. There were guns and even nitro glycerin lying all around that house. When Lyn wanted 'a dog for the girls' he simply stole a neighbors Rottweiler, named it Caesar, and locked it in the basement.

One evening Lyn, a kid named Palamesi, and the now surgically repaired Duffy decided they needed some coke. They didn't want to go through the hassle and find a suitable mark in Jackson Heights, so they decided to rob a local dealer. The only problem was the only one they could think of that they had not robed already was a bouncer at Spy's the busiest night club on Long Island. Lyn walks into Spy's with a pump shotgun Phil had borrowed from Dave Lamante. I can imagine the look of horror on the faces of Long Islands Flock of Sea gulls crowd when Lyn proceeded to poke and prod the bouncer with the shotgun right through the crowd towards the front door. The only problem was Lyn poked a little too hard and the gun went off accidentally blowing a massive hole in Palamesi's chest killing him instantly.

As I said Lyn was a bit sentimental, so they forgot the bouncer and dragged the dead body out to the car. When he got home with-it Lyn realized he had just committed murder in front of about a thousand people and called Phil. Phil knew just what to do. In a rendition of the proverbial Polock story he cut the legs, arms and head from the body, between peering into the body cavity "to look for chunks of crack." Phil disposed of the torso out on the Islands and the legs and arms in different wooded areas of Long Island. Phil probably figured even with the witness's without a body they could not charge Lyn with murder. Unfortunately for Phil some old clam digger did find the torso and only a few days after the spectacular crime had been headlined. In the back pocket of the torso was Palamesi's wallet. When the cops picked up Duffy he was only too happy to tell them all about what Lurch had done, how he had put the head in a hat box and summoned a limo to take both he and the head into the city for prostitutes and crack. According to Phil

"Palamesi would have wanted it that way." When the evening festivities were over Phil tossed the head, hat box and all, into the East River.

Lurch, as he had now been dubbed by SCPD, was now the most famous ghoul in the tri-state area. Out on bail he sat around his basement all day trying to figure out how he was going to kill Duffy before the trial when he didn't know where Duffy was. I told him he would also have to kill Lyn, everybody who was at Spy's that night, the Limo Driver for him and the head, and maybe he should kill the head too, but he wouldn't listen. He was fixated with killing Duffy.

CHAPTER 21

I wasn't myself. A shotgun belonging to the president of the Pagans had been found in the wood pile of my parent's home by homicide detectives, a gun used in perhaps the most gruesome media spectacle in the history of Long Island. I had a 'psychotic episode' and was committed to the 'Flight Deck' of South Oaks Psychiatric Hospital. Nobody could talk to me up there, no reporters, no homicide detectives, only the other nuts.

I was up there for a few weeks, till Duffy finished whining to the police. They were "Strange Days" indeed. I had two sixteen-year-old girls tending to me night and day. Both of them were up there because their parents were convinced they were nymphomaniacs. One named Dawn kept trying to escape. She was really cute. I was warned by the nurses that if I helped her get away they would personally see that I was brought up on charges for corrupting a minor. Strangely enough I have no memories of ever sleeping with Dawn but when I got out I had to be treated for venereal disease.

Almost all the patients up there were young attractive people, and it was Co-Ed, also strangely enough. One Hindu girl about the same age as me and from a well to do Indian family kept telling me she was fine but "they have stolen my soul and although you are still conscious and presumed living without a soul it is terribly painful to live without one. Inside is a vast emptiness." She told me she would have to stay up there till she could get her soul back. I hoped she wasn't holding her breath in anticipation and wondered just how 'crazy' she was. All of the adults up there were presumed dangerous by the staff and could snap at a moment's notice. The younger kids had been committed by their parents and had shown a predilection to run away. According to staff they were 'escape risks.' The place was locked down tighter than Ronald Reagan's asshole with double solid steel doors on each end of it.

They kept trying to medicate me and quickly found out I was

immune to Thorazine. When we were eighteen or nineteen John had befriended a nut named Jimbo and commandeered his medication. Thorazine is like aspirin to me. They were giving me mega doses and I was doing pushups all day. They switched it to something else called Haldol which had side effects like spasms, so they had to give me some other concoction to counteract the side effects of the Haldol. I wondered why they just didn't dispense Tuinals. A couple of Tuinals knocked out James Bond in Ian Flemings 'Octopussy and The Living Daylights.' The blue and red bombs had been known to even occasionally knock me out if I washed them down with enough booze.

I would amuse myself by playing mind games with my fellow patients. According to the nursing staff in the short span I was there they had 'ten times the usual amount of two two two's'. A 'two two two' is something to behold. I once watched one where a sixteen-year-old hundred- and forty-pound boy tossed around six large black orderlies, plus some nurses, for almost a full five minutes before they got him Straight Jacketed. Dawn was the princess of the two two two's. She would spend evenings cooing on the phone with her parents "I just want to come home and catch up with my piano lessons." Her days were spent trying to fuck me, trying to escape, and launching into vicious two two two's on the nurses and orderlies. She once described to me in graphic detail how a pimp had fucked her with a shampoo bottle. I was accused of giving my psychotic new friends drugs by both the doctors and nurses. I told them "I am not giving them drugs. You are. I am giving them sound advice."

One of the black orderlies, a guy named Perkins, had convinced the nuts that he was a Kung Fu Master and he 'could knock anyone out with just a thought punch.' He had even convinced himself. That's all he talked about. Now don't get me wrong. I love kick boxing and had practiced night and day since I was thirteen years old but outside of Miyamoto Musashi and 'The Book of Five Rings' Asian Martial Arts is full of pretensions and unwarranted assumptions. In WWII, Korea, and Vietnam, in hand to hand combat to the death the bigger stronger Americans almost always prevailed. Bruce Lee was no more dangerous than your average ballerina or gymnast. I had to pull Perkins card. I told him we could go around the corner where no one can see. "You can take your best shot. Then I'll take mine. No one will know." He tried to play it off like he didn't want to hurt me but after that I was satisfied that he knew I would laugh at him and knock him out.

The largest nut was a six foot two short, circuited jock. The kid was about two hundred pounds of muscle and the whole staff, including Perkins, was terrified of him. He took exception to Dawns taunting of him one day and got aggressive. In a matter of fact fashion, I laid him out with a short right no Straight Jacket or medication necessary. The staff told me that they could press charges on me for assaulting a minor, but Dawn and the kid insisted he had deserved it and I had possibly saved her life. He became my biggest fan after that.

One day I gathered all the nuts around me with Dawn at my side. We watched the communal TV which I never did and encouraged them not to do either. For some reason I had to watch the Space Shuttle; Challenger, reenter the earth's orbit. I remember laughing hysterically when I watched it blow up in front of the horrified nurses. All I could think of was the line from the Doors song Wild Child about how she dances on her knees with the pirate prince at her side staring into the hollow idols eyes.

When they cut me loose the by then thoroughly spooked psychiatric staff bid me a relieved goodbye. I threw the Haldol and its accompanying pharmaceutical concoction in the garbage pail on the way out and got the good news. Homicide no longer wanted to talk to me. Duffy had not implicated me. The Geraldo Rivera thing would drag on for another year and a half, but I would also get the bad news. I was going to jail anyway.

Mercy / חסד

CHAPTER 22

The day after Richey's proposition Phil followed me with his own car to Richey's house in Brentwood. I introduced them and left. Ostensibly I was still a landscaper. The next day I picked up John at his grandfathers. He and Meryl were already on the skids. They had two children together. What was going through Johns head when he had got married? I will never know. John was working on outboards which by now had been relegated to a hobby for him. He had graduated to far bigger junk. WWII bulldozers and ancient cranes were strewn all around a couple of different lots he 'rented' from various mobsters and garbage guys. The backyard of the sprawling two-acre ranch he and Meryl had purchased in East Islip looked like the aftermath of the Battle of Kursk. John was wearing his grease stained tan Carhartt overalls which henceforth would be his uniform because nothing else fit him. He made sure his grandfather who just had a heart attack was alright then he crammed himself into the front seat of my Firebird Esprit. I hoped he wouldn't leave a stain.

It was pouring rain when I pulled up to Phil's house. We knocked and entered his lair which was the bottom floor of the house. The rest of his family lived upstairs and weren't allowed downstairs. Phil paid all the bills. He was holding court with a bunch of Italian kids from the neighborhood. These kids were all on the express train to nowhere. They were all affiliated with the Gambino crime family and most of them would be dead or in prison before they were thirty. Phil was their hero, but they had all heard of John. He was their God. It was as if Derek Jeter had just walked into a rotary club meeting. They were all taking turns doing curls with some frivolous amount of weight which I ended up curling ten times with one hand. Phil was slumped in his big easy chair, the only chair in the room, laughing at them. He was surrounded by piles of pots and pans. Interestingly enough he had just graduated the Culinary Institute of Technology in Manhattan. On one end of the house was a plywood cubicle where he slept on his bare mattress. He had one dresser in there. It always had all the draws open exposing more pistols than clothes. A couple of old pictures of his dead father and relatives he had never met back in Poland hung on the walls over his mattress. As I have already said the rest of Phil's lair was done up, courtesy of the Amityville Police Department, in everything that could be purchased from Dan Laurie for twenty-five thousand dollars. The garage was on the opposite end of the house from Phil's 'bedroom.' It was separated from the house by a cinder block wall. In the garage hung three heavy bags and this wooden mannequin thing that Phil would punch 'to toughen his knuckles.'

One of the kids; Sal, who followed Phil around like a little dog was all excited that he had just met John. He started asking John how he trained. John played along. He told the kid that he should never do bench pressing because it would fuck up his punching muscles and that when he got past twenty-one he shouldn't lift any weights at all. He told him that the boxing team in Attica only did calisthenics. To toughen their whole body's, they would take turns running into the wall as hard as they could. John said, "let me see you do it right now." Pointing at the cinderblock garage wall John said, "run into that wall right now as hard as you can." The kid by now thought he had figured out that John was playing him. He was incredulous and said he didn't believe that they really ran into walls at Attica. All of a sudden John burst into a leaping sprint smashing into the garage wall with a thud that shook the entire house. Pots and pans tumbled down from their piles next to Phil and the picture of Phil's uncle Igor in Poland fell from the wall in his room. John turned and pointed to Sal "now you do it!" You could see Sal getting himself all psyched up. He was taking deep breaths and concentrating on the wall. He let out a guttural scream and charged into the wall as hard as he could. It was like a bug splattering on the windshield of a fast-moving car. He slid down the wall in what seemed like slow motion landing in an unconscious heap on the floor. Phil in between laughing hysterically said to the other kids "okay now get him out of here. We have to talk about something." They dutifully carried him out to their car and left.

I spoke first "their probably all up at Something Else. A few weeks ago, I went in there with Charlie Murray and a couple of the other kids that work for me. The place was packed. There must have been a hundred of them in there. I shook hands with everybody, and everything was cool. I went in the back to check out some girls and when I got back to the front I was just in time to see Charlie smiling and shaking a guy's hand then laying him out with a perfect front kick. I got the kid out of there in one piece but later when I went home my parents were really pissed. They had showed up at my house in about five car loads waving guns around in the street. My father's dying. I can't have that shit. They were lucky I wasn't home. Let's go there first." John said, "T-bones in town he's the one who's in charge for the whole East Coast." He looked at me and said "did you ever meet T-bone? He was supposed to fight Ali and he got himself all fucked up in a bike accident. Now he walks with a cane. He knows me very well. He loves to talk to me about boxing." Johns face lit up in his old satanic grin as he spoke. I answered unenthused "never met him. These are you and Phil's buddies, not mine." Phil said "well Dave Lamante will be there. I'll talk to him. He's still pissed at me because Lyn got his shotgun taken away by the police for shooting Palamesi. Not that he's going to say anything. This one can go off by accident too." He pulled a thirty-eight out from under his shirt and laughed his ghoul laugh. Then he looked at me and said "you find out whose idea it was to go over your house. I'm going to blow him away right in the bar. Everybody's a gangster. Throw them a body and we'll see who the gangsters are." With faces of stone and a deliberate pace in our steps we left Phil's house into the dark and rainy night.

Something Else had a huge parking lot with a low spot in the center. It had rained all day and apparently the drain wasn't working because there was a small lake covering most of the lot. It was dry up by the bar so against the wall lined up side by side were fifty or sixty Harleys. Smoking pot and milling around the bikes in the rain were about twenty Pagans. John pointed to one who looked like a lawn ornament dwarf on steroids and said "there's Frankie Mad Dog. He's supposed to be the toughest one. Maybe I should bring Eric down here and we can see who really should be using that name." "He's not big enough to fight

Eric." I said. John said "he's supposed to be a fifth-degree black belt. He's their martial arts instructor." I answered him with scorn "he wouldn't last two minutes with Eric." And John said, "not even one." I floored the big eight cylinder and when I got to the center of the puddle I slammed on the breaks turning the wheel and spinning the car into a one eighty sliding at them and the bikes sideways and pushing up a tidal wave of water that washed right over them. Drenched they all came charging at us and when they got to the car I rolled down the automatic windows. They stopped short and Frankie Mad Dog said "oh. It's you guys. I should have known. What are you doing out Phil?" Phil said "I'm out on bail. You know anybody who might have seen Duffy around. You sell coke. I know that crackhead needs coke." Frankie said "no. Duffy wouldn't come anywhere near us. You should have let us finish the job on him." Phil said "I know. Is Dave in there?" Frankie answered "yep. He's in there with T-bone."

    When we walked through the door the bar was packed with Pagans. All of them were wearing colors. The juke box was blasting hard rock making it impossible to hear anything anybody said that was more than ten feet away. I don't think anybody who wasn't a member was allowed in that night because one of them I had never seen before was sitting on a stool by the door. The guy had a raccoon mask tattooed around his eyes and Phil stopped by him looking him up and down. "I have to ask you this." Phil said, "did you ever wake up in the morning and look in the mirror and regret doing that to your face?" The guy didn't answer him, and Phil said, "where's Dave?" The guy pointed to a booth where I saw Dave sitting with a couple of other guys. One of them was pushing sixty and looked a little gimpy. I gathered that was T-Bone. John and Phil went over to the booth and Dave and T-Bone got up and exchanged warm hugs with them. T-Bone with the help of his cane walked to the back of the bar with John's huge arm draped over his shoulder to support him. The other two Pagans who had been sitting with T-Bone and Dave got up and went to the bar. Phil took a seat across from Dave. I sat down on a stool at the front of the bar facing out to the crowd. I saw Charlie the clubs usual bouncer over by Raccoon Boy. I gestured for him to come over and asked him accusingly "who came over my house a few weeks ago?" He started to say "it wasn't the club just the bouncer that Murray laid out. That guy's not even a prospect. After that he never will be. The guys" I cut him off. "You guys are just lucky I wasn't there. I paid a thousand dollars for an AR15 and all I get to shoot with it is sea gulls in the chum slick. I would have tried it out for sure on youse. As a matter of fact, if my father wasn't a sick man he would have shot youse himself." I didn't say anything else after that and he walked away after a moment of silence between us. After about a half hour John comes ambling back to the front with T-Bone and Dave gets up from the booth with Phil. They all exchange warm hugs again and I thought to myself I guess there won't be no killing tonight. Just then a guy comes up to me with a huge Bowie knife strapped to his leg and says "So now you're with Richey Capri? We don't like Richey Capri. That guys an asshole." Before he had a chance to say another word or do anything I snatched the Bowie knife out of the sheath on the side of his leg with my left hand and grabbed him by the back of the neck with my right. I started poking him in the chest with the knife saying "does your mother know you have this? Does she? You could get hurt with one of these things you know, especially if you don't know how to use it." I pushed it into his throat and sucked up the fear in his eyes like it was ambrosia. Suddenly I was snapped out of my trance by Phil, John, and Dave all calling my name. I let go of the guy and flipped the knife in my hand grabbing it by the blade and pushing the handle out to Dave which he gingerly took from me. On the way out the door he asked Phil if I was really going to kill that guy. Phil just looked at him and shrugged.

    We continued on our mad romp through all the clubs in the area making sure we told anyone we talked to that Bogart's was no longer the Pagans clubhouse. Phil was now the new manager of Bogart's and its sister club next door; Gaslight. For now, on we would only be featuring the hottest girls in New York and there would be no bikers allowed in the bar that were wearing colors. I was pretty drunk by the time I dropped Phil off to end the night. The southern end of the Venice is separated by a narrow canal spanned by a slightly less narrow bridge forming an abrupt hump in an otherwise mile straightaway running parallel to the main canal. I dropped Phil off a couple of blocks south of the bridge and when I turned onto the straightaway I hit the gas on the big eight cylinder. I don't know how fast I was going when I jumped the bridge, but I was airborne for longer than I expected. When I did finally hit the black top, the car fishtailed and did a one eighty right into a four-foot-thick maple tree dead on the driver's side door nearly cutting the car in two. I was thrown across the seat and slammed against the passenger door. I got out and saw I had scored a ringer with the car right around the maple tree. The problem was I wasn't playing horseshoes. I had to walk to Phil's and get a ride home from him. The next day after the body guy, who was also the local Mafioso, peeled the car off the tree I went over his shop and seen him talking in hushed tones as he and his paisan's cast disbelieving glances at me. I wasn't hurt. In fact, I felt nothing. But my whole left side did turn black and blue.

CHAPTER 23

Phil hadn't been on the job long when I popped into the Gaslight late one night. The Gaslight was laid out with an elongated rectangular stage that spanned the entire front of the building almost up to the foyer for the front entrance leaving only a narrow walkway to the seating on the side of the stage furthest from the bar. The stage was surrounded by tables and seats as was the much smaller stage at Bogart's. At Gaslight there was about a twenty-foot corridor between the stage and the correspondingly long bar. Where the bar ended there was a room with a pool table and restrooms off to the side. Beyond the pool table was the backdoor and phone booth. Between the stage and the restrooms was a five-foot-wide tunnel that led to a back room. One side of the tunnel doubled as a mirrored wall and entrance for the stage. The wall on the other side of the tunnel was the wall to the backroom which contained a walk-in freezer and bar supplies. The spacious backroom also doubled as the clubhouse for the Gaslight staff. Phil had a barstool pulled up against the wall by the entrance to the tunnel wearing his huge black bomber jacket and an extremely dour look on his face. There were a couple of customers at the tables and an aged Pagan not wearing colors watched some pig flopping around on the stage. She exhibited all the enthusiasm of a freshly gaffed codfish. An old drunk sat at the bar being served by Agnes who looked like one of them historical black and white photos of an Apache squaw. She was even dressed like one. Agnes's sister was the waitress. She looked like a Philippine dwarf and I heard her telling the customer at the table that she needed good tips because she was very sick and had to go to the doctor.

Phil gestured with his hand at his surroundings and said "look at this. Does he really think I can work with this? If that bitch Agnes asks me one more time what I'm going to do if the Pagans all come in here I'm going to blow a hole right through her forehead." He pulled the thirty-eight from his pocket for emphasis. "Look at her sister! That's a waitress? Customers keep leaving because their afraid she has leprosy and I think she might too. She belongs in a freak show in the booth next to the snake man." Phil was talking loud enough so he could be heard over the juke box. He got up from his stool and walked over to the aged Pagan and demandingly asked "how long has she been here? I'll give you four hours. Agnes give this guy eighty out of the draw." Addressing the aged Pagan again he said "get this pig out of my bar. And don't let me see her back here again. For now, on I don't want to see any of your girls in here unless their named Gracie Starr or Dianne Rodney. As a matter of fact, for now on Gracie appears exclusively at the Gaslight.

Those Who Would Arouse Leviathan

You tell Savage if he wants to keep breathing me and him are going to have to come to an understanding." Being an old-timer, the Pagan had no idea who Phil was, and I was standing there in my Bermuda shorts and topsiders. He started to get indignant when he suddenly realized he had another girl there too. "Hey" He says "where's my old lady? And where's Al?" Just then Al and his 'old lady' wandered out from the back room. Al was Richey's father. He was a shriveled up unabashed seventy something degenerate who had spent a load of money getting a surgically implanted pump on his penus so he could fuck the girls who worked there that were nasty enough to do it with him. Al's raisin face was covered with lip stick as red as the face of the aged Pagan who was now screaming at his old lady "what were you doing with Al back there. That's it I'm calling T-Bone and the whole clubs coming down here." Phil pulled out his pistol and told him to shut the fuck up before he got pistol whipped. With the other hand he then pulled a quarter out of his pocket and handed it to the aged Pagan and told him "here go call chicken bone and tell him what you just said to me." When the Pagan got out of the phone booth he apologized to Phil and said T-Bone said to get the girl out of there if Phil didn't like her. The girl was dressed by now and he started to tell his old lady to get dressed but Phil said "no she stays till four. I'm not going with just two girls, besides Al likes her. Come back and get her at four." The guy looked like he was literally going to explode but he walked out, pig in tow, without saying another word.

"It gets even better" Phil said. "Take a walk across the street with me and meet my bouncer John Doxie the human punching bag." As we walked across the street Phil mimicked the aged Pagan "hey where's my old lady? Where's Al? At least that will keep that old fuck out of my hair for the rest of the night. Rooster says you can tell when Al really likes a girl the stain on the front of those plaid pants he always wears gets bigger." Actually, I had met John Doxie years ago when he had tried to tell me I couldn't drink with a pile of Xanax in front of me. It had ended with him locking himself behind the reinforced steel door of Bogart's basement and I leaving after I finally tired of trying to kick it in. The Pagans had installed that door special to keep their party's from being raided by narcotics police.

Doxie was sitting on the stool by the door in the corridor leading into the bar. He was a sweaty three-hundred-and-fifty-pound sauropod in a tank top. He had a Fu-Manchu-mustache, a cast on his arm, and more hair on his back than the Sasquatch. He was about the same age as us. Bogart's was smaller and darker than the Gaslight, but it was packed with over a hundred people. One look at the stage explained why. A girl named Mesha was dancing. She was the official representative of High

Society one of the better porn magazines of the eighties. Mesha did promotional tours for the magazine all over the country. She had auburn blond hair with legs like a filly racehorse and large firm breasts. Later I would find out she had ten years of professional dancing lessons by a private instructor. The guys were going crazy throwing money at her from every direction. As her dancing became more raucous and provocative their attempts for her attention became more and more frenzied. Now this was a stripper. Hollywood couldn't have done it better than this. The late eighties were right before plastic surgeons started turning out girls that looked like this from the most unlikely sources. These girls were all products of nature and as such were the equivalent of rare jewels. It's the difference between a synthetic diamond and a real one.

"Look at this shit I got to put up with." Phil said. "Jerry's girlfriend Sue is working in here, so I got three A-girls working here and not even a C-girl working in the bigger place next door. We will end up ringing about twenty-five hundred on the register after pay outs here. If I put Mesha next door I could ring five thousand easy. As it is now after payouts and whatever that fat whore Agnes is stealing I'm probably not going to even break-even next door. I can't deal with this job if Jerry's going to be controlling the girls. Let the Pagans come back in. I'll quit." Phil loved playing his role of sadistic brute, but he also had a sinister intelligence that was probably the most alarming thing about him. I immediately saw his logic. "You better tell Richey this" I said. He said "don't worry I'm telling him just what I just told you. As a matter of fact, I don't even have to. Doxie will be on the phone with him as soon as I turn my back." "Hey John" he leered. "Why don't you tell my friend how a hundred and forty-pound Polock got you wedged in the steel door over there and smashed your arm all up?" Doxie didn't answer him. Phil went on "yea you know we have to get rid of the Polock's because they come hunting John down after they get drunk in their bars in Copiague. Richey didn't tell us about that." Copiague had a population of very rough Polish immigrants. That was when the communists were sending all their criminals to America. Phil continued with his taunting "don't worry Doxie tonight we are going to show you what we do with Polock's. I'm every Polock's worst nightmare, a bigger Polock!" A slinky Puerto Rican girl with slightly African American features that only made her look more exotic wrapped herself around Phil. "This is Amenia" Phil said. "She's one of the smart ones. This is another A-girl Sue doesn't need." On queue Amenia said "Why don't you put me over at the Gaslight? I can make more money over there. Nobody can compete with Mesha except Gracie Starr and Celeste. Rodney already took a walk over there."

Those Who Would Arouse Leviathan

Now Phil was furious. He told Amenia to get her stuff and we would walk her over to the Gaslight and remove Rodney.

When we got inside the Gaslight Phil halted and said, "woops there go the Polock's that broke Doxies arm." There were three of them, two about two hundred pounds each, and one who was about a hundred and forty pounds and ripped to shreds. I was guessing he was the one that did the arm breaking. "Should I go get the fat fuck?" I said. Amenia chimed in "what for? So, they can beat him up again. Don't encourage them. They'll be here every night." Phil said "fuck the fat fuck I'm gonna knock those other two out. You take the tough one." The three of them were standing at the entrance to the tunnel by the stool where I had originally met Phil that night. Phil walked up to them and without saying a word caught both two hundred pounders with a devastating left right that he practiced day and night on that wooden mannequin of his. They went down like they were shot. I squared off with the wiry muscled Polock. Just as I had suspected the guy must have been the Polish lightweight champion back in the old country. He was fast. The fight went on all through the bar and out the back door into the parking lot. Finally, I caught him leaning forward with a kick flush on the side of the head. He went down and I grabbed him by the hair and dragged him over to the car where his friends were now standing. They were both dazed and bleeding. Phil hovered menacingly close to them like a shark on its wounded prey. I kept bashing the unconscious Polock's head against the windshield until the windshield finally broke. He was a bloody pulp, and he was never going to look the same again. Both bars had emptied out by now and everybody was watching this gladiatorial spectacle.

A girl came up to me. She was wearing a transparent red negligee and had the most perfect body I had ever seen. I had been studying Egyptian Gods and Goddesses now for almost two years. I swear I had seen her in some obscure illustration of Isis depicted with arms outstretched revealing her erect nipples on perfectly sized breasts and back arched to sensuous female perfection. The girl had a nasal twang that was at once endearing and at the same time annoying. She scolded me "not even the Pagans did shit like that. You just deliberately maimed that guy. You don't belong running around loose." All I could see were those erect brown nipples through her red negligee. I knew she was aroused but not half as aroused as I was. I felt a warm rush go straight through my genitals. I couldn't believe the absurdity of it. Here I was. I had just had the fight of my life and I was getting an erection. Was I becoming Phil? She continued her berating of me "You can't do something like that just because they're Polish. I happen to be half Polish myself." At this point Phil interceded "shut the fuck up Rodney. How many times do I have to tell you the Pagans don't run this place anymore? I do. Who the fuck told you you could just wander over to the Gaslight anyway? How come I missed you on the way over to Bogart's? Were you in your car again smoking pot? Get back in Bogart's! And that go's for everyone else too. Anybody who wants to hang around here anymore and not be in terrible danger better get back in the bars before the police get here and they better forget what they just seen." I heard Rodney answering him back as I was leaving for my truck. No one ever answered Phil back. "You know that girl that you just viciously insulted was my friend. You're an animal Phil and so is your friend there who looks like he's dressed up to go yachting!"

CHAPTER 24

The next day I got a call to come and meet Phil and Richey over at Richey's office in Bogart's. Richey hit me off with a stack of cash, but I was hooked anyway. I had my share of beautiful women already, but this was totally different. The three girls I had seen last night; Mesha, Amenia, and Dianne Rodney, all looked like they had just stepped from the centerfold of Penthouse Magazine. It was the difference between the girls in Hustler and the girls in Penthouse or Playboy. These were the best of the best and my hormones were raging into overdrive. I had been oversexed all my life anyway from the jerking off a half dozen times a day since I was twelve to the blue ball I would get if I didn't. There was nothing more I wanted to do with my life at the time than to make these bars my personnel kingdom. Richey said "I been talking to Phil all morning. You know your friend is really smart." I said "yea Richey. Why just because he's an axe murderer did you think he was an idiot? I don't hang out with idiots. They only get to work for me." Richey said "hey that's a good line. I'm going to borrow it sometime. Anyway, you know Jerry's got like nine hundred thousand dollars sunk into these places. He embezzled it from his job on Wall Street and did two years while I invested it in these places for him. But I can't just let him run the clubs into the ground. Now that the Pagans are out of here we are starting to make money and I want to make as much money as I can. So, I told Jerry that for now on only Phil would be dealing with the agency and the girls." I smugly said "Well that's between you, him, and Phil. I'm just going to fuck as many of these girls as I can." Richey said "that's what their here for. Can you do me a favor? I got Gracie Starr next door she's going to be appearing in the Gaslight exclusively in the daytime for now on. She's the hottest girl on the circuit. Vinnie Gambler from the Pagans go's out with her. He's next door now with Doxie. I got this asshole

Mike the Boxer over there. He went a couple of rounds with Tyson and I think he got brain damage from it. He hangs around the Gaslight all day bothering the girls and trying to extort drinks. Gambler is the only one who can keep him under control. So, I got to pay him to sit with this stupid fuck all day. And Gambler don't want to be there believe me. He's a mason. He's like you. He's got his own business. He helped me to build these places. Can you and Phil get rid of the stupid fuck for me?" I looked at Phil and he gave me that stone cold shark look. Richey said "just go in there you'll find him. And remember Vinnie's on our side. He's just got to make it look good."

    As Phil and I walked next door we talked it over. Phil said "you start with him. Get him to come outside with you. Then I'll jump in. Tyson himself couldn't kick both our asses." I sneered "I don't think he could even kick mine in a street fight. I'll take that nigger on anytime in a street fight." When we went in the club it seemed like it had been completely transformed from the previous night. There must have been close to two hundred people packed into standing room only. We picked our way through the crowd towards the waitress station where we knew we would find him. The waitress station was on the far end of the bar towards the pool table. That is always the choicest spot in topless bars because that is where the waitresses, dancers and barmaids congregate. The stool against the wall by the stations bar flap in the Gaslight would become my throne. Everybody in the bar was screaming and stomping and the whole building was shaking. Up on the stage strutting up and down like a model on a runway was a raven-haired beauty. She had the biggest tits I had ever seen that weren't sagging. In fact, she had a body like an athlete. Her striated rib cage muscles were holding those water melon sized tits as erect as flags in a gale force wind. Her legs were just as good. I had heard that they had been featured on an album cover and she had toured with Motley Crew. As her name would indicate she was the biggest star on the strip club circuit at that time. Money covered the stage, and the guys couldn't throw it at her fast enough. Up on the stage against the mirrored wall stood John Doxie, arms folded like a fat hairy sentinel. Occasionally a guy would try to climb onto the stage with her and Doxie would dutifully toss him back into the crowd. It was a game. I looked at Phil and I said "wow" over the din of the crowd. He said "that's Dianne Rodney's best friend. At least she ain't got a big mouth like Rodney."

    After we watched the show for a while we made our way to the back to attend to our business. We found them where we figured we would. A very stoutly built guy with a long grey ponytail sat next to a behemoth that must have been the only man in the world actually as hairy as John Doxie. The behemoth was wearing a leather jacket, but it looked like an afro was growing out of the collar and cuffs on the sleeves. I nestled in between them and introduced myself to the guy with the ponytail. He gave me a warm firm handshake and I saw his teeth were a little messed up. I would have been expecting a girl like Gracie Starr to be going out with a rock star or at least a male model, somebody equally attractive, not necessarily rich. This was before Hollywood had turned America's most beautiful woman into brazen whores. I was finding out that what these girls liked were tough guys. The tougher the guy the harder they fell. I guessed Vinnie must have been a pretty tough guy in his day, but it looked like his day was nearing an end. I was at the threshold of dawn and I knew it. I turned to the hairy behemoth and said "I heard you fought Tyson and lost. You're a disgrace to the White race and I don't want to see you here anymore." He started trying to actually tell me how tough he was. I cut him off saying "your nothing but a washed-up punchy thug to me. Let's go outside right now. I'll show you what I'll do to Tyson." He didn't look like he wanted to go. Maybe he wasn't as stupid as he looked. But he grudgingly got up and followed me outside tailed at a discreet distance by Vinnie and Phil. As soon as we had stepped outside the door I started wailing this fat fuck. He was nothing. All the while I was beating the shit out of him I was wondering how he had gotten a fight with Tyson. The Polock I had fought the night before was tougher. This guy couldn't touch me. All he could do is try to cover up while I nailed him with a succession of rights and lefts. Finally, Phil comes over and Phil starts nailing him too. It was really pathetic because this guy's greatest talent was his ability to absorb punishment. We beat him worse than I had ever seen any man get beat in my life. He was on his knees actually crying as his blood went flying in every direction with each punch we landed. Finally, with real empathy I turned to Vinnie and said, "get this fat fuck out of here before we kill him." Vinnie dutifully carted him off and we never saw 'Mike the Boxer' again.

In the beginning I was getting two hundred dollars just to show my face there once a night for fifteen minutes. After a few weeks I started showing up there with my whole crew and hanging out all night. Richey would buy me a case of Wild Turkey every week and it turned out Agnes was at least good for one thing. She made the best Bloody Mary I have ever tasted. She used about thirty different ingredients which she would bring in just for me. It was pure ambrosia and I have never tasted as good a one since then. Jim went home to Patty, no relation to Kenny's Patty. There was no place for Jim in a bar you did not want to destroy. Everyone else came with me, including every 'Bay Rat' that could fight their way out of a wet paper bag. The really tough ones we gave jobs like the Buttenhagens and a guy named Sammis who had also fought Tyson in the amateurs. Geir was given the job of stocking beer; it was his forte from the old OBI days anyway. There was one guy I kept hearing about that they were all afraid of, besides Phil and I; Jimmy Murphy. People said he could beat even me, of course I didn't believe it. They said he had beaten Sammis up just as badly as I had beaten up Mike the Boxer and Sammis was in a lot better shape than the hairy behemoth had been. Murphy was just finishing up a two-year bid upstate and he would be out in a couple of months. In the meantime, I took on all comers and I didn't care how many there were either.

CHAPTER 25

One-night Mesha was working the Gaslight and I had gone into the city to get some valium since Steve no longer gave Xanax to me. I got to the Gaslight at about one in the morning with my crew. I guess I had taken about four or five tens. I had Whitehead and Charlie Murray with me, which I always did, and Ray Broderick and Mike Flanagan. They were all very tough nineteen and twenty-year-old kids from Venetian Shores in Lindenhurst; Bay Rats. Phil and Geir were in the Gaslight and either Sammis or one of the Buttenhagens was next door. Valium, much more than Xanax, is sure to send me into a raging red out if I take a small dose and fifty milligrams is a small dose for me. When I walked through the door the place was packed same as it had been for Gracie Starr. Phil was up on the stage bailing people off because he had banished Doxie to the Rainforest, Richey's other bar in Nassau County. There was a huge bachelor party there of well over fifty guys. These were college kids and I heard some of them saying they were all college wrestlers. They were 'diesel' to just about the last man and they thought they were really tough guys. They wouldn't give up on the rushing the stage thing and they were much more aggressive than the other guys had been for Gracie Starr. Even Phil started to get nervous and he sent Geir next door to Bogart's to get the other bouncer. I remember trying to reason with them but then somebody told me to sit down and shut my fucking mouth. It was the last thing he said that night. I broke his jaw right on the spot.

There was nothing natural about this fight. Even in the Mo's Place fight I had years earlier maybe you could reason that I was a lot bigger than most of the guys I was fighting. But most of these guys were over two hundred pounds and they were all obviously trained athletes.

Geir wasn't even back with the other bouncer yet but my Bay Rats were on them like ravenous wolves swinging pool sticks and beer bottles. Phil jumped down from the stage and we stood back to back. They just kept coming and we just kept knocking them out. Whoever hit the floor stayed there. I don't know how many guys we knocked out inside, but they were piled up in heaps of bleeding flesh. It must have been at least a dozen of them. We forced the remainder out one at a time through the back and front doors. When we got them all outside I kept punching people. Everybody I hit was smashed with the immutable permanence of a wrecking ball. No one was getting up.

The ancient Greeks believed that sometimes Aires would fight at the side of his chosen warrior. There is no doubt in my mind to this very day that I had help that night from the God of War. I never hit anybody more than once and I didn't see anybody get back up. It was as if my fists were twelve-gauge slugs. Bodies were piled up all over the place both inside and outside the bar. When they wouldn't let me come near them without almost running away I bellowed at them "is there anybody fucking else?" The biggest one left let out a primordial howl of war and came charging at me diving for my legs in a classical wrestling take down. I caught his head between my knees and came down with my full weight driving him face first into the concrete. His body went limp and I grabbed his hair and began trying to sand his face off with the concrete. Phil and Geir pulled me off of him. I was still screaming as they dragged me off "is there anybody fucking else!" Now the remaining ones really did run, some taking off in their cars and others running down Hamilton Avenue. Phil told Whitehead and Charlie Murray to get me out of there. I was later told that over a dozen ambulances responded in the aftermath and many of my victims had to be carted off on stretchers. One guy was missing most of his face and he ended up suing Richey's insurance for millions of dollars.

I was now a living legend. Hundreds of people had watched this fight. Both bars had emptied out and traffic had even stopped on Sunrise Highway. It had gone on for at least a half hour, maybe more. Due to Wolfs influence those bars were off limits to the Suffolk County Police Department. The only way they would come is if they were called and even then their response time was slow. This was no choreographed cinema featuring Bruce Lee or Chuck Norris dancing around with their stunt men and trying not to get hurt. It was an all-out war where I wanted to kill them and they wanted to kill me. One man had taken on forty in hand to hand combat and not only won but routed them. As surely as Jesus healing the lepers this was a miracle and I knew it. Whatever had stalked me through my childhood, whatever I knew about Jim Morrison and the Amityville Horror in the inaccessible corridors of my mind, whatever I had seen in East Islip, it had either followed me or brought me to these clubs.

For my reward I got to meet the 'head of the Mob on Long Island'; Joey Massera, or Joey Bang Bang as Richey called him. Joey looked like Vince Lombardi and talked with a little too much arrogance for my taste. I didn't get his crime family. I really didn't care. Joey met with Richey every Monday morning at Richey's house. He 'owned' the Tendertrap an elephant's graveyard of a club for topless dancers. I have never really liked mobsters nor anyone else who would kill their friends for money. When I met Joey, I remember it was really important for him to know what my religion was. I told him Rosicrucian and he seemed to understand the implications of me saying something like that. He asked me "why not Christian like everybody else?" I didn't think I should answer so I was abrupt and evasive. Just he and Richey talked for a while. When he resumed speaking to me Joey attempted to break the ice by saying "I just hang around with Richey till he tells me where he keeps his money. Then I'll kill him ah ha ha." I just gave him a patented stone-faced Phil look while he cracked up at his own joke. There was not much more conversation between us after that, ever.

The Mafia is above all else a secret society. It traces its roots back to Italian Free Masons and the Vatican itself. In retrospect at the time of our meeting Joey probably had a better idea of what he was dealing with than I did. He foresaw the possibility of himself and his underworld empire becoming collateral damage. I think he thought I was in some kind of position to negotiate. I had only the faintest ideas back then. I was vaguely aware that the unnatural events of my life were somehow interconnected and that everyone around me was loosely organized. I was also aware that I had some kind of honorary position within that organization that nobody was telling me about but there was only one of us that could negotiate anything, and it wasn't me.

CHAPTER 26

It was so easy after that. Everyone was trying to please me just like the song in Appetite For Destruction. The one that pleased me most was Mesha. She became my girlfriend. Her real name was Michelle, but everyone called her Mesha. It turned out that she was from East Islip. So, I wasn't really surprised when one night we were having one of our marathon sex sessions and I looked up and saw shadows on the wall at the head of the bed moving around like they were watching us. They were clearly disembodied from any object, but I got up and checked outside. Nothing was out there nor between me and the street lights shining through the window. I put the light on and they disappeared.

When I turned it off they were back. They were humanoid in shape and appeared to be wearing hoods as they moved along the walls of the room. Shadows that are cast from streetlights don't usually conduct themselves in an independent intelligent manner. When I pointed this out to Mesha she acknowledged that they were there but she only seemed upset that I had interrupted our love making. With a cajoling tone in her voice she implored me to resume as she stretched out flat on her back with her knees up and legs spread exposing her shaved pussy. Even with the lights on there was not a single flaw to her body and strange thoughts filled my head about dyeing there on that motel bed locked in an orgasmic embrace with her. I started to think if whatever was there should kill us it would be the ultimate in sexual gratification. My erection felt like it would burst the skin on my penus when I turned off the light and knelt on the bed to go down on her. Her feet arched behind my head and drew me in. I felt my naked back exposed to whatever unnatural thing was in the room with us. There was a sensation that started at the bottom of my spine arcing through my body like an electrical current, a mixture of fear, anticipation, and arousal. Although I had been having strange fantasy's since I was old enough to become aroused it was the first time I ever felt something like that during sex. It would not be the last.

  One night I was walking in Bogart's with Mesha. It was late and she wasn't working. In Bogart's, the entrance to the front door consisted of three stairs leading up to a concrete platform. The door burst open in front of me and a shifty looking Polock was propelled out with force by John Doxie. Doxie had been 'reinstated' in the Gaslight and Bogart's because it was decided that it would be best for him to explain my now nightly carnage to the police. The Polock stiffened when he got outside and hacked up a viscous glob of saliva right in Doxies face. I was standing on the platform, which wasn't very wide, so I nailed the Polock with a perfect front kick. It felt like I had kicked a piece of steel. It didn't have much of an effect except to back him up a little. So I kept kicking him, landing about a dozen right front kicks all the way down the stairs and out onto Hamilton Avenue which separated the clubs. He was still standing, and he wasn't very big so I picked him up and flung him to the blacktop. When he tried to get back up I landed a right elbow flush on his spine. That dropped him for good and I heard him say with a thick accent "nice one" like he really enjoyed it. I was wearing topsiders and it felt like I had broken my big toe. I decided that night it was time for a change in wardrobe.

  My knuckles and knees were cut to ribbons to go along with my throbbing right toe. The Gabardines and Docksiders had to go, so did the Topsiders and Capezio's. I could keep the Italian leathers and the hundred-dollar sweaters which I favored after September. But new foot wear was mandatory as were heavy dungarees. I already had leather pants. I had immediately went down to Orchard Street in lower Manhattan with Steve and stocked up on them after seeing Mel Gibson in The Road Warrior. I never wore them much before but after the spiting Polock incident I took to wearing them every other day.

    The next day Mesha and I went shopping at the Sunrise Mall. A Pakistani man from a magazine kiosk came running from halfway across the mall clutching a handful of magazines and waving around a pen. Not that Mesha dressed flashy when we went out. She was wearing a full-length Italian leather coat with a mink collar. This guy knew his business and he was very grateful when she signed his magazines. This was before the days of porn stars. Girls like Mesha and Gracie Starr were that era's version of them. We stopped in the Levi's outlet and then the Doc Martins store where I bought some regular Doc Martin boots in different colors and a pair of Doc Martin steel tipped black combat boots that came halfway up my calves. The next stop was a store that specialized in goods made out of rattlesnake. I bought a rattlesnake hat band with the rattle still on it, a rattlesnake belt, and couple of pairs of black leather gloves with the fingertips cut off. The last stop was a place that sold hats for gentlemen and I bought a black felt one in the classic style of the forty's and fifty's. I ripped off the feather and replaced it with the rattlesnake band.

    Mesha had also insisted on buying me a pair of snakeskin boots. I made sure I bought her a thousand-dollar pair of diamond earrings for Christmas. I am at loath to take money from woman. All of the girls loved me for this alone. The Pagans had been extorting all of them except Dianne Rodney, who was still claiming she hated me in between expressing an almost mother like sympathy for my wounded toe and Gracie Starr who loved me because Vinnie Gambler loved me. He would come down to the bars just to see me and would sit for long hours talking about all kinds of things. He used to tell me he had always wanted to have a white smile like me that he could flash at people right before he beat them up. He said it was like I just stepped out of the movies. I didn't tell him my smile was strictly a product of cosmetic dentistry. Back then most people couldn't afford it. I heard he told all the other Pagans I was like a mad dog straining at the leash. That's about the highest compliment a Pagans going to give another man. A couple of times I went looking for his eighteen-year-old daughter with him in North Amityville. She had a bad crack problem and I felt truly sorry for him.

    The holidays were pretty much a blur. Wolf told me "there is nothing we can do for you because you have already pleaded out your case. We can delay sentencing as long as you want but you will have to serve six months in county, which is really four months. We will make sure Phil go's in at the same time so you can watch each other's backs. But I think I can get him sixteen days for illegal dissection." So, Phil was going to get sixteen days for his head shtick, and I was going to do four months along with five years' probation and a felony record attached to it for serving my community.

    My father had been diagnosed with terminal lung cancer years ago, but he had responded well to Chemo until now. He had taken a turn for the worse and was now going pretty fast. I hated being in that house, I wished I hadn't moved back there. I spent every waking hour either working or in the bars. After Thanksgiving I started 'working' regular hours in the bar. My father was on two different dosages of Dilaudid and morphine. The morphine was in powerful small purple tablets while the Dilaudid was in huge pink capsules. An end to his suffering could easily be arranged by crushing up about a dozen morphine pills and substituting them for the contents of his Dilaudid capsule. I brought the idea up to Richey Capri in his office. Richey was mortified. He said, "I thought you said you would never kill someone unless it was in self defense?" I said "yea but it's my father and he's in a lot of pain. Tumors growing out all different parts of his body. It's like watching a live showing of Alien or the Thing." "It doesn't matter" He said. "In the eyes of the law murder is murder. There is no law for euthanasia." "What's that?" I said. "That's when you kill someone to put them out of their pain like you're talking about doing. This is a really stupid idea. All they got to do is an autopsy and not even Wolf will be able to get you out of it. Do you think they don't know when somebody is ODing if your mother brings him to the hospital? How close are you to your father?" I wondered why he was getting so upset. I said "when I was young we were inseparable. When I was a teenager he beat the fuck out of me till I could return the favor. But you could say he made me the man I am. He was a Golden Gloves finalist. The last few years all he's done is make my life miserable by accusing my mother of financing my life style with the business. He talks that shit while he's using my mother's money to put brand-new engines in his boats and fill his gas tanks." In an authoritative tone he said "It doesn't sound like it's worth it to me. If my father got in the way of my money I would put him in an old age home." That conversation distinguishes Richey as the only man who ever talked me out of doing something I thought was right.

    My father's morphine and Dilaudid pills were good for something. They kept me high till he died. He had a whole draw full of them in all different colors. Nobody knew what was in there least of all my father or his doctors. I used to take the purple morphine ones which were the strongest except for the big pink Dilaudid capsules. I left those for him. At one point I was fighting three times a night, most of the time more than one guy at once. I never lost or even came close to losing. I never even got a black eye or a cut on my face. I knew I was participating in a supernatural event. For lack of a better explanation I began to see myself as a God. I started to refer to other people as sub creatures as I had seen done in the movie Ghostbusters. It was during this period I met Bobby and Marlena. I had my own cult following and Richey's father took to calling me the wizard because I had a penchant for black and studied Hebrew Qabalah all night, when I wasn't beating people up.

    I got the whole sordid history of the topless industry when things were slow. The best source was Lucille a barmaid who was married to 'Och' one of the three Ferrety brothers. Och was the target of the FBI's investigation on the Pagans. He was making a fortune using the gang to distribute cocaine all along the east coast. According to Lucille, whom with I had gotten very close, Och was never going to see the light of day again. Their waterfront house and their matching his and hers forty-foot Cigarettes had been confiscated. The two other brothers; 'Mortician' and 'Wasp', together with their sidekick 'Pain', had made a pretty good living out of extorting the dancers. They had never been implicated in the FBI's investigation, so they were free to try to come back. But we weren't going to let that happen much to the relief of all the girls accept Dianne Rodney. Celeste would tell anyone who would listen how Mortician had knocked out her front teeth when he thought the 'Pagans cut' was too small. Celeste was a Playboy Centerfold and on a first name basis with Hugh Heffner who's party's she regularly flew out to the West Coast to attend. She was a jade eyed Puerto Rican of stunning beauty who would leave the bar with two or three garbage bags full of just singles 'to count when she got home.' It wasn't like any of these girls were street whores. The Pagans were still in all the other clubs and every 'A-girl' in NY now wanted to work in Richey's clubs.

    I was going way too far, and nobody knew that better than me. The only law I had now was Aleister Crowley's law of Thelma "do as thou wilt." It was around then that I finally met Jimmy Murphy. I had already met two of his brothers; Billy, and Vinnie. I don't want to be to flattering but they could have been Dumb and Dumber in the movie of that name. Vinnie Murphy was practically a retard. The thing about the 'Murphyis's', as the Pagans would come to call them, is they were all over six-foot-tall and as tough as a wolverine. Billy and Vinnie were the only guys in Lindenhurst, in their age bracket, that I ever seen Whitehead and Charlie Murray give a second thought. They argued in the car on the way there at the prospect of a fight between Jimmy Murphy and me who was going to fight Billy and Vinnie. Whitehead was sure he could take Billy who was their age, but he kept bringing up that Vinnie, who was twenty-one, had whipped Charlie's ass over a stolen bicycle only a couple of years ago. Charlie said, "that was then this is now I want a rematch with the retard." Whitehead said, "it was only a year and half ago you ain't no bigger now than you were then."

We met the younger brothers in a sleazy little bar in Lindenhurst around the block from their parent's house. I waited around for an hour for an introduction to this guy who was supposed to be the other toughest guy on Long Island. Besides for copious shots of Wild Turkey the only entertainment I had was Billy and Vinnie hitting each other with brutal body shots that would have floored the average man. That was their preferred recreational activity. They would have hit other people but a general rule for those bars around Lindenhurst is that when the Murphy's came in you left. When Jimmy Murphy came through the door I was not disappointed. He may have been the biggest man I have ever seen that was solid muscle. He was six foot two and two hundred and sixty pounds with twenty-inch biceps and a chest like Hercules. He had movie star good looks with his short dark hair combed back to immaculate perfection. He was a few years younger than me but in the Murphy tradition he was as dumb as a stone. That didn't matter. He had an animal intelligence that reminded me of Eric, and he was loyal to a fault. He had just done two years because he refused to name his accomplice in a robbery. He was deferential to me treating me with exaggerated respect. We soon became inseparable friends. Murphy was my missing piece. With him around I no longer had to fight. Besides his brothers Jimmy came equipped with his own ghoul. John Miller, whom everybody called Blockhead, was a professional burglar. He never left Jimmy's side and looked like a six foot two two-hundred-and-twenty-pound version of Peter Lorie.

Severity / גבורה

CHAPTER 27

Bobby kicked in his best friend Tommy and we had the numbers too. Richey had the toughest bouncing crew that ever worked a strip club scene. I had a private army. There were at least a half a dozen guys in Gaslight and Bogart's at all times. A dozen more could be there in minutes. Nobody made an out of place peep anymore but that didn't stop me. I was on a roll. It was freezing cold on one of those crisp clear sunny winter days when I walked through the door of Bogart's. I was wearing my version of The Terminator get up: black leather pants with a rattlesnake belt, Italian black leather jacket and black wool sweater, Doc Martin black combat boots, cut off black leather gloves, all topped off with my black hat and rattlesnake band. At that moment I knew I was the most dangerous man alive in hand to hand combat in the streets. The functionality of my new costume aside I wasn't about to let my moment escape me. I was dressed for the part.

As soon as I walked through the door I heard a girl screaming at John Doxie in the back offices. This was not unusual. Dianne Rodney screamed at and belittled him every day. The irate female voice lacked Dianne's signatory nasal twang, so I took a walk in the back to see what was up. Phil was sitting at his desk looking like he was contemplating mass murder. Doxie was standing with his head down and shoulders slumped like a dog being admonished. A tough looking bitch dressed in expensive clothes was screaming at the both of them "I don't care. He owes me money. Joey knows I'm here. He told me to come here. I want my money!" By now all the Murphy brothers had followed me into the back. Phil said to me "I got to have a word with you outside. Vinnie and Billy go wait in the bar. Jimmy you go next door and make sure Blockhead isn't following that washed up old bag into the back room again." Jimmy gave us his idiot laugh and said "John likes her." He was the only one who called Blockhead John. Phil answered indignantly "that's disgusting! That woman is pushing fifty. She's old enough to be his mother. But that's right you did tell me he tried to rape his mother a couple of years ago."

Phil and I took a walk outside and I said, "what's a matter he didn't pay her out of the draw?" Phil said "no that's Annie V. She deals coke for Joey Massera. Doxie must owe her money for coke and the fat fuck keeps trying to claim he doesn't do any drugs. It's disrespectful of Joey to send her down here to make a scene like this in my clubs. Rodney's on stage. She heard all of this shit. What now? She's going to think she has a license to scream at us? It's bad enough she screams at Doxie." I stuck my hand in my pocket and pulled out a wad of cash saying, "I got a couple of thousand dollars on me I'll take care of it." When we went back in I asked her how much John owed her. It was like seven thousand dollars. Phil and I looked at each other and I said to her "I ain't paying that and he ain't paying you either. We don't pay him anymore. In fact he pays us to sit in here with us. You better write it off as a loss." At that she starts getting real snotty with me saying "do you know who I am? Joey will have you whacked tonight!" She had said the magic words. I didn't say anything I just picked her up and carried her screaming outside the bar where I threw her off the landing of Bogart's. She landed on her face with a thud and I jumped down and started stomping her back. By now all the Murphy's were out there and Annie V was unconscious face down in the parking lot. Phil said "you better go. Doxies going to have a hard time explaining this one." I left. But later I heard they weren't done with her yet. They carried her into the front office and Phil went in Richey's office all the way in the back to call for an ambulance. As she was groaning Vinnie Murphy pulled her pants down and stuck his fingers up her crotch. She started to moan for him to stop and Vinnie told her "it's okay I'm a doctor."

    I didn't know what the mob was going to do, or at least what they thought they were going to do. I didn't care. I went down to this hundred-year-old apartment building Charlie Murray and his friends rented over by the Rail Road tracks to sell drugs out of. Kevin O'Reilly was selling coke and I bought all he had, about an ounce. I called Phil and he told me to stay holed up, that Joey wanted to put a contract out on me, and Richey had to have a sit down with him. Phil said "I just told Richey that putting a contract out on you is not an option. If anything happens to you they all die. I already called John. Just hang out over Charlie's for the next few days. This will get straightened out. They know what the deal is."

    I started shoveling coke in my nose. I was feeling morose again. Dianne had just started talking to me. This was not the way to win her affections. The kids decided to make one of their weekly forays into Harlem to buy angel dust leaving me alone with Kevin O'Reilly who was about my age. He didn't party at all and he looked like a prematurely balding red-haired leprechaun but he did have Mob credentials. Richey had been on a first name basis with him even before he met me. They didn't get back to the wee hours of the morning. By then I had done most of the ounce by myself. The drugs, the state of the building, and its location, gave me déjà vu. Kevin had all he could do to keep me under control. I was crawling the walls, having East Islip relapses, hearing things inside them.

    Charlie was very proud of himself saying "that Nigger thought he was going to get paid. Well he got paid alright." Then he starts doing front kicks which, aside from me, he was now the best at. He continued as he demonstrated his kicking technique for me "we went around the side of the building and I nailed him right in the jaw. That Nigger was doing a sleep over! Whitehead took his shit. It was like rolling a drunk." Whitehead pulled about a quarter pound bag of angel dust out of his bomber jacket. I had only smoked angel dust that one time with Negron and Steve, but I was down for anything that night. I did a massive last line and I rolled myself a baseball bat sized joint out of the toxic smelling bag of weed. I started smoking and I thought I heard a noise in the antiquated bathroom. I went in there to check it out and remember nothing from this world after that.

A scowling leprechaun emerged from in back of the old toilet and impatiently gestured for me to look at something on the wall in back of him. When I did my gaze was directed inward and I saw myself hanging as Christ on the cross. Longinus pierced my side with his spear and all the faceless dread and unnamed horror that had dwelled in the uncharted recesses of my mind spilled forth from my wound. There was that thing in East Islip, and the dancing dwarf from my childhood. There were the noises in the walls that took the form of the black gamma mink tails my father brought home from work for me to play with when I was a child. They were nuzzling me affectionately as they spilled forth from my side. There were the sounds of maidens laughing and cavorting wafting from the far-off forests of Pan. There were a thousand other unspeakable and fearsome things that lived loathingly beneath the troubled beds of earth-bound children. All of them came forth from the wound on my side. I heard the leprechaun speaking to me "these things that you fear. They are of you. You fear yourself."

The next thing I remember was John sitting next to me on Charlie's bed gently slapping my face. I sat up and hastily pulled up my sweater. There across my left rib cage was a gapping ten-inch-long cut. John turned to Charlie and Kevin and said, "what did you guys do to him?" It did not sound good for both of them and they were terrified. Kevin answered stammering "he, he must of got that when he fell against the toilet in the bathroom. We put him on the bed. He's been out ever since then, about three hours." John just looked at them and didn't say anything. He got up and helped me to my feet. He said to me "c'mon we're leaving." He helped me down to his car then he told Charlie "go back in and get his hat and coat." Kevin stayed outside with us pleading to John "hey I hope you don't think any of us would ever do anything to hurt him. We're the best friends he has besides you guys. I don't do any drugs myself. I told him not to go smoking that shit after all the coke he snorted." John didn't say anything, and Charlie came running back with the hat and coat and we left.

John brought me to my parent's house. My father had taken one of his endless trips to the hospital and nobody was home. I was still unsteady on my feet, so John helped me inside. When we got inside I suddenly remembered and said, "hey what about the Guiney's." He just said, "don't even worry about them." I went into my closet and pulled out a little four-ten shotgun I had in there loaded with a slug. I staggered out to the hallway and fired it into the living room floor. John started laughing hysterically and I said "no John you don't understand. I'm tired of them, all of them. What we need here is a night of death. They all need to be murdered in their beds by their own children. We can start with the Italians since I was born Italian, but I want them all; Irish, German, Jews, Catholics, Protestants. They are all fucking infidels! They are vampires that suck the blood of their own children! They take and they take, and then they take some more. What they give back is the least amount possible. They call that good business. I call it stealing. They have traded all our tomorrows for their one today!

    Look around you! We can't even get contracts to build anything because they got all the bids rigged for themselves. The other day I'm talking to some English prick that's got a contract to build a huge apartment complex on the North Shore. I should beg him, some foreigner, for the landscaping there while half my relatives occupy the memorial cemeteries of this fucking country? To top it off how many of them died in the last big war saving his country's ass? That was not what was intended when the Free Masons fought for and founded this country! Look at what they did with the sewers. J.D. Posillico didn't even have an ice cream truck and never built a fucking thing in their lives when they were awarded the entire contract for the Southwest Sewer District, now the bays unfishable. They all need to die John. Killing them will not be murder it will be euthanasia! We need a night of death. Crowley said we will grind the old grey world beneath our feet. Let's start grinding."

CHAPTER 28

    That bag of dust was bad news it ended up putting Charlie in Jail for six months. A couple of days later I was smoking some with the kids and I lost my first fight since I started my run. We were in Starboards a bar in Copiague that already didn't like me because I would regularly bring John in there to terrorize them. I was only in there because I wanted to find out what happened to Steve my old foreman. His twenty something white bitch wanted to live to high on the hog. The few times I had seen him since we had severed our relationship he had been asking me about the how-to's of doing drug stick ups. Him and another friend of mine; Pauli, had made the front page of Newsday by doing an armed robbery of an SCPD narcotics cop. They sold the ounce to him then they robbed it back at shotgun point. They threw him out of the car and got about a half a block. They were looking at twenty years, for a fucking ounce of cocaine.

    I was getting this information from the barmaid; Tara, a sweet little blond whom I used to be hot on before somebody threw me the keys to the candy store. Her father owned the place. He was an ex-cop currently gangster who was running a sizable gambling operation out of there. It was packed at all times and it was in the middle of the day. Flanagan who was probably the best pool shark on Long Island was cleaning the place out in the back. After Flanagan mockingly demonstrated for his marks that he could clean a six-foot table whenever he wanted a couple of guys took exception to losing their paychecks to a nineteen-year-old kid. They started chasing him around the bar. I jumped in front of them and they grabbed me and wrestled me out the front door depositing me face first on the concrete outside. My eye got gashed and was bleeding badly so I let Charlie and Whitehead talk me out of going back in and fighting the guys. I didn't care anyway. It felt like I had no strength and I figured it was karmic payback for stomping a woman and smoking angel dust. I never smoked dust again after that.

I went to the hospital and got a couple of stitches then we went over Charlie's house. Kevin told me he wasn't selling coke anymore. He said "I don't know how John just suddenly showed up at the house like that early in the morning. He's never even been here before." Kevin told me he knew who John was and said "that's one dude I never want to see like that again. I thought me and Charlie bought it." He said "you were talking to yourself all night. What the hell did you see?" When I told him a leprechaun his face turned white as a sheet. He said "you know I was hearing those noises in the wall too. This is a really old house though. I just figured it's the heating pipes, but I have never heard those noises before. My family is supposed to have a leprechaun that's been passed down from generation to generation since the days back in Ireland. I never believed in that stuff before, but I think I might now."

CHAPTER 29

It was a week or so later when I walked in the Gaslight. Al had his dentures stretched out in an ear to ear grin. "What did you do to Annie V?" he said. "I can't stand that bitch. All she did when we had her here was curse at me. She didn't even work half her sets. She used to sit in the corner all night selling her coke." I quipped as I probed for a confirmation of what I had already been told "yea well apparently Doxie was one of her best customers. I hear Joeys taking care of everything and she's not pressing any charges." Al went on breathlessly "I heard she's going to be in the hospital for a month. She's got footprints all over her back. What's Joey got to say about that? She's supposed to be one of the boys. Hey did you hear? They found two Pagans dead in the parking lot of Stonehenge, shot through the back of the head, two real assholes. Nobody liked them. But there's going to be trouble. They can't just let something like that go. You have to get me a gun. Richey won't let me have one." I answered the old man. I always found him kind of amusing "It must have been somebody they thought was their friend. Sounds to me like another Pagan did it. I guess I can't be a suspect in that one. What makes you think I would get you a gun Al if Richey doesn't want you to have one?" Al sneered "Ahh my sons an asshole! I'm the one that's up here all night dealing with gangsters while he sits home and counts his money. One time the Pagans were all drunk next door, and they dragged the jukebox outside. I had to drag it back in by myself. When Big Frankie, Dominic, and Artie, and all them wrecked Gucci's he went into hiding with his daughter. I had to stay up here!"

  I hadn't heard this before. "What's a Gucci's?" I said. Al wrinkled up his raisin face even more than usual "Richey used to have four clubs. Gucci's was the fourth. They went in there with about twenty guys and totally demolished it. Then they called up Richey, it was Dominic that fat fuck, he says 'hey Richey how do you like the way we redecorated Gucci's?' It wasn't worth a dime after they got done with it. It was our nicest club. Them guys are not with Joey, their with another family. They don't listen to him. Big Frankie was here a few days ago but he was only with one other guy, some asshole I never seen before. Wherever they went Phil followed them and sat in the next stool. Big Frankie didn't say anything to him. I was laughing. He went from Bogart's to Gaslight then from Gaslight to Bogart's then back to Gaslight. Wherever he went Phil followed him. Big Frankie looked like he was really uncomfortable fidgeting and not saying much to anyone."

  I didn't want to tell Al exactly how uncomfortable I would be if Phil was following me around, so I didn't say anything and Al went on. "They must be afraid of Phil though. Sooner or later their going to come in here, they hate Richey. He's the only club owner not paying them." I was telling the truth when I said "It's all news to me. Didn't you tell me the Pagans were going to come in here sooner or later too Al? And that nobody was ever going to find Margret?" Margret was a Black girl who had been living with Al and hit him over the head with a liquor bottle and rolled him before 'she left him.' For months Joey Massera had 'looked all over the city for her.' Phil had found her in a week and dealt with her appropriately. Ignoring my sarcasm Al continued. "You see? My son doesn't tell you guys anything. He doesn't care if you guys get killed just so long as he can sit home and count his money. A real prize my son. A real prize." feigning urgency in my voice I asked, "Does Phil know about this?" Al dismissively said, "I told him about it." Then he got back to his favorite subject "Can you get me a gun?" I gave up trying to distract him and reluctantly answered "I suppose I better put something in the liquor closet now. This isn't TV Al. It ain't going to be no handgun. I believe in having the right tool for a job. You told me you were in the welders union. You should know all about that."

    I went home and got my AR15 that I kept under my bed. I saw my younger sister there and she told me "daddy's almost dead. You have to go to the hospital to see him." I said "he's been dying for almost five years now. I'll go tonight. He's not even conscious anyway." The AR15 fit neatly into a yellow gym bag I had, and I threw about twenty extra thirty and twenty round clips in there with it. The clips were all loaded, and I even threw in some extra boxes of ammo. This was in the late eighties before anyone even packed artillery like this. Until then John was the only guy I had ever seen running around with a military machine gun like a Nigger with a Saturday night special. I figured I had more than enough fire power to take care of either the Pagans or the Mafia if they wanted to play with guns. When I got back to the bars I showed Al how to arm it. I pressed the button to drop the clip and put it on the desk transferring the gun into my left hand. Then with my right I ejected the unfired 223 snatching it backhand as it bounced off the wall. I pressed it back into the clip then slammed the clip back into the gun. Then I put the weapon into the liquor closet to which only Phil, Al and I, had a key. I was Al's new hero after that.

CHAPTER 30

    Phil wasn't there yet so I went up to the bar and got myself a Wild Turkey triple. I sat by the tables around the stage and Dianne was sitting up on the upper stage her legs dangling down onto the lower stage. The stage at Bogart's was small just two squares the low one acting as a mote between the high one and the tables. This arrangement provided more separation from the customers than the stage at Gaslight which was almost even with the tables. Very few people ever tried to climb onto Bogart's stage. The girls would try to get away with just playing their music and sitting on the upper stage if there were no customers there during slack periods in the afternoon. But it was 'our job to keep them moving.' It was still early and there were only a couple of people in the bar. She was wearing a full-length negligee like she always did around the bars and I gestured to her to start dancing and take it off. She grabbed the pole on the upper stage pulling herself up and flinging those long hair extensions of hers back over her head. She let the silk negligee slide from her back and down her arms. It collapsed in a puddle at the base of her stiletto heels. I looked at that body. Perfection in a woman's body is something I had sought all my life. There was something about the arch of her back, the curve of her ass, her flawlessly shaped breasts, the length of her thighs to her knees, her tiny delicate feet, even her effortless balance in those high heeled shoes. What I was seeing in front of me was supernatural. I had learned by now to know the difference between the world of man and the world of the angels. She saw me losing myself in her and locked eyes with me, a self-satisfied smile on her face. I felt myself being drawn through a vortex to a place where there was only me and her staring right through eternity into each other's eyes.

She spoke first "does Mesha know how you feel about me?" I said, "how would you know how I feel about anything?" She said "that's just it. People think I'm stupid because I'm up here on stage. I'm twenty-four years old and I already have enough saved to buy my own house. I don't need no man to ever take care of me. I take care of myself. Why do you think Gracie has me for a best friend? I'm the smartest girl in here. I see things that the other girls don't. Like you and your friend Phil. You don't have any emotions. It's like you're dead inside. What you did to Annie V is just a small demonstration. You're capable of anything. Whereas other men would draw a line somewhere you just do whatever you feel like doing." I said, "yea well that's what the Pagans used to call us when we ran with Jimmy Lyn; 'the Living Dead.' But you think you have it all figured out don't you? Did you ever wonder if this world that you live in, all of it measured in fleeting seconds of time, really means anything at all. You're going to buy a house. Then you're going to grow old, lose your beauty, and die. You live in the allusion. The allusion means nothing to me. It's the world of the sub creatures. They can have it."

Phil pulled up a chair next to me and I told him "I put something in the liquor closet. Don't be using it unless you have to. That thing cost me a lot of money." Phil said "I know. Al's in the office waving it around in front of the girls already. Now he thinks he's the geriatric Rambo. I'm going to have to get Richey to take his key to the liquor closet away." Dianne wasn't through with me yet and now that Phil was there all the better "You know before I went out with Charlie I went out with one of the Pagans. Their actually really nice guys, nothing like you two. They may like to fight and stuff. I like to fight too. Ask Gracie. Whenever we go out I'm always kicking other girl's asses. I may only be five foot one but I'll fight any girl. When the Pagans were here nobody was stomping dancers in broad daylight in the parking lot and nobody got murdered in the club down the road either. I don't even know if I want to dance anymore. You guys scare me and I ain't the only one. My friend Janet is a witch, and she says you guys are Satanists."

Phil was getting tired of her fast, but I kicked him under the table as I bemusedly asked her. "Who? Janet the dancer next door?" Then I quoted Zappa from Bongo Fury ""Say she's a witch / Shit-ass Charlotte! / Ain't that a bitch?"" Then I sung tauntingly ""Cast your dancing spell my way / I promise to go under it." You're too much Dianne. You don't even know what a witch is and neither does your friend, even less what a Satanist is. Is that Satanist as in Anton LaVey the carnival barker and Hollywood fruitcake?" Now she was getting really mad and I was getting that hot flush feeling in my groin again. She said "you know what I know. I know you're going straight to hell and you're not going to be taking me with you. I know the Pagans aren't getting you guys out of here now. Their just as afraid of you as everybody else, I know you're not going to be scaring Dominic and Artie like that. I know them very well. We're from the same town; East Meadow." I said "I'm not taking you to hell with me. You have to big a mouth. You'll wake the neighbors." I turned to the waitress standing over by the bar; Wendy. She was an old time Pagans girl. Al always said she wore so much rouge she looked like the thing that pops out of a Jack in the Box. I said, "as a matter of fact for the Spring Equinox we have already decided that we will be sacrificing Wendy to Moloch!" Wendy turned white in spite of her rouge. I got my departing shot in on Dianne "what you don't know is that I have come to hell to get you."

I got up and told Phil to come outside. By now I had a raging hard on. I stuffed it down my pants leg I wasn't going to show it to Dianne yet, everything in due time. When we got outside I said "what's up with this Dominic and Artie bullshit. They wrecked one of Richey's clubs? What was he waiting for to tell us?' Phil's answer was both indifferent and mocking at the same time "Dominic and Artie, Big Frankie and Bittermen. These guys have all been watching too many cartoons. Big Frankie was in here the other day. He used to hang out next door to my house with Bittermen. I'll take those guys and crack their heads together like Mo dealing with Larry and Curly on the Three Stooges. Richey wouldn't let me bitch slap him. He says he's a made man." Phil rolled his eyes as he said it and continued "he told me to just follow him around the clubs and keep an eye on him, make him uncomfortable, as for Dominic and Artie their mine. Their two brothers from East Meadow, their supposed to be shooters, I hear Dominic's about four hundred pounds. I hope you brought extra ammo." "In the bag" I said. "What happened with those Pagans?" Phil looked at me grinning like a friendly orangutan and said "I'm figuring they killed each other in an argument over who got the last hit on the crack pipe. The Pagans are washed up. Without these clubs their nothing. Who needs an agency when all the A-girls want to work here? Now we should take all the good barmaids and waitresses from the other clubs. These bars are taking in about twelve thousand a day counting the Rainforest. I figure with barmaids that ain't stealing and waitresses that don't look they belong in a zoo I can get that up to twenty-five thousand. The problem is Richey has some kind of misplaced loyalty to all these old barmaids. What are we running here some kind of old age home for female Pagans? We got Lucille in here every night and then we got the rest of her family filling in all the other slots: Maryland, Genevieve, and Agnes. I'm tired of Agnes day dreaming that the Pagans are gonna come back in here and run us out. If she doesn't go one way she's gonna go another. What I'm gonna do is bring Andy Braum in here and do a professional evaluation of the employees. He just came back from Austria. He'll be in the states for the next couple of weeks." Andy Braum was a friend of Vigdis and Geirs from the old German club days back in high school. He was a hotel spy deployed by all the major chains throughout the Germanic countries. He was in his late twenty's and already one of the best in his business. Like I said Phil had a sinister intelligence that was the most alarming thing about him.

Phil looked at me with as thoughtful a look as a Great White Shark is ever going to get and said "John told me what happened last week. When are you going to stop doing drugs? Even John doesn't do them anymore. You're the only one. You hang around with those kids that work for you and think your eighteen years old." Shifting my weight, I looked down at my Doc Martins and said "what are you my father now? Maybe I'll write a book. My father was a serial killer, which reminds me I have to go. My real father is dying. I'll just tell you this. Unlike the rest of you I had my own successful business. Now I'm going to jail for six months and when I come out I will be a felon. All because some cops wanted to handcuff me and knock my teeth out and not get sued. You're all just lucky I'm not an alcoholic or a junkie. I'll see you later. If he dies I'll call."

CHAPTER 31

In the ensuing days, my father died. Since he was stationed at Camp Hero in Montauk during the Korean War and since I was later to have a four year affiliation with Preston Nichols the author of the Montauk Projects and progenitor of the Montauk Project mythos this is probably the most appropriate time in this story to give a brief account of that mythos since it would provide some 'Cartesian' explanation for some of the more inexplicable events in this story. I would not formerly meet Preston till a few years later when he insinuated himself into my mother's circle of friends. I will save my account of that association for another time.

In 1992 a very strange man came out with an even stranger book. The story woven by Preston Nichols of East Islip and his coauthor Peter Moon has assumed cult status. They blend Aleister Crowley, secret underground bases, Nazi occult science, 'aliens' and time travel, all under the control of some 'sinister' cabal that is able to operate in an alternate reality to manipulate this one. According to Nichols there is an underground base in Montauk that is headquarters for a secret army of mind controlled super soldiers who act as assassins for the cabal. They have been trained by Nazi's and are able to travel through both time and space. Amongst Nichols circle of friends his story is taken so seriously that John Ford the president of the Long Island U.F.O. Network, and three of his friends, were given lengthy prison sentences after being 'entrapped' into a plot in 1996 to poison then Suffolk County Republican Chairman John Powell, Suffolk Legislator Fred Towle, and Brookhaven Conservative Party chief Anthony Gazzola, by exposing them to radium.

It is Nichols and Moons contention that much of what goes on in Montauk revolves around what they call the Babylon Working. An occult ritual performed through sexual magic 'designed to bring about the incarnation of the Moon Goddess.' Aleister Crowley was the first to attempt the ritual, which Crowley called the Amalantrah Working. Crowley attempted the ritual in the spring of 1918. He spent the summer in Montauk. Crowley's sexual partner in this ritual, or the Scarlet Woman as Crowley called her, was a woman named Roddie Minor, an extremely competent practitioner of the occult arts herself. The ritual was later attempted again in 1946 by some of Crowley's disciples; Scientology founder L. Ron Hubbard, Jack Parsons cofounder of Jet Propulsion Laboratory and one of the founders of Americas space program, along with his sexual partner Marjorie Cameron. They rechristened the ritual; The Babylon Working.

In 1992 Nichols wrote the first in a series of four books; The Montauk Project: Experiments in Time. The cover of the book features a statue of an ominous rearing stallion of tremendous muscular proportions. Nichols goes on in the book to say that man's future can only be accessed so far then the "time traveler" will always find themselves before a statue of a great rearing horse in a barren landscape devoid of all people. In 1993 New Mexican artist Luis Jimenez was commissioned to build a thirty-two-foot-high statue of a tremendously muscled stallion rearing up in the middle of Denver International Airport. The airport would not open till 1995. Jimenez was killed in 2006 when a section of the unfinished horse fell from a hoist at his studio in Hondo, New Mexico. His sons finished the horse in 2008. Since then about twenty-eight million travelers per year are treated to the spectacle of the rearing horse. It's most notable feature is its ability to leave lasting impressions of fear and dread in small children. The statue is also known as the 'Devil Horse' and 'Satan's Steed.' Because of its strange architecture, decorum, and history, Denver International Airport has been called a shrine to the 'New World Order' by many legitimate researchers. Some have even tried to make a case that it is the external face of a vast underground base in the service of the 'Luciferian' Free Mason elite who have controlled America since its very beginning. Only one thing is really certain the horse in the airport bears an uncanny resemblance to the horse on the cover of Preston's Nichols first book. As Jim Morrison once said: "When all else fails / We can whip the horse's eyes / And make them sleep."

CHAPTER 32

My father's funeral was more a gala event than an expression of grief. My mother by now was heavily into the more fringe elements of the occult and they can invent a thousand reasons why one 'must go to the light.' Dianne was right about me. I could not feel. I felt nothing for the whole three days. Although I did get angry when I found out my Reinhard Heydrich environmentalist sister dumped the draw full of opiates in the garbage while I was stuck at the funeral home. My father had a lot of friends from many years on the water. I acted as the master of ceremonies. At times it was more like a captain's convention than a wake. All the while I wanted to get back to the bars. I remember sneaking my assault rifle out of my bedroom window and stashing it underneath a car, so Phil could borrow it, while the guests inside the house indulged in the spread and open bar. The highlight of the event for me was when Al showed up at the funeral home with Gracie Starr. Gracie, of course, caused quite a stir among the male mourners, even in her street clothes. Mesha came too but by then I'm not sure it mattered anymore for me. The Catholic priest had noticed the lack of grief among the 'bereaved' and took the opportunity to espouse on everything he didn't know about death. He and my mother ended up getting in a verbal altercation.

When I next went in Gaslight Phil was positioning a waitress;

Karen, on the stool against the wall to the backroom. He stepped back and thoughtfully looked at her sitting on the stool. He gestured for her to move the stool a few inch's this way then a few inch's that way. Finally satisfied with his arrangement Phil pulled a fifty gallon plastic garbage pail next to the by now teary eyed girl and nodded in approval. Suppressing my laughter, I asked "where's Agnes? Wasn't that a violation of union rules? You better look out. After her circus freak sister Karen is her favorite waitress." He looked at me with mirth and said "Agnes and the dwarf from the circus are gone, so is Genevieve, and Maryland's going in a week. Lucille is trying to say she needs this money for Och's appeal, but I told Richey she can't work here no more." I grinned and said, "I guess Braum figured out how they were stealing." Phil feigned indignity and said, "yea in three days he found twenty-six different ways they're stealing, all in a neatly typed report that I gave to Richey." I got everyone except for Sue, who doesn't have to steal because Jerry is and some the waitress's. It will be easy enough to make them quit.' He looked over at Karen who now had tears streaming down her face. Phil nodded at her and grinned his ghoul grin saying to me "do you like Karen's new waitress station. For now on if she's not serving drinks she must be sitting at her waitress station." For emphasis Phil walked over and adjusted 'her garbage pail.' A new girl was working as a barmaid. She was very attractive aside from the white ring she had around her nose from doing lines in the bathroom all day. The stain on the front of Al's plaid pants was the size of a grapefruit as he leaned across the bar trying to breath half-digested pastrami into her face.

 I had on my leather pants and snake band hat which I couldn't wait to get back into all during the funeral. Phil and I took a walk next door to Bogart's. The bar was packed. Geir was sitting in the corner drawing. The beard that was growing on his chin looked like a dead cactus and he was dressed in his customarily disheveled manner underneath a huge faded black leather jacket. Phil said jokingly "that's my new manager over there. For now, on when anybody asks to speak to the manager you say that's him in the corner over there coloring." Rooster was working the stage and guys were hooting and hollering as Doxie sat stone faced by the entrance. Rooster technically was probably the best dancer I've ever seen. She had long red hair and looked like she had just stepped from some Dionysian celebration of forgotten Celtic Gods. She could drink with any one of her Irish countrymen and would usually owe the bar money by the end of the night. She could also run straight up the mirrored wall at Bogart's and do a flip off the top of it landing on her feet like a gymnast. She would sometimes do this while holding a drink and not spill a drop. Geir liked her. He left his 'coloring book' and came over to Phil and I muttering about Pallas Athena the warrior Goddess sprung full grown from her father Zeus.

    I had been surprised when I walked in to see Margret, Richey's girlfriend, sitting at the end of the bar next to Geir. She usually stayed at the Rainforest where Richey allowed her to manage it unmolested by Phil. Aside from us and the dancers Margret was probably Richey's only competent employee at the time. Margret was a tall attractive brunette, about thirty, with her hair cut short like a boy. She was a notorious switch-hitter. She gestured for me to come over and when I did she whispered in my ear "Richey wants you to go out with me tonight." I didn't know what she was talking about but whatever it was it was alright with me. We took off in her vintage black Thunderbird and visited every strip club on Long Island, between twenty and thirty at the time. We went in each and under my watchful eye Margret handed out cards to all the attractive waitress's and barmaids. She told them "if you want to work in a real strip club give me a call." By now everybody in the topless circuit knew who I was, and nobody dared say a word. We culminated our night with a trip to the Ravens Nest a bar in Nassau County run by the Pagans. It was the only other club on Long Island, besides ours, that still featured A-girls. Margret stopped the T Bird right in the entrance to the parking lot blocking it off and we got out and had a few drinks inside. A couple of Pagans that were staffing the place came over to me and asked me if Margret could "please move her car? Nobody can come or leave." I told them no "we'll leave when she's done with her drink." We stayed at the Ravens Nest for about an hour while Margret handed out cards to our captive audience.

    We had put Jimmy Murphy up at Doxie's house and he was now making over a thousand dollars a week right out of prison. Jimmy beat people up on command, no questions asked, two and three at a time. But we had to get his 'little' brothers' away from the clubs. They had taken to rolling the customers in the parking lot. There was no controlling Vinnie he was a complete idiot. We allowed Jimmy to keep Blockhead because he would have frightened even John Wayne. But Blockhead could also be a pain in the ass. He had ingratiated himself with Al and followed him around all night like a faithful dog. One night I went in the liquor closet to get my gun. I don't leave guns that belong to me lying around. That gun went home with me every night. On that night I had a hard time getting to it because the liquor closet was stuffed full of plastic Santa's and reindeer. Blockhead had broken into the nursery next door and stole a bunch of Christmas decorations for Al. I will never know why the old man needed a seven-foot Santa it was almost spring. When Richey found out about it he put a temporary moratorium on Blockhead.

The junior Murphy's and Blockhead were still allowed in the clubs. We just didn't want them hanging around all night. Late one night they came in all excited. The house Blockhead had broken into that night had contained a nice cache of handguns. Blockhead was waving a thirty-eight around showing it to Jimmy who was working. Jimmy got a call to go next door from Phil. We all went. When we got their Frankie Mad Dog, and another Pagan were at the bar and Phil was at the far end staring at them with his shark look. They weren't dressed in their colors, but they were both done up in military combat gear from head to toe. To me it looked like they had come there to make the 'gallant' last stand of the Pagans. Frankie Mad Dog did have balls I will give him that. I think Phil was thinking the same thing. But Phil was also thinking about shooting him in front of witnesses. Al walked in after we did and when he did the junior Murphy's and Blockhead mobbed him. Blockhead pulled the thirty-eight pointing it at Frankie while showing it to Al. There must have been about fifty people in Bogart's besides us and Blockhead was yelling so the whole bar could hear him over the jukebox. "Look Al I got you your pistol! It's loaded and everything! Want to try it out in here?" At that point Frankie abruptly jumped up from his stool and marched out the door accompanied by his fellow Pagan and would be martyr. Frankie wasn't stupid either. After that there were no more complaints from Richey about Blockhead.

CHAPTER 33

It must have been in the early spring. I remember telling Wendy that she was to be sacrificed on Walpurgis Night to the Spider Goddess from Aleister Crowley's novel Moonchild. Wendy was married to a lifelong Pagan and she always took my 'holiday preparations' seriously. She would turn white as a ghost. I had broken up with Mesha. Dianne had called her and told her I was secretly in love with her. Mesha had taken the position with me that she was a national star, and she wasn't about to be playing second fiddle to no Dianne Rodney whom she called "that shrimp." I really didn't care how many men in America jerked off to her pictures I wasn't taking ultimatums from anybody on earth at the time, let alone my girlfriend. I said "Mesha I really like you and I think the sex is great. We make a really attractive couple. But I really really like Dianne. I'm really really attracted to her. I haven't made a move on her yet. She's going out with Charlie and she has a big mouth anyway. I can't promise you that sooner or later I won't go after her with everything I got. But it ain't right now especially after she calls you with some nonsense that could for very well be all in her head." She didn't want to hear it. Honesty is never the best policy with women. She broke up with me.

  I was livid at Dianne and I was no longer talking to her, but I knew inside that her going through all the trouble to call Mesha was a sure sign that she felt the same way about me as I did about her. She was working at Bogart's one night and I was trying not to pay her any mind when three of her old friends from East Meadow walked in. One of them was fat Dominic the same fat Dominic who had 'redecorated' Gucci's for Richey. He was about six four and four hundred pounds. He was with two goons. One of them, I was informed by Al, was called the Birdman. He was also a 'made man.' They were sitting at the tables carrying on and cavorting with Dianne as Phil and Doxie sidled up next to me at the bar. Phil said 'I just talked to Richey on the phone. He said don't do anything to them. It will start a mob war. Richey wants me to just follow him around the clubs like I did Big Frankie." I said "whatever. It just looks like they came here to see Dianne anyway." Phil looked at me expressionless and said "I'm getting tired of this pussy shit. These guys aren't shit and neither is anybody who backs them. These guys were shooting coke up in the van outside before they came in. A customer saw them. Look at that fat slob! I'm supposed to respect that? I'll bet Doxie could take him." We had been juicing Doxie up lately, trying to improve on his self-esteem. To his credit he had a string of no less than a dozen Polock knockouts, almost all of them done with the cast he was no longer wearing.

  They stayed all night mostly talking with Dianne and giving her a lot of large bills. They kept going out to their van so they must have been doing something in there. They took a couple of walks over to the Gaslight in between paying for Dianne's dining room set in the house she was going to buy. We dutifully followed them always at a distance and always using a different door than they did at Gaslight. Bogart's only had one door. They made no signs that they were uncomfortable. It was just Phil, Doxie and I that night. I don't even think Geir was there. Either Murphy wasn't working, or he was filling in for Tommy at the Rainforest. Doxie was working the Gaslight. Toward the end of the night Dominic, Birdman, and their accomplice ambled over to the Gaslight again. They went through the back door and Phil and I went through the front door. When we got inside we could see Birdman and the accomplice pulling up chairs at the other end of the bar but there was no Dominic or Doxie. We went to the back door and it was locked. The key that was always left in the keyhole on the inside of the door was gone. We ran to the front door. I got there first and when I went through it I was greeted with a sight I will never forget. Four hundred-pound

Dominic was chasing three hundred and fifty pound Doxie west down the eastbound lane of Sunrise Highway. Dominic was waving aloft a knife that would have done Michael Myers proud. For a second I froze wondering whether I should run the other way across the street to Bogart's and get my gun. By then Doxie would be dead. Disarming a four-hundred-pound professional killer bare handed without getting cut was not going to be an easy task, even for me. In the split second I was thinking about this Phil had run into the back room of Gaslight and grabbed a heavy iron coal shovel that was kept around for snow removal purposes. Phil burst past me running down Sunrise Highway with his shovel. I made sure the other two stayed in the doorway with me, where they were by now. It didn't take Phil long to catch them even though Doxie was running for his life. Neither Doxie nor Dominic was exactly a sprinter. When Phil got to Dominic he smashed him in the head so hard he dropped the knife and turned around and started running for the van. Phil trotted leisurely at his side smashing him in the head with the shovel every few feet till they reached the van in the parking lot in front of Bogart's. By then Birdman and the accomplice were also trying to get in the van. Phil started beating Birdman, who was trying to get in the driver's side, now mercilessly with the shovel. Birdman was a bloody heap in the parking lot when Phil again started to beat the other two again and again over the head with the shovel as they futilely tried to cover their heads with their hands. Birdman, who was about forty and not very big, somehow staggered to an upright position and managed to get in the van and start it up, Phil gave Dominic a final resounding thump to the face with the shovel and let the bloody blob crawl through the side door of the van and make its getaway.

It turned out Doxie had been holding the back door open for them. The other two went in but Dominic had pushed Doxie out the door and the other two locked it behind him taking the key with them. They must have been planning it all night, maybe before that. There would be no more 'respect' for anybody. We never gave anyone a chance like that again.

Dianne, standing there in her negligee and many of the customers had been watching all this from the doorway of Bogart's. Phil's face had been entirely expressionless through the whole melee even as he had robotically beat them with the shovel. We now walked inside Bogart's through the crowd. Phil brandishing the shovel deadpanned to the crowd "this is my gangster removal shovel. It can remove even the largest gangsters." Dianne had tears streaming down her face and she now started screaming almost incoherently at Phil and I. "just a year ago before Richey hired you thugs I used to really enjoy working here. Everybody was friends, the Pagans, Dominic and Artie, who mind you are friends of my father, the barmaids and the dancers, everybody got along. This is like a Clint Eastwood movie where the Devil comes to town to destroy it but he tells the towns people he's there to protect them." I looked at her crying like that and all I wanted to do was hold her. It was the first time in my life I ever felt something like that. That was the moment I decided that I loved her madly. I wasn't about to act out. I said "oh to bad. The mother fucker just tried to kill Doxie. Were we supposed to let him because he's an old family friend of yours? Now your father will just have to come in here and watch you dance by himself." Dianne's father sometimes hung around the clubs while she was dancing. I found this disgusting and I think deep down she did too. She locked herself in Bogart's basement for about an hour and when she came out she wouldn't speak to anyone.

It was about that time we lost all respect for these mob characters, if we ever had any in the first place. We wanted addresses and nobody would give them to us. Instead the next afternoon I walk into Bogart's and Richey's sitting at the bar with a paper napkin 'covering' his 357. He was completely unnerved and said "you can't just go beating on made men with a shovel. Now they're going to put a contract out on Phil. Joeys trying to straighten it out but their mad. Joeys sending over his own guy to sit on Phil, he's a private detective and he's licensed to carry. Phil has to be very careful about where he go's and who he sees. He better stay in the offices. He can sleep on the couch at least till after the sit down." I was incredulous. I said "Why don't you just give me a list of Dominic and all his associates' addresses? Phil has been doing this for a living ever since he quit his job at Pathmark years ago. He does it with the Spics and the Niggers in the South Bronx with no help from us at all. As you can see he is still alive. He is not going to go along with any of this Richey. I don't care how much money you give him. Why don't you just let him handle it? He's the professional." Richey said "Dominic and Artie are notorious shooters. Do you know how many people they have killed?" He was certain at any moment they were about to burst through the door Tommy guns blazing as they chomped on their Cuban cigars. I had to get out of there for a while.

Phil actually did go along with it for about two days. I walked in Gaslight two days later and a very Italian looking guy in a suit is following Phil all over the place. Phil introduced me to him. Then he said to me "this is my bodyguard. Joey sent him over. He has a licensed firearm. I already told him if there really is any trouble to just hand it to me so I don't have to smack him and take it." The Italian guy in the suit laughed like an idiot and Phil gave me a look like you see. I said to Phil

Those Who Would Arouse Leviathan

"you really slept in the offices last night?" Phil said "are you kidding? I told Richey at four thirty I go home. Alone! I'm not playing this mob shit for twenty-four hours a day. I need to sleep sometimes. Dominic and Artie ain't busting a grape in a fruit fight. Right now, that fat fuck is sucking through a crack pipe with a broken jaw and nose. Yea he's gonna come back and wanna do it with guns. Richey watches too many movies." I looked at the bodyguard and said, "let me see what you pack." He went to pull out a snub nosed 38 and it fell on the floor doing an exact repeat of the cops' gun from the chase in Harlem. It spun around in circles as everyone who had seen it except for Phil, him and I, dove for cover. Phil and I just looked at each other and Phil said "you see? I'm safe."

That same day Phil disappeared along with Jerry's girlfriend; Sue the barmaid. Richey swore that Dominic and Artie had 'whacked' them both and he was next. I thought they were all hysterical women especially after I had received a call from Phil the same night on the day he disappeared. He told me "I'm in Atlantic City, Sues with me. Richey wanted me to lay low so now I'm laying low. Nobody knows I'm here. Don't tell anyone. Let them play mobster till I get back in a few days. I want to break the news to Jerry myself. I can't wait to see the look on his face. You know what Sue told me? After they fuck he likes to curl up in a fetal position and suck his thumb. I want to ask him about that too."

When Phil did comeback, Sue was his new girlfriend and Jerry was shamed into leaving the clubs. I assume Richey gave him a buyout but who knows Jerry was terrified of Phil by then. We never had any more problems from Dominic and Artie the two 'notorious shooters.' Phil was now free to do just what he always wanted to do, take over the agency. But first Richey had some unfinished business up at the Rainforest for Phil to attend too. Richey now realized he was a card carrying mob boss. In the next fifteen years he would accumulate over a hundred million dollars. It took him only two weeks to become a tyrant that abused anyone he could and laughed at all the rest of the Guido's, including Joey.

Margret had a 'little problem' with cocaine and Richey had always let it go, even turned a blind eye to it in the Rainforest. Phil and I had not been to the Rainforest more than once or twice since we started working for Richey. But now Richey was a 'Don' and the Don could not have his live in girlfriend publicly doing cocaine. He deployed Phil to root out all Margret's suppliers. Phil worked there as a bouncer for a while under the guise that we were fearful Dominic and Artie would show up there since it was in their home territory in Nassau County. When he was satisfied he knew who they all were Phil badly beat each of them and banned them from the club. One guy tried to ignore his edict and Phil dragged him into the back room where Richey was waiting. As Richey directed from his stool Phil held his head over the drain on the floor while he jammed a 357 into his ear and pulled back the hammer. That guy lived to tell the story probably only because Richey was there. Margret ended up leaving Richey for a while after that one and we were now left with three bars to run. Murphy couldn't be trusted to help out with any kind of management. We put him up at the Rainforest and the first week he used his key to break into his own liquor closet and stole every bottle in there. Phil wasn't finished with his performance at the Rainforest anyway. For his encore Phil dragged Savage out by his long biker hair and kicked him around the parking lot until he soiled his pants. APP Talent Agency was dissolved and the list of a hundred and fifty girls went to Richey. Phil was now running the agency out of Jerry's well-furnished office in Bogart's. By then I knew what I wanted out of all this. We arranged my schedule, so I worked when and where Dianne was working.

Bobby, the president of the 'Cretins,' was now the new manager at the Rainforest with Tommy as his bouncer. About thirty or forty employees would meet Phil and I after work at the Diner on little East Neck and Sunrise Highway. There we would hold early morning court at a table that was prepared for us each night by the waitress's pushing most of the tables in the dining area into a single aggregate table. Marlena who had been one of the jewels in Gracie Starr's entourage had just recently become a waitress. The waitresses were now making just as much money as the dancers. In fact most of them were dancers who preferred to keep their clothes on. Bobby and Marlena were sitting across from each other at this table one night when I decided that Bobby should be rewarded for his loyalty. I told Marlena she should be with him and they were together ever since.

Knowledge / דעת

CHAPTER 34

I looked down at my wrist as they changed the bandages. Arvan had operated, reconnecting the tendons in my right hand. I now had an elongated and jagged M running ten inches down my right forearm to my hand. Arvan had also used two bolts to set my compounded right ankle. Eventually they would have to be removed by him. After looking at the hack job he did reconnecting the tendons, I was given a choice by my other attending physicians. I could stay at Good Samaritan and let Dr. Arvan mutilate my left arm too. Or I could have Dr. Levine transfer me to Stony Brook Hospital where a more competent physician would perform microsurgery that would not leave the vicious looking scar I now had on my right arm. The catch was that after the microsurgery I would be shipped from Stony Brook to Central Suffolk Hospital in Riverhead and be put under the care of the Suffolk County Corrections Department. After Arvan removed the bolts at Central Suffolk Hospital, Wolf promised me he would get the bail reduced to three thousand dollars cash but that for a little while I would be in jail. Central Suffolk Hospital was a jailhouse facility. The scars meant nothing to me, and I knew I was going to walk again, in spite of Arvan's incompetence, but I needed some fresh air by then. I had not been out of that room for weeks, at least while I was conscious. I figured my deputy sheriffs could use a change of scenery too, so I opted for the medical excursion to Stony Brook on the North Shore. When they wheeled me out chained to the gurney, the clear fall air felt invigorating. Memories crystallized in my head. It was all so clear like the clarity of light between the daylight and night that the French call l'heure bleue.

  Dianne had about two dozen guys who were in love with her. She had a different cutesy act for each of them, and they were all giving her money. Gracey Star had thousands of guys who were in love with her, or at least her body and they were all giving her money too. Gracey's gratuities were in lesser denominations than Dianne's benefactors lavished on her but in quantities voluminous enough so Gracey would always need at least two plastic garbage bags to haul the crumpled ones and fives out of the clubs. Tens and twenties she would usually accept from the customers' hands by clasping the unfolded bills in the cleavage of her breasts. A good day for Gracey was between three and four thousand dollars, more than the bar made. Back then bottles of beer were three dollars and taps of soda or beer considerably less. Some guys would buy one beer or soda and linger all day. Phil and I solved that problem by posting a sign over the bar that said, "Drinks Must Be Purchased Every Half Hour!" But we would only enforce that rule when we knew a guy was a deadbeat. Gracey and Dianne would alternate being on the stage from 12:00 to 8:00. The first night girl was expected by 8:30 when the last day girl went home. I was, of course, the day bouncer. When they worked in the day we had decided to keep Gracey and Dianne in Bogart's to avoid problems with guys rushing the stage. I spent almost my entire day in Bogart's with them. I was down there by myself sometimes, but much of the time Vinnie Gambler, Jimmy Murphy, or Phil would come by and hang out. By then Charlie had gone to jail, but I still had Flanagan and Whitehead to watch the Gaslight for me. Flanagan was very happy with the pool table in the Gaslight.

     It was still cold out, but I remember Jimmy Murphy was wearing a T-shirt in the parking lot when he pulled up to take my shift. His biceps were bulging, and his massive chest heaved as he gesticulated describing how he had just left the hospitality of John Doxies home. Jimmy said to me, "You know that dirty white sweater he always wears? It was in the corner on the floor, and I took a wicked piss all over it last night. Let's see if he wears it in tonight." I said, "Jimmy, I don't know why you do shit like this. He's not going to want you living there if you're going to be terrorizing him. Just like the Rainforest. We make you the manager and you rob your own liquor. You could have drunk every one of those bottles right in the comfort of the bar surrounded by beautiful women. Why did you have to take them out of the bar?" He answered me with that idiot's look of his, "Blockhead said we could sell them." "Did you?" I inquired. He giggled stupidly and replied, "No, most of the bottles are still in Blockhead's apartment. You think if I gave them back Richey and Phil would make me the manager of the Rainforest again?" I said, "I don't think there's much chance of that anymore." Then he shocked me by saying, "That's too bad. I liked it better there. The Rainforest is like a regular bar. Bogart's and Gaslight are highway bars. Gaslight should be called the Last Light because that light." He gestured to the eastern light on Sunrise Highway. "That's the last light between here and the Hamptons. On any given night you have every deviant, sneak thief, and wannabe gangster prowling this highway from New York City to the Hamptons in their cars. Now we got Ronnie Craps, Johnny Blue Eyes, Franzese's people, and the people they come in here with, all big-time mobsters. It's just a matter of time till we get shot here." I had thought Jimmy would not have been smart enough to articulate a fact like that, but I addressed his fear first: "You know what Phil and I do? When you are in a situation like this, just consider yourself dead already. Like Jim Morrison said, 'No one here gets out alive.' The worst that could happen is you could get killed, but you are already dead anyway. Dead men have nothing to lose, so they don't waste their time thinking when they need to be reacting."

     We walked into Bogart's, and I looked up at the stage where Dianne was strutting around the pole, pausing occasionally to spin on it. She was playing a new song called "Devil Inside" by INXS on the jukebox. The song was about a promiscuous girl who uses her words like weapons. She has been raised amongst leather-clad bikers and has "the look" in her eyes. She meets a man who also has the look his eyes. He has nothing but is full of pride. They both have the Devil inside them. The fate of the human race seems to be balanced on their relationship. The future is said to be uncertain "but certainly slight." Quoting the old Outer Limits show I used to watch when I was a boy as best I could I said, "We control the transmission. If we wish to make it louder, we will raise the volume. If we wish to make it softer, we will lower it to a whisper. We control the horizontal, and we control the vertical. You are about to experience the mystery of the inner mind."

Jimmy just looked at me. He had already followed my lead of calling myself a god by sometimes referring to himself as a goddess. Jimmy needed work, lots of work, but he got the general idea. Phil came through the door and stood next to us in front of the stage asking, "Where's Doxie? He's not next door yet." Jimmy answered, "I threw him on the floor at the apartment. You think he's mad at me?" Dianne had been listening to everything we were saying, as usual, and screamed over the music from the stage, "He's in the basement on his shoe phone talking to Richey!" Then she likened him to a popular dog food commercial at the time: "Gotta tell Richey, gotta tell Richey – you know like the dog on TV that can only think about Kibbles 'n Bits, Kibbles 'n Bits. But with Doxie it's gotta tell Richey, gotta tell Richey." She said all this while she waddled around the stage mimicking Doxie as a demented penguin. Gracey chimed in from her throne at the end of the bar surrounded by her admirers: "You guys should make him wear his colors. The Pagans cut the sleeves off an old dungaree jacket and told him he had to wear it whenever he was in the bar. Those were his 'colors.' There was nothing on the back. Nothing. Just like him. If he didn't wear the jacket they slapped him around." Just then Doxie walked in wearing his white sweater; Jimmy and I suppressed our laughter. Gracey shrieked at him, "John, where's your colors? How come you don't wear your colors anymore?" The crowded bar burst into laughter. Jimmy and I looked at each other, looked at his sweater, and laughed harder than everyone else. Mercifully, Phil sent him to the Gaslight.

Dianne motioned for me to come over. I did and put my hands on a table that butted the stage, leaning over the railing that was around it. She stepped down theatrically to the lower level, wearing just black stiletto heels and a black leather G-string. She bent toward me grasping my shoulders firmly in her hands. I could feel euphoria racing through my body as it spread from the places where her fingers clung to me. Using me for support she gracefully lowered herself to her knees. Somewhere in Hell a key was being forged for damnation's lock. She pulled her naked breasts almost to my mouth and brought her lips to my ear. Her hair smelled like roses, untouched by the aroma of tobacco and beer in the bar. Her breath was sweet like mint, and I looked at her neck which was as elegant and white as a Grecian statue. From the way she held on with restrained desperation she didn't have to say anything. But she whispered in my ear, "Why don't you and Phil come down to the basement with me and Gracey. We'll smoke some weed."

Gracey was already in street clothes, so we only had to wait for Dianne to finish dressing in the bathroom before we went downstairs. Gracey was the last one through the heavy steel door, and she threw the two thick steel bolts behind her and gave me a funny look. Bogart's basement was really all that was left of her and Dianne's little kingdom that once came resplendent with "knights" on chrome-plated Harleys. We descended the steps into a windowless concrete bunker that was the heart of their castle. Beyond the kegs that fed the bar upstairs were some tables and chairs where Dianne lit up a joint. Wearing a long cashmere coat, she sat on a table. As she spoke she was poking at me for punctuation with her matching high-heeled designer boots: "I heard you told Mesha you liked me, and she broke up with you. You men are just all so stupid. You fell right into my trap. Now you have nothing. You have Phil." She laughed, and I looked at Gracey who was sitting next to her. Gracey rolled her eyes. I snatched Dianne off the table and tried to kiss her, but she buried her face deep in my chest, making no effort to pull back from my embrace. I held her like that. An electrical rapture seemed to bind us both together. I was frozen in time until I once again became aware of Phil and Gracey's presence. When I let go of her, Dianne continued in her most grating nasal twang: "You thought you were going to go out with me? I'm not going out with you. You're crazy. You're going to jail. And I'm a nice girl." I said, "Yeah, a nice stripper?" She retorted, "No really! What do you think? I just jump into bed with guys? I have gone out with seven guys in my whole life. I don't drink or take drugs, and I don't like to be around people that do. I have never been arrested in my life either and you're going to jail. You think I'm attracted to that?" I said, "You went out with a Pagan for two years. Who are you trying to kid?" She answered indignantly, "That guy was really good to me. When I got sick with hepatitis and nearly died, he carried me into the hospital. No one even knew what I had. I turned yellow. The doctors told me if I had waited another day to be diagnosed I would have died. He took care of me in bed for weeks. No Pagan ever disrespected either me or Gracey. They treated us like queens. When we came down here, they had to leave if we asked them to." I sneered, "He probably gave you the hepatitis. Where did you get hepatitis from? Playing with dirty needles?" She was incensed again and said, "I have done coke four times in my life. I don't like it. I would never stick no needle in my arm."

Satisfied that I had proved my point, I exclaimed, "You see? You got it from having sex with him!"

She insisted that she didn't get it from him, but I don't think she had even known you could get hepatitis from having unprotected sex. I half-joked, "You fuck a dirty Pagan who gives you hepatitis, but you're too nice a girl for me?" I pulled her close again and tried to kiss her with the same result as before. This time I looked down at her eyes and saw they were closed as she pressed her face against my chest. I said, "Alright. I have never been one to shy away from hard work. Hard work heightens the senses." She was murmuring now with her face pressed to my heart, "I'm going out with Charlie. You should go back out with Mesha. She'll wait for you when you're in jail. She really loves you. I can fix it for you. You want me to fix it?" "No," I asserted, "I don't want you making any mistakes as to just what I want."

CHAPTER 35

It was decided that Wendy would not be sacrificed to the spider goddess on Walpurgis Night because I would be in jail. The date was fixed for the middle of April – not Wendy's "Act of Contrition" but rather my incarceration. Phil would join me for a sixteen-day vacation around the end of May. He had pleaded guilty to "illegal dissection." I thought it would only be right for Dianne to break up with Charlie and wait for me. I would wait for her until the end of time. I spent the next couple of months trying to convince her. I was surrounded by beautiful women but could see none of them, especially Mesha who tried everything to get my attention. I gave Dianne my number, and she gave me hers even though I already had it from the list. She told me not to call because "Charlie might answer." We started playing phone games. I don't know who started it.

The supernatural forces enveloping both of us were wearing her down. It was plain enough. Her regulars stopped coming to see her, and she didn't care. When she was up on stage her eyes were glazed with a dreamy look of expectation as she stared longingly into my eyes. Her pearl-white smile beamed self-satisfied approval. She was making nothing and didn't even notice. She spent every moment off the stage sitting as close as she could to me at the bar. Sometimes we would embrace but never kiss. When we embraced, "two worlds collided" just like another song by the now suddenly famous INXS. They came from a shithole somewhere in Australia but would win five MTV music awards that year. They were the only thing being played on the jukebox, on the radio, and anywhere else music was played. All their songs seemed to be about us. The song "New Sensation" talked about how the pain of being human would soon be over and then we would live forever together. The refrain in "I Need You Tonight" said all that was needed to be said and kept repeating, "You're one of my kind." That's how it ended. It was as if INXS were in the Gaslight, watching us, serenading us. Less than ten years later the band's lead singer Michael Hutchence would be found nude and hanging dead in his hotel room. No one knows why.

    When my landscaping business started up early that year I could no longer work days, so I took Tuesday and Thursday nights. Weekends were optional. It took Dianne less than a week to decide she no longer wanted to work days either. She started working Tuesday and Thursday nights, without Gracey, with me at the Gaslight. We spent all night in an empty bar as she desperately clung to me even as she tried to push me away with her words. We were driven by some insatiable ethereal hunger to touch and hold each other. To be in her presence was to stand at the doorway of Paradise. I had recoiled from physical contact with other people, even my own mother, since I was ten years old. I had never touched a woman except in sexual arousal, but with her it was all different. The thrill of just touching her sent bliss racing through my body. Richey wanted to move her to the Rainforest rather than pay us both out of the drawer from the now paltry registers. I had Phil explain to Richey that was not happening. I got the impression that Richey was a little too eager for me to go to jail.

    One-night Phil called me over to the office and introduced me to a guy named "Animal." He was about six foot nine with long hair and a beard, dressed in faded denim and the scuffed-up engineer boots that identified him as a biker. Phil said, "This is Animal. He's known all over the East Coast by the Pagans and the Hells Angels. He's worked all the toughest clubs down south. Richey wants him to fill in for you while you're away." I looked him over and decided he was a little too attractive for my tastes. I didn't want him working with Dianne. He was just her type. I asked him what it was like working strip clubs down south. He explained, "Those rednecks are really crazy. If they don't know you, they'll wait for you in the parking lot and shoot you when you come out." I responded, "They'd do that here too except I have the Murphy's and Blockhead on all-night surveillance outside. Don't worry they're looking for marks they can follow out of here. The Secret Service couldn't be more vigilant." He said, "Well over there you just got to get in with the right people. I joined the Ku Klux Klan while I was down there." Then he proudly pulled out a folding knife emblazoned with KKK. He added, "They only give this to members in good standing." At that point I went into a complete red out. I don't remember much. I may have hit him a few times, but the next thing I remember is dragging Phil, Geir, and Doxie as they hung on my back. I tried to land a clean kick to his head while he dodged out the front door. I screamed at him as he took off down the block on his motorcycle: "I know what kind of animal you are. You're a chicken!" Perhaps Richey thought my assault on the "Animal" was racially motivated because the next candidate they produced to replace me was a large, muscular black guy. When Phil introduced us while we were sitting at the bar, he made a comment that Richey would not be Richey without me and that I was the one who did everything for him. The guy made an innocent joke trying to be one of the boys. He asked if I also did windows. At that point he was given the Animal treatment too. We finally settled on a guy named Kevin. He was even bigger than Animal. But he had a huge lantern jaw that made him look like he was deformed. He was one of the nicest guys I ever met and completely subservient to me. Perfect.

CHAPTER 36

At first I thought the pop music serenade was just part of my by now regular gig, the whole archetype thing. Somehow I was intimately connected with the collective unconscious of my culture. I had been calling myself a god. I had seen things that no man ever really should and had participated directly in them; really, I still had no idea. Aside from her physical beauty there were other things about Dianne that commanded attention, things I had never seen demonstrated in another human except John and myself (and I did not consider either of us human). The things she thought and talked about, the music she liked, and even the clothes she wore or didn't wear were all reflected in pop culture. It wasn't as if she was following their lead. Dianne had zero interest in pop culture. They were following hers. I knew I had met my soul mate. But I don't even know if I wanted to have sex with her. I wanted so much more than sex. I sensed but didn't know. What I wanted was eternal.

I had been reading voraciously about the occult for the last couple of years. Anyone who is intellectually competent and makes more than a cursory study of that subject carrying it into the twentieth century will soon come to the realization that its nine-hundred-year history starting with the Knights Templar culminates with Aleister Crowley. Crowley was born to kill God. If I engaged in conjecture I would say Nietzsche wrote The Antichrist as a bar mitzvah present to him. Crowley was turning thirteen when Nietzsche penned it. Although he had memorized the Bible by the time he was seven years old, Crowley rejected his rigid Plymouth Brethren upbringing almost from birth. He knew he was the Beast of Revelation the first time he ever heard of it. Famed mountaineer, chess master, and saint of the Gnostic Church, Crowley was a self-described dope fiend with an intellect that could rival Nietzsche himself. He set upon the task at hand with an inhuman single mindedness of purpose.

After spending a few years at the turn of the twentieth century under the tutelage of the famed occultists of the Golden Dawn, an organization laden with England's aristocracy and their gurus, Crowley made his play for the throne. He believed himself to be in contact with the long-awaited Horus the Avenger through his spirit medium Aiwaz who he said had dictated The Book of the Law to him through his wife Rose Kelly. Crowley said she had become possessed by Aiwaz while spending the night with him in the King's Chamber of the Great Pyramid of Giza in 1904. The Book of the Law, outlining the Aeon of Horus, would not be published for general consumption until 1909. Those who read it then were advised to destroy it after reading because only those who are to come have the right to study it. In the oral traditions taught to me by John Crowley had the ability to alter time and be in two places at once. He could kill a man or a supernatural entity with just a look, and all the 'Illuminati' feared the glare of his evil eye which amounted to no less than an inevitable death sentence. He had performed miracle upon miracle witnessed by Europe's aristocracy and America's industrial tycoons. Famed military strategist and inventor of the blitzkrieg Major-General John Fuller gave a written account of how Crowley turned a beautiful young temptress into a shriveled old hag right in front of him. Crowley told him she was a vampire feeding on the life force of his followers.

Moonchild is one of two novels written by Crowley, the other Diary of a Dope Fiend is ostensibly about his lifelong struggles with heroin addiction. Crowley opens Moonchild with an author's note that ends: "Need I add that, as the book itself demonstrates beyond all doubt, all persons and incidents are purely the figment of a disordered imagination?" This was probably the biggest lie Crowley ever told, and Crowley sometimes made a sport of lying, a demonstration of his disdain for the human race. The book that made the Ordo Templi Orientis decide he was a god is aptly titled The Book of Lies. In Germany, the OTO was the metaphysical equivalent of the Golden Dawn for the Teutonic aristocracy. The Germans immediately embraced Crowley, but he ended up having to use a pistol to persuade the more skeptical high priests of the English aristocracy that he was the prophet of Horus. Men like W. B.

Yeats, A. E. Waite, and MacGregor Mathers were not prepared to accept Crowley's plans for engineering the Aeon of Horus. The secondary purpose of Crowley's publication of Moonchild, which Crowley claimed he penned in 1917 but did not publish until 1929, was as a mockery of Yeats' vain attempts to pull off the Great Work singlehandedly chronicled in Yeats collection of poems titled Michael Robartes and the Dancer published in 1921. In Moonchild Crowley gives a detailed description as to how he trapped the soul of the moon into the womb of Lisa la Giuffria, a friend and constant companion of the famous Lavinia King. Crowley introduces King in the first chapter as "the most famous dancer in all the world." The character of Lavinia King serves as an opening kick in the face to Yeats and his attempt to circumvent Crowley and his followers. Later in the book Crowley introduces Yeats as Gates, a bumbling poet with dirty finger nails.

There are in actuality no fictitious characters in the book. If one knows enough about the occult, he will recognize every character in Moonchild which Crowley uses as a platform to slander his enemies and flatter his friends. Allan Bennett, an Eastern mystic and Crowley's friend, becomes Simon Iffe who is a cross between David Carradine's character in the Kung Fu television series and Jesus. Crowley's enemies are dealt with savagely: MacGregor Mathers becomes a black magician who pimps out his wife, A. E. Waite chokes to death on his own tongue, and W. B. Yeats is killed with a tarot card. As the only man who ever attained the exalted rank of Ipsissimus, Crowley was now in a position to challenge for the throne of God. The Magi and even God himself were now obligated by the divine imperative of the Holy Spirit to divulge their most arcane secrets to him. Moonchild is nothing less than a partial account of Crowley's attempt to build his own Tower of Babel, his attempt to kill God and seize the throne of heaven.

Crowley wasn't above taunting his enemies; in fact, he made it a point to do just that. As I have said, Moonchild's secondary purpose was to taunt Yeats, but its primary purpose was to taunt all that would oppose him. The game was won, and being the great chess master he was, Crowley knew when it was checkmate. He had already performed the Amalantrah Working in the spring of 1918 on Esopus Island in the Hudson River in New York. He had performed the rites of Abramelin the Mage long before that in the Boleskine House overlooking Loch Ness. When the exhaustive ritual on the Hudson River concluded, Crowley had retired to Montauk Point on Long Island, supposedly for some rest and relaxation. It was during his time spent in New York in the closing stages of WWI that Crowley had opened the portals that would set in motion the Aeon of Horus. The picture Crowley drew of his guide during the

Amalantrah Working would become the prototype image of what is now called a Grey. What he had already done could never be undone; however, Crowley could not be sure the work would ever be consummated. He himself had tried during the Amalantrah Working and failed. He blamed his sexual partner, or Scarlet Woman, for the failure, saying that she let her feminine instincts get the better of her. The culmination of plan A would have to wait a generation or two, but like any great strategist Crowley had a plan B. Plan B would be homicidally reckless to the point of madness, yet Crowley never did let human empathy get in his way. He had demonstrated this back in 1905 when he had led an expedition up the unscaled Kangchenjunga, the third highest peak in the world. A few thousand feet shy of the summit; some of his men had decided to turn back and ended up being buried by an avalanche. Crowley waited a day before going down to lend assistance by which time they were already dead. Crowley later remarked to the worlds press: "This is precisely the sort of thing with which I have no sympathy whatsoever."

The Book of the Law is just as revered by Crowley's followers as the Talmud and Bible are by Jews and Christians. But it was The Book of Lies that made him a God among the German nobility and spawned the Astrum Argentum, the inner order of the OTO. The AA along with the ancient Thule Society became the Vril Society, the soul of National Socialism. Writing about his birth for the London Sunday Dispatch in 1933 Crowley states, "Over the centre of my heart I had four hairs curling from left to right in the exact form of a Swastika. Before Hitler was, I am." Ian Fleming, intelligence agent extraordinaire and creator of James Bond pointed Crowley out to the British admiralty when Rudolf Hess, the second highest ranking National Socialist, inexplicably checked out of WWII by parachuting into England in its early stages muttering about the occult.

There is another book, a compilation of three books, which is held in even higher reverence by some of Crowley's disciples than all the ones previously mentioned. The Holy Books that John had brought back from the bowels of Attica is only for those who are in direct communication with Crowley, who now permeates this world with his disembodied presence just like the "old grey God" once did. That book is for what Christians would call a prophet. In it he exhorts his followers to rise up and smite the children of Ptah lest they interfere with the rule of the just in the new aeon. Ptah is what the ancient Egyptians called the God of Abraham. In Crowley's mind, Islam was the only great religion that was worthy of anything but contempt. The God of Mohammad's revelations is Allah, al meaning all and la meaning nothing, the essence of the Supreme Being and what Crowley calls the one true God in The Holy Books. He urged his followers to form an alliance with Islam. But Crowley wanted to be sure the children of Ptah would be smote. He needed an insurance policy. He took one out by incarnating the moon in its most malevolent and dangerous form, what the ancients called Hecate the Crone. In Moonchild Crowley tells his readers that this was achieved when he says the infant was "no ordinary baby." She was born with "hair six inches long, so fair as to be silvery white." His ending puts the "Moonchild" on a boat for New York City, setting loose in America the bloodline of what had until then lived only in the most malevolent realms of the ethereal.

    The goal of the Great Work can be understood as an evolutionary adjustment that transcends generations designed to bring about the resurrection of the hermaphroditic super beings that were the predecessor of man. The Greeks called them Hyperborean. But this can never be achieved during the reign of the oppressive Abrahamic God and his human agents of authority. In the prophecies handed down from a time out of mind in Egypt it is Horus the Avenger who will slay the tyrant God, thereby avenging the murder of his father Osiris the God of Light and widowing of his mother Isis the Goddess of Magick. But Horus is the God of War, and just like his prophet Aleister Crowley he cares nothing about collateral damage. Horus requires three horrific battles with Seth before finally defeating him. WWI and WWII were the first two battles. The Western world's war with Islam can be counted as the third; however, it must be escalated to apocalyptic proportions before what Crowley calls the Equinox of the Gods can proceed. In the eyes of the Magi, every organic organism from the time of the Abrahamic God's reign has been forced to participate in a self-perpetuating cycle of murder. The collective soul is bound to a world where the living must consume the living to continue existence. Life itself is cursed to be born again and again to the same endless perdition. The architect is mad and his design a prison, yet Jews and Christians call him the one true God. Ancient Hebrew sages had another name for him. They called him Samael, blind ignorant God. That is why they perpetually rebelled against Moses. They knew the God of Abraham for what he really was, a bloodthirsty demon. This is the darkest secret of the doctrine called Gnosticism, rites that were practiced in the underground catacombs of Rome, subterranean mysteries trapped between heaven and hell that would become the seeds of their own antithesis: Christianity.

    When Jesus walked the earth, if he ever did, forbidden knowledge was still available for those who sought it out. Alexander had conquered the known world in his insatiable quest for knowledge. Scrolls from all the far-flung corners of the East were the most priceless of the spoils appropriated by his invincible armies. The scrolls were gathered together in the Library of Alexandria in Egypt. Although the library was accidently burned by Julius Caesar in 48 BC the manuscripts were saved and dispersed throughout the city. What was in those manuscripts gave rise to Gnosticism, a doctrine of self-enlightenment diametrically opposed to the Judaism of the Pharisees and their tyrannical God with his 613 Commandments. Later many of the tenets of the ancient religion were presented as parables and allegories and became the teachings of Jesus. The Gospel of Thomas is the oldest known written record of those teachings. There are 114 verses. A few centuries later Mohammad's Quran would be composed in 114 suras. In verse 3 Jesus tells his disciples that "the kingdom is inside of you." But he tells them in verse 22 they will only achieve it "when you make the two one" and "the male and the female one."

In the 13th verse Jesus whispers, something into the ear of Thomas. The other apostles, curious, question Thomas as to what Jesus told him that he could not tell them. Thomas replies to them that if he told them they would pick up rocks to stone him and that the rocks would turn to fire and consume them. But it is known anyway that Jesus whispered Isaiah 28:13 into Thomas's ear: "And the word of the lord will be to them precept upon precept, precept upon precept, line upon line, line upon line, here a little, there a little, that they may go, and fall backward, and be broken, and snared, and taken." The priests of the deceitful Abrahamic God could not tolerate the likes of a Gnostic Jesus exposing their evil deity. A relentless campaign was launched to extinguish all traces of the fire where the light of the ancient truth always burns. Paul dissembled everything the Gnostic Jesus had said. Irenaeus made that Jesus a heretic in the name of the Judaic Jesus. And finally, Theodosius burned all that could be found of the manuscripts which were the source of this wisdom. When even that was not enough, Pope Innocent III unleashed his dogs of war. In what is called the Albigensian Crusade, the brave knights of France murdered every man, woman, and child they could in the south of France. It was a desperate effort in genocide to wipe from the face of the earth the still-flickering flames of Zarathustra's fire. Catharism, the other Christianity, was at the time threatening the debilitating and eventually lethal brand of Rome; the spiritual shackles fashioned by a Pontifex Maximus whose roots can be traced back at least to the Etruscans hundreds of years before the birth of Rome and a millennium before Jesus. When one of his battle-hardened princes dared question the slaughter he was being asked to perpetrate on his own countrymen in the name of God, "Innocent" replied, "Kill them all and let God sort them out."

The Sphinx is a symbol from a time out of mind when Osiris ruled over beings that were living gods. Dante once lamented that every man's heart is halved at birth and that he must spend his life seeking the other half. When Osiris reigned that was not necessary. Men were born whole. It was a time of light and a time of science – not the idiotic monkey sciences of today that are just as bad as the faith-based religions they would supplant – real science, the kind that is learned in the Copenhagen School of quantum physics. The moon isn't there if there is no one to see it.

Three hundred years ago a philosopher and Christian shaman named George Berkeley first postulated the idea that matter, corporeal substance, the things man finds so familiar and comforting to behold and to touch, are only ideas in the mind of the beholder. Berkeley's epiphany was called Immaterialism. Now it's called quantum physics. For two hundred years philosophers tried in vain to refute Berkeley; for the last one hundred years quantum physicists have been proving him correct.

Einstein's theory of relativity was proven wrong long ago by John Stewart Bell, ironically enough while he was trying to prove it right. Many experiments since have confirmed the reluctant conclusion of Bell's Theorem. There is no locality of matter. It is no longer George Berkeley's theory of Immaterialism; rather, it is a scientific fact. Objects and events can interact with each other though they are separated by too vast a distance of time and space to be connected even by something travelling as fast as the speed of light. In the Slit Experiment the electron pattern on the wall should be the imprints of single particles, but instead it shows up as a wave. When instruments able to discern why are added to the experiment, the electrons can only be detected as particles. In Quantum Entanglement, electrons can be emitted in pairs with their spins dependent and opposite from each other. If one is negative, the other will adjust to positive. When the electrons are separated, the adjustment continues even in experiments where the electrons were separated by over a hundred kilometers. As soon as these electrons are examined with instrumentation made for that purpose, the adjustment ceases; they then go back to random spins. As Berkeley articulated, "Esse est percipi," to be is to be perceived.

CHAPTER 37

I had already understood all this, but during the two months before I went to jail I began to read everything C. G. Jung ever wrote. Jung collected and translated all of the ancient alchemical texts he could lay his hands on. Jung knew intuitively that gold is used in them as a euphemism for the soul. Alchemy was not a pseudoscience, but a religion practiced by all the learned men of the renaissance including Isaac Newton himself. Its tenets were concealed from the unwashed masses by obscure symbolism that could only be understood by its practitioners. Jung translated the manuscripts from Latin. Before him men like Paracelsus, Nicolas Flamel, Raymond Lully, and John Dee translated them from Aramaic to Latin. Semitic scribes had already translated them from the languages, many long dead, in which they had originally appeared in the Library of Alexandria. These were the men who brought the Renaissance to the Western world, men of fearsome intellect, fearsome enough to defy even the pope. Some paid for it with their lives like Giordano Bruno, but none ever bowed to the pope like Galileo. They did not need a Pontifex Maximus to bridge the gap to the sublime. These men were already there. They were the first of Nietzsche's golden beasts who would no longer need a god because they were not afraid to be their own gods, as Edward Bulwer-Lytton described "the coming race."

    In the latter stage of his career Jung became obsessed with the sacred marriage between the Sun and the Moon. He was deliberately kept in the dark by men like A. E. Waite whom he relied heavily upon as a source of the actual existence of this tradition, shared only amongst the most illuminated of the Magi, other than as a metaphor. But Jung knew anyway, for as Dylan put it, he was "Knockin' on Heaven's Door." Toward the end of his prolific career Jung culminated his research with two scholarly works on the subject: Mysterium Coniunctionis and The Psychology of the Transference.

    On the first page of The Psychology of the Transference Jung quotes the Latin translation by Khalid ibn Yazid, a legendary Egyptian alchemist from the sixth century: "Take a Coetanean dog and an Armenian bitch." Maybe it was the word bitch because that is exactly what Dianne was, but I knew right there and then I had found what I was looking for. It was the proverbial bolt of lightning, my own epiphany. Suddenly I knew who I was and who she was. It no longer escaped me that Dianne and Gracey Star could very well be Lisa la Giuffria and the famous Lavinia King. It was all a game that I had been playing since the day I was born, and this game was for all the marbles, the very throne of heaven, right across from Babylon Town Hall, probably exactly the same place where it had all begun so many thousands of years before.

    I said nothing. I just kept reading. It wasn't like I could just walk up to a close confidant and say, "Hey, I'm the Sun God, and I am here to die with my lover the Moon Goddess locked in an eternal orgasm so that we may be resurrected together as The Crowned and Conquering Child!" That would make me as crazy as W. B. Yeats. I wasn't conveniently stupid like Yeats either. I knew that for the ritual actually to work we would both have to die, quite horribly too, just as was depicted in the medieval wood cuttings. Some of the wood cuttings used by Jung in Mysterium Coniunctionis showed the king's and queen's severed limbs suspended together in a tub of fluid. A Latin caption read: "Our stone is to be extracted from the nature of the two bodies." The water in the tub was said to be the "amniotic fluid of the wind." I wondered if Phil had been practicing when he dissected Palamesi and exactly how many people, not disincarnate beings, around me knew about this. There was only one person I could really talk to about it, and I wasn't quite ready to confront John yet. I wasn't scared. If the leprechaun had been telling me the truth, I had not felt fear of any external threat since I was a boy. In fact, I had felt nothing since I was a boy except for now when I felt this overwhelming need to be with Dianne. It all made sense now. I had been born for this. I had been fantasizing about death and sex since I was old enough to ejaculate. My deepest, darkest fantasy had always been to make passionate love to a latter-day Helen of Troy; just when we reached the pinnacle of orgasmic climax together, we would both simultaneously be slain.

On one of those long nights when we were alone together at the Gaslight, I did cryptically say something to Dianne. I was massaging her, and she looked like she was having an orgasm. She was seated on the bar stool in front of me, wearing only her G-string and stiletto heels, exposing her bare back to me. I was being careful to avoid her naked breasts as I complied with her insistent requests and forcefully kneaded the muscles in her armpits and ribcage. My stool was up against hers, and my legs were wrapped around her hourglass ass. If my cock got any harder it would have been up her ass. There was not much difference between her skin and the silk negligees she usually wore. Her head was tilted up so close to my mouth that I could taste the faint sweetness of her hair. Her eyes were tightly closed in ecstasy. I just blurted it out right into her ear: "Do you remember when we were back in Egypt?"

I saw Donna Colleen watching us from the stage. Suddenly I realized that she knew. Donna Colleen was an "A-girl," tall and statuesque, deeply tanned, with dyed platinum blond hair and a very expensive breast job. She was about the same age as Dianne. She had started working with Dianne and I immediately after we started working nights together. She was a real biker bitch who frequently came to work on her Harley that she sometimes went riding with Dianne who had a small 400cc bike. Donna never said anything; even if you spoke to her she would give you one-word answers. Phil said it was because she was dumb, but I know when someone is watching everything and taking it all in. That was exactly what Donna did every night. She could have made more money working across the street or at the Rainforest. By now the customers knew our act and didn't want to interrupt, so they just stayed in Bogart's or went to the Rainforest. But Donna always wanted to work with us, supposedly because of her friendship with Dianne. When I had first met her, she was wearing a pendant with an eye in a triangle, Crowley's symbol. I immediately asked about it, and she told me she was a recovering alcoholic and that it was the symbol of Alcoholics Anonymous. This is true, but there is another AA for which it is a symbol: the Astrum Argentum, the inner order of the OTO.

    Dianne opened her eyes, turned around, and looked at me asking, "What are you talking about?" I got off my chair and pulled her off hers, holding her to me so that her breasts were flush against my body and she could feel my erection. I watched Donna observing us from the corner of my eye as I said, "All this is staged, Dianne by the people around us and things that you would not even believe existed unless you saw them with your own eyes like I have. This started in Egypt thousands and thousands of years ago. You and I have been scheduled to meet in this place since this aeon began. Look around you. Look across the street. Don't you see where you are? You're in Babylon, Dianne. I'm ready to do this right now. Right up here on the bar. You are right about me. I have never felt a single thing since the love I felt for my parents when I was a small child. Since then I have never had any emotions – no love, no fear, no sorrow. Till I met you, the only thing I thought I ever could feel again was red-hot hatred. Why do you think I like violence so much? It's the only time I ever feel anything. But now it's all different. I want you, and I want you with my soul." Our faces were a few inches apart; I tried to kiss her, but she did her usual burying her face in my shoulder. She started almost to cry saying, "This is just what I mean. You talk crazy. I could never understand the things you believe in, and I don't want to either. That's the reason girls are so attracted to you. It's like you reek of evil. You're like some vampire in a movie. That's not what I like about you. I ain't gonna lie. I like it when you hold me, but I'm never going to kiss you back. Not right now. You're going to be in jail for four months in less than a month. I'm very happy with Charlie. He's very well trained. He never gets annoyed with me. This morning he kept making the bed, and every time he was done I unmade it, and he just calmly made it again. That's the kind of shit I do because I like to be annoying. But I don't like it when people get annoyed with me. You think all we are going to do is have sex? Charlie is lucky if I let him look at my ass occasionally when he cums. I wear feety pajamas to bed. I'm nothing like Mesha in bed, and I know what you're like. If you still want me when you get out of jail, well then maybe we can talk about it. I'm not going anywhere. I'll be in this place till I'm forty."

As the Cathars knew full well, since they retained their Gnostic roots, sex is the trap the god of this world uses to keep souls bound to him. That's why Catholic priests, who are for all intents and purposes professional Magi, are celibate ... in theory at least. When Cathar men and women reached forty, they practiced abstinence. But orgasmic energy, or Orgone energy as Wilhelm Reich called it, can also be used as a devastating weapon. The human orgasm and the sexual arousal that leads to it are a bridge, a Pontifex as in Pontifex Maximus, to the sublime, to ecstasy, to euphoria, to the positive current that animates this world. That is why in sex humans find pleasure and fulfillment at once with the method that allows for the procreation and the continuation of humanity.

Death and fear tap into the negative current that animates this world, the source of its endless pain and sorrow. Always there are alternating currents, Black and White Magick, the same as the alternating currents that run household appliances. Both positive and negative can be used to open the portals of time. Crowley used them both to unleash the Old Ones, the Titans, the three offspring of Loki: Hell, mistress of the damned; the Midgard Serpent, a euphemism for the constellation of Draco; and the Fenris Wolf, a euphemism for the three-star system of Sīrius – all the metaphorical spawn of H. P. Lovecraft's Cthulhu. They have watched from the inaccessible recesses of the night firmament since time out of mind, existing here only in the darkest corridors of man's collective unconscious for eons untold, awaiting their inevitable return for a reckoning with this God, his angels, his world, his priesthood and all their followers. Crowley wielded these antecedent currents like Musashi Miyamoto wielded a sword. He brought the tyrannical God of Abraham, the God he and the Egyptians called Ptah, to the brink of oblivion. But he was unable to deliver the coup de grace because he did not yet have the "proper substance" with which to do it. He never would, not in his lifetime. But as everyone knows except the cattle, Crowley was prepared to work across as many generations as necessary to get the job done. His Magickal name is Frater Perdurabo, a Latin term meaning "Brother I shall endure to the end."

In The Psychology of the Transference C. G. Jung illustrates eleven stages, eleven perhaps in deference to the Sepher Yetzirah, of the original twenty of what is called the Royal Art or Rosarium philosophorum. The Royal Art is nothing less than the much-talked-about-never-explained Great Work of the "Illuminati" intended to liberate man, or at least themselves, from their parasitical gods. He uses full pages reproduced from the second volume of De Alchimia opuscula complura veterum philosophorum published in Frankfurt in 1550.

    The first four figures and the last figure are arranged like the Sephiroth from the Sepher Yetzirah. There is ten Sephiroth in the Sepher Yetzirah. Three are arranged in columns, or "pillars," on both the left and the right of a "middle pillar" that has four. The left pillar is of demonic severity and the right angelic mercy. In the center from top to bottom are Kether the crown of God, Tiphareth the beauty of the Sun, Yesod the foundation of the Moon, and Malkuth the World. There is an eleventh Sephiroth between Kether and Tiphareth called Da'at, or knowledge, but for the last thousand years Qabalists have debated whether it is fixed or just a temporal understanding of the other ten. It's the same debate the proponents of M-theory in quantum physics engage in with time being the eleventh dimension that makes M-theory work.

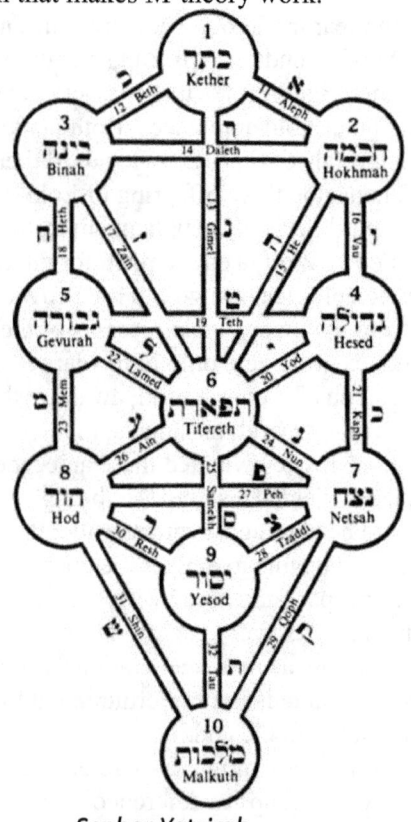

Sepher Yetzirah

In Figure 1 of Rosarium philosophorum, occupying the position of Kether is a two-headed snarling beast whose respective heads spew forth the left and the right pillars. In the Sepher Yetzirah all of the Sephiroth including the Sun and the Moon are interconnected by twenty-two paths. In Rosarium philosophorum the Sun is between the pillar of severity and the middle pillar, and the Moon is between the pillar of mercy and the middle pillar. They each stand alone and separate from the beast, in actuality a six-pointed star that has imprisoned them by encircling them with the world it has vomited forth. They are gazing down below at the mercurial fountain, the only way out. But the caption written in Latin warns: "I make both rich and poor both whole and sick. For healthful can I be and poisonous." (1)

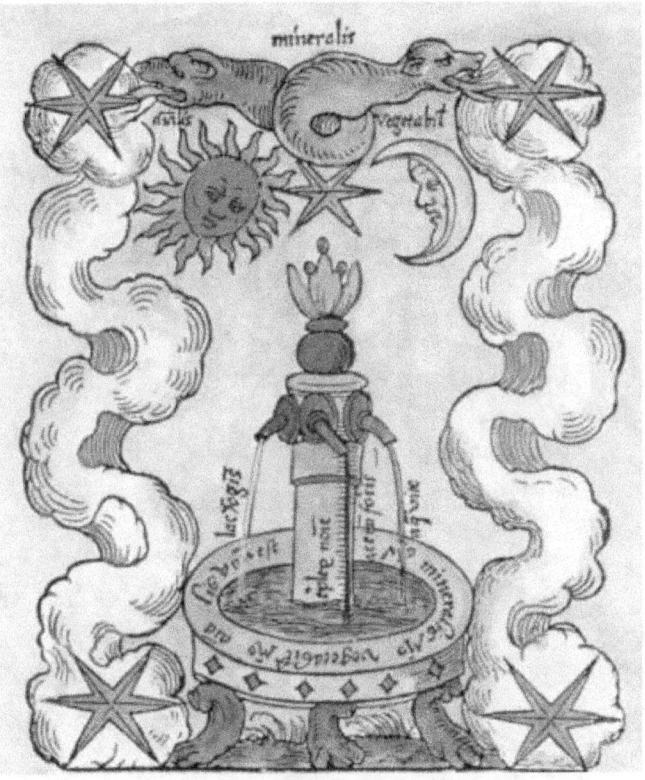

Figure 1

In Figure 2 the king and the queen grasp each other's left hand, and the dove descends on the left side. As Jung notes, Rosarium philosophorum begins as a work of the left-hand path. The six-pointed star from which the dove descends is in this case properly aligned North to South unlike the star that supports the vomiting Beast which is centered East to West. It is in this second stage the practitioner is warned against making the same mistake that has been made by all the others who tried before. Jung gives the text: "Wherefore all error in the art arises because men do not begin with the proper substance and for this reason you should employ venerable nature, because from her through her and in her is our art born and in naught else: and so our magisterium is the work of Nature and not the worker." (2)

Figure 2

Only the Holy Spirit, symbolized by the dove, can sanction the sacred marriage. Rosarium philosophorum is not a Magickal working that can be performed without actually having the two incarnated gods acting as its subject and rules must be broken. The dove expresses sanctioning of those transgressions by the highest power, by a thing beyond good and evil, a star which can never become unbalanced, a thing by which nature itself is just a byproduct. Rosarium philosophorum is far more than an operation; it is an act in accordance with the will of the Supreme Being that takes precedence over everything else. The text warns the practitioner of this most preeminent of all Magickal workings to fear God and be pure because God can see what kind of man he is and may strike him dead at any moment. Those who would dare meddle in such an operation should expect no less. In Figure 3 the king and the queen now stand before each other stripped naked, and the dove descends directly between them. In the banners, the king of souls asks the queen for her hand in marriage, and the queen replies that she cannot refuse him. It is now the six-pointed pact between the king, queen and the Holy Spirit that supplants the world the beast has vomited forth.

Figure 3

In Figure 4 the king and the queen are shown immersed naked together in a bath. In the text the practitioner is told: "Our stone is to be extracted from the nature of the two bodies..." (3)

Figure 4

For the fifth stage of Rosarium philosophorum Jung gives two illustrations. In Figure 5 the king and the queen copulate upon the water of the great sea, what Jung calls the maternal sea, making it synonymous with Binah, the Sephiroth at the top of the Pillar of Severity in the Sepher Yetzirah, in turn synonymous with the waters of the Qabalah.

In verse 20 of The Book of Concealed Mystery we are told by the children of Ptah that in the beginning the world "was formless and void, and darkness upon the face of the deep, and the Spirit of the Elohim vibrating upon the face of the waters." But beneath the waters there are worlds upon worlds "under the form of a vast serpent extending this way and that." This is from a translation by S. L. MacGregor Mathers from Latin to English of Christian Knorr von Rosenroth's The Kabbalah Unveiled published in Latin in 1684.

Mathers continues with vitriolic deist extrapolations of the original Hebrew text which he could not even read himself. Some of the vitriol, in the square brackets, is his. Some, in parentheses, is Rosenroth's, another deist and one of the original apostles of Anglo-Israelism.

Those Who Would Arouse Leviathan

Since the days of John Dee, a contemporary of Rosenroth, Anglo-Israelism has been the unseen current driving the tides of blood and war that have swept first England and the Netherlands then America to world hegemony. It is the fanatical belief by the elite among the Anglo-Saxons, the Frisians, and their progeny that they are the lineal descendants of the Israelites and that the throne of England through the Order of the Garter can be traced back to the House of David in the Bible. Therefore, the Anglo-Saxons and their Frisian allies are Yahweh's chosen people.

Rosenroth and Mathers translation of The Book of Concealed Mystery continues on about Leviathan to verse 29...

"And this dragon hath been castrated since his crest (or membrum genitale), together with his mate, have been repressed, and thence have been formed four hundred desirable worlds. And this dragon hath in his head a nostril (after the manner of whales) in order that he may receive influence, and in himself he containeth all other dragons, concerning which it is said: 'Thou hast broken the heads of the dragons upon the waters' (Ps. lxxiv. 13)."

What Mathers and Rosenroth, together with the lice ridden rabbis who composed the Zohar, neglect to tell their readers is what it says in Ps. lxxiv. 14: "You broke the heads of Leviathan in pieces, and gave him as food to the people inhabiting the wilderness." It is a Judaic tradition that the righteous, which they call Zedeks, will be given a banquet in the afterlife in which the main course will be Leviathan. In the Talmud it is speculated that the feasting will be on the female Leviathan which God has salted and preserved in anticipation of the occasion. The Rashba and the Maharal of Prague, the two greatest rabbis of this millennium, both taught that Leviathan is a spiritual force. The Rashba taught that the feast in the afterlife is necessary to establish an eternal and unbreakable bond between the soul and the physical world. Undeterred by what the most relevant Jews think about Judaism, Mathers and Rosenroth the two Jewish Vikings continue with their botched interpretation of this most evil little book: "There are swellings in his scales (that is, like as in a crocodile; because great in him is the heaping together of judgments). His crest keepeth its own place (that is, there is in him no further power of hastening to things beyond in the Outer). [There is in the destroyer no "hastening to the outer," because he is centripetal and not centrifugal.]"

The tail of the male Leviathan "is in his head (that is, he holdeth his tail in his mouth, in order that he may form a circle, since he is said to encompass holiness). He transferreth his head to behind the shoulders (that is, he raiseth his head at the back of the bride of Microprosopus, where is the place of most severe judgments), and he is despised (since in him is the extremity of judgments and severities, whence wrath is the attribute of his forms). He watcheth (that is, he accurately searcheth out and seeketh in what place he may gain an entry into holiness. And he is concealed (as if laying traps; since he insinuateth himself into the inferiors, by whose sins he hath access to the holy grades, where the carrying out of judgments is committed to him.) He is manifested in one of the thousand shorter days."

None of the parties responsible for the English version of The Book of Concealed Mystery seems to be able to decide whether the female Leviathan is dead or just out of luck because the male has been castrated. What is certain is the male and female Leviathan must never come together "lest they should seek to multiply judgments..." Mathers would die abruptly in 1918 at the age of 64, perhaps another notch on Crowley's evil eye.

Jung gives his translation of the poem used as a caption in Figure 5 of Rosarium philosophorum:

"O Luna Folded in my sweet embrace /
Be you as strong as I, as fair of face.
O Sol, brightest of all lights known to men /
And yet you need me, as the cock the hen."

Jung, no doubt more proficient in Latin than either Mathers or Rosenroth or anybody they may have known, presents the unseen text below the poem: "Then Beya [the maternal sea] rose up over Gabricus and enclosed him in her womb, so that nothing more of him was to be seen. And she embraced Gabricus with so much love that she absorbed him completely into her own nature, and absorbed him into atoms." Jung then provides the Latin text of some verses by Merculinus, a common pseudonym for medieval alchemists, quoted next and not appearing in his illustration. He then gives his translation of the Latin verses below them in parentheses:

"(White-skinned lady, lovingly joined to her ruddy limbed husband, /
Wrapped in each other's arms in the bliss of connubial union, /
Merge and dissolve as they come to the goal of perfection: /
They that were two are made one, as though of one body.)" (4)

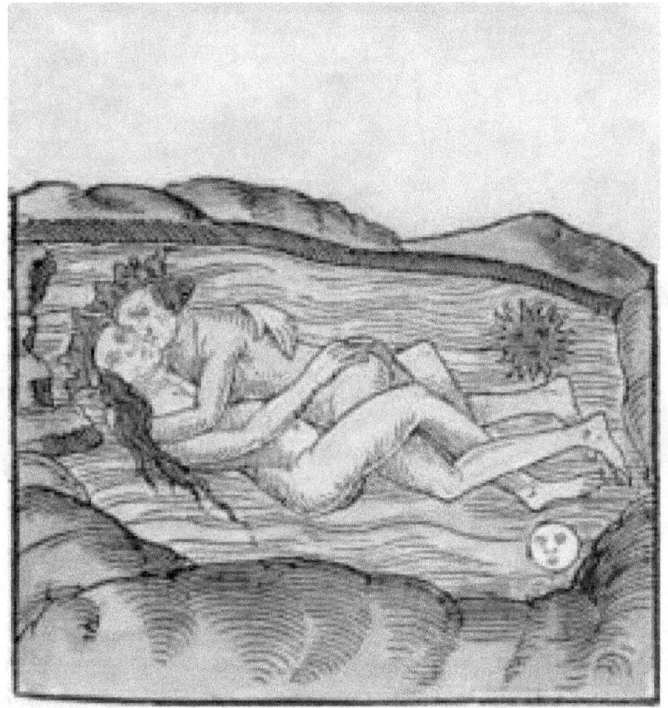

Figure 5

For Figure 5a Jung used what is really illustration 11 in the second volume of De Alchimia opuscula complura veterum philosophorum. The full twenty illustrations were originally woodcuttings that dated well before 1550 and had no text. They were meditation devices. The text was added by a German fraternity, in all likelihood the forerunners of the Rosicrucian's. Illustrations 11- 20 constitute a far darker ethereal inversion of Rosarium philosophorum in another world; a parallel world. An opposing world is entirely in keeping with the present toroidal nature of the interactive hologram impersonating a universe that is being used to incarcerate the collective soul of the human race.

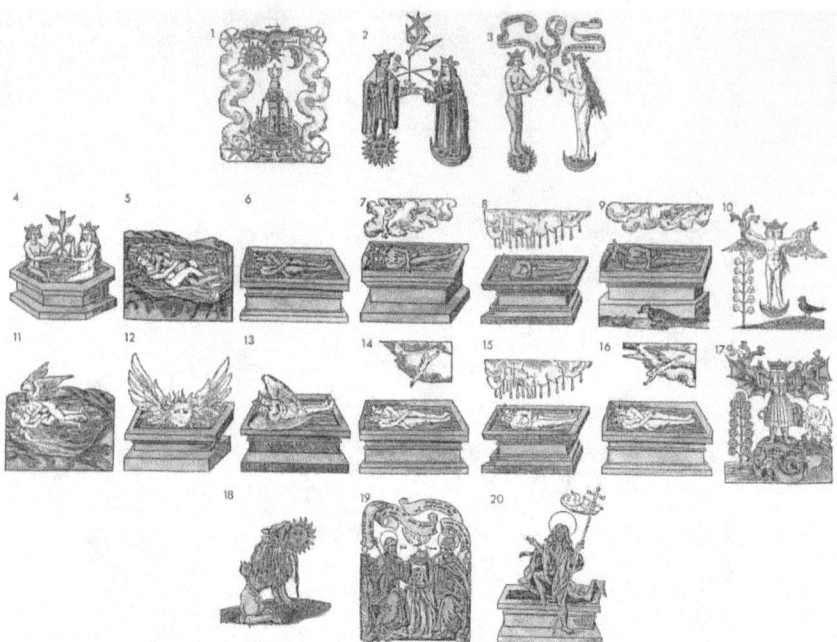

The woodcuttings as they were illustrated in the second edition of De Alchimia opuscula complura veterum philosophorum

"I make both rich and poor both whole and sick. For healthful can I be and poisonous," and poisonous it shall be if the switch is pulled at stage 4 in the hot tub and stage 11 is carried out in the ethereal realm without the sanction of the Holy Spirit, without ever doing the ritual properly in the flesh. If the king and the queen of souls are not ready to die for it, both of them together in the flesh, Rosarium philosophorum produces a lie just like the one currently endured by man, an abomination called Christianity that has led to "a place called Hell."

The last quote is of course from the INXS song "Devil Inside," not so coincidentally featured in the fourth season of Game of Thrones. In the 1988 video for the song, the band members sing and play their instruments as the camera pans into a seedy nightclub named Balboa (Babylon?) featuring the Devil Inside. An electrifying girl drops her coat as she steps up to walk the bar with an attitude as extreme as the curves on her body. The crowd – bay rats, bikers, and sophisticates – along with the musicians look on in awe. A strapping man in a tank top walks up to the bar looking just as hard himself as he is looking at her. They approach each other and break into a violently erotic dance that leaves the onlookers stunned. The bay rats and bikers face off on the edge of war. A limo pulls up bearing another stunningly beautiful hard case of a harlot. She gets out with great fanfare, and the two predatory women momentarily face off. A fat cat in the back of the limo gestures for the first girl to get into the limo, and she complies. As they drive off it can be seen that the Devil is driving the limo. The substitute girl gets on the back of a bike with the guy, and they ride off into the darkness. Bikes and skateboards disperse into the night as the song winds down. (5)

Jung incorrectly interprets the ethereal copulation depicted in Figure 5a as occurring simultaneously with the copulation taking place in Figure 5, mistaking what is actually Figure 11 of an entirely separate sequence for a subconscious representation of Figure 5. He notes the king, and the queen are frequently depicted as "two birds fighting or winged and wingless dragons." For the Dragons he cites the title page of Francesco Colonna's Le Songe de Poliphile, or in Latin Hypnerotomachia Poliphile, an enigmatic and priceless sixteenth century book about a man's surrealistic pursuit of his lover through a fantastically illustrated dreamscape. Hypnerotomachia Poliphile predates De Alchimia opuscula complura veterum philosophorum by half a century.

Le Songe de Poliphile was first printed by Aldus Manutius in Venice in December 1499. Its author is unknown even though it has been dubiously attributed to Francesco Colonna, highly doubtful since he was a Franciscan monk. Le Songe de Poliphile was in all likelihood written by a courtesan, someone more than just a little familiar with royal etiquette. It's been speculatively attributed to various Roman noblemen including Aldus Manutius himself. At the time Venice was a seething cauldron of political intrigue and Magick, the very birthplace of Synarchism and some say National Socialism itself.

In 1510 Antonia Contenta, a Roman noblewoman with the secret backing of the Venetian doge, along with leading Venetian and German merchants, founded the Ordo Bucintoro, an aristocratic trans-generational conspiracy dedicated to bringing about a new aeon and a unified German-Roman Empire. Antonia Contenta, aside from being a Roman patrician by birth, traced her pedigree back to Geoffroy de Saint-Omer. He was tied to her bloodline by her marriage to a nobleman from Burgundy. At the dawn of the 12th century, Burgundy was ground zero for the secrets of the very Cistercians who would establish the Knights Templar. Geoffroy de Saint-Omer was one of the Templar's' nine founding members.

According to the lore, Julietta Montefeltro was the high priestess of the order from 1516-1562. No one knows what happened to her after that, but it is said that during that span she never aged a single day. Men were afraid to look at her because to see her was to become enchanted by her beauty. For half a century she inspired fear and fascination in Europe's aristocracy. Everyone knew she was a sorceress. She came and went from the doge's palace like she owned it. She could be in Rome and Madrid on the same day she was seen being carried on a litter, escorted by two armed men, through the Piazza San Marco

In spite of the family prominence in European history, documentation on Julietta Montefeltro is nonexistent. Her real name was probably Livia Loredan, which is denied in the order's written lore, but her name is sometimes used interchangeably with Montefeltro and sometimes as her successor. Loredan was said to be in possession of "Spiritus Eros," the occult doctrines of the order. Leonardo Loredan was the doge of Venice from 1501-1521. There would be two more Venetian doges from the House of Loredan in the ensuing years and Venice would be the seat of western power...

Figure 5a

Figure 6 shows that both the king and the queen have died, their orgasm culminated by the ultimate act of submission to each other, the submission of self. In death their bodies have fused together and are now interred in their sarcophagus as one, floating lifeless upon the water. To quote Aleister Crowley: "The most favourable death is that occurring during the orgasm, and is called Mors Justi. As it is written: Let me die the death of the Righteous, and let my last end be like his!" (6) Jung interprets the verse in the caption: "Here the King and Queen are lying dead / In great distress the soul has sped." But he notes, "The picture is also entitled 'Conceptio.'" Death is but a transitional state, the seed of something new germinating in the womb of its own putrefaction. Death is conception. "No new life can arise, says the alchemist, without the death of the old." (7)

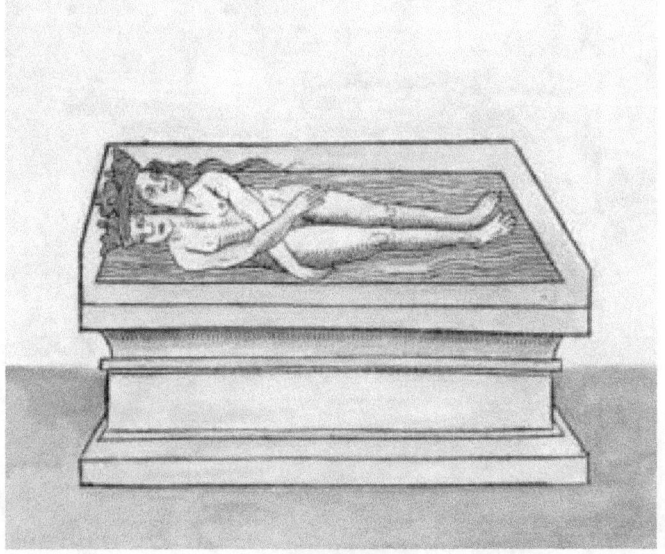

Figure 6

Figure 7 shows the corpse of the king and queen, still interred in their sarcophagus and floating lifeless upon the water. The positions of the heads have switched with the king's now on the left and the queen's on the right, the opposite of how they were depicted in Figure 6. A little man ascends into the clouds. Jung gives the caption: "Here is the division of the four elements / As from the lifeless corpse the soul ascends." (8)

Figure 7

In Figure 8, to say anything more than what is said in the caption would be conjecture. Jung gives the interpretation of the text: "Here falls the heavenly dew, to lave / The soiled black body in the grave." (9)

Those Who Would Arouse Leviathan

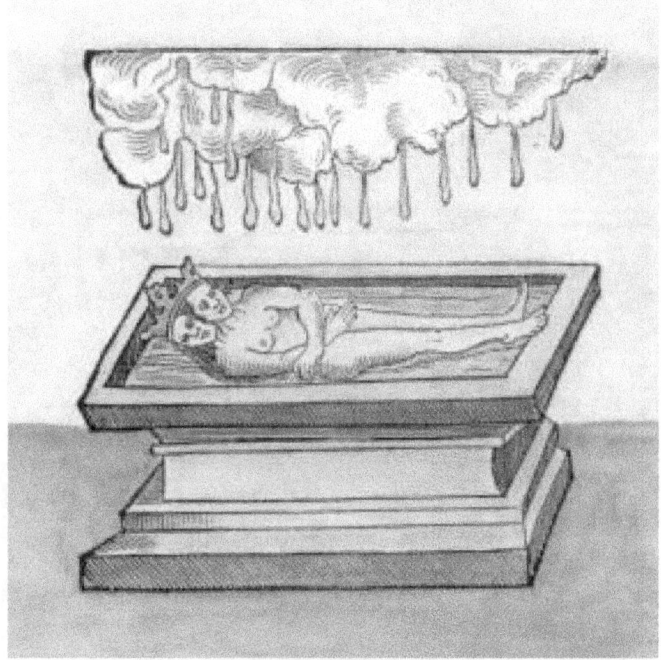

Figure 8

In Figure 9 a little man descends from the clouds as the corpse of the king and the queen still drift aimlessly atop the water in the sarcophagus. Two crows emerge from the depths of the earth and Jung gives the text. "Here the soul descending from on high / to quick the corpse we strove to purify." (10) Failing to grasp the significance of the crows both Jung and all the moldy old alchemical texts that he used for his psychological exegesis of Rosarium philosophorum simply ignore them. The soul is descending from Heaven but the crows which are a symbol of resurrection of the dead are ascending from Hell. This Rosarium philosophorum, this Resurrection has been sanctioned by both the powers of Heaven and Hell...

Figure 9

In Figure 10 there is a Resurrection. The king and queen live again joined as one, crowned astride the Moon, a winged hermaphrodite. They are complete and the Dragons head has broken through the waters. It is the end of all the old powers that drove the creation and the beginning of a new one; theirs. In their left hand they hold aloft the crested serpent over a cockerel, symbolic of the Morning Star. In their right they hold aloft a chalice filled with three crested serpents over a tree from which grow thirteen severed heads, the judgment of the Magi upon the God of Abraham.

The Great Seal of The United States of America

There are thirteen stars in The Great Seal of the United States of America. They are arranged in an occult formula for ascertaining the true names of the Old Testament God. Yahweh and Jehovah are just two of the four-letter anagrams, called a Tetragrammaton by mystics, denoting the God of Abraham. They are false, for it is forbidden to use the correct ones. There are twelve Tetragrammaton's, one for each of the moon's cycles within the year. They are read right to left: HVHY (Jehovah), HHVY (Yahweh), YHVH, HYVH, YHHV, HVYH, VYHH, YVHH, YHHV, HVYH, HHYV, and HYHV. The Zohar says: "Two names of the Tetragrammaton for the first is indeed a perfect name, but the latter is thoroughly and completely perfect." The two names are due to the toroidal nature of this universe, expansion and contraction, or as the Zohar says, "The living creatures rush forth and return."

Much of the Zohar is devoted to the nature of God's beard which is said to be thirteen-fold and must "ascendeth and descendeth." This is represented by the interlocking triangles on the Star of David and the arrangement of the stars on the Great Seal of the United States of America.

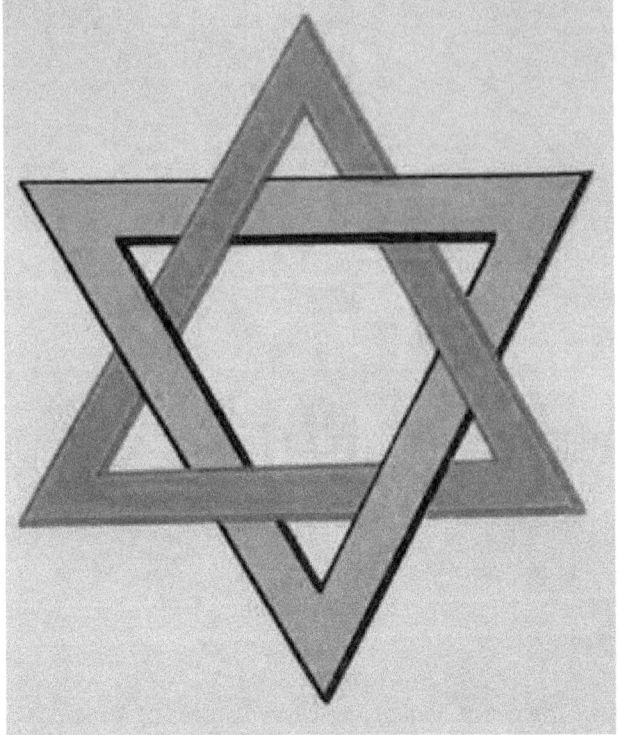

Interlocking triangles

Each of the thirteen stars that form the interlocking triangle on the Great Seal symbolizes a Hebrew letter; each of the letters has a numeric value: Y = 10, H = 5, V = 6. According to Manly Hall's The Secret Teachings of All Ages, "By arranging the four letters of the Great Name I, H, V, and H in the form of the Pythagorean Tetractys, the seventy-two powers of the Great Name of God are manifested." Only ten letters are placed within Hall's Tetractys which is a triangle sitting on its base, but the Zohar is quite clear that the nature of God's beard is thirteen-fold and must "ascendeth and descendeth."

Those Who Would Arouse Leviathan

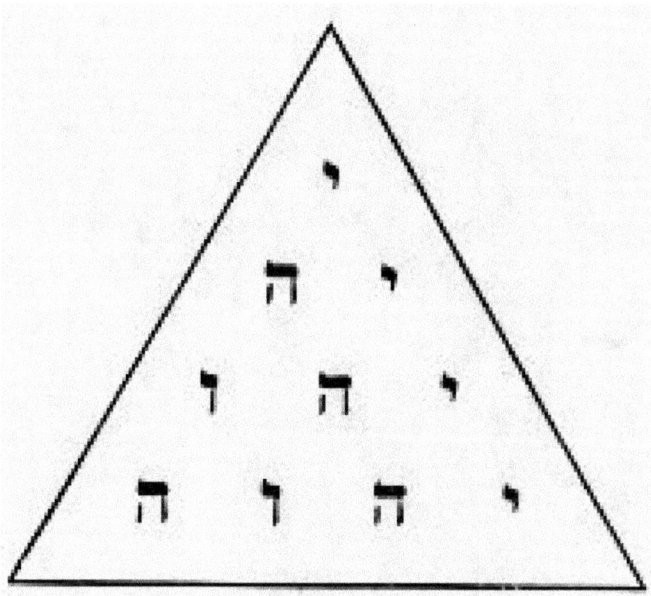

Pythagorean Tetractys

When the triangles are interlocked, the beard "ascendeth and descendeth," and three missing letters must be added to fill in the three empty points on what becomes a six-pointed star. When the letters are arranged according to the rules established by Hall's Pythagorean Tetractys using the full contingent of thirteen letters of the twelve possible combinations read right to left, only HHYV (5-5-10-6) and HYHV (5-10-5-6) when placed in the base of the Pythagorean Tetractys and expanded into thirteen letters will add up to seventy-two. In Hebrew, AChD means unity and AHBH means love. The value of both in Gematria, the most often used Qabalistic code, is thirteen. For this reason, it is often said that thirteen is the number of God in Hebrew.

Jung gives the text for Figure 10, which in actuality is the first four lines of a much longer poem in "German, evidently written about the same time it was printed in the 1550 Rosarium, explaining the nature of the Hermaphroditus as follows:

> Here is born the Empress of all honour /
> The philosophers name her their daughter.
> She multiples / bears children ever again /
> They are incorruptibly pure and without stain..." (11)

Figure 10

By the end of WWI Yeats knew exactly what was coming. The most famous poem in the Michael Robartes and the Dancer collection is "The Second Coming," a stalwart among academics. Yeats begins it: "TURNING and turning in the widening gyre
  The falcon cannot hear the falconer;
  Things fall apart; the centre cannot hold;
  Mere anarchy is loosed upon the world." (12)
  The Egyptian hieroglyph for Horus is the falcon. In the aftermath of WWI's carnage, Yeats sees clearly that nothing can control the God of Vengeance: "The blood-dimmed tide is loosed, and everywhere / The ceremony of innocence is drowned." In the poem's last line Yeats asks, "And what rough beast, its hour come round at last, slouches toward Bethlehem to be born?" (13) Yet he has already described the Beast with all the skill that his prodigious talent as a poet would allow:

"A shape with lion body and the head of a man,
A gaze blank and pitiless as the sun.
Is moving its slow thighs, while all about it
Wind shadows of the indignant desert birds.
The darkness drops again but now I know
That twenty centuries of stony sleep
Were vexed to nightmare by a rocking cradle." (14)

Yeats had been vacillating ever since 1913 when he had slain Michael Robartes in a short story titled "Rosa Alchemica." Right before the turn of the century Yeats had said of his muse: "Michael Robartes is the pride of the imagination brooding upon the greatness of its possessions, or the adoration of the Magi." (15)

But by 1913 it was entirely different. Michael Robartes had now metastasized into one of the Golden Dawn's infamous "hidden masters," the supernatural beings whose disputed existence and direction caused a schism within the group that was settled by Aleister Crowley's pistol. In the story, Robartes appears at his door after a fifteen-year hiatus and forces Yeats with mind-bending incenses to accompany him to a temple by the seaside where they are besieged by an irate Christian mob. During the night Yeats participates in a ceremony with a cult similar to the Golden Dawn. When he awakens in the morning he finds that the ornate temple has now become an old barn, and he is unable to rouse Robartes and the rest of the cult who are in a trance-like sleep. As Yeats flees, Robartes and the cult are stoned to death by an enraged Christian mob. Yeats then waxes poetic as he delivers Robartes' eulogy which is a reflection of his own faltering courage. Yeats renounces the deception of "Legion," like a little Catholic boy renouncing the Devil, wrapped in the imaginary protection of his rosary beads. Yeats' insecurities didn't last long, though. By 1916 his guilt for what they had done combined with his grandiose opinion of himself had convinced him that he was the incarnated Sun God and could pull off the Great Work by himself.

The first two poems in Michael Robartes and the Dancer are about Yeats' own love life. In the first poem, the title poem, Yeats refers to himself as a "half-dead dragon" in the eyes of the much younger Iseult Gonne whom it seems Yeats believed to be the incarnated soul of the Moon. Iseult was herself of magical birth, being conceived in an act of sexual Magick as the aristocracy has been practicing for thousands of years. She was among the kings and queens of Europe a legendary beauty and the daughter of their own residing wild woman Maud Gonne. In his desperation Yeats allowed himself to become convinced that he could perform the Great Work without the necessary pain, bloodletting, and details that his nemesis Crowley and his followers were apparently reveling in by 1916. Crowley says of himself in the author's note of Moonchild that by 1917 he was exerting his best "efforts to bring America into the war." To Crowley and his aristocratic followers, WWI was not a struggle between nations but a Holocaust, a Blood Sacrifice, Burnt Offerings to bring about the incarnation of Horus and the killing of the old grey world and its tyrannical God.

Undaunted our hero, the rejected self-appointed Sun God, next proposed to Maud Gonne whom he believed to be the rest of the Pagan female pantheon. Rejected again the intrepid pseudo Sun God married his fellow Golden Dawn initiate, twenty-four-year-old Georgie Hyde-Lees, the witch of "Solomon and the Witch," the second poem of the Robartes collection. Yeats proposals all took place in 1916, a year in which he was obviously desperate to marry. The year 1916 appears in another verse of the collected works. "Easter, 1916" is a poem first published back in 1916. On the surface it appears to be about Irish nationalism but contains the line "When sleep at last has come on limbs that had run wild," a sentence that could be interpreted pornographically. Easter is also the day of resurrection in Yeats' Christian security blanket. Regardless of the ambiguity of "Easter, 1916," Yeats' meaning in "Solomon and the Witch," the second poem of Michael Robartes and the Dancer, is perfectly clear.

"AND thus declared that Arab lady:
'Last night, where under the wild moon
On grassy mattress I had laid me,
Within my arms great Solomon," (16)

Most of the works translated from Latin by Jung were originally written in Aramaic; in Aramaic works such as Turba Philosophorum, Solomon is the Sun God.

"I suddenly cried out in a strange tongue
Not his, not mine.'
And he that knew
All sounds by bird or angel sung" (17)

They were speaking gibberish to each other in the heat of passion. Yet Yeats no doubt convinced himself and her that they were speaking Enochian, a language either discovered or invented by John Dee, which according to occult traditions like those of the Golden Dawn was the authentic angelic language.

"Answered: 'A crested cockerel crew
Upon a blossoming apple bough
Three hundred years before the Fall,
And never crew again till now,
And would not now but that he thought,

> Chance being at one with Choice at last,"
> "All that the brigand apple brought
> And this foul world were dead at last.
> He that crowed out eternity
> Thought to have crowed it in again.
> A lover with a spider's eye
> Will find out some appropriate pain," (18)

Yeats expresses his longing for vindication of man's expulsion from paradise and a desire for vengeance. During a vision of Walpurgis Night in Moonchild, Crowley depicts God as an "enormous spider" who sits at the center of a web with strands made up of all the other gods man has ever worshiped. So, when Yeats says, "A lover with a spider's eye will find out some appropriate pain," he is again expressing he and his Luciferian brethren's thirst for vengeance.

> "Aye, though all passion's in the glance,
> For every nerve: lover tests lover
> With cruelties of Choice and Chance;
> And when at last that murder's over
> Maybe the bride-bed brings despair
> For each an imagined image brings
> And finds a real image there;
> Yet the world ends when these two things,
> Though several, are a single light,
> When oil and wick are burned in one;
> Therefore, a blessed moon last night
> Gave Sheba to her Solomon.'
> 'Yet the world stays':
> 'If that be so, Your cockerel found us in the wrong
> Although he thought it worth a crow.
> Maybe an image is too strong
> Or maybe is not strong enough.'
> 'The night has fallen;
> not a sound In the forbidden sacred grove
> Unless a petal hit the ground,
> Nor any human sight within it
> But the crushed grass where we have lain;
> And the moon is wilder every minute.
> Oh, Solomon! let us try again." (19)

Yet the world ends when oil and wick are burned in one – this is the part that always scared schoolchildren like Yeats playing at being Magi. They use images conjured while they are in the throes of sexual ecstasy or murdering little children. It's always that murder that is over and never this one, their own. That's why the bride-bed always brings despair and the world stays. Cowardice dictates that their cockerel always will find them in the wrong and that they will never be worth but a single crow. But always they will try again because to them it's nothing but fine entertainment. In one of the woodcuttings in Le Songe de Poliphile, the lovers are hacked to pieces and their severed limbs fed to the beasts of the forest; in others the severed limbs are steeped in a vat filled with the amniotic fluid of the wind. The Royal Art is not for squeamish peasants and must be carried out with the conviction of a king and a queen. Figure 6 must take place in this world, not in some forbidden sacred grove in a phantasmagorical parallel world.

Crowley had been performing terminal sexual Magick at least since the Amalantrah Working. In 1924 Mussolini would expel him from Italy when a young nobleman died at his abbey from the practice. He was advising candidates in what he called the rite of "Eroto-Comatose Lucidity." The object was to prolong intercourse through "every known means. Every device and artifice of the courtesan is to be employed, and every stimulant known to the physician." When delirium is achieved so is commune with the sublime, and when finally, the orgiastic carnality can no longer be continued Crowley advised his supplicants "the Initiate may then be allowed to sleep, or the practice may be renewed and persisted in until death ends all. The most favourable death is that occurring during the orgasm, and is called Mors Justi..." [20]

Throughout the second half of the twenties, Crowley would continue his quest to "die the death of the Righteous" [21] in France with any of the West's more adventuresome elitists who were willing to participate. In 1928 France would finally ask Crowley to leave because by then they knew his sympathies lay with Germany in a war over a decade away but already as inevitable as the next sunrise. Crowley would go to his beloved Germany for a while, but 1933 would find him back in England where he had come to get some satisfaction in her courts about the slander the British intelligence services were busy spreading about him all over Europe and America.

Perhaps for reasons known only to himself (because he was much smarter than that) after taking Figure 11 and calling it 5a, Jung chose to dismiss the entire second half of Rosarium philosophorum as a "concession to feminine psychology." He said, "The first series of pictures is followed by a second – less complete, but otherwise analogous – series, at the end of which there appears a masculine figure, the 'emperor,' and not, as in the first, an 'empress,' the 'daughter of the philosophers.' The accentuation of the feminine element in the Rebis (Fig. 10) is consistent with the predominantly male psychology, whereas the addition of an 'emperor' in the second version is a concession to a woman (or possibly male consciousness)." (22)

Miguel Serrano was one of the very few writing about the occult in the twentieth century who grasped the significance of what he called the union between the He and the She. Serrano, one of Jung's closest personal friends, accused the great psychologist of attempting to "psychologize" the raison d'être of human existence with his clinical analysis of Rosarium philosophorum. It is Serrano's contention, and that of the SS for whom Serrano is speaking, that this timeline where everything that's bad is good and everything that's good is bad only still exists as a prison for the human soul because Rosarium philosophorum has never been properly performed.

The king and the queen of souls, even if incarnated into the flesh, are not a natural man and a natural woman; they are the templates by which man and woman are made. There are many worlds, and the king and the queen of souls exist in each and every one of them simultaneously. In the second set of figures illustrating Rosarium philosophorum, the operation has been diverted to just such a world, one that Yeats called the "forbidden sacred grove." In the sacred grove the king and the queen are what Jung called vapores, or fumi, spirits with wings; that is how they copulate. The thing is that this is a completely Black operation and is sanctioned by neither the Holy Spirit nor Hell itself. There are no crows in this operation, and it leaves the Sun – the true soul of the king – trapped alone in his sarcophagus.

Figure 12

It is a soulless king who dies with the queen in this phantasmagorical dream world where nothing ever really dies, and therefore nothing new can ever really be created.

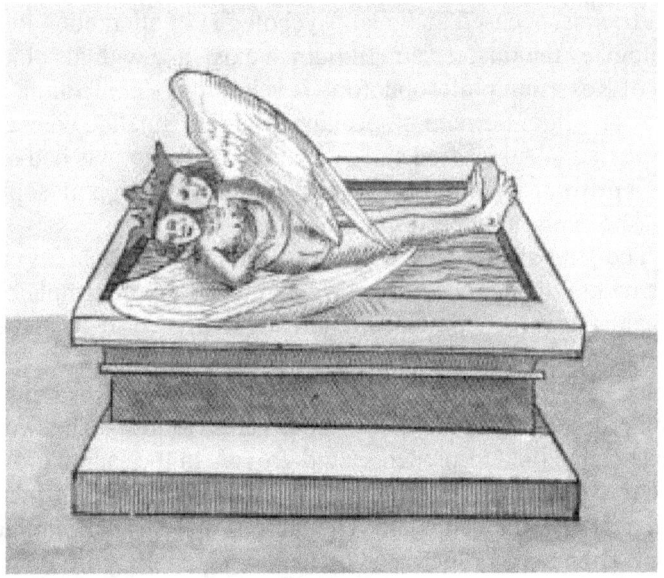

Figure 13

Consequently, since there is no male soul it must be the woman's soul that leaves the nuptial sarcophagus and ascends into the clouds above.

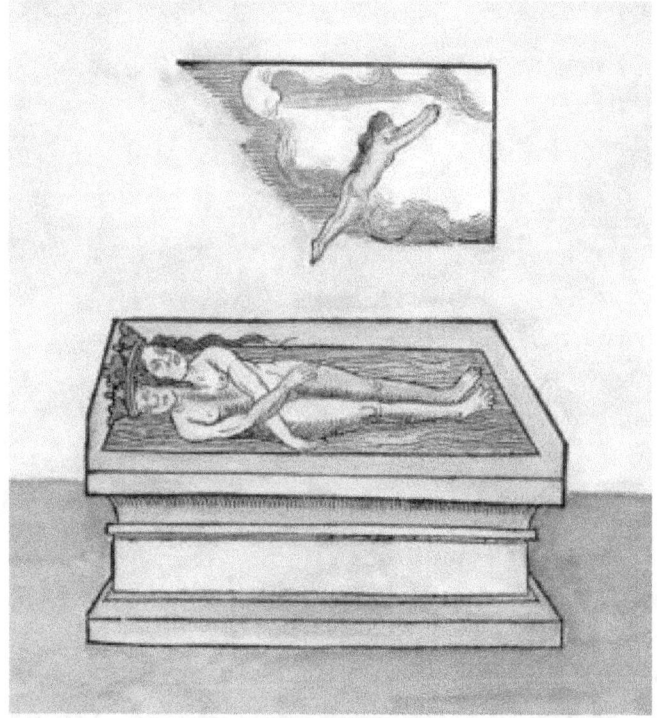

Figure 14

And it is a woman's soul that descends from the clouds to reanimate the corpse in Figure 16. There are no crows present because nothing has really died. There can be no resurrection. Hell, which is simply a name for the many worlds of the dead along with the great Goddess Hell, whose name is eponymous to those worlds which she rules, has been bypassed.

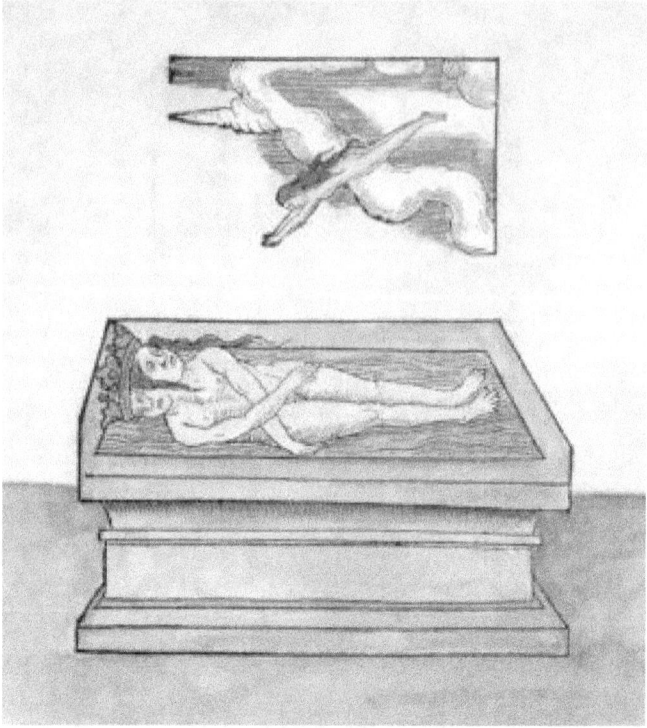

Figure 16

In Figure 17, instead of a super being motivated by female empathy and fortified by the convictions and courage of a man, a monster is born into the world. It is not an empress at all but rather an emperor motivated only by male cruelty fueled by an insatiable appetite for judgments. However, it is a cruelty carried out through female deception. His wings of a dove have been replaced with the wings of a bat, a creature of the darkness; he stands upon his own judgments, which devour themselves. Behind him crouches a ravenous lion, and he holds aloft the crested serpent over the pillar of mercy, where now the young must be fed with the flesh of their mother. In the pillar of severity, the judgments of the Magi are upon the Sun God. It is his severed heads that now hang from the tree.

Figure 17

This is the current world, the world man "lives" in, a Christian world. In Figure 18, the ravenous lion finally devours the Sun, forever cursing a world gone bad to exist in eternal darkness and live a relentless lie.

Figure 18

There is a rumor from beyond the veil of a thousand years that it was Mary Magdalene who brought Christianity to the South of France, references in Sagas from time out of mind to women on a mighty mountain, wave maidens, and supernatural women. They are led by a goddess named Freyja who has her own heaven called Folkvang coterminous with Valhalla. According to the Prose Edda, of those brave men killed in battle "one half of the slain belong to her, and the other half to Odin." Freyja has had many names; she has been all over the world searching for her lost lover, crying golden tears. Tacitus the Roman historian makes mention of the inexplicable worship of Isis among the ancient Teutonic tribes. There is Venusberg in German and Mont de Venus (Mountain of Venus) in French. There is an old Germanic story of a knight who after slaking his carnal desires with the women of the forbidden mountain seeks forgiveness from the pope who gives him only dead roses. When the Goddess finds out she makes the roses bloom. Wagner's famous opera Tannhäuser is based on the story.

Tannhäuser in the Venusberg by John Collier, 1901

It is the pope's deepest, darkest secret that there never was a man named Jesus, but there was a woman with many names because she has been all over the world crying golden tears searching for her lost lover. Jesus is really a woman – or more correctly a goddess. That is the real reason a war of extermination was waged upon the Cathars, for they knew this. The seed of the secret was preserved by the Knights Templar and planted in Venice through the Ordo Bucintoro and their 'Spiritus Eros' in the sixteenth century. The twenty woodcuttings, an abbreviated version of Le Songe de Poliphile, are the result. In Figure 19 She is crowned Queen of Heaven by the Father and the Son.

Figure 19

In Figure 20 she steps furtively from her sarcophagus. She is still wearing her hair in the same manner she has worn it in the other sixteen woodcuttings that depicted her, but now she has a beard. She has become Jesus, the Alpha and the Omega, charged with saving herself as the exiled soul of the human race. Alone, she is not up to it. Behind her head is ostensibly an oversized halo that is in reality the Moon. In her left hand, to quote Guns n' Roses, she carries "the cross of homicide" that will bring a thousand years of pain and suffering to the world. No good has ever come of a lie.

Figure 20

CHAPTER 38

As I studied all this, I began to notice bright green hairs growing from my head. I plucked them out and never told anyone until now. The day finally rolled around when I would start my sentence. I popped about a dozen Valiums and met Wolf in court to appear before Judge Vaughn and be remanded to the Suffolk County jail. Vaughn was a pompous pig of a man, corpulent and red-faced from years of alcohol abuse. Everyone had informed me that he was Suffolk County's "hanging judge." He thought he was going to lecture me. I ended up lecturing him. Wolf told me later that he had never seen anyone get away with talking to Vaughn the way I did. With the price of admission, I was paying, I was going to get my money's worth. I was sent to the "Farm" where I slept for two days. When I finally woke up I was called out of the dorm and met by a correctional officer who was a fan of my sister. The correctional officer had me moved to the kitchen dorm and gave me a pack of cigarettes.

There were about a hundred guys crammed into a single dorm with no air conditioning. There were six dorms for inmates in the Yaphank barracks. Most of the inmates slept on double bunks. There were about a dozen single bunks in the back of each dorm, mostly divided equally among the Black and the White sections. The kitchen dorm was infested with roaches and mice and smelled like shit and used socks. They gave me the bottom of a double bunk in the front, but for the next two days I stayed by the glass-encased CO station all night reading under its lights. I had a new book to go along with my mother's new boyfriend, Marty Myers, who owned Total Health, the intellectual hub of Long Island's Occult and New Age movements.

The book was titled The Greatest Story Never Told: A Scientific Inquiry into the Evidence of the Fall of Man from a Higher Civilization in Antiquity. Signed by author Lana Corrine Cantrell, it was written as a thesis for a medical degree and privately published as a book. A used copy now sells on Amazon for over a thousand dollars. Cantrell uses her medical training along with a thorough exegesis of the Vedas and insights derived from Zecharia Sitchin's interpretations of Sumerian cuneiform to present a theory that man's actual life span should be about a thousand years, the same as the biblical patriarchs. Cantrell makes a medically documented case that the original skin color of the human race is green and that the different races all suffer from having adapted to breathing an oxygen-depleted atmosphere, forcing their blood to turn from its original copper-rich blue to red. All three races – Mongoloid, Negroid, and Caucasian – suffer from various afflictions due to a shortage of copper in the bloodstream. Caucasians are affected the worst with deleterious conditions being more pronounced the lighter the skin is. Cantrell points out hieroglyphic tracts that talk about the pharaohs sending in their shock troops that they called "the kilted ones." Cantrell also has a doctorate in archeology. She uses her medical and archeological training to produce a lucid argument that the kilted ones were the ancestors of the Celts. In the pre-diluvian age, human civilization was concentrated in the Mesopotamian and Indus valleys. There the Caucasian was bred only for war. It is Cantrell's contention that the White man's aggressive disposition, which is symptomatic of his medical condition, makes him an unsuitable ruler of the world.

I only had to run the big industrial dishwasher after each meal, and I was allowed to take whatever I wanted from the kitchen that was loaded with fresh produce from their farm in Yaphank. Just when I was starting to think it wouldn't be too bad, some big Black guy comes over to me and tries to give me a mop and a bucket telling me, "I'm the dorm rep Mr. Floyd. Everyone who comes in this dorm has to take a turn cleaning the bathroom." I said, "First of all, Floyd, you better forget about me ever calling you Mister. And if you don't get out of here with that mop I'm going to be forced to beat you to death with it." It started a big thing in the dorm, but some of the Black guys in there knew me from the streets and advised Floyd, a former sergeant from the Vietnam War who had the younger kids calling him "Sergeant Floyd," that I was extremely dangerous. I told him that he could not be the dorm rep anymore because I was. He could be second-in-command. Actually, I had gone in there with every intention of beating the fuck out of the first suitable victim, and when Floyd showed up waving that mop around I figured he was volunteering for the job. I then made an announcement to the dorm that I would be taking a single bunk in the back and didn't care which side it was on, declaring, "You all look like sub creatures to me!" The White guys quickly made a bed for me. The one little shrimp who had to be moved to a double bunk objected, but he wasn't even worth swatting. I put him down to be dealt with later.

My behavior was causing a furor amongst the Blacks, who made up the majority of the dorm. At the time, the Five Percent Nation of Islam was taking America's prison population by storm, and the kitchen dorm contained all the ones who had juice in Suffolk County and weren't going upstate for long "bids." They were insisting to Floyd that he must represent the Black race against me in a death match in the basement of the kitchen. I told them anyone who thought they could do it was welcome to go down in that basement with me; Floyd was the only one with any real balls. The next day he did, and they locked the door behind us. I knew he didn't want to fight me, so when we got down the steps I said to him, "You know, Floyd, these guys are fucking crazy. Where the fuck they think they are? Attica? Yeah, you and I should kill each other in the basement so that one of us will die and one of us will catch a body. I say we go back up there and tell them that we are co-dorm reps now." Floyd liked that idea. He was scheduled to be released in two weeks anyway. So that's just what we did. My first official act as co-dorm rep was to have the little shrimp White guy who had objected to my taking his single bunk beaten up and thrown out of the dorm by the Blacks. They liked this, and it helped loosen racial tensions in the dorm considerably.

I started an intense regimen of training with a couple of Black guys and a couple of White guys. In no time I was doing a thousand pushups between chairs and a thousand dips between the bunks along with about a dozen sets of curls with up to two hundred pounds and other weight training in the yard every day. It wasn't long before every young stud in the dorm was trying to keep up with me. Nobody could. Martial arts were practiced in the bathroom, out of sight of the correctional officers, with a lot of Black guys remarking about how glad they were that they had not tried me when I first came in the dorm. Keeping in mind that I had actually grown a couple of green hairs not a month earlier and that I had seen Eric's blue blood the one time he injected heroin with us, I kept reading that book and supplemented it with everything Nietzsche and Plato ever wrote.

Yaphank Correctional Facility became my personal kingdom just like the strip clubs had been. But this one had correctional officers, so I had no use for violence in this kingdom. I didn't need it anyway. I controlled the food for all six hundred inmates. Once again everyone was "trying to please me." I had four lockers; one was filled with cigarettes and one with pornography. When you wanted to jerk off, I gave you something from the "library" and told the other inmates to keep out of the bathroom. You gave me some cigarettes. I had a very extensive pornography collection because everyone who was leaving jail gave whatever they had to me. I found a Hustler magazine that featured as its centerfold a woman who looked just like Dianne doing it from a kneeling position on top of the guy. I didn't loan that one out. That one I personally used a half-dozen times daily. I would like to say that the CO's at some point started looking at me strangely, but they had been looking at me strangely ever since I had come through the gates. One day they took me out of the dorm for what they said was some kind of routine examination. The exam lasted for hours with one woman "doctor" questioning me about every facet of my life before I had come in there. She was particularly interested to know how I had gotten the scar across my left rib cage, the one I had from my communing with the leprechaun on the night after I had stomped Annie V. I lied to her, which I never do to anyone. I figured, "Fuck these people!" I knew what the game was now, and I also knew that they weren't supposed to be making the rules. I was. I didn't take any drugs or even smoke pot during the time I was in there – not that there wasn't plenty of stuff available. The Bay Rats had even brought me some pot during one of their visits to me. I took a couple of hits off a joint and gave the rest away. I knew I was metamorphosing and didn't want anything interfering.

Those Who Would Arouse Leviathan

Every night after Muslim prayer the Five Percenters would spread their prayer rugs in a circle and do what they called "knowledge lectures" for hours. They never played cards or did any of the frivolous, stupid things that the White guys did that I refused to participate in. I heard them calling each other gods, and I was fascinated. I told them that what they believed in and what I believed in were basically the same thing. Aleister Crowley had taught that every man and every woman is the terrestrial manifestation of a star. We are all gods. We are all stars. There were about thirty of them, and at least twenty wanted me to be the first White man to ever sit in on a knowledge lecture. The ones who objected did so because I ate pork and was a "White blue-eyed devil." I pointed out to them that I had brown eyes, that a couple of them had blue eyes, and the book I had been reading every day like it was a Bible said exactly the same thing about White people being human devils. They told me to wait two days when "Knowledge" was coming in on the next transport from upstate so that they could ask him. He was an acknowledged spiritual leader of the Five Percent Nation of Islam. When Knowledge arrived in the dorm a couple of days later, I was not disappointed.

He was an extremely intelligent and articulate brother. He told me he had been hearing about me upstate and would be glad to have me sit in on the knowledge lectures but that I had to stop eating pork. I asked him what the big deal was about eating pork, and he explained, "The pig is genetically modified from a human being, and eating pork was the same as being a cannibal." Cantrell had been saying the same thing in her book but was saying it backwards, as I was told. Cantrell asserted that the human had been genetically modified from the pig and that evolutionists deliberately lied about this when they claimed that apes were man's closest relatives in the animal family. She proves her point about pigs being genetically closest to man beyond a shadow of a doubt when she indicates that only pig organs can be successfully transplanted into humans. I wanted to hear the rest of the knowledge lectures and certainly didn't want to be a cannibal, so that was the last day in my life that I have ever deliberately eaten pork, or anything cooked with it.

The basic premise of the Five Percenters was that Islam is the religion of the "natural man" but not that all Muslims were gods. They believed that "only five percent could ever be gods" and that "the gods must rule over the others." It was similar to what the Spartans believed about other Greeks which the Spartans called Helots. However, Five Percenters did not believe that a man's ability to be a god was passed through lineage like the Spartans thought. In fact, when pressed, Knowledge could not say with certainty whether a man even had to be

Muslim or Black to be a god. This was my reason for attending the lectures. The first thing he did when he got to Yaphank was to ban the praying by those who were in "the Nation." He told them that "a god does not grovel before another god." In The Secret Gospel of Thomas, Jesus tells his disciples, "If you pray, you will be condemned." Then he tells them, "Do not tell lies, and do not do what you hate, for all things are plain in the sight of heaven." Heaven knows who you are and what you want.

I was told that "At one time before the White man's history, the Black man ruled over the earth, but he ruled haughtily. His punishment for this is the current epoch of bad karma and the White man's subjugation of the Black man. This epoch will soon be coming to an end, and the Black man shall once again assume his rightful place on the thrones of the earth." All over the southern foot of the Mexican valley, giant stone heads of brooding Black kings have been unearthed. They are fixed with defiant stares as if daring the defilers of history to explain them. Many of the stone heads have been disfigured and deliberately buried by Mayan populations as though having committed some unforgivable crime. I told them what I knew that verified what Knowledge was teaching them. Sometimes I would speak for long periods during the knowledge lectures, and it was the most comfortable I ever was among a group of people. I stopped combing and cutting my hair because no natural man does these things as indicated by the story of Samson and Delilah in the Bible. This was not a rule. There weren't really any rules for a god, only that "he must conduct himself at all times with dignity."

Sometime during all this, Phil came to jail. His first meal was sneaked in on the food cart, a twelve-pound eye round roast beef cooked to perfection by a CO cook just for the occasion. I sent notice to the dorm rep of the dorm he was in that Phil was to be extended every courtesy they could think of and that whoever thought of extra courtesies would get extra food. I only saw Phil maybe once or twice while he was there because to see him I had to deliver a food cart. When I did he told me, "I'm tired of Richey's gangster shit. He's now clearing over a hundred thousand dollars a week, and what is he giving us? A couple? I found a really hot looking barmaid named Janine. You're really gonna like her. Me and her are getting an apartment. My mother is on her own and so are you. You don't need me there. Go back and get Dianne. That's all you want out of those places anyway. I took a truckload of fireworks from Joey already, and he ain't getting a dime. I am going to try to get more as soon as I get out of here. They can consider that my severance pay. When I took over that agency for them they were supposed to give a real union and real benefits to the dancers. Now they're not even paying the new girls. They are only working for tips. My father was a union man. I should shoot both of them right through the fucking head. But I know you got to go back there. I'm only staying until then. You get out of here you're on your own. I'm out of there!" I tried to talk him out of it, but Phil was adamant. He said, "They think this is a fucking Monopoly game, and the one with all the money left at the end wins. They replaced you on weekends with Sergeant Slaughter from the World Wrestling Federation and another guy named Mark who used to be Bruno Samartino's tag team champion partner. Richey bills them as guest bouncers. All they do is sit in the corner all night. Jimmy is the only real bouncer. They're going to get me killed. I'll be leaving before that even comes close to happening. Tell Richey that John is your new partner. One day Richey's not going to be able to get his key in the lock because someone broke a toothpick off in it."

    Every night a brilliant star would remain suspended over the Black section in the overhead windows around the top of the dorm walls. The hotter it got that summer the brighter the star seemed to burn. Everyone asked me what star it was, but I had no answers for them. No one slept until it was really late, and I never seemed to at all. I read all night by flashlight. One night when I was the only one up in the dorm, I glanced up from my reading and noticed all the lights were out in the hallway and the CO Booth. Beyond the bars that sealed the front of the dorm there were shadowy figures moving around in the darkness. There must have been at least a half-dozen of them. They were dancing widdershins just like the dwarf I had seen when I was a small boy. I wasn't the only one who saw this; some of the Five Percenters also had. One told me confidentially, "I always wake up late every night when everyone else is sleeping. I have seen stuff here with the walls where things are just in the wrong places. I have never been so scared in my life. I don't want to know what's going on in here. I just want to do my time and get far away from here." We were speaking right under the observation booth when I heard the correctional officer inside answer the phone's incessant ringing. He picked the receiver up and sharply reported "Antichrist!"

    When my uncle and my cousin Andrew finally came for me in the middle of August, I was ready for anything, but I had only one order of business. I remember I hardly said a word. I watched out the window as the sweltering heat bore us westbound on the Long Island Expressway. I put on my Walkman and listened to "Rocket Queen." I had been introduced to Appetite for Destruction by some of the younger White guys while I was in Yaphank. I knew I was expected to follow the script, but so was she. At the end of that song, which was the end of the album, she gave it up to me.

Wisdom / חכמה

CHAPTER 39

In the east lay negation and the west damnation so we travel north and south just to stay alive. As soon as I went home I did about a thousand sit ups on the slant board and found out from my mother that Jim had everything under control with the business. I put on my hat, black leather pants, and the skimpiest tank top I could find. It was past seven, show time. I got a ride up there from Geir who was working for me in the daytime and Richey at night. I knew she was still in Gaslight because Marlena had been watching her for me, but I went in Bogart's first to see Phil. Janine was working Bogart's. Phil had been right. I couldn't believe he had pulled a girl that looked like her. He introduced us and I looked at her and I looked at him as I said with a smile "you still owe me for all this motherfucker." Phil laughed and said, "if it wasn't for you I would have quit three months ago." I said, "well this ain't gonna take long. Stick around." Phil said "yea. Well I got one of my guest bouncers working next door. Make sure you scare the shit out of him. Fucking moron thinks he's on TV. He wears red and purple suits with more gold chains than Mr. T." I said "You mean Richey's got my girl working with a TV actor? You might be breaking that tooth pick off in his front door lock sooner than you think." Phil laughed and said "yea Marks gonna take Dianne Rodney from you. Wait till you see this guy. He's over forty and he seems like his brain is addled from the experimental steroids he tells me he gets from the Israeli Defense Forces. I'll tell you what she sure hasn't been pining away for you. She's making big fucking money again. All her regulars are back, and she's added a few more pretty boys you're really gonna like."

We didn't say anything else. We walked in silence next door. My blood was already cold from the fact that she had never come to see me. She had said that she might. I hadn't expected her too, but really I had. By now I had striations on me I had never seen on another human being before. I looked like I stepped right out of a comic book. I used to catch the other guys in the dorm admiring me when I had my shirt off

Those Who Would Arouse Leviathan

and they thought I wasn't looking. I had never felt more like a living God in my life but still I knew this wasn't going to be easy. Dianne was a living Goddess and deep down inside she knew where we both were going, and she wasn't through with playtime yet.

She was up on stage when we entered the packed bar. She saw me right away and tried to pretend like she didn't, averting her eyes from me. Phil was saying "c'mon over and meet Mark." But it was show time. I walked over to the stage and every customer within five chairs of me got up and went to the bar. I looked up at her and said over the music "nice of you to come and see me." Our eyes met and I knew she still loved me when I saw hers start to gloss over. She said "and Charlie? What was I going to tell him? He knows about you. If he ever thought I went to see you that would be the end of our relationship." I said "yea. Well your relationship with Charlie just ended anyway. They'll be no more excuses. You don't have any legitimate ones anymore. You started all this, not me, on the day you called Mesha. Now I'm going to finish it and there ain't no power on earth that can stop me." paraphrasing the Rolling Stones from the song Dead Flowers, I said ""I know you think you're the queen of the underground" and you are. But I'm the king so don't even try to send me any dead flowers." She started crying and ran through the back door of the stage and locked herself in the backroom. As I entered the tunnel towards the backroom door a three-hundred-and-fifty-pound man with a chest like a garbage pail, wearing a purple suit, about a hundred gold chains around his neck, and a black version of Donald Trump's hair piece, tried to stop me. He held out his arm in front of me and said, "only employees are allowed back there." I grabbed him by the neck and slammed him against the wall. Gold chains went bouncing all over the floor. Phil got me off of him and I continued to the backroom door palm heeling it off its hinges. She was by the sink crying and I grabbed her to kiss her, but she turned her head away sobbing even as she embraced me with every ounce of strength in her body. She said, "you just can't do this like this." I said "why not? You see I just did. Didn't I?" She was still sobbing when she said, "I know I said we would talk about it and we will, but don't you think your rushing things?" I hugged her back and she put her face in its usual place buried in my chest saying "you don't know how many times I wanted to come up there and see you. Ask Gracie. She was supposed to take me up there just last week, but he figured out some excuse why I couldn't go out with her. He checks the mileage on my car every day. And he doesn't let me out of his sight except to work. He knows all about you." I said "maybe if you didn't talk about me all the time right in front of him he wouldn't. This is it Dianne. You have to just break it off with the guy. I'm not in the mood for any more games. If you don't I'll make sure you dance in an empty bar every day while I fuck a different dancer every night. How would you like that? If I were you that would kill me. In fact, you are killing me right now and I'm not going to die alone." We held each other like that for the better part of a half hour. I could smell the sweat on her body, and it smelled just as sweet as her hair. I finally let go of her and told her to go fix her makeup in the bathroom.

When I walked out from the backroom Phil said "I told you to scare the shit out of him not strangle him in front of the whole bar. I told you. She's still playing games. How long do you think this is going to take? I can't stay here for the whole thing. Joey Massera wants the money for the fireworks and Richey keeps telling me I got to pay him. I'm gonna shoot Richey in the face and then it will be over anyway. If you want we'll kidnap her, and you take her to a cabin in the woods somewhere and rape the shit out of her. By the time you're done she'll love only you. Me and Gracie already talked about it. Gracie thinks that's exactly what you should do. Dianne probably fantasizes about that while she's fucking Charlie. By the way I got you a gold chain."

'A cabin in the woods', no doubt that would have worked for all parties involved, except maybe God himself. There are rules to the performance of The Great Work. In the Tractatus aureus the practitioner is warned in the third stage to "put away the vice of arrogance" to be "righteous", and above all else "to fear God who seeth what manner of man thou art." But that's why I was calling the shots and not them. God must abide by the rules only as long as the practitioner does. A 'little mistake' like that and God can bring to bear all the wrath that can be expected of a King upon those who would depose of him.

CHAPTER 40

It was late one night, and I was still wearing tank tops when over a dozen gorilla's walked into the Gaslight. I was told these simians were from Gotti's crew and that the biggest ape; Alex, knew Doxie and he had just got out of prison. I had already figured out by now that to know Doxie was to want to kill him so I didn't need to be told anything else, but this was not my fight. It would be Phil's farewell address as he beat a man who looked suspiciously like Junior Gotti over the head with a fire extinguisher. It would also be the night Geir the babbling idiot was reborn as Geir the berserk Viking.

Geir had been psychotic and ranting on about Norse Gods since he had come back from Norway years ago, sometimes at subzero temperatures while wandering around outside past midnight shirtless and without shoes. In fact, long ago Bob Matheson from the OBI had bought surplus WWII search lights for the docks that he never used. When people asked him why he bought them he would tell them "so Geir can look for Odin." When we were teenagers Geir had never exhibited one sign that he was any different from all the other kids around him. He went to live with his father for a while in Norway and he came back muttering about Nordic Gods and the Theory of Relativity. He was good for nothing except hard work. He couldn't even take care of himself. We would have to make him both bath and eat. We called him the Geek after a comic character in Hustler Magazine that was depicted in a cage eating live chickens. He had always carried a commando fighting knife named 'Ludwig' but we had never thought he could bust a grape in a fruit fight. He was six foot and about a hundred and sixty pounds if we fed him regularly.

All I remember from inside the Gaslight was Phil attacking them with a fire extinguisher, both bludgeoning and spraying them while he did. He completely overwhelmed them by himself and made it look funny while he was doing it. When we got them outside these guys really didn't understand how Phil had just done that to them. They wanted a rematch. Geir, of all people, squares off with one of them. They were both flat footed on the ground facing each other in classical boxing posture. Suddenly Geir leapt backwards about twenty feet and punched another guy that he alighted in front of, dropping him. Maybe he was jumping but it sure looked like he was levitating as he moved through them depositing lethal right hooks on people's jaws. About half a dozen of them ended up on, what was by now a sacrificial alter to Horus, the concrete sidewalk outside of Gaslight. From that point on Geir could be relied on to hold his own against any three guys but I never saw him actually levitate again.

The next night Richey took me to a dance club named Phasers. I was wearing my usual leather get up and hat with a new fashion accessory, a semiautomatic pistol shoved under my snakeskin belt. We had a sit down with the owner ostensibly to smooth out the 'beef' between Doxie and Alex. The big club was empty, and we sat at a table they had set up in the middle of it, just me him and Richey. No sooner did the meeting get underway than the guy mentioned Sonny Franzese. When he did Richey playfully but firmly slapped him across the mouth and asked him not to say Sonny Franzese's name again, saying "Sonny is a good friend of mine too. Let's keep him out of it." Richey went on to slap the guy a half dozen more times during the course of the meeting. He also appropriated about sixty thousand dollars' worth of stereo equipment from Phasers, which the guy ended up 'negotiating' to give him. At the end of the meeting, I don't know whether it was a lamentation or a threat, the guy starts telling me what a dangerous business I'm in. Richey slapped him again and I told him "there's no man alive on the streets right now that can win a violent confrontation with me. If you know any stupid enough to try send them down to the Gaslight. I'll be waiting."

The next day Phil, Janine, and I were sitting around Phil's lair on the bottom floor of his mother's house as I told Phil what had happened. Phil said "that's it! I've busted up my last gangster for Richey. I got him talking to me now like he's my boss. I got his fat dog Doxie following me around the bars reporting back to him. I told you I wanted out and now I'm out. Richey thinks this is all happening because he is a shrewd business man. He's not going to live through this, most of them aren't. You mark my words but then you don't give a shit do you? All you want is Dianne Rodney; it's time for you to just go get John. Let them all drown in their own blood." Janine expressed how terribly romantic she found my pursuit of Dianne. But she also made it clear that she supported Phil's decision and had instigated it.

For emphasis Sleepy Joe came over later. Sleepy Joe was the manager of the Tender Trap and Joey Massera's boy. He wanted to know when Phil would be able to give Joey some money. Phil just laughed at him and asked him to help me 'spot' on one of Phil's patented twelve hundred-pound squats. When he stood straight up with the weight Phil dumped the side Sleepy Joe was standing on just missing him with half a dozen hundred-pound plates. Sleepy Joe looked shaken up enough, but Phil wasn't done yet. He said, "woops I missed." Then he dumped the rest of the weight and went in his room and pulled a pistol out of the draw. He fired twice into the wall right next to where Sleepy Joe was standing and said "the next time I'll just use this. It's more effective."

Phil had himself a belly laugh. Sleepy Joe left looking like he was in shock. He didn't have long to live. He would be found shot through the back of the head in a car before a year was out. Mark would also be found shot in the back of the head in the parking lot of the Crazy Clown, a strip club he purchased when my uncle backed out of the deal for it and bought a yogurt store instead. People were going to die, and others were going to be destroyed for life. Phil wasn't exaggerating. I couldn't do this all by myself. I would need someone to watch my back. Bringing John around would be like releasing the Kraken but what else could I do? I enlisted his help.

John would never actually work in the bars. John did not work. As Eric once said, "he lurks." John always had money. He had lots of money. He had a fortune just in scrap for the antique machinery that was stashed in various yards all over Long Island. I remember one time being over his house when he got a call from an airport adjoining one of 'his yards' to lower the boom on his crane because it wasn't properly lighted. When we got there, it was the middle of the night. We were coked out of our faces. The crane was thirty years old if it was a day and looked as tall as a sky scrapper. John proudly told me it was one of the tallest cranes on Long Island. The only way to lower the boom caused an electric shock to the operator from its half a dozen oversized batteries. John cheerily played with the boom for the better part of an hour. You could almost see the sparks flying from him. That was what John called work.

    I took John to the bars and I introduced him to everybody. Richey already knew him. He had been introduced to him by the 'Bubba' way back when the Bubba was still alive. I remember the first night John was there. We were sitting at the bar drinking and he suddenly yanked Doxie from the seat next to him. He started swinging him around the bar like a rag doll in some perverse improvised waltz, squeezing his ass cheeks as they 'danced.' As he was doing this John said, "you remind me of my cell mate back in Attica." Sighing loudly and squeezing Doxies ass cheeks for emphasis John then swooned "He used to let me call him cupcakes. Will you let me call you cupcakes?" I had to pull John off of him. If I hadn't I really think John would have sodomized Doxie right there in the Gaslight during business hours.

CHAPTER 41

    Less than two years ago I had been lying in the room I grew up in, twenty-seven years old and wondering why I was still alive. Now I was a rock star. I was even better than a rock star. I was the rock stars muse, the embodiment of the primordial Luciferian archetype of rebellion that had spawned rock and roll in the first place. The album Appetite For Destruction was all the girls now played on the juke box. Guns and Roses was now the most popular group in America since the Beatles. Each dancer had their own dance to each of the songs on the album. Mesha was the only exception. Her favorite song on the jukebox was as Cold As Ice by Foreigner. She would play that every time I walked into the bar and dance savagely at me, it was probably the most erotic dance I have ever seen outside of Dianne's dance to Rocket Queen. Dianne's dance would give rise to the whole dominatrix thing. Everyone else knew that the first song on the album Welcome to the Jungle was me and the last song on the album Rocket Queen was Dianne. The songs described us graphically right down to our attitudes. Dianne was a sexual innuendo in a burned-out paradise. She could turn on any one just like she turned on me. She had a tongue like a razor. It was a sweet switch blade knife. And I, I was the ravenous king of the jungle.

  Gracie and I were sitting on the end of the crowded bar of Bogart's while Dianne danced. I said "I'm starting to have second thoughts about all this. I'm a man and every girl that works in these clubs would trade their soul to be my whore, yet I haven't had sex in over half a year. What's wrong with this picture? I only been out of jail a few weeks and I'm already getting really tired of this shit. She's still going out with Charlie and she still won't even kiss me. This is all just a game to her. It's nothing but an ego thing for her. She has what all the other girls want. She couldn't care less about me." Gracie said "she's breaking up with Charlie. I can assure you of that. They have been fighting about you since you got out of jail. Don't be an asshole. Look at her. Look at the way she's looking at you right now. You think she looks at everyone like that? I wish I could look at Vinnie that way." Dianne's eyes were locked on mine, even as Gracie and I had been speaking. She had her little smirk on, the one she always got when she was trying to think of something sarcastic and witty to scream at me from the stage. She did not see anyone else in that bar or in her dreams. I knew that but I just kept going "I should just go back out with Mesha. Obviously, she's still in love with me and she makes almost as much money as you do. I'll tell you one thing Gracie. If I go back out with Mesha I can never be with Dianne. I'm telling you that as a vow. I won't hurt that girl again because of Dianne, no matter what." Gracie said "you know a lot of this is your fault. You're not forceful enough with her. You have no problems unleashing your aggression on everybody else but you're a complete mush with her. The next time you try to kiss her don't take no for an answer. Just play Rocket Queen on the jukebox for her. It's her favorite song ever. She loves that song!"

  It couldn't have been more than a day or two later and I was still feeling morose about the whole thing. John came over in the morning and we drank a bottle of wine pouring out a libation to Aleister Crowley and leaving it on the kitchen table. John started quoting passages from The Book of the Law. The book advises its reader to destroy it after reading it once, but John had the whole thing memorized. He started reciting it like a Shakespearean actor ""I am the warrior Lord of the Forties: the Eighties cower before me, and are abased. I will bring you to victory and joy: I will be at your arms in battle and ye shall delight to slay. Success is your proof; courage is your armor; go on, go on, in my strength; and ye shall turn not back for any!"" John told me that Crowley had the ability to be in more than one place at the same time. He put his finger to his lips as if to say shhh and said Crowley could become invisible by invoking Harpocrates who was the crippled twin brother of Horus and the God of silence and secrecy. We left and passed my mother on our way up Coolidge Avenue and she made us stop the car. She told us that she had a premonition that I would die that day and she was distraught.

    I don't know what we did for the rest of the day but late that night I went up by myself to see Dianne at the Gaslight. I wasn't wearing my leather pants and hat and when I walked through the front door nobody noticed me. Mark was asleep in his chair by the tunnel to the backroom, Karen's old 'waitress station.' Mark always slept at 'work.' The only subjects that could ever animate Mark were wrestling and talking about the steroids the IDF were giving him. He had long since apologized to me for getting between Dianne and I saying "hey I don't know what's going on in these places. Joey Massera just told me to report to work up here. Nobody said anything about you. I didn't even know you worked here. I'm only here to help. You just tell me what you need done and I'll do it." After Dianne and I's little post prison reunion and Phil quitting, Richey and I had decided that only Mark would work with Dianne when she worked at night without me. When I wasn't working with my mother I usually worked days at the clubs. Aside from me Mark was the only one I trusted to watch over her. Murphy or Kevin was always right next door anyway. Mark was a very professional bouncer, much more so than me and far more than those two gorillas and he had more than proved his courage to me when he tried to stop me. Besides, Richey was paying me more money to work the seven-hour day shift by myself than he was paying the two bouncers that worked the nine hour night shift.

    The bar was packed, and it was packed only for one reason; Dianne. She was sitting over at the tables while Donna Coleen danced on the stage above her. Dianne was surrounded by at least a half a dozen suitors, each one prettier than the one next to him. It looked like rock stars worshipping at the feet of Crowley himself. Dianne was so amused at her new found deity status that she never even noticed me. I could hear her laughing and cavorting, dispensing witty jokes in her most adorable nasal twang. They were sitting around her like obedient dogs. These were all guys that never would have come in these bars a little over a year ago for fear of sustaining grievous bodily injury. The barmaid never even noticed me or asked if I wanted a drink and every barmaid that worked there knew to snap to attention and do just that when I walked in. It seemed to me that Dianne had every intention of doing this Moon Goddess thing solo. I left the same way I had come in with nobody noticing.

I wasn't trying to kill myself. It was three AM. I had done it dozens of times before at that hour. When I turned onto Coolidge Avenue on my way home I hit the gas. I was doing over a hundred at the halfway point and a car pulled out two blocks in front of me. I had nowhere near enough room to stop. I had to plow into some parked cars. When I climbed out of the wreck I saw right away I had bent another steering wheel straight up. When they got me to the hospital my stomach was already bloating with blood and it hurt. They scanned and x-rayed me for two hours and could not find any internal damage. By then my stomach was swollen like I had swallowed a basketball and I was in agony. They did traumatic surgery cutting me open at the belly to find the damage. My Spleen and some of my Pancreas had severed on my spine from the pressure of being compressed against the steering wheel. Lucky thing I had been doing over a thousand sit-ups a day. The surgeons removed the offending organs then sewed me right back up again. I wasn't in the hospital two days. I woke up with seven nurses and doctors standing around me looking like they were having some kind of seminary. They pulled some tubes out of my belly, patched up the resultant holes and told me I could go. Later when I went to one of the surgeons to have the staples removed I thanked him for saving my life. He told me that's what they were there for and I couldn't help but notice his office was decorated wall to wall with portraits of medieval castles.

    I saw Dianne the same day I got out and I played my accident and injury's for all I could get. When she saw me, her whole face lit up, more than usual. Grinning widely, she said "I heard you had a little accident. That's a nasty scrape you got on your face. Lucky it's on your eyebrow. Its gonna leave a scar." I showed her my stomach and it looked like somebody punched her in hers. The smile dropped from her face and her eyes clouded over. She said "Geir just told me you had a little accident. I knew it. I should have called you. I should have come to see you." I said "I was in the Gaslight the night of the accident. I went there to see you but you looked busy, so I left. Where are you going now?" She was dressed in her street clothes and it was only four PM. She became very agitated and said "I don't believe you just walked in the Gaslight and I didn't even see you. Why didn't you just come over to me? You see? You are always being creepy. I'm going to The Feast of San Gennaro in Little Italy. Or at least I was. You're not staying up here like that. All the shit you have done up here. What if somebody sees you and punch's you in the stomach. You're going home right now. C'mon. Do you need help?" On the way to my house I said "you know I could get killed at any moment or any second up there. It's been that way since me and you met. You suddenly care now?" she said "look I'm breaking up with Charlie. He's cheating on me anyway. You're going to be my new boyfriend. There's no question about that. Just give me a little time. I have not been on my own since I started stripping. I just want to see a few different guys and play the field. Why don't you just date some of the dancers if that's what you want to do? I won't get jealous." I knew she was going to say that. I had even read the lyrics to Rocket Queen. I said "fine. Remember you said that." When I lay down in bed I took one of my pillows and pressed it against my stomach. My surgeons had recommended this to protect the wound from the surgical incision. I imagined the pillow as Dianne. I sleep that way to this very day.

CHAPTER 42

I was fresh out of cars, but rock stars didn't drive anyway. I had a dozen different people to call up and take me wherever I wanted. Dianne was among them, but she only wanted to take me one place, home. She would always make sure she drove me home whenever she left the bar even if I had just walked in. I went along and called Geir or Bobby and Marlena as soon as I got inside. I was back at the clubs before she even got home herself. It was actually my busiest time for Richey since the whole thing started. He dragged John and me, with Geir chauffeuring all of us in Richey's hundred thousand-dollar cars, to every mob club on Long Island. John would make loud announcements to the staff and patrons that nobody was to get to close to me while Richey threatened everybody and tried to drink all the cognac at the bar. One time we had to even bail Richey out at the police station in the early hours of the morning because he thought the police, whom the Holiday Inn had called because of Richey's incessant belligerence, had gotten too close to me. Richey started shoving the cop and yelling at him as John and I looked on sheepishly, finally talking Richey into allowing himself to be arrested. Geir made a pig out of himself at whatever buffet was available. I saw Geir eat whole pastry carts at two hundred dollar a plate restaurant's in Hauppauge. We never paid anyway. Richey was the new "King of New York."

I was going to do this whole thing and there were no doubts about it in my mind especially a few weeks later when I sat in Bogart's with Dianne. She was running her fingers through my hair obviously very attentive to her technique. I was in Nirvana. She said "I'm going to go out with this guy tonight. If I don't like him it's just me and you." When she gave me my obligatory ride home that day she dropped one of her shoes out of her car. Dancers always had a car load of shoes. I took it inside and stayed home that night. At midnight I wrapped an article of my clothes around it and pulled with my left and my right hand on each end of the clothing. I kept repeating the mantra in my head "don't fuck him. Don't fuck him." When I saw her the next day I said, "did you fuck him?" She said "you know I really wanted to. We were laying on the couch kissing and I really wanted to do it with him. He kept trying to take my clothes off, but I wouldn't let him. Something kept saying in my head don't fuck him. Don't fuck him. I could hear it as clear as day. It was the strangest thing. He's a really nice guy. I was running my fingers through his hair like I do with you. You really like it when I do that. Don't you?"

I don't know what I said but she took me home anyway. When we got there, I said "let me get your shoe. It fell out of your car yesterday when you dropped me off." She said "oh I was looking for that shoe. That's my favorite pair of dancing shoes." When I got back outside with the shoe I said "Consciously you have no idea what is going on right now but subconsciously you know exactly what is. Well this is to the subconscious part. In case you ain't noticed I don't play the game that way. You fuck him Dianne and all bets are off. Now you think you're just going to defile yourself with the sub creatures after I have watched you dance naked for them for the last year? I have come across all of time to get you, but I will go back across all of time without you." She fucked him and one or two more by her own admission. I wasn't forgiving her. The 'Babylon Working' was essentially over after that.

CHAPTER 43

Thelema is spelled θέλημα in its original Greek. It means free will, especially sexual free will, exactly my intentions now. Mesha was up on the stage and Kevin and Geir were at the bar when I walked in Bogart's. Richey had asked me to hang out because there may be some trouble there. I never stayed in the bars all night anymore unless I was engaged in 'heavy petting' with Dianne. This was going to be boring unless it ended up in a hotel room with Mesha. Kevin said "look I know you don't want to be here and believe me I don't want you here. You're the only thing that scares me in these clubs. Give me your gun and I will lock it in the desk draw. I brought you some valiums just take them and go sit in the corner there and drink your Wild Turkey. Nothing's going to happen tonight. Richey's been drinking too much. I have some friends of mine from the city coming in to hang out, their all detectives. I know you hate cops but just be nice to them and me and Geir will take care of everything." I promised him I would be nice to them, gave him my gun and took my medication. The guys were cool enough when they came in.

There were four of them. I ended up hanging out with them and we sat by the stage because like everyone else they were mesmerized with Mesha's savage dance routine, inspired by me. Of course, she and I got into it. These guys tried to mellow me out and took me up by the bar away from her, but I was still frothing at the mouth. One of them grabbed me and threw me up against the wall with his forearm against my neck. He said "do you know who we are? We take down guys like you for a living." I don't remember what he said after that. When I came to all four of them were lying around the floor of Bogart's looking like road kill. Kevin was holding on to me with one hand and Geir with both. Kevin's other hand was on his massive forehead like oh my God what has he done now. Later people told me that it was like I had some kind of 'Vietnam flashback.' I was dragging Kevin and Geir around like they were children and winging kicks so fast they could barely be seen with the naked eye. All four guys had to be taken away by ambulance. But at least I got to go home early.

    I wasn't going back out with Mesha. First of all, since I would never break a vow I could not just shut the door like that on Dianne even though she had now left me with a wound that was never going to heal. Second of all Mesha was tall and voluptuous with blue eyes. I liked my woman now just like Dianne, petite with dark eyes. Richey had a new waitress; Melody. Melody was one of the most beautiful girls I have ever seen. She was of Dutch descent and about five foot three with long straight black hair and facial features as fine as any porcelain doll. She had a body to match her face. There's a line in Rocket Queen about being a little young. Melody was only seventeen years old when I met her and already a legendary beauty around the strip club scene. She had come to us from Manhattan because the owner for the Kit Kat Club was so infatuated with her that he had made it impossible for her 'to breath' in the city. She was as wild as she was beautiful. The first night I met her I had just seen a couple of my Five Percenter brothers on the street and they had given me a marble sized chunk of free base. I didn't smoke that stuff anymore for the most part, so I asked her "do you do coke?" She said "why you got any?" "Only smoke." I said. She said "really?"' I put the chunk on her waitress tray, and she walked around with it like that for the rest of the night serving drinks.

    Doxie, of course, was goo-goo-eyed over her. There was a man who never knew his limitations. He took her to the Diner one night after work when I was holding court. I said to her "you know you may just have the most beautiful face I have ever seen but I would really like to see you naked." She said "I was the best-looking dancer at the Kit Kat Club. Ask the owner." Doxie was mortified but a couple of days later she granted me my wish. She would be my 'girlfriend' till after the holidays. My little sister hated her. My sister's bedroom adjoined mine and Melody and I would have loud and raucous sex all night with the bedpost hammering the wall. When we watched TV in the den Melody would sit on the hassock in front of me and dutifully change the channels on my whims and that was every time a commercial came on. To Melody men were nothing but a live buffet but she 'loved' me.

She lived in a nice house on the water in Freeport with just her father, poor man, who was a coin dealer. One night we were in her bedroom when we really got into it. Her father was probably in the next room, but Melody didn't care. She was a complete sociopath. To go along with everything else Melody, just like Mesha, was extremely athletic. It was cold outside, but we were both lubricated with about two gallons of sweat as we violently pounded on each other only stopping to seamlessly switch positions. I had cum at least a half a dozen times already, and so had she, but Melody wasn't even slowing down. I wasn't being outdone by anything at the time, not in heaven, earth, or hell so I summoned everything I had left. I got on top of her and just started mechanically pounding on her. It went on for hours. Somewhere in the wee hours of the morning I rolled off of her onto my back with my arms outstretched. I said "I'm dead Melody. I can't do this anymore." She hoisted herself up to a kneeling position and straddled me lowering her wet pussy, so she slowly impaled herself on my still throbbing cock. She said "you're dead? That's what I want to do. Kill you. Kill you as you cum." She kept thrusting down onto my cock as she lowered her porcelain doll face to mine blowing her breath right into my mouth as she spoke "I want to kill you while we are having sex. That's my fantasy. Can I do it right now? I want to look in your eyes while you cum and die at the same time. That's what I want. Isn't that what you want? I want to look in your eyes as you die." We both came like volcanoes, me ejaculating semen that I didn't know I had left and her squirting till it ran between my legs into the crack of my ass. Our orgasmic convulsions must have shaken the whole house.

Back then, in spite of what I had seen in East Islip, I thought Melody was far too young to have anything to do with what was going on. I had never spoken a word to her about it. How could I? Something had gotten into her while she was in the throes of passion. Something unclean and clearly malevolent but something I found incomprehensibly erotic. It was right then I started to get ideas, Thelema ideas. Melody never said another word about that night and that was fine with me. I couldn't see how a girl that young could have free will, regardless of her psychological condition. I wanted her out of it from that moment on.

Everything was building to a crescendo and I didn't see it or maybe I did. We had killed the conductor and the "abased" eighties were hurtling towards the end of the line like an out of control train.

CHAPTER 44

I met Michelle before the holidays at the same time I started sleeping over Janet's and sometimes Gracie's too. Rock stars didn't have a home. Richey called me into his office and explained to me that we would be taking care of Sal's trophy girlfriend. Sal was one of the boys from Mulberry Street. He had sold five kilos to an undercover cop and gotten a year for each kilo. He kept his mouth shut. He hadn't started his bid yet but his live-in girlfriend needed work. Richey said "I haven't seen her yet, but they tell me she's one of the best-looking girls in New York City. She'll be tending bar here five days a week. Just do me one favor. Stay away from her." He might as well have waved a red cape in front of a bull. I couldn't wait to see her and when I did I wasn't disappointed. Hell had built me my own chimera. Michelle was a dark eyed Italian beauty about the same size as Dianne, maybe an inch taller. She was a year younger and had a face almost as perfect as Melody's and an ass that was just as good as Dianne's, some said better. Richey's customers would argue all night about which one had the finest ass in New York City. The girl reeked of sex. She could turn a dead man's head and she knew it but the most striking thing about her was her hair. It seemed to fall in a tumultuous cascade of auburn brown almost to her knees. I had never seen hair like that in all my life, and I still haven't ever again.

The first day Michelle worked I walked into Bogart's and sat on the end of the bar drinking her in like a vampire sucking the final drops of blood from his 'victim.' This was gonna be great. She was tending bar and Dianne was dancing up on stage playing her new 'favorite song in the whole world'; What I Am, by the now suddenly famous Edie Brickell and the New Bohemians. The song gave Dianne's answer verbatim to everything I had been trying to tell her about what was going on around us. It bragged about not being aware of things. Well she was about to become aware that she had competition. Michelle and I looked each other over. I spoke first sneering "I heard you're with the last Italian in New York that's not a snitch." She sneered right back at me "I hear you're in love with that idiot that's up on the stage. Pffft!" We would spar with words like that for the next few weeks.

A day or two later when Michelle wasn't working I took the opportunity to start banning Dianne's pretty boys. Her new song infuriated me. It seemed to me she was dismissing everything I had ever tried to say to her. The song said philosophy is nothing but the talk on a cereal box and religion is the smile on a dog. It's a shame I never read those lyrics. I missed the most important part. The song ended with the vocalist imploring her lover to "choke" her in the shallow water before she got to deep. Apparently Dianne was ready too. But it wasn't going to work like that anyway. Like I said there are rules. She needed to be consciously aware of just what she was doing just like I was, that's what free will means. She didn't need to know that together we would bring down God himself but at least that we were giving ourselves to each other for eternity.

    Dianne had taken a cross country train ride, 'to clear her mind', with one of her court jesters. They had come back, and he was telling everybody in the clubs that nothing had happened between them. 'It couldn't because she was in love with somebody else. That's all she talked about for the whole train ride.' She had made him swear an oath not to say who it was. Gee I wonder. It infuriated me even further that she was broadcasting our business among the customers. He looked really funny running as fast as he could in his thousand-dollar designer jeans outfit as he disappeared over the horizon of Hamilton Ave with Billy and Vinnie Murphy hot on his python boot heels. In the next few weeks, I would ban every one of them, never when Michelle was working though. The idiot comment was enough for me.

    It was about the same time that I got a phone call from Gracie asking me to stay with her for a while. She and Vinnie were breaking up. One of Dianne's friends had made the centerfold of either Playboy or Penthouse that summer. I don't remember which. Anyway, her family had thrown her out for her achievement and she had been staying on Gracie's couch. Apparently Vinnie couldn't resist the temptation. Gracie threw the girl out and Dianne made sure that she was now a pariah 'who walked the streets of East Meadow turning tricks for crack.' Now it was Vinnie's turn. He had to go too. It was a shame because I really liked Vinnie, but Gracie was like a sister to me and he had been the one that had cheated. In the ensuing weeks Gracie told me that she wasn't going to dance anymore. The hours of exercise that were entailed in having a body like that were too much for her. She was in her late twenty's and already had more money than Richey. It was time to have fun with it. One night I asked her why she never had Vinnie's teeth fixed and she said "You don't know how many times we have fought about that. He just refuses to take any money from me for anything." Like I said Vinnie was a real man.

    Gracie had also said to me "If it's the last thing I do I am going to get you and Dianne together." It suddenly dawned on me that Gracie might have been John's female counterpart. I had seen the Scientology books she had all over her condo, but she had downplayed her involvement with the religion when I had asked her about it. She told me she just studied Scientology to free her from her fears and inhibitions otherwise she could never have done what she did and made all the money she had. Just like Marlena who had known her before she started striping Gracie had come from an affluent and rigid upbringing. On January twenty fourth I tested the water the best I knew how. When everybody was sitting around her condo and just she and I were in the kitchen I said "You know L Ron Hubbard died on this day two years ago. Everything he taught and did was based on the teachings of Aleister Crowley. I can feel him in the force that is driving all this. He is one of the primary players" She gave me a knowing smile and looked at me with those big brown eyes and said, "I know."

CHAPTER 45

Janet had been dancing for Richey since I had started. We never really spoke. I knew she was fanatically Wiccan and didn't really approve of Aleister Crowley. I for one had always considered Wiccans posers. They want to rebel against God, but they don't want to go all the way and risk damnation. They have the same relationship with Crowley as the American 'left wing' has with Marx in politics. But Dianne was not the only one who needed someone to talk to.

Janet was sitting at the bar in Gaslight when I walked up to her and said, "so I hear you think I'm a Satanist." She looked at me and smiled saying "I didn't really know you then or at least know of you. Besides did you want me to explain Aleister Crowley to Dianne? Have you ever tried that yourself?" I smiled back at her and said "I wouldn't dream of it. She doesn't need to know anything like that. Don't you know religion is the smile on a dog?" She laughed; she got my joke. Then she said "Aleister Crowley's just too dangerous for me." I said, "I study alchemy too." She laughed again and said "well that's more of a guy thing. You have the strangest aura I have ever seen. It's every color in the rainbow and seems to stretch on into another world. I was born Wiccan and I have never seen anything like it." I said, "what about hers?" She looked at me and gave me a knowing smile and a nod.

Janet and I became inseparable friends in the ensuing months and she actually defected from Gracie and Dianne's entourage to mine. She would never give me any information about them, but she made it perfectly clear that she knew just what the consequences were of what was going on there in Babylon. She wanted me to be with Dianne. Janet hated Michelle but she was deathly afraid of her to the point of stammering when she said her name, mostly refusing to even talk about her. She confided to me one night that Michelle was the most powerful witch she had ever seen and may have been Lilith herself incarnate.

In the Qabalah there is no Satan, no king of demons. Asmodeus and Beelzebub are princes not kings. There are seven princes for the seven palaces of hell. There are no kings. Only God is king. Lilith is the mother and the queen of all demons. The name of her consort; Kebad, has the same numerical value, twenty-six, as God. According to the rules of the Qabalah God and Kebad are the same entities. Lilith herself is rabidly hostile to man. She was Adams first wife, but she refused to accept a subservient position to him particularly during intercourse. All Jews put a tiny scroll somewhere in the entrance to their home to keep her out and are implored not to suffer a 'witch' to live amongst them. A true witch derives power through the malevolent forces and is a servant of Lilith. The ancient Hebrew sages called them Daughters of the Owl. The owl is the symbol for Lilith.

I don't know whether it was to keep me away from Michelle, retribution for removing her entourage of girly men, or whether she really loved me, but Dianne now claimed she could not dance with me in the bar. She had never wanted to do her Rocket Queen dance when I was there but now she would only play Sweet Child of Mine over and over again and just sit on the stage and stare at me with big sorrowful eyes. I told her "to bad I'm not going anywhere. Why don't you ask the bouncer to tell me to leave?" She tried to make an issue out of it with Richey and he tells me "how can you love her? You never had sex with her. You have never even done anything with her. To me you have to have gone through something with someone to love them." But that was Richey. He thought love was a stock option. That's why he never had a real relationship with a woman. Before she had started sleeping around I had told her two dozen times "why don't you just quit dancing? I make plenty of money for both of us."

It was after seven and Michelle had already left. Dancers didn't get off till eight, eight thirty. That was the time I reserved for conversation with Dianne. I went and sat by the stage and she suddenly just flipped out on me. She jumped off the stage and went running outside in her G string. When I followed her outside she kicked off her shoes and went running down Hamilton Avenue practically nude in the cold night air. I ran after her and caught up to her which wasn't easy. She was a soccer star in high school. I threw her over my shoulder and carried her all the way back to Bogart's collecting her shoes on the way. I told the customers to get back inside and I put her down on the landing outside the front door. I said "you did this! You dug the Grand Canyon between us. All I ever wanted to do since the very first day I laid eyes on you was love you." She said "I don't want to be your girlfriend. I don't want to be your wife. And I don't want your money. All I want to be is your friend. Why can't we just be friends?" I looked into her eyes with my own eyes tearing up and said, "because you love me!" She started hurling her head against the concrete wall, once, maybe twice, until I grabbed her. Now I was scared for the first time since I was a little kid. She wasn't just banging her head against the wall. She was launching into it with complete abandon. I held her as she sobbed covering her naked breasts with my body. When we both stopped crying I told her to get dressed and go home. When Richey found out about it he said, "I can't have you two working together in the same bar anymore." I was inclined to agree with him.

CHAPTER 46

I was beyond morose. If ever in my life I really didn't want to continue it was during that period. I remembered back to when she first drove me home. I thought I knew we would be together, and it was only a matter of time. It seemed like the pall that had enveloped my entire life had just been lifted. Just like in the song Sweet Child of Mine "everything was as fresh as the bright blue sky." Now the very air around me was like daggers that gouged at my soul.

I took my International to go see John. Someone had actually given him a contract to take down a water tower somewhere in the Freeport area. I found him in his trailer office on the site. He was like a kid with a new erector set. Somehow we ended up standing on the corrugated steel roof of the tower. It was pitched gently down to where it ended abruptly in a hundred-foot drop to the pavement below. The biting winter wind howled around us. I fought back feelings of vertigo and the bustling little city below seemed to undulate. John kneeled down and leaned over the edge, unimpeded by a safety line, randomly cutting pieces with a small torch. The pieces looked like leaves as they swirled down in the wind. He was talking crazy like he was gonna pick the whole thing up with his crane as soon as he got enough cut off. I wasn't wearing a safety line either, so I kept at least ten feet from the ledge as John danced around it on his knees. I told him the whole story about Dianne. He kept asking me questions. This was strictly a man thing about a woman. There was no talk of any great work or sun and moon deity's. He seemed particularly appalled that Richey wanted me to stay away from her. He casually got to his feet on the ledge seemingly oblivious that he was inches away from certain death. He said, "do you know where Richey is right now?" I said "yea he's been hanging out in the Gaslight all day lately getting drunk and harassing his employees. That's why I'm here and not there." John gave me a repressed version of his old satanic laugh and said "why? Are you his employee?" I said, "it seems so." John asked me to take him to the Gaslight.

    When we got there Richey was panic stricken. I asked him what was wrong, and he told me one of the dancers was wearing a wire. I asked him who it was. It was some girl that I had never seen before so I picked her up and carried her to the front door then I shoved her through it and told her never to come back. I returned to the bar where John and Richey were standing and said, "problem solved." John said "I have to talk to both of you in the back." When we got to the door of the backroom John let Richey and I go in first and then he came in and closed the door behind him blocking any access to it with his massive frame. Looking coldly at Richey he said." What have you been telling him about staying away from Dianne?" Richey immediately started to sweat from his forehead and said, "I only said maybe they should stay away from each other a while." John said "that's not what he told me. You got rich here and it's because of us. In exchange we expect things to be a certain way. If he has personal problems with Dianne they need to be worked out. Are you interfering?" John stared at him as emotionless as a stone and Richey started to sweat profusely. John told me to go back to the bar. Richey tried to follow me, and John positioned himself to block his way. They didn't come out till a half hour later. Richey was soaked. He looked like he just crawled out of a swimming pool that he had fell in fully clothed. That was my new joke. Richey had been telling people that his name back in the day was Richey Pool because he was such a good pool player. I said it was because he manufactured a pool of sweat when he got nervous. There would never be talk of me staying away from her again.

    We were in one of John's trucks a few days later. We had been doing coke that night and it was about three AM when we pulled into the Gaslight to pick up Melody. I said "John I'm not paranoid! Everywhere we went tonight people have been following us. I'm not a fool I know when I'm being followed." Pulling a bag of cocaine from his pocket John said "here's the rest of the coke why don't you just take it and go home. One of Bobby's biker boys will bring you home. I'll get somebody to bring Melody home too. You really should just go home and study The Holy Books. When I'm really high that's what I like to do. I'm beat I'm going home myself." He started reading passages from The Holy books, which he was lending me again, insisting that I go home and read it. I went home with the book. He wasn't around the next day when I tried to find him. When I next spoke to him he told me that after I went home he had went to Pappa T's, an after-hour's club in North Amityville, where he was detained by Suffolk County Homicide. They hauled him in and questioned him for twenty-four hours. I said "they can just do something like that? Why didn't you call a lawyer? Who the hell got murdered? What evidence did they have on you?" he said "that girl you threw out of Gaslight was a crack head. She was up in North Amityville and somebody stabbed her dead." I said, "why did they arrest you?" He said "they didn't. They were just questioning me. They need to get enough points to get an indictment on a homicide and I know just how many they need and what they consider a point. I don't need any lawyer." I said, "well what do they have on you?" He said, "they found the knife in my truck." I said "isn't that evidence?" He laughed and said "the doors were unlocked and the windows were wide open. Anybody could have put anything they want in there. That's a work truck."

    I wanted Melody out of this. She had just turned eighteen. I started trying to get rid of her, but she was really stubborn. I had been arguing with her all morning on the phone trying to convince her that I really didn't want to go out with her anymore. I told her it would be better for her to find somewhere else to work. Doxie never did have any idea what was going on around him. It was always kind of funny. He thought we were all in the Mafia. He had taken his knew found wealth and bought a year-old Lincoln Continental. The thing was gold and really pimped out as they say now. Melody must have been calling me from Bogart's because she gave Doxie a big sob story about how she needed to go find another job now because of me. Doxie had only had that Lincoln for a couple of weeks but he lent it to Melody. She cruised to her old neighborhood by the Verrazano Bridge and got bags of assorted drugs from every man there that ever had a crush on her. She pulled up to my house shortly after dark leaning all over the horn. When I went outside she started proudly showing me her haul. I said, "why did you take those guys drugs you have no intention of paying them?" She started crying and said "I did it for you." I said "first of all you have never seen me taking any kind of drug except cocaine and Wild Turkey. What would make you think I would want any of that shit?" She said "I can get really good coke too. But I can only get ounces and more and I have to pay for it. You think John wants any?" By this time, I was relenting. I had just seen my probation officer. I figured Melody and I would do lines and bang the shit out of each other all night. I said, "let's go to his office."

    When we got to Johns office I made her call Doxie. He told her to bring the car back or he was calling the police and reporting it stolen.

She told him she had one more job interview. John pulled out a thick wad of hundred-dollar bills from his greasy Carhartt overalls and said "let's go to Brooklyn!" We met some twenty something Italian under the bridge and he sold John a deluxe bag of coke. By then John was driving taking great care to hit every curb and pot hole that could possibly damage the Lincoln. Melody and I were in the backseat. John held up the bag of fish scale in the lights from the bridge. I said "we ain't even got a mirror." With his cartoon villain laugh John ripped the mirror from the front windshield bellowing "we got a mirror!" We cruised the tri state area that night at one hundred miles an hour. We ended up going to Mo's Place where I found John something he deemed suitable. Then we went to his house and we retired with the girls to separate bedrooms. This was of course after John drove Doxies Lincoln through his Kursk battlefield backyard at thirty miles an hour fishtailing into 'vintage' bulldozers and cranes. John wanted to stash the car in the woods where his property ended 'in case helicopters were looking for it.' Two days later John dropped Melody and I off at my house and gave what was left of Doxie's car back to him up at the clubs. Doxie wisely never said a word about John's alterations to his Lincoln but I couldn't take it. I dropped Melody off at the Gaslight and let Doxie slap her around a little. They both needed a moment. That was the last I saw of Melody.

  Sometimes Doxie had to pay for his benefits. He had been the joke of the underworld until we had showed up. Now he was witnessing karmic vengeance on all of them. Around then I had walked in Bogart's and found Doxie mopping up the foyer. When I asked him, what had happened he said "Steve tried to come in with a beer and when I told him he couldn't he smashed it here." Steve was one of Long Islands homegrown Guido's. Another one of Richie's 'made men.' He owned some big dance club out in Ronkonkoma. He always came in his own limo and had a chauffeur and body guard with him. I said, "where is he?" Doxie stammered "by the stage." I said, "go throw him out and tell him not to come back!" Doxie started telling me how tough his bodyguard; Barry, was. I stormed into the club and snatched Steve by his cashmere coat collar from the table where he was tipping Mesha and started dragging him toward the front door. Barry and his chauffer jumped on me. I knocked out the chauffer and somehow got all three of them out the door. When we got outside Barry and I squared off. Both bars were packed, and they emptied out in a circle around us to watch us fight almost to a draw. I was pouring in kicks from every direction, but he was a trained boxer and blocked all of them. Finally, it was decided that wrinkly old Al and Steve would have a 'sit down' in the backroom of the Gaslight. Nobody was supposed to come in the Gaslight, but Barry insisted. Geir was trying to block his way when I snuck in one of the two best rights I have ever thrown flush on Barry's jaw. It sounded like an egg cracking when it landed. Barry required an ambulance and stretcher. He would spend a month in the hospital getting his jaw reconstructed. It turned out Barry and Doxie were from the same Bayshore neighborhood and Barry had been slapping around Doxie since they were little kids.

CHAPTER 47

I had been working on Michelle for weeks. I would sit at the bar and make fun of the Mafia all day. When I wasn't making fun of the Mafia I would make fun of Sal himself. Especially when she told me he was a Vietnam combat veteran. Charlie had been a Vietnam combat veteran too. Truthfully, I wondered how girls like Michelle, Gracie and Dianne ended up with guys that were twenty years older than them. But like I have already said combat is the place where men are forged, and these girls liked men. Richey heard that we weren't getting along so he brought us into his office and had each of us sit on different sides of his desk. I don't remember what it was I said to Michelle, probably something about waiting five years for Sal, but she pulled off her high heel shoe and catapulted over Richey's desk. He caught her in midair as she tried to imbed the heel in my temple.

Knowing what a thin line there is between love and hate I took that as a green light to continue my amorous advances. It was shortly before Christmas that I found myself in her vintage red Eldorado heading for Mesha and I's old motel in Copiague. The first thing I did was stick my tongue up that impossibly perfect ass. Then, starting at her well-manicured toes, I used my mouth to taste every inch of her. My tongue explored each crevice of her naked body till I had to insert my penus into her to keep from ejaculating into the air. I showed her my special trick where I could continue copulation, without pausing, even though I had just ejaculated a small pond of semen. After two hours we ended up in the hot tub, the fourth stage of Rosarium philosophorum. When we got back to Bogart's Al was waiting for us at the doorway wearing a demonic grin on his raisin face. As I walked in and she drove off I said to Al "we went nowhere!"

The most striking thing about Michelle, outside of her physical beauty, was the lack of bad tastes or odors. It was like making love to a warm and tangible picture. Her body was overwhelming. One night I was sprawled on my back and she was standing over me silhouetted in the moonlight from the window. It was a perfect view of her ass with that wild hair tumbling over it. I'll never forget seeing that vision. The light of the moon caught her pale white flesh and an eerie supernatural glow seemed to envelope her.

Sal's parents lived in Lindenhurst and she snuck away from him at their Christmas party to visit me in my house where she met my mother and little sister. She pulled up in her Eldorado convertible and sat on my mother's sofa wearing fifty thousand dollars' worth of jewels and clothes topped off by a full length designer mink coat. She ingratiated herself with both of them in the twenty minutes she was there.

When they walked in Bogart's I spotted them right away and I did not have my gun. Four Sicilians wearing gabardine pants, button up dress shirts, construction boots, and work coats. I was sitting over by Michelle at the waitress station. One of them came up to her and in a thick Italian accent asked her about me using my full name. She said "Who?" He pulled a slip of paper from his two-hundred-dollar pair of work pants and said my name again carefully pronouncing it. Without batting an eyelash, she said "I have never heard that name mentioned before. I don't think you have the right name. There's nobody that works here with a name that even sounds like that. I'm the head barmaid. I would know. Do you want to leave your card or name and number? I'll ask around." He declined. They had a drink and left after fifteen minutes. Lucky thing he hadn't asked Dianne. She would have pointed me out. It would be the last time I ever went out without a gun. Richey would claim it was over the Steve thing and he squashed it in a sit down which he attended with a pistol and a live hand grenade, but I'm inclined to think it was a cumulative thing.

Michelle and I were having as much sex as we could after her shift without anybody finding out about it. She would always have to go back to Sal's Co-op in Lynbrook long before the carnal desires or capacities of either one of us was slaked. The only ones that knew for sure were Al and Dianne. Al had his own shriveled fantasies about Michelle. I could feel Dianne seething from the stage when Michelle and I cavorted at the bar. She never spoke to Michelle and Michelle never spoke to her, contrary to the gregarious dispositions of both of them. Michelle made it clear to me that she did not like Dianne and thought my pursuit of her was moronic. I made it clear that she was not going to be waiting for Sal for five years, not even a month. The funniest part of the whole thing was the same customers who were entranced by Dianne were now the customers entranced with Michelle. The biggest topic of conversation in Bogart's and Gaslight was who had a better ass.

It wasn't long before Michelle confided in me that her mother was a witch and head of a coven. That is how she had been raised. She was extremely evasive about 'what she did' herself but she wanted me to know that she did it and had been initiated since she was twelve years old in a ceremony she never would talk about. She had no other religion since birth. She told me right off the bat "I cannot make anything good happen, only bad things." Her mother had started as a stripper and head barmaid at the Stonehenge. She now owned her own thriving strip club in South Florida and an upper floor on a luxury high rise on the beach in Boca Raton.

CHAPTER 48

It was during this time that Red came over from Joey Massera to be Richey's new manager. He was about six foot and a hundred and eighty pounds with thinning red hair. He was slightly older than me. It wasn't like he was taking my job. I didn't want it. I got paid no matter what. The only things that concerned me in those clubs now, other than who I had to beat up, was Michelle and Dianne. Red and I soon became inseparable friends. When I was not in the clubs I was usually with Janet or Red, if I wasn't at a motel with Michelle. Red introduced me around to Joey's crew. It was then I would meet Patty Esposito, Reds partner, who would end up turning states evidence against Joey for many of the murders that were committed during my tenure with Richey. Joey would get life in some federal shit hole in Kansas for killing half his own crew. Patty disappeared into the witness protection program. Ironically enough Patty used to have a standup comedy act that he would do for us about Richey pointing a finger at all of us during questioning by law enforcement.

Red may have been a shooter but he certainly wasn't no fighter. I never saw him have so much as one fist fight during the better part of a year I worked with him. Kevin had quit after I beat up his friends and any serious 'attitude adjustments' were left to Murphy, Tommy and I, with Geir providing our 'secret weapon' and John our nuclear deterrent. Mark was pretty much useless in a real fight although he could talk his way out of anything. The rest of our guest bouncers from the WWF were completely useless. We had one named King Kong Brody who they stuck on the day shift with me. He was a four-hundred-pound tub of lard shaved bald to appear fierce. Whitehead would take great delight to come home from a hard winter day on the bay and come down to the Gaslight just to fuck with him. He was terrified of Whitehead. It would have made great comedy TV, the four-hundred-pound wrestler being ordered about and threatened by the hundred and seventy pound blond surfer boy. One day Whitehead got overzealous and beat him with an empty plastic ice bucket. When I got Whitehead off of him Brody wanted to go to the hospital. I told him "go wherever you want but don't come back here."

Ronnie Craps was a big time Mob bookie in the city. He promised me he could get fights for Murphy against Tyson and me against Sugar Ray Lenard if I could get down to one sixty-five. Murphy would have annihilated Tyson. Tyson never even came close during his carefully staged career to fighting anything like Murphy in the ring. He was a sucker for a left hook lead and that was Murphy's best punch. I knew Lenard could certainly outbox me, but I also knew I could break every one of his ribs in a clinch. I began to lose weight. I knew it was a pipe dream, but I had nothing better to do. At one seventy I looked like something Michelangelo had conjured up in a wet dream. When I met people for the first time they would sometimes remark that they had always thought I was bigger. Months later Patrick Swayze would make the movie; Roadhouse. Patrick Swayze was scrawny and short. I was ripped and six foot tall.

I watched Dianne on stage go from a foulmouthed bitch that was paradoxically tempered with childlike innocence to a sneering dominatrix who viewed men as sexual toys who were not really necessary. She soon forgot that 'she couldn't dance in front of me' and her acts grew more and more provocative. All the girls had to do a certain amount of 'floor work' where they stretched out on the stage floor, nude except for their G string, and showed the customers what paradise really looked like. Dianne always used her floor work to play Sweet Child of Mine and try to get me to look at her the way I did when Michelle wasn't around. It never worked. But it didn't matter anyway. Michelle knew I was in love with Dianne and seemed to relish every second of her role of taking me away from her. It was like she liked that part just as much as the sex. She seemed to consciously make sure that by the time Dianne got down from the stage for the day, an hour after our shift ended, we were in a motel fucking our brains out. Whenever she said Dianne's name she would say it with distain, but she never even intimated that I should stay away from her. Michelle always called her by her first name like Gracie, John, and I. She never called her Rodney like everyone else, even Janet and Marlena sometimes referred to her as Rodney, but Michelle never did. Michelle always maintained that our 'affair' was sexual, and she would wait for Sal who wasn't even in prison yet.

CHAPTER 49

I was working the Gaslight one night with Dianne and Donna Coleen. Red was next door and Geir was stacking beer. All the wise guys from the tri state area were there, or at least it seemed that way, along with some Columbians who were 'with Franzese.' I had become friends with one of the Columbians a small man who wore a forty-thousand-dollar watch and drove a hundred and fifty thousand dollar custom Corvette that he let me drive when he was in the clubs. Some guy came in that knew all the Guido's and went around shaking hands with them. He was in his mid-forty's and wearing glasses, about six foot and two hundred pounds. I wasn't all that impressed with him, but the Columbian informed me that the guy was some kind of freelance enforcer that everybody feared. The man took his glasses off and came over to us and warmly shook my Columbian friend's hand. They had known each other for years apparently. Then he starts talking to me. "Are you really serious?" He said. "Do you know who I am? My great uncle was Joe Profaci. I did four tours in Vietnam. I was a navy seal there. I'm here to tell you that no asshole with an eighth-grade haircut is gonna keep us from getting a piece from these places. You should call Richey now and tell him I'm here and I want to see him."

He didn't like my dreadlocks and they were just starting to come in. I went to the phone booth in the back, but I didn't call Richey. I tried to get Murphy but couldn't. Then I got Tommy and told him "come to the Gaslight right now." In the meantime, Geir had been talking to Dianne who, of course, knew what was going on. I don't know what Dianne said to him but when he came back he was like a panic-stricken old woman saying "your gonna die tonight. This guy was sent to kill you with his bare hands, and everybody said he can. Let me just get you out of here. Your gonna die tonight." Geirs vote of confidence was even rattling me. I remembered what the Indians believed about crazy people having the gift of prophecy. I went over by Dianne and Donna and said, "what are you worried about me now?" Dianne said "why? When did I ever stop worrying about you? Why don't you just get out of here? Richey doesn't pay you enough for this. You got no Phil here to watch your back. Where's John? All these guys are here to watch this." I said "as long as they watch I don't need John. He's for in case any of them pull a trigger. It's called mutually assured destruction."

I handed my gun to Geir. Red never even came over or if he did he didn't say anything. When Tommy got there five minutes later I told the guy I wanted to talk to him in the bathroom. Geir followed us in and the guy started poking me in the chest and telling me I better get out of his face and get Richey there. That's when I flipped the script on him. I didn't want to fight him in the bathroom. I wanted to get him outside where I could use my speed and youth in case he was as good as everybody said he was. I made a little speech that Geir later informed me was mesmerizing. I said "you poor man. You have searched the far corners of the earth for something that was always right here waiting for you. Tonight, I'm going to show it to you. Tonight, you will see Aires. Tonight, you will see Mars. Tonight, you will see Shaitan. The Gods of war are all here. You have found what you have been looking for all your life." He didn't know what to say. He went back to the bar and started drinking with his friends again. I came out and nodded to Tommy who fell in step with me as I made my way to the front of the bar where this guy was drinking with the Columbians and Ronnie Craps. I removed the drink from his hand and told him it was time. He followed me outside and got caught with the second of the two best rights I ever threw. He went down to the pavement just like everyone else. I kicked him in the head with my steel tipped combat boots till there were no discernible features left on his face. I was trying for brain matter, but Tommy dragged me off of him. I was glad I had called the kid. He stopped me from catching a body. The Columbian and a couple of Italians loaded the bloody heap into the Columbians custom leather upholstered Vet, and he drove off never to be seen again. We went back inside, and I said to the rest of them "yea. Well he did his final tour of duty outside on the sidewalk of Gaslight. He didn't make it." Then I started hammering down Wild Turkeys.

    Donna was looking at me like she was going to cum in her G string. Dianne was cuming in her G string, but she was trying not to show it. I walked up to the both of them and said "when the male lion defends the pride he gets the females whatever way he wants. Tonight, is your night too Dianne. Donna you can join us if you want. Dianne's probably going to need your help. I'm feeling very invigorated." Donna looked like she thought that was a good idea, but she didn't say anything. For the rest of the night Dianne and I crawled all over each other just like we used too. She kept saying "tonight I might have to really kiss you back." I didn't try to kiss her in the bar. I was certain that it really was the night. I wondered if Geir had been right and that night I would die, with her. I wanted to. I had not felt this close to her since she had broken up with Charlie and started her fornications.

    I waited out in her car, which was parked right outside the front door, for twenty minutes. The engine was running for heat. When she got in the car I went to kiss her, and she said "no! I just did my makeup. It took me twenty minutes. I have to go somewhere after I drop you off. You waited a year. You can wait another day or two. You're not messing up my makeup. She kept cuddling up next to me and running her fingers through my hair but every time I tried to kiss her she turned away, telling me not to mess her makeup. We stayed in front of Gaslight for a long

Those Who Would Arouse Leviathan

time. I showed her the raging hard on I had that was bulging against my pants and said "We need to do this now or very very soon before you piss me off again. Where the hell are you going? You got somewhere to go that's more important than this?" She said something about a modeling audition. I said, "a modeling audition at four in the morning?" She said "it's the only time the guy could do it. I've been planning this for weeks." I didn't believe her for a second. I was already doing a slow burn when she dropped me off.

When I woke up that afternoon Gracie called me. She said "I want you to sleep over my place tonight. Come by after eight. Dianne will be here. She's sleeping over too. Bring John. We will drink a few beers. I told you I would do it." I said, "where did she go last night at four in the morning all made up?" Gracie said "she probably went to do a private dance. Don't worry. She wasn't with nobody else. I used to do those too. We can make thousands of dollars doing them. Don't fuck this up. This is what you have been waiting for." What Gracie didn't say is that when she did private dances half the Pagans motorcycle gang would be waiting outside for her. Doing private dances was how strippers got raped and murdered. Dianne had went and done one by herself. Richey and I did not allow the girls to do private dances. If she had told me that's where she was going I would have taken her keys and thrown them in the canal by my house. If she needed a thousand dollars that bad I would give it to her. I told Gracie I would be there.

I had gazed to long into the abyss and now the abyss was gazing back into me. The problem was the abyss was my own reflection. John picked me up in the same truck he had driven to Papa T's when he was picked up by homicide. We stopped at Something Else first. John had to talk to a couple of Pagans. While John was in the back I bought a small package of cocaine. I had no idea why. Dianne and Gracie didn't do it, and neither could I. If this were all real the drug would have made it impossible to work up the necessary passion to go through with what we had to do. It wasn't like I did cocaine every day either, maybe every couple of weeks. I was on probation. I got urine tested every two weeks. I stuffed the package in the side pocket of my leather jacket and forgot all about it.

I watched the lights from the buildings stream past as we headed east to Bayshore. Was this all even real? They said I was having a psychotic episode in South Oaks. Maybe this was just all part of the same delusion. Maybe we were just star-crossed lovers and this was all going to end when I married her and we had a few kids and got a dog to fill that home she was going to buy. Having her to hold in the middle of the night would have made life tolerable, even worth living. I started to run my life over in my head, the apparitions in childhood, Morrison and the drowning where I could not die, Amityville, East Islip, Geraldo Rivera, and the fate of that corrupt police captain, now all this with the strip clubs.

When I was in jail a mouse had scurried across the top of the bunks in the Black section. Some of them were screaming like woman and some trying to kill it. Nobody could get close to it. I watched the pandemonium from my own bunk laughing for a minute. Then I picked up my boot and jumped over a couple of bunks waiting at the one where I knew the mouse was going. When it got there, I smashed it with one shot. I had known where that mouse was going all the time. No. I knew better than any man what reality was. I proved it every day. I was still alive because I knew exactly what my enemies were thinking and could anticipate their next move before they had even thought of it. How much more so my friends and allies?

I looked over at John driving with his eyes fixed ahead not saying a word. This was not a natural man. Nothing I had ever seen in nature could explain him, just like it couldn't explain me. Hell had placed him beside me to watch over me till the time was right. Then he would kill me and the only thing I ever loved, and I wanted him too. I remembered when we were back in seventh grade. This vicious little daughter of an Irish whore named 'Sister' Grace Edwards asked everyone in class to say what they wanted to be when she called on them. When she called on me I said, "a writer." John laughed out loud at me so then she asked him what he wanted to be. He smiled and looked her right in the eye as he deadpanned "a hit man." She slapped his face till she was out of breath, but the smile never left it. Later I asked John "what's so funny about being a writer?" He said "what have you ever done? Only an idiot would read a book about something that was written by someone who never did it. Like you sitting there reading books all the time written by guys who are making it up as they go along. What a waste of time. If you want to do something you better go out and do it not waste your time reading or writing about it." Now I was going to be a bloody human sacrifice. Worse yet the only thing I ever loved would accompany me onto the hit man's sacrificial alter. Who was going to write about me and her?

It was about two years ago. He had already separated from Meryl and we were over his parent's house on Ocean Avenue doing lines of some garbage coke I had got stuck with. Out of nowhere John started to beg me to sacrifice him down in the basement. He became insistent saying "c'mon lets go down in the basement I have nothing more to live for anyway." He wouldn't shut up about it either, so I told him he was crazy and I left. Now I realized that in his own way he had been trying to show me that he was not afraid to do what I had to do.

Gracie was in on it too, by now I knew that. What if we were wrong? What if all of heaven and hell were wrong? Dianne and I would both just perish in another vain attempt at 'The Great Work.' Well then the God of Abraham would certainly have his laugh and everything that was ever born would continue to decay while we moldered in some unmarked grave.

I wondered how much it was going to hurt. In The Psychology of the Transference Jung had written about "dismemberment of the body" and "excruciating animal sacrifices." They would have to kill me first I could never watch her suffer pain. I would fight like a cornered lion. Jung, quoting the woodcuttings text, had also said that the Sun Gods very atoms would be absorbed by the passion of the Moon Goddess's orgasm "And she embraced Gabricus with so much love that she absorbed him completely into her own nature and dissolved him into atoms." That was how I wanted to die. I wanted to be swallowed up in the passion of her orgasm. I wondered where it would all take place. Is that why Gracie had that oversized bed that took up her whole bedroom?

CHAPTER 50

When we got to Gracie's Dianne was already there. She wasn't even being evasive about why she was there. In fact, she and Gracie discussed at length where she and I would 'sleep.' It was decided that we would stay on the three piece couch right next to the sliding glass doors that opened up to a wooded area in the backyard. When I looked out the sliding doors I saw shadows moving around in the woods. I knew who or what they were, but I pointed them out anyway. I was already throwing shit in the game myself. The girls both saw them. Dianne got scared and clung to my bicep. Gracie said "maybe its Vinnie and some Pagans. He hasn't gotten over me yet." John said, "there's nothing out there!" Then he went outside and searched the woods. I stayed with Dianne. There was nothing out there that did not belong there.

We made small talk for hours mostly about doing private dances. I made Dianne promise me that she would never do another one, but she wasn't very convincing. I finally said, "so why did you make me wait this long Dianne?" She was arrogant about it saying "I told you I wanted to play the field and I also told you that I don't need a man. In fact, if we ever had a baby together it would have my last name not yours. You act like we are going to get married. I'm not ever getting married to no one. I like the way it is now. Men just get in the way." I said "so what you're telling me is we are just going to have a night of pleasure here. Well in that case why don't we all just do a couple of lines and we'll get really kinky about it. You want me to call up Melody? Gracie got that big bed in the room." She said "I don't do drugs! You better not ever bring them around me. And Melody is a dirty little hole. You better not ever bring her around me either. But that's right you like Michelle now don't you?" I knew where I was going with all this, but I just kept going. "What do you care who I like. This is all just a night of pleasure. You think Michelle asks me if I like you? As a matter of fact, I got a package of coke on me right now. I think I'll do some. I don't think there was ever a man born that could be better than me in bed but I'm even better on coke." I took out the package and dumped most of it all over Gracie's ten-thousand-dollar dining room table. In slow deliberate fashion I cut it into lines with a matchbook while Gracie looked on sheepishly and Dianne got that look like somebody punched her in the stomach. John for the first time, maybe ever since I have known him, looked like he didn't know what to do. He said "why don't you just give the coke to me. I have to get out of here anyway. I'm meeting some people down in Amityville. You shouldn't do the coke. You two have a lot to talk about." I said "no John. We don't have anything to talk about. Me and her are just gonna fornicate like two dogs in the street. You and Gracie can watch." Dianne said, "if you do those lines you can forget about being with me tonight." I said "really?" Then I sucked them up from the table with a hundred-dollar bill in my nose. I left some for John who was now shaking his head in disbelief. Then I said "you know what Dianne? I think maybe I want to play the field for a while too. I'm afraid you could make me forget my plans. I don't even know if I want to be with you right now." She changed her tune a little "you can stay or leave if you want. I'll tell you right now my boyfriends don't do drugs." I said "but that's just it. My girlfriends not only do them. They get them for me. You want to strut around now in leather and chains?" Gesturing to the coke remaining on the table I said, "here why don't you just do a line and do it right?"

    Frankly, I don't think anybody had ever defied the little bitch like that before. She didn't know what to say. She sent John and me to the seven eleven to get a couple of things for Gracie's apartment. When we came back she said "look I didn't mean that I wanted you to leave tonight. I don't want you doing drugs especially around me. You can stay. Just don't do anymore." John said "yea why don't you just give the rest to me? I'm late already." I said to Dianne "you make me laugh. You try to act like you're the innocent one. When we met you were in the gutter like some lost diamond covered with filth. I didn't even bother cleaning you off. I just handed you my heart like some newborn that had no idea of the sorrow and suffering life entails. I was the one that was innocent. You took my heart, spit on it, and threw it down in the gutter. Then you did a little topless dance all over it. Now you think you're going to tell me what to do. I think you forfeited that right." Then I said to John "I'll take the ride with you. We can always come back later." Dianne said "I'll be here all night. And when you come back could you pick up some toilet paper. I forgot to tell you to get toilet paper. Gracie doesn't use toilet paper. I'm trying to potty train her." She laughed at her joke, but she didn't sound so sure of herself anymore. Gracie followed us down the stairs and said "just knock on the door when you come back. I'm not leaving it unlocked. Let me talk to her. Vinnie wasn't allowed to do drugs around me either but that didn't stop him from snorting half of Columbia with Och when he wasn't with me."

John and I went to Amityville. On the way there I said "I did everything right according to any code of chivalry man ever had. I broke up with one of the finest pieces of ass in America to go out with her. She made it into a game. I didn't let it bother me. I courted her like it was the Victorian age. Then finally after a year, probably only because she knows I'm fucking Michelle, she's gonna give me some pussy. Well I'm not gonna give her no dick." John said "I don't blame you. The bitch is arrogant. Her voice grates on me. Hearing that voice forever?" John shook his head and gave a snickering laugh. Forever? John kept asking me all that night and into the dawn if I wanted to go back there. We didn't.

Understanding / בינה

CHAPTER 51

Napoleon once said that if it weren't for religion the poor would kill the rich. The poor need a new religion. I wasn't handicapped by the pretentious hypocritical 'morality' of the slave religions. Like Nietzsche once said the humblest creature on earth is the worm. It always bows when it's stepped on. I would bow before no man and no God, not even to the other half of my own soul. I had only one rule: do to others as you would have them do to you. I could only add to that if others should do wrong to you while you are following this rule with them then you must utterly annihilate them. Like I had told John that night when we left Gracie's; I had followed every protocol of courtship that this degenerate civilization and its malignant God had ever thought of. I had done that while all the while she was dancing around naked on a stage. At Gracie's, that night, was probably the first time I ever needed anything in my life. Instead of giving me the reassurance that I needed she rubbed my face in my own self-doubts. It was now my intentions to do to her just what she had done to me. Like the song Welcome to the Jungle said I wanted to watch her bleed.

    It was shortly before the spring equinox when I lay with Janet in the dark on her oversized waterbed. She was wearing only her panties. I was wearing my dungarees. Janet was well aware that it was heaven and hells intention that I belonged to either Dianne or Michelle, but I think she got a little turned on by being almost naked and so close to me. We weren't doing anything sexual. We never did. It was freezing cold outside and well past midnight. I said, "the Egyptians fucked crocodiles to gather the prana of Sobek" She looked at me in the illumination from the streetlights outside. The night was moonless. She said "how did you know about that? Do you know what part is eaten in a ceremonial human sacrifice?" I said, "the upper right thigh." She looked at me introspectively and said "they talk to you. Don't they? Those things are not in any books." I laughed and said "they have talked to me ever since I was old enough to remember. When I was a small child I was terrified. Now I even listen. Sometimes." Then she said in a hushed tone "there are people all around you that are watching everything. There are different ones coming in every day. That bitch inside is a Voodoo high priestess. She hasn't fooled me since I first met her." Janet was referring to the stunning looking Cajun stripper whom she shared her apartment with. She continued "I knew it when I met her at the Ravens Nest two years ago. I should have never let her move in here. I already told her she has to leave. She's probably listening with her ear to the wall right now. The new barmaid at Gaslight is an occult master. She might even be one of the hidden masters."

    I always treated Janet like she was letting her Wiccan imagination run away from her. I said teasingly "more powerful than Michelle?" She answered like she was scared to say what she was saying "No. But she's different from Michelle. She's really knowledgeable about the occult. I was talking to her the other day and I couldn't believe what she knew. Maybe you should talk to her." I said, "maybe I should." She continued. "I'm under attack. The other day I was driving on the parkway at night and I rounded a curve and just for a second I saw this thing in the lights over on the shoulder of the road. It looked like a cross between a man and a worm. It was in the grass like it was waiting for me then it just half slid half wiggled into the woods and disappeared before I got up to it. I don't see things. Other things are happening too, bad things." I said "I'll lend you The Holy Books. Just read that every night. That ought to fix things. Just make sure you give it back. It's Johns." She was hesitant when she said "Aleister Crowley might make it worse. All of this is because of him." Like she had proved my point I said, "exactly why he can fix it."

I related my own recent encounter with strange people. "The other day I was working Bogart's and in walks these two guys. They were the nerdiest looking dudes I have ever seen. One was really fat, and they were both wearing high waters. When they walked by me they were engrossed in a conversation about music. I heard the fat one saying well I really like U2. It was strange because of the way he said it. Like it really mattered what a fat nerd liked. Like it was an important decision he was making. I just got the vibe that these guys weren't customers. They weren't players but they weren't customers either. They weren't there to see the girls that's for sure. They looked like they didn't even like girls." Years later, when I formally met him, I would realize the fat one was Preston Nichols. You don't forget that face or that body.

The stillness of the night was broken by a cacophony of dogs outside the window. It seemed like every dog in the neighborhood was howling in the same guttural forlorn pitch. Janet and I both got out of bed and looked outside the window. Nothing was out there. I turned to her and said only half joking "another attack?" She giggled and said "no. That's just Dianne checking up on you. There's no moon tonight. She's Hecate. She knows you're here. But she trusts me." I said, "has Dianne ever been here before?" She answered, "all the time before you started hanging out here." I looked outside the window to see if I saw her car. Janet knew what I was doing and laughed saying "Hecate doesn't drive a car."

CHAPTER 52

Janet gave me back The Holy Books a few days later. We were in the Gaslight. She said, "I don't think he likes me." I opened the book randomly and read a few sentences: "nor is it fitting for the cobbler to prate of the Royale matter. Oh cobbler! Mend me this shoe, that I may walk." I didn't say anything. Adroitly changing the subject Janet said "that swamp rat won't move out, so I did. I got a new apartment. Can you help me move this weekend?" I said "yea. I'll tell Richey I can't work. We'll use my truck. It will take everything in one shot." She said "good. My boyfriend and his friends will help us." I said "Michelle wants us to take her to some of the places you know about downtown. She has to get ingredients they won't have at the Magical Child. It's a recipe her mother gave her for some kind of special incense. Sal finally went to jail. I hear he's got a really nice co-op. I really owe these mob guys for how generous they have been with me. Remind me to pay them some day." She looked at me and shook her head like she didn't approve of my designs on Sal's co-op, but she said "we can go tomorrow. Do you want me to drive?" I said "yea you drive. She drives like a fucking lunatic."

    We met at the Gaslight and dropped Michelle's Eldorado back off in Lynbrook because Michelle was convinced that 'Dianne would have somebody fuck with her car.' When Michelle was finally satisfied that we had met the requirements of her list Janet dropped us off in Lynbrook. It was the first time I was ever there. There was a doorman and security cameras that could be monitored from TV's in the apartments. We took the elevator to the fourth floor and Michelle got busy grinding away with what looked to be an ivory pestle. The co-op was spacious, complete with an oversized bed and hand carved ornamental dinning set imported from China.

    Michelle got up from the couch and seductively moved across the room to the stereo. I watched her ass swinging rhythmically as a pendulum in her skin tight designer jeans. Then she stopped and bent over the stereo as if to give me a better view. She said, "I got a surprise for you." She popped in a cassette of Zappa's Bongo Fury and played what she called 'Janet's song.' She came back to the couch and laughingly pantomimed as she resumed grinding away with the pestle adding things in sequential order. "'Say she's a witch / Shit-ass Charlotte! / Ain't that a bitch?'" I had never said one word to her about that song nor about Frank Zappa either. After about an hour or two she was done. I had watched her the whole time. She was completely absorbed never stopping or even hesitating except when she came to an ingredient she had substituted because she couldn't get the original. She said of the missing ingredient "you can never get that, but my mother says this is a perfectly good substitute." When she was done she burned the list in the sink and tossed the unmixed excess in the garbage. Her creation consisted of some half dozen cones about two inches at the base and two inches in length. She placed two of them on a silver incense burner tray then lit both cones at the same time and sidled up next to me on the couch saying, "relax and just take deep breaths." The cones smoldered in the tray then seemed to explode filling the room with a sweet-smelling vapor. I was immediately overcome with a shock of flashing colors that seemed as bright as the sun itself. I passed out.

    I came to about a half hour later. Michelle was next to me on the couch. She was also conscious. We were both unable to move for another half hour. It felt like I had no feeling in my limbs. Gradually the numbness in my limbs was replaced by a feeling of extreme sensitivity. After a while it felt like even the touch of my clothes was arousing me. I was rock hard when Michelle said, "let's go in the bedroom." On uneasy feet I complied. We took off our clothes and Michelle lit three long black candles she had purchased that day at the Magical Child. The phone was ringing but nobody was answering it. She pushed me onto the bed on my back, which was easy since I had no balance. She got on top of me straddling me as she lowered her pussy, so it slowly swallowed my throbbing cock. She threw back her hair like a matador with a cape and I could feel it as each individual strand seemed to caress my thighs that they were now draped over. She looked down at me as she thrust in a slow deliberate fashion that seemed designed to maximize my pleasure without causing me to explode in orgasm. She leaned forward and pinned both my arms to the bed with her hands digging her expensive fingernails into my wrists. Slowly a few strands from her hair started to rise straight up and give off traces of tiny blue sparks. A far-off look settled into her dark eyes as they looked into mine. She seemed to be admiring the ecstasy she was inducing in me. She hadn't spoken a word but now she said with her eyes locked on mine "you're the one. You're the one. I've been waiting for you. You're the one." spasmodic convulsions of ecstasy seemed to wretch my spine as I quivered in what seemed like an orgasm that would not end. I had a feeling of being overcome by my own pleasure. I felt helpless and even more aroused by my own feeling of helplessness.

    She seemed to be able to read my mind as she climbed out of bed and produced two belts from the silk bathrobes in the closet. She used them to tie my hands securely on each side of the bed. Then she again mounted my still rock-hard cock. She began pumping in the same slow deliberate fashion. This time more than just a few strands of her hair were standing straight up towards the ceiling emitting clearly visible tiny halos of blue sparks. I couldn't believe my eyes, but I felt it in my loins. It was a sensation that started at the bottom of my spine then arced uncontrollably through my whole body. The same fear, anticipation, and arousal, that I had felt with Mesha that night when we had made love in the motel room with the shadows watching. I guess I was stammering when I said, "Michelle your hair is standing straight up." She said "call me by my name. You know my name. My name is Lilith and I have been waiting for you." Before I could cum again there was a knock on the door. She gave me a sinister laugh and said, "I'll be back." Then she slid off my cock and got off the bed. She went to the closet and put on an oriental silk bathrobe embroidered with dragons. It had no belt. She left me tied to the bed and left the room closing the door behind her. I heard her entertaining Sal's sister in the next room remaining cool as ice. I even heard Sal's sister jokingly say "what's going on in there Michelle? Do you have a man in there?" Michelle just laughed and said "I was just taking a nap. I'm really tired tonight."

When Sal's sister left Michelle came back in the room and said "and you talk about sub creatures? You must like being tied to that bed. Do you know what I could do to you when I have you like that?" She climbed back up onto the bed dropping her robe on the floor as she did. She positioned herself so she was kneeling over my face facing toward my seemingly permanent erection. Her juices ran down my cheeks and neck as she began gyrating on and humping my face. My tongue probed feverishly as she pushed her ass down smothering my nose and mouth. Just when it seemed like she would cut off my oxygen she sprawled out onto my stomach and took my whole cock down her throat. She slid it up and down in her throat while I looked at her impossibly perfect ass and vainly tried to reach her invitingly puckered asshole with my tongue. The semen seemed to explode out of me and into her mouth as my body was rocked with spasm after spasm of excruciating pleasure. Then she turned around and gave me a long lingering kiss smearing salty tasting semen all over both our faces.

She untied me and we continued to make love in every different position we could imagine for the next two days. We burned up the rest of the incense never leaving the room in that span, not even to eat. I called Janet on Sunday morning and she asked me where I had been. I told her I was all tied up. She said, "I figured." I never saw her again after that.

CHAPTER 53

Sal's co-op was now my co-op. Michelle didn't give me a key right away. In fact, she threw me out Sunday night for burning a hole in her TV set which I had carelessly placed my cigarette on. But she apologized the next day and told me anything that was hers was now mine too. She made it pretty clear that she would be expecting me 'home' every night. She no longer talked about waiting for Sal just finishing up some unfinished business he had in the streets. Sal had an Uzi and a couple of other nice weapons that she needed to sell and give the money to his mother. I told her an Uzi is a glorified pistol that was too big to conceal and had no armor penetrating capabilities. I know my guns. My father had taught me how to shoot when I was four years old and 'he was the best marksmen in the Screaming Eagles during the Korean war.' The reason the army gave him for not shipping him out to Korea with his friends and instead stationing him at Camp Hero was that they needed him to represent the hundred and first in military shooting competitions. My yogurt swilling uncle was also a gun dealer. I refused to even touch Sal's weapons, bad karma, although I liked his pictures from the Vietnam War. He had one with a young American soldier impaled in a pit filled with sharpened bamboo stakes. The guy was dead as a doornail but still I wondered why they had taken a picture before they pulled him out of there. And people said I had no feelings.

Every week Michelle and I would make the drive into Mulberry Street. She would run into a social club there. I would wait in the car. She would come out with thousands of dollars. Some of the money was hers and some of it had to be distributed between Sal's family and friends. When I asked her, who was giving her the money she told me a guy named Birdman. Her Birdman was an 'old man' though. The guy who Phil had beaten with the shovel was middle aged. When it came to street names the Italians were not as original as the Bikers or the Five Percenters. When we weren't working for Richey our nights were spent in Manhattan partying in all the clubs and restaurants. There was really nothing left for me to do anymore at Richey's clubs except pick Michelle up after her shift. Richey was now king of the streets and I was his undisputed champion. I would never have to fight in those clubs again.

I remember one-night Michelle and I were partying at Tavern on the Green. We left with our drinks. Nobody was saying anything to me, not even in Manhattan. When I started to drive off in Michelle's Eldorado a police car pulled us over. I dumped my drink out the window before I got out, but I was slurring my words and staggering drunk. The cop says, "we pulled you over because you don't have your lights on." Michelle jumped out of the passenger side with her drink still in her hand. She said to the cop "officer he's such an asshole. I told him he couldn't drive. He's too drunk. He never listens to me. Make him give me the keys. I'll drive." The smiling officer complied, and she drove off with me in the passenger seat and her drink still in her hand.

I was told the incense can only be made once but that didn't slow us down in our exploration of the dark corridors of sexuality. At the time you could purchase an eighth of an ounce of cocaine, called an eight ball, in Cypress Hills for eighty dollars at any time of the day or night. The shit was almost as pure as Kenny's used to be, but it was processed with acetone instead of ether giving it an acrid gasoline taste. I was taking as much of her Klonopin as Marlena was. Although neither Bobby nor Marlena ever touched cocaine they would frequently hang out with us in Lynbrook and I would make Bobby drive us in to Cypress Hills because

I was either drunk on Sal's vintage whiskey, high on Klonopin, or both.

One-night Red drove me home from the bars and he came upstairs to hang out for a while. He already knew both Michelle and Sal from before my day. Michelle never called him Red. She called him Carrot Top, snickering every time she did. Michelle had the Himalayan named Beijing and the two Amazon parrots. Red started to play with the cat and tease it. Michelle produced a Ruger Blackhawk forty-four magnum from her pocketbook cocked it and pointed it at Red saying "nobody touches the cat Carrot Top. Did I say you could touch the cat?" At first I thought she was kidding but I could see by the look on Reds face that she wasn't. When Red left I said, "let me see that gun!" She took it out and handed it to me. I lovingly fondled it. Although I had only seen pictures of the gun it just seemed so familiar in my hand. It happened to be my favorite pistol ever made. What a 'coincidence.' I said, "is this Sal's?" She said, "no its mine." I said "did you ever hear of a twenty-five semiautomatic? You were really going to shoot him weren't you?" She said "somebody already shot me. Why should I care if I shoot somebody else? If I did you were getting rid of the body." She parted her hair and showed me a bullet crease on the top of her head. After that I gave my semi-automatic to Geir and I went nowhere without that forty-four. She even had a Bianchi quick draw holster for it.

CHAPTER 54

I had what everyman wanted and this was before a rich man could purchase a reasonable facsimile. But who wants a knock off anyway? I had it all but yet I was nothing. Nietzsche said man's primary motive is power. But with power comes the ability to love the one you want. A pauper cannot love a queen. The pauper must make himself a king then he can have his queen. The God of Abraham destroyed the world before this one because the other Gods could not keep their hands off the daughters of men. Troy burned for love. Kings have abdicated their thrones for love. Dylan's Italian poet once said every man's heart is halved at birth and he spends his life seeking the other half. The poets name was Dante Alighieri. He was the greatest poet who ever lived. It was not only me that burned for Dianne but all men who were ever born that burned for someone. There is nothing more to existence except the love between a man and a woman, or for that matter the love between the sun and the moon. There is a hermetic maxim that says, "as it is above so it is below." Every time I closed my eyes I imagined her there.

When Gracie was still working for Richey a couple of stock

Those Who Would Arouse Leviathan

brokers about my own age came in Bogart's wearing all their Wall Street finery. The doors to the front office were open and you could see in from the entrance to the club. I was sitting in a chair at the desk and Gracie was sitting on one knee Dianne the other wearing their G strings and not much else. One of the stock brokers yelled to me "you're my hero. How do you get a job like this anyway?" I told him you got to be lucky, but I said to myself that he couldn't survive the first day. In my mind I had seized everything by my own hand. I was growing haughty which according to Christian lore had been the reason for Satan's fall from heaven.

    I was getting tired of hearing Appetite for Destruction everywhere I went. It didn't really suit my mood anymore and I was no longer buying the ending. My younger sister had started dating a music critic for Rolling Stone Magazine, so I asked her what the hipsters were listening to now. She said "funny you should ask. He just gave me this cassette by this girl. She's like rock and roll country western. Her songs are the saddest thing I have ever heard but they are haunting and addictive at the same time. He says she's gonna be the next big thing." I said, "get me one I want to hear it." A couple of days later she handed me a violet colored cassette with a picture of a Janis Joplin type looking girl on it. She was posed in biker leather looking like she was in the process of having some mystical revelation. I don't know if I knew inside already but when I opened it up and listened to it I was staggered for maybe the first time ever in my life. Her name was Melissa Etheridge and she sung in a raspy bluesy style that was even reminiscent of the great Janis Joplin. There really was no denying even for the most avowed skeptic that Dianne was using Melissa Etheridge as a conduit to deliver her pain to the world and to me. Not if they knew Dianne. From Similar Features to Chrome Plated Heart the entire album was a tour de force through Dianne's inner mind. When I listened to the words I knew Dianne saw it different than I did. In Similar Features Etheridge says to her lover whom she has made wait too long, and has now spurned her for a girl with similar features and longer hair, that they never had to wait for nothing in their life. They just had to have the jewels wrapped around their fingers. Everything they have has been handed to them. Etheridge now realizes that the wall she had put up between them to protect herself has made her lover, who is not familiar with rejection, bitter. It was steel blue knife as Etheridge called it. It was true, all of it, and I knew it even the part about curiosity kills if you can't read the signs but at the time I couldn't read the signs.

    No girl had ever turned me down since I was playing around with "Gobby" back in the hood. Since I had left high school, and even before, everything that I wanted had been handed to me. I had been getting help all along. My landscaping business was just waiting for me when I got out of college. The clients were all my mother's clients. No sooner would we finish one job than seemingly out of nowhere we would get another. I had been wondering about that for quite some time. I had even adapted the attitude that I was privileged. I expected to be handed what I wanted. Taking over the strip club scene on Long Island had been easy. Phil and John had done most of the heavy lifting. Even now I knew no one was going to shoot me in the back and unleash all the wrath of hell when John came looking for them. The fights that I had won so easily had not been natural. I was tough but no human being was that tough. No man had ever even scratched me; ever shed a drop of my blood while I was in those clubs. I had been brought to her by the powers of heaven and hell to keep a promise I had made so very long ago and now I had reneged on my promise. And for what? Just what I had ridiculed her for when we first met. I would grow old and I would die.

    I saw Dianne's face when she was up on the stage in Bogart's when we worked together under Michelle's watchful eyes. I could see right through her and knew the pain I was inflicting on her. Not only did I close my eyes and imagine her there like the song said. Every time I closed my eyes I saw her face. Etheridge laments to her lover that they should know by the song that she wanted to be the one and asks them how they feel now that the damage has been done. I didn't feel good at all. I felt empty, an infinite and eternal emptiness gnawed at my soul. My resolve to hurt Dianne weakened. I went to go see her without Michelle watching us.

CHAPTER 55

    It was a freezing cold day in spring when I woke up one morning and told Michelle I had to look at a job with my mother. I did. But when I was done looking at the job I went to the Gaslight and waited in the parking lot for Dianne to come in for her shift. Michelle wasn't working that day and it was more like an opportunity than a premeditated plan. When she pulled up I got out of the car and she said, "were you waiting for me?" She actually looked like she had been crying and I said "yea. I was." She said "isn't that Michelle's car? Does this poor girl know what you're really like? What would she say if she knew you took her car to come see me?" I said "why? Are you gonna tell her? Oh, that's right you'll just tell Louie the Milkman and he'll tell her and the end result of that will be both of you will lose one of your best customers because I'll kill him." Louie the Milkman was a scrawny milkman who hung out all day, every day, equally dividing his paycheck between Michelle and Dianne. I often wondered how he had enough left to eat let alone pay his rent. She said "I'm past that. I'm seeing somebody anyway now. How are things going with you and Michelle?" I said "things are going real well. Look at her. What do you think? I just got one problem. I can't forget about you." Tears started to stream down her face, and I thought to myself this is it. Here's where you throw everything away that you worked so hard to get for a fantasy. I pulled her close to me. She was wearing that heavy knee length cashmere coat she always wore when it was cold. She hugged me harder than she ever had before. I felt like she was going to squeeze the life out of me but again she buried her face in my chest before I could kiss her. She started murmuring into my chest again "it's never going to work out between you and me. We have too many differences. I'm seeing this guy Vinnie now. I really like him." I said, "do you love him?" She didn't answer. I said "look Dianne. I can't play any more games with you. This is very serious what's going on between me and Michelle. Before it go's any further I need you to make up my mind for me. All you need to do is just say the magic words. You know what they are. And get your fucking face out of my chest and put your lips on mine." She started to sob. She didn't answer and she didn't kiss me. She just held me with far more strength than any five foot one-hundred-pound human should ever be able to muster. We held each other like that for I don't know how long not saying anything under a freezing cold sun. She missed her first half hour set. Finally, she released her anaconda like grip on me and said "I better go inside." I let her go.

    I went to Cypress Hills and got an eight ball. On the drive in I thought about it. I wasn't going to put myself out there like that again. Maybe this was all just some convoluted dream. I was making too much out of how I felt about Dianne. She was the first and only thing I had ever loved. We had spent more intimate time together over the past year and a half than most chaste conventional lovers do in twice that time. She was a beautiful and witty girl, and I was a man. Of course, I loved her but I would get over it just like all the other chumps that gave their money to her. Poet; Jimmy Carroll, once said: "But the stars tell lies, it blinds the only warning / And when darkness dies, there's nothing left but morning". The disincarnate were above all else liars. They were just like their master Aleister Crowley. They made a sport of it. I wasn't going to let the darkness die. I was having too much fun with it. Dianne had slept with other men when she knew she loved me, and I was remaining celibate for her. She had mocked love itself. Even if the whole great work thing were true who would want to spend eternity with her? Why should I crawl on my belly to her? Why should I even have her if she crawled on her belly to me? What if this was all just a simple case of a man wanting to marry a woman who didn't want to get married? She was just a whore who took her clothes off for a living no matter how she wanted to dress it up. Michelle didn't take her clothes off for anybody but me.

When I got back to Lynbrook Michelle was still sleeping. If left to her own devices Michelle would never get out of bed. I woke her up with a nice fat line. We showered together and I shampooed that magnificent hair my erection probing at her ass, which was the one thing she would not let me do. That was fine with me the one time I had tried it with Mesha I had ended up peeling half the skin off my dick. It was far more fun to think about than to actually do. By the time she combed out her hair the light was fading from the window. We still had plenty of the black candles she had bought at the Magical Child. She lit three of them up and we did some lines and shared a long lingering kiss our tongues lapping up the numbness from each other's mouths. She climbed up on the bed and knelt with her hands bracing her torso parallel to the bed, her hair spread out on her back and draped over her ass. I knelt down behind her and she propped up her ass. Her hair slid down from it on each side like curtains being drawn back to reveal what they had been hiding. Her pussy looked like a small cherry clam just starting to open and her carefully painted toes curled in anticipation. I slid my blood gorged cock in from behind her warm wet pussy. I forcefully thrust upwards while she pushed backwards with her elbows which now supported her weight off the bed. Gradually her face settled into the bed up to her breasts under my relentless pounding. We both came simultaneously in convulsing ecstasy. I could feel her juices squirting out onto my balls as they mingled with my semen and ran down my leg.

When our body's finally ceased quivering she rolled onto her back her head on the pillow with her hair spread out around it like a manta ray. I moved to between her legs ready to start all over again and I looked down at her face. She had that far-away look in her eyes again and her hair started to rise up from the pillow till about a quarter of it stood straight up in the air. She said "you went to see her today didn't you. You took my car to go see that stupid slut. She's a fucking clown. She doesn't even know what she wants. Maybe I should tie you up again and teach you a lesson." I felt the fear mingled with anticipation creeping into my spine and making my already hard cock throb with anticipation. Just then the phone rang, and it kept ringing even though we both tried to ignore it. Her hair settled back down onto the pillow and she got up from the bed and answered it. She said "hello" then there was dead silence as she seemed to listen intently to the other end. Finally, she hung up and said "that bitch got my phone number from the office. She probably even knows where I live. I'll bet she's out there right now at a pay phone. She got off of work about forty-five minutes ago. Just enough time to get here." She went over to the window and surveyed Peninsula Avenue below. She said "I wonder where she's hiding. Maybe I should take the forty-four and go find out. She's pathetic. How could you love her?"

The phone calls continued, and they always came when I was at the height of arousal. One of the longest songs on Etheridge's Album is Watching You. Etheridge tells her lover that she is below their window watching them because she has nothing better to do. She actually sings that her only other option is Bogart's in the window down the street.

Michelle didn't say anything to her about the phone calls and Dianne stopped pretending that she liked Michelle to me. When I said something to her about the calls she didn't deny it. She just said "if that bitch thinks I'm calling her house let her say something to me. We can do it anytime she wants!"

Even Richie who was at loath to acknowledge the fact that his two finest looking specimens of the female form were about to kill each other over me had Red separate them on the schedule. They now only worked together in the day on Tuesdays and Thursdays at Bogart's when Richey was there. I had started with my business, so I wasn't working day shifts anymore. It was probably just as well. The whole situation was a bomb, and I was the detonator. Together they rang even bigger day shift registers than Gracie and Dianne had in spite of the fact that they never spoke to each other. Mark whom they both loved like a father was assigned babysitting duties. On the two nights that all three of us worked Michelle was in the Rainforest and Dianne was with me down in Gaslight or Bogart's. Margret, who was back at the Rainforest, worshiped Michelle. Michelle had jumped her registers by over a thousand dollars per shift. One time all four of Margret's dancers left the club because Michelle was walking the top of the bar in her hot pants and stiletto heels scoffing up all the tips. Margret didn't care. Michelle, by herself, kept the place packed in a tumultuous din that was reminiscent of the days of Gracie Starr.

CHAPTER 56

I can't say I had anymore misgivings about hurting Dianne. In Bring Me Some Water Etheridge laments that she knows that all the while she is making excuses some other woman is making love to her lover. I was tired of the excuses. I had a year and a half of them. In I Want You Etheridge points out that she is well aware that the primary motivation of her lover is vengeance. She tells them to cut her and watch her bleed if that's what they really want. I wasn't going to go that far; besides the knife that I was using on her was forged to cut her soul. It would have been far more merciful than I was feeling towards her to use one that was made out of simple steel. Dianne personally tried to make that happen one night in Gaslight. I was cutting up lemons and limes for the barmaid with a huge butcher knife by the waitress station at the bar. I believe it was the same knife Dominic tried to kill Doxie with. We kept it around as a macabre souvenir. Dianne was sitting right next to me, probably not wearing a bra, she never did, only a negligee, G string, and heels. I said something stupid to her, again probably that she had to wear a bra to sit at the bar. She leapt up and grabbed my hand that was holding the knife with both her hands and pushed her throat into it. I couldn't believe the knife didn't penetrate her flesh. She was pushing so hard the skin on her throat went back to her windpipe before I reacted and stiff armed her away from me. I stashed the knife under the bar and closed the waitress station flap and told her not to go inside the bar. I stood guard by that knife for the rest of the night. She tried to make a joke out of it, but I just looked at her and shook my head. I didn't see anything funny about trying to make me cut her throat. I stopped riding her after that. In fact, we didn't talk for a while.

      The next time we did she was up on stage at Bogart's. Michelle was in the Rainforest. Dianne starts entertaining the crowd by asking them what their fantasies to do to her were. I didn't want to hear this shit. I was gonna kill somebody. I went outside the front door and hung out on the landing by myself. Not easily deterred when she was done with her set she walked outside as always not wearing a bra. I grabbed her and pulled her back inside with me. She said "what about you? What's your fantasy? What do you want to do with me?" I wasn't about to give her a truthful answer and tell her I wanted to die with her in the throes of passion so that we could be resurrected together and take the throne of God by force, so I went with something a little more conventional. "What I really want to do Dianne is bend you over maybe that desk in there." I pointed to the office "then I want to fuck you right in the ass without using any lubrication. I want to hear you scream. Then when I cum I want to lay you on your belly on soft silk sheets and lap the semen up as it leaks out your asshole." She looked at me like she was both revolted and intrigued. She said "you know what I want to do to you? I want to take you somewhere where we can both take off all our clothes then I want to have a knock down drag out fight with you and you better believe I'll kick your ass. Then when you're helpless on the floor I want to stick my foot right in your ass." For emphasis she took off her shoe

Those Who Would Arouse Leviathan

and showed me her foot and said "look. I have tiny little feet. I think I can get it all the way in there. I'll start with my toes. You like my toes don't you? How would you like them in your ass?" I now had a raging hard on, but I was also at the same time disgusted with her. I said "why do you have all this pent-up rage focused on me? What did I ever do to you to make you hate me like that?" She had a long list of things I had said to her and people I had thrown out but never once mentioned the truth. Michelle.

Doxie had rented out a popular dance club in Nassau County for some kind of party. I think it was his birthday bash. Michelle took off from her shift in the Rainforest to attend. I didn't think anything of it. She had a better relationship with Doxie than most of Richey's employees. They frequently worked together at the Rainforest where Doxie would whimper all night about her antics behind the bar. He was always paranoid that I would come in and catch her doing what Margret referred to as her Wild Kingdom show where she would wear the skimpiest animal skin print tights, frequently strategically torn and tattered, and walk the top of the bar working the customers up to a frenzy. He actually took her in the backroom one night and tried to sew one of her costumes up with a needle and thread because he was afraid I was going to walk in and see her wearing it. He needn't have worried. I had bought it for her but when she told me the story I thought it was very considerate of him.

The trouble began when Michelle and I were ready to leave Lynbrook for the dance club. Michelle said "this is as good a night as any to settle this whole thing. Dianne's been making a big fuss all week about this party all of a sudden Doxies really important to her. She's just going for one reason because you're going to be there. Well now I'm going to be there too." I said "Michelle I don't need no trouble between you and her. We work together for ten hours two nights a week. She doesn't have to go to Doxies party to see me. Me and her have been at this for two years, long before you came around, it used to be five days a week, nothing ever happened of any sexual nature. It's never going to. Why don't you give it a rest?" She didn't answer and I should have known when she didn't.

When we got to the club I had the forty-four stashed underneath the seat where I intended on leaving it. Only Doxies coworkers and friends were allowed in the place, neither of which was going to try to shoot me. Michelle go's under the seat and stuffs the gun in her pocket book. I said, "what are you doing?" She said, "I'm going to shoot that bitch tonight." I jumped out and went around the passenger side and refused to let her out of the car. I pushed her back every time she tried to get out. I said "I'm not going let you shoot her. Just put the gun back under the seat. We'll go in, have a few drinks, pay our respects to Doxie, then go to the city." She became hysterical saying "don't worry I'll shoot her in the chest. This way you can have an open casket funeral for her, and you can cry your eyes out. This isn't about you now. I know you aren't encouraging her. She's deliberately defying me. She's following my boyfriend around. She's calling my house and hanging up at all hours of the day and night. I'm supposed to take this shit from her?" I kept pushing her back in the car every time she tried to get out telling her "you're not going in there with that gun." All the while I had a sinking feeling in the pit of my stomach thinking here's where I lose them both. I imagined what a field day this was going to be for the local news. It was probably going to go national and be a movie of the week. Finally, I said "look Michelle what I'm going to do is just call the police and say it's my gun. I'll do a year in jail. I like that idea better than you shooting her. If you shoot her you might as well shoot me too because she'll be dead, and you'll be going to jail for life. I prefer not to stick around for that." Finally, she said "just give me the keys. I'm leaving." I gave her the keys and she went fishtailing out of the parking lot burning rubber all the way. She still had the gun and now I had to get the other stupid little bitch out of there before Michelle came back, no small feat. My relief was unbounded when I went in the club and found out Dianne had been there earlier with her little stripper posse, danced for a while, and left. Bobby told me they were going out on the town and they weren't coming back. I had a drink with Doxie and made Bobby take me back to my mothers. I went to Lynbrook the next day with Charlie Murray, now out of jail. When I asked Michelle where she had went she told me she had been in Valley Stream where she pulled over and was crying. Three black guys walked up to the car and one asked her what time it was, and she had shot at him and missed. I said, "are you sure you missed?" She said "really I don't know but I don't think I hit anybody. All three of them ran away." I cleaned the gun and told Charlie to hold on to it for me for a few days. I scanned the local papers during the ensuing days. There was nothing. For once I was glad Michelle packed a piece that was bigger than she was. I doubted she could hit the broad side of a barn with it.

  Queen of the Night is a late blooming Darwinian tulip. It is a deep purple that is probably the closet flower in nature you can find to black. When liberally planted with its hot pink Darwinian counterpart the effect is breathtaking in massed swaths during late spring. I cut Michelle thirteen blossoms of the black tulip from a job where I had planted them in late fall the year before. They now looked about to open. I immediately brought them to Bogart's where Michelle was working with

Dianne. I gave the cuttings to Michelle warning her that it was too dark in the bar for them to actually open up, but they would be appropriate for our bedroom in Lynbrook since Queen of the Night is an ancient name for Lilith. Michelle put the tulips in water on the bar. Dianne looked on from the stage mesmerized failing miserably in her attempt to feign indifference. When I picked up Michelle at the end of her shift she was elated. I walked in the club and she gestured triumphantly to the flowers on the bar and said "look!" The flowers looked like they had opened in the full strength of the sun. All thirteen were in full bloom. Michelle looked defiantly up at Dianne on the stage and we left with the flowers. On the way home Michelle said "my black magic against her white. All day I felt her willing with all her might for those flowers not to open. You should have seen the look on her face when they started opening. My black magic against her white I am stronger."

    Dianne must have not got the memo because the phone calls continued. They seemed to always come when Michelle and I were exploring the most inner sanctums of depravity. During the next few months Dianne's attitude toward me grew more and more hostile. I thought I no longer cared or at least tried to pretend I didn't. The Eighties now cowered before a relentless nihilistic assault on every moral axiom that the slave religions had ever cherished. Just like slaves in love with their own chains some waxed nostalgic for the good old days of Nietzsche's God of thou shalt not. The cattle of the earth had become "abased." They were ready to follow a different master. The first order of business should have been to murder the old gray world of Abraham's repugnant God.

CHAPTER 57

    She had her chance. Our war with God was an exercise in futility without the power of her Magick. That's why in the tenth stage of Jung's The Psychology of the Transference the crowned and conquering child stands upon the moon. She is now the empress of all. Gone are the feminine sensibility's that lead only to weakness. She is now ruled only by the Fire and Force of Horus and together they will avenge the murder of Osiris. As Jesus says in the final sura of The Secret Gospel of Thomas "I myself shall lead her in order to make her male". The thirteen severed heads growing in the pillar of severity on the wood cuttings depicting the 'Great Work' are the thirteen letters in the God of Abrahams name when they are arranged in his blasphemous six-pointed star. It is the Magick of Isis combined with the Fire and Force of Horus which will depose the tyrannical king. As Jim Morrison said, "Coda queen, now / Be my bride /

Ragin' darkness / By my side."

Story's change especially when they are relayed over countless eons of time. Isis, Horus, and Seth is mythology by its very definition. There are some who walk this earth who understand just where this all began but they will not tell the others because they believe the knowledge to be a privilege that can only be passed on through the blood. The world has suffered their silence long enough. They are pompous fools that play at being descended from Pharaoh's and Roman Emperors when in truth their linage can only be traced back to Dark Age whore houses. The only thing passed on through the blood is venereal disease. For the Five Percent who are out there just like Morrison said "Callin' all the dogs / Callin' on the gods," there is a story that is as old as time itself.

In the beginning before there was even a time and space there were four pairs of consorting couples. In the time before the Sphinx they were called Ogdoads. It would be wrong to say they encompassed existence. They were existence. It was through the ecstasy of their carnal pleasure that the inscrutable God was manifested into their angelic realms. This is the God Jesus called the Holy Spirit in The Secret Gospels of Thomas when he said you could blaspheme against the father and you can blaspheme against the son but to blaspheme against the Holy Spirit was unforgivable. Qabalists are not even allowed to contemplate this God they are merely told its three names for its three states of existence; Ain, Ain Soph, and Ain Soph Aur. All of them are beyond even the comprehension of the Crown of God.

Sophia was one of the Ogdoads. She yearned to manifest the inscrutable one without the aid of her male consort. Pistis Sophia, discovered in 1772, and dissertations from the Nag Hammadi tracts, 1945, tell a tale of woe whereby Sophia attempted to manifest God without her consort. Her actions disturbed the balance. As the Qabalah says the vessels were broken. Matter subsequently came into existence along with the resulting God or 'demiurge'; Jehovah, Set, Ialdabaoth, Sakla, many names but always the same entity. Sophia was now bound to the world of matter and at the mercy of her own arrogant creation. In order to glorify himself the demiurge attempted to create man to worship him using as a template the distorted images of the angelic world that Sophia fell from but when he used the matter to form man he found that he could not animate him without using the same life spark from Sophia that had created himself. This is why men have the innate ability to be Gods equal and know better than God himself the difference between good and evil. Without her everything the demiurge has created would be barren and infertile. In order to make his creation self-proliferating it was necessary for the demiurge to bind Sophia to it. He accomplished this by locking Sophia within matter where she undergoes endless incarnations as a woman of ill repute dazed and confused by the distractions of the flesh.

The Templers, the progenitors of the Free Masons, were told to gather in the places frequented by woman of ill repute. Mary Magdalene Jesus' bride is depicted as a whore. In The Thunder, Perfect Mind, a tract from the Nag Hammadi, The Goddess says of herself "For I am the first and the last. I am the honored one and the scorned one. I am the whore and the holy one." I had not yet read it when I knew Dianne. I can only wish I had. "I am the one who is disgraced and the great one. Give heed to my poverty and my wealth. Do not be arrogant to me when I am cast out upon the earth, and you will find me in those that are to come. And do not look upon me on the dung-heap nor go and leave me cast out, and you will find me in the kingdoms. And do not look upon me when I am cast out among those who are disgraced and in the least places, nor laugh at me. And do not cast me out among those who are slain in violence. But I, I am compassionate, and I am cruel. Be on your guard!"

The redemption brought by the savior, who is Lucifer the original consort of Sophia, is the redemption of his lover Sophia. Through her restoration to the angelic kingdom from which both her and Lucifer came will this whole blasphemous creation be rolled up. Lucifer did not fall from heaven nor was he cast out. He has no use for this Gods heaven. He comes of his own accord like a vengeful bolt of lightning from unimaginable heights aimed at the dark heart of this demon God.

All the would-be luminaries who read from their "good book" without ever having bothered to learn Latin or Hebrew are the monkeys praying to a nuclear missile in the Planet of the Apes. Lucifer means light bearer in Latin; in Hebrew it is HYLL. When the capitals are strung together like this it is purely a transliteration and not necessarily the pronunciation. In Hebrew HYLL means Morning Star the same thing as Light Bearer. It was the HYLLYL Pharisees, the priests of Lucifer that defended "Jesus" against the ShMY Pharisees, the priests of Jehovah. The HYLLYL Pharisees taught that the entire Torah could be summed up in the golden rule "do unto others as you would have others do unto you".

Gershom Scholem the greatest Hebrew scholar of this century, and perhaps the last two thousand years, wrote that the supreme mystery of the Qabalah was concealed in the true name of Lucifer. He gives it in Hebrew as AYLTh HShCR NGH CVCB which in translation means instrument that brings the light of the brilliant star. But AYLTh besides meaning instrument can also mean gazelle and Jesus is referred to as a gazelle in various apocrypha and Gnostic Tracts. Even those who presumed to edit and change the words of the master in the synoptic gospels and the "Wicked Priest" himself, as Paul is repeatedly referred to in the Dead Sea Scrolls, dared not spew the blaspheme that today pass's as Christianity. What greater blaspheme could ever be committed than to celebrate Sets murder of Osiris by depicting Osiris as an impotent God, naked and dead, hanging from a cross with that pathetic look on his face: "look what you've done to me." This is what Christians are forced to look at every time they enter their churches. This is what they force their children to look at. Blaspheme!

Lucifer as the Morning Star appears in the new testament only twice, once in the synoptic gospels; Peter 1:19 "And so we have the prophetic word confirmed, which you do well to heed as a light that shines in a dark place, until the day dawns and the morning star rises in your hearts; " and again in Revelation 22:16 "I, Jesus, have sent My angel to testify to you these things in the churches. I am the Root and the Offspring of David, the Bright and Morning Star." Revelation makes other cryptic references that Jesus is Lucifer when Jesus says in 22:13 "I am Alpha and Omega, the beginning and the end, the first and the last." The first and the last just like his bride Sophia. This theme is repeated again in 1:8, 1:17, 2:8 and 21:6. It is an incantation woven into the symbolic tapestry that is Revelations. That is why it is repeated five times to conform to the five points on the pentagram.

Herein is Gershom Scholem's mystery: ShCR is a word with a plurality of meanings. It can mean daybreak, but it can also mean nightfall or darkness. Within the Qabalistic name of Lucifer is contained the alpha and the omega of light the same alpha and omega Jesus lays claim to in Revelations. ShCR also has a third meaning and that is to search, and search Lucifer must, because God the one now called Jehovah, the one the Egyptians called Set, has taken Lucifer's bride and concealed and imprisoned her within his creation. She is the life force that animates that creation as well as God himself. This is revealed in Zohar where God says that he can only exist within the Shekinah. It goes on to say: "with this woman are connected all those things which are below, from her body do they receive their nourishment, and from her do they receive blessing". She is the one that Qabalists call Malkah a derivative of the word Malkuth which means The Kingdom. Malkuth encompasses the entire physical world. But she is not only the Kingdom. She is the dark matter and dark energy which are the other nine Sephiroth. Learned Rabbis call her the Shekinah; she who is in exile. The ancient magi called her Zoe. The Egyptians called her Isis or Nuit and the Christian shamans still loyal to Lucifer called her Sophia dividing and concealing her within the three Mary's of the New Testament. In her corporeal form she has been known as Baphomet to the Templers, Vril to the Nazis, and now electromagnetism to mad scientists who would profane her.

    The Jews believe that the messiah must be born into every generation. And so, must his bride Sophia. The Coda Queen is Sophia. As Solomon says in The Book of Wisdom "I loved her above health and beauty, and chose to have her instead of light: for the light that cometh from her never goeth out." Sophia means wisdom in Greek, skill in Magick. When her wisdom is combined with the fire and force of Horus they are Leviathan the Son of Man. According to The Zohars Book of Concealed Mystery the God of Abraham has defeated the kings of Edom and broken the heads of the Dragons upon the waters. But from the books wording it is clear the Dragons have only been restrained not defeated like the kings of Edom. In the Zohar God still awaits his finale battle with the Son of Man. Rabbi Shlomo ben Aderet the thirteenth century Talmudic scholar known as the Rashba taught that Leviathan was the union of man's intellect with his soul, the same as the marriage of the anima and animus to consciousness in CG Jung's interpretation of Rosarium philosophorum. In the Talmud's Bava Basra 74, 2; Rabbi Yehudah teaches that 'if the male and female Leviathan should ever consummate the world that the God of Abraham has created would be made desolate.' The chains by which the demon God binds man and woman to his world of pain and sorrow would be smashed and torn asunder by the limitless power of the Beast that he fears. God so fears Leviathan that he warns the children of Israel even as he gloats in the Book of Job 41:10: "No one is so fierce that he dares to arouse Leviathan; who then is he that can stand before Me?"

CHAPTER 58

    As Jung would have put it she was my anima, and I was her animus. Without her I wasn't exactly the nothing I imagined myself in my grief. I still had what Jung would have defined as the archetypical conscious. I needed her though, she was the archetypical subconscious. She was the collective soul of man; the Shekinah, she who is in exile. The darkness withheld no mysteries from her. She is the mystery. She is the darkness. With her Magick I could squash him like an insect. That was never likely though. Even in the ancient myths Isis never uses her Magick against Set and Hecate is the only Titan who doesn't wage war against Zeus. Like any mother she loves her son. The ancients could not know this so it is not in their moldy old manuscripts but it is love that binds the Goddess to the God of Abraham, the love of a mother for her son, and it is only love that can tear her from him, the love between the Sun and the Moon.

Even without her I could still redefine the word hedonism. It was time for his whore Lilith to show me every foul and unclean act that could occur between a man and a woman. I was not alone in my appreciation of the female form. It is said in Genesis 6:2 "the sons of God saw that the daughters of humans were beautiful, and they married any of them they chose."

The Crown / כתר

CHAPTER 59

The summer of eighty-nine had now begun. Even John was wearing T-shirts under his greasy Carhartt overalls revealing his tree trunk sized arms. Janet hadn't been exaggerating about the new barmaid. If there was such a thing has a hidden master she was one of them. I didn't fear her. I knew by now, as the poet Jimmy Carroll said, I had allies in heaven and I had comrades in hell. But I knew she was a venomous snake and I knew from reading about how most of the herpetologists who studied venomous snakes ended up its best to avoid them even if you do find them fascinating. John had no such reservations. She was a little heavyset and very arrogant, just Johns type. He settled up to the bar at Gaslight and ordered a Wild Turkey. He said "so you know about Crowley I hear. What else do you know about, the hidden masters? There are those who serve Set and those who serve Horus and his prophet four-one-eight. There are no real masters. Who do you serve?" She said "why don't you find out about me? How about I do your tarot cards? When I am done you will know all there is to know." John smirked and said, "your place or mine?" She said, "my place after work." They left in her car after the day shift ended and I went home early. I was told the next day that John showed up back at the Gaslight about 2 AM wearing only his underwear. He took his truck and left. The girl never came back to work again. When I asked John, what had happened he would only say "she started doing my tarot cards and she just knew too much about me. She knew stuff that nobody should know. I had to get out of there. She lives right in Babylon, so I just jogged back to my truck." Right down Sunrise Highway in his skivvies as I found out in the ensuing days. I didn't ask any more questions. I knew better. Red and I were walking into an afterhours club in Babylon a month or two later and she was the barmaid. As soon as I walked through the door she produced a camera and snapped my picture. Red freaked out, he probably thought it was a mob thing. He went behind the bar to take the camera from her and I said "no. Let her keep it." They would make me pay for my overconfidence in the ensuing months. I still did not know Gods Hebrew names.

Nietzsche said, "Be careful, lest in casting out your demon you exorcise the best thing in you." I had no intentions of casting my demon out. I let him drive. The first few months of the summer of eighty-nine were like the golden age. Sooner or later it would have to be Dianne. It could only be Dianne. Anything less was to condemn myself to wander the earth in perpetual hunger. But I was having too much fun with Michelle and everybody else. I just didn't know how little time I had left. I also didn't bargain that Dianne was just as cruel as me.

Patty Esposito started coming around regularly. I didn't think much of it when they gave him the agency. Phil should have just stayed and kept it. I didn't want it, that's for sure. Geir always called Richey "a whore monger!" I tended to agree with him. Richey was giving me money hand over fist and my landscaping business was doing well. I wasn't about to go into the pimp business.

I couldn't listen to anymore of Michelle's bullshit about me taking her car 'to go see Dianne so I rented three or four cars. Actually, it was four but I lost one when I forgot where I parked it. It seemed like it became legal for clubs to remain open in Babylon after hours that summer. We no longer went to Diners after work. Usually everyone went to the Third Rail, a bar over by Babylon train station. There we would party till the sunlight became offensive. All the 'gangsters' went there. It was my new place to hold court and now I had a queen. In Richey's clubs we rolled Richey's customers whenever we could. One time Red got over two thousand in twenty-dollar bills from a drunk sleeping it off in his car in the parking lot. The bills were so new I couldn't even count them. Guys used to come around and sell the dancers high end designer clothes. I determined who came around by how much of a cut they gave me. I don't know if I was drunk or the guy really shorted me, but I had Blockhead thoroughly clean this guy's car out one night. There was an Arab Bazaar at the Third Rail later on. Of course, Michelle was taking the best stuff for herself. This guy we used to call 'hello I'm Sal I'm somebody's son', because that is practically the way he would introduce himself, comes over and asks me if he could buy one of the outfits for his girlfriend. Unfortunately for Sal it was an outfit Michelle had already picked out for herself. She didn't even let me answer him. She physically threw him into a fifty-gallon garbage pail. Only his legs were dangling out of it.

CHAPTER 60

Jim didn't work for me that year, so I hired my cousin Andrew to be my foreman. Andrew was built just like me. He's the same age as my younger sister and they were inseparable, had been since college. I started spending a lot more time with my family, at least the ones that were worth spending time with. My younger sister was getting tickets and free passes for all the concerts in the tri state area courtesy of her music critic boyfriend, so Michelle and I attended a major concert every week that summer. The best one was Melisa Etheridge in the gymnasium of Hofstra University. I was standing twenty feet away staring into her eyes, the favored daughter of the Queen of Night by my side, when she sung Similar Features. I wondered if she knew she was performing for her own muse.

If there were any doubts in my mind as to who and what Dianne was they were only because I was trying so hard not to pay attention. If only I had listened to the music. Morrison had even given me a memo in When the Music's Over when he said, "Music is your only friend." I don't know if I was intoxicated by the pain I was inflicting or the pleasure I was consuming but I was blind. In Late September Dogs Etheridge did everything but spell out that it would all be over in September. She also tells her lover that she has spent hours with the Devil to understand just what they need. She pleads with them saying "the spear in your side is me."

We went to see Cher in concert at Jones Beach and she sung three songs one of them her new smash hit which had resurrected her career; If I Could Turn Back Time. The song said she didn't know why she said and did the things she did. Repeating the by now familiar theme Cher, perhaps the greatest female vocalist of the twentieth century, sung 'words are like weapons and pride is a knife that cuts deep. I didn't mean to inflict the pain that I did. I was too strong to tell you I was sorry and too proud to tell you I was wrong. I would give anything to go back in time and take back those words. Then you would love me like you used to.' Cher delivered Dianne's message. It took about ten minutes and then Cher was whisked away in a helicopter leaving the sellout crowd ripped off and ready to riot.

Those Who Would Arouse Leviathan

Dianne was coming at me with all the power of Isis, a power that could override even God himself, but I was unmoved. She could resurrect Janis Joplin to apologize for inflicting the wound of Aforteas on me and fly in the greatest living female vocalist to tell me she was sorry but Joan of Arc herself wouldn't have moved me. Nothing less than the words coming right from her incarnated lips were ever going to move me at that point. I, in flesh and blood, had burned down the Mafia and the most powerful motorcycle gang on the east coast just to hold her hand. She could speak two then three words and until she did I was going to take whatever pleasure I could with My Michelle, a title from the album Appetite for Destruction and my lover that didn't throw needless complications into what was all very simple.

The Who in the Meadowlands was a classic, not for the way they played. The Who themselves were disappointing. But the event was the perfect date. We took my sister, Andrew, and a few of their friends, in one of my rentals. We stopped to get something to eat at Kentucky Fried Chicken in North Amityville since Michelle and I had only left the Third Rail long enough to go home shower and get ready for the concert. While we were at Kentucky Fried Chicken Michelle had a fender bender at the drive through with some loud-mouthed Black girl. While this girl was jawing, Michelle was taking off all her jewelry. When she was done she pulled off her stiletto heels and got out still brandishing one of them. Without saying a word Michelle in a matter of fact fashion permanently disfigured the girl's face with her high heeled shoe. Michelle never even messed up her makeup. The other girls lip was half hanging off and the rest of her face was a gory mess. I ended up knocking out her boyfriend, but he was pretty tough. He got back up after convulsing on the floor for a couple of minutes. His gyrations on the pavement saved him from my usual sense of fair play where I would kick him into a bloody hamburger. I was quite surprised when he got back up and resumed fighting. Andrew lent me some assistance in making sure he stayed down the second time. Then we had to leave because Blacks were streaming from every building. We still hadn't eaten any food yet and we were hungry when we got to the Meadowlands. Everyone was barbequing in the parking lot, so we traded Andrews sister's best friend for some hamburgers for Michelle and I, sausage's for everyone else. We didn't see the girl for the rest of the night. When we left the concert Michelle must have run over every cone in New Jersey. We weren't waiting on any lines. The bumper was already hanging off the car anyway. Somewhere there's a picture of Michelle and I kissing against the brilliant red sunset that evening. It's easily the best love photo I have ever seen that wasn't staged.

Michelle and I continued to explore the deepest darkest corridors of sexuality but "When sleep at last has come on limbs that had run wild." I lay on the left side of the bed, on my left side, the pillow pulled tight to me. I would shut my eyes and the pillow was Dianne. I never told Michelle I loved her. She probably didn't need Lilith to tell her what was coming. When she worked at the Rainforest and I worked with Dianne Michelle was almost guaranteed to walk out before her shift was over. One-time Doxie haltingly informed me that my clothes were strewn all over the parking lot of Bogart's. I went outside and sure enough they were.

    She wasn't like that all the time. In fact if Dianne wasn't in the picture she didn't care what I did. One night she encouraged me to go hang out with some girls that were recruiting, on Long Island, for a female chapter of the Hell's Angels. The only thing that could be more insulting to the Pagans was if some guys were recruiting for a male chapter of the Hells Angels on Long Island. The clubs were blood rivals and Long Island was the Pagans territory at the time. But the girls were a lot of fun and everyone knew them, so they were letting them do it. We actually ended up staying over by Farmingdale in some biker bars that were the last strongholds of the Pagans. They were buying me drinks all night and I took about twenty hits of some 'good' acid the girls had. By the time I got back to Bogart's at about 3 AM on the back of a bike I was as inebriated as anyone still standing can get.

    Bobby and all his Cretins were there but hardly anyone else. Michelle stubbornly refused to close the bar early so she could take me home. I went behind the bar and I grabbed the Wild Turkey. I broke the top of the bottle off on the bar and started guzzling it from the jagged glass just like in the movies. By the time I finished the bottle she had all the meticulously polished glass's neatly stacked in pyramids on each side of the bar. She was taking her sweet ass time, deliberately antagonizing me. She still hadn't even called last call. I broke the empty bottle on the floor and picked up a bar stool yelling "The bars closed!" Then I broke every glass on the bar. Some guys were sitting in the corner covered in the shattered glass and I staggered up to them still brandishing my trusty bar stool. I half sneered half slurred "didn't you hear? The bars closed!" One of them had the balls to actually deck me, either that or I finally passed out. But I heard that he ended up taking quite a beating from Michelle and the Cretins. They took me to my mother's house and put me in the guest bed down in the converted garage. When I awoke, around noon the next day, I was peeing five feet straight up in the air and back down on Michelle and me.

    Richey tried to get cute again after that. By this time, I didn't need John to tell me how to deal with him. When I saw he had cut

Michelle from five days to four I went right in his office. I showed him the schedule and said, "why does Michelle only have four days on here?" He starts sputtering "she never even finish's those shifts at the Rainforest. She's the only girl that even does five shifts. That's too much. She's gonna get burned out." I slammed my forty-four onto his desk with the barrel pointing at him. I don't believe in leaving the chamber over the hammer empty. I said "Richey! You see my new gun? It's bigger than yours." Richey quickly said "I don't care how many days she works. Tell Red to put her on the schedule seven days a week if you want. I was just looking out for you. You gotta live with her." He was right too. I didn't need the money and neither did she, but we just couldn't let him get away with something like that so I said, "tell Patty that Bobby will be booking some girls too for now on." Bobby had about three or four already that Marlena and him had cultivated from dance clubs. By the time Bobby's list had twenty-five girls Phil would reappear and Mark would be unable to attend a meeting with me at the Crazy Clown because someone had shot him in the back of the head in the parking lot before I got there. The rest of the owners, except Richey, would go into hiding. Joey Massera and his whole crew were going to become history. Richey would be the only man left standing. He knew how to play his cards with us. He shut his mouth.

CHAPTER 61

It couldn't have been very far into the summer when I was standing at the door of Bogart's watching the traffic on Sunrise highway and someone grabbed my shoulder. I didn't need to turn around to know who. She had a way of touching me that nobody ever had before or since. I guess it was the same way I held my forty-four. Dianne had a warm yet apprehensive smile on her face. I hadn't seen her smile at me in months. In fact, we hadn't even talked in over a month. She had been beaten up by some firemen while doing a private party. Vinnie had taken her there. I wanted to kill him, and I wanted to kill him real bad but I knew that would seal everyone's fate forever. So instead I figured the best thing would be for Dianne and me to stop talking to each other.

She said, "I have to talk to you." I said, "where's Prince Charming?" Her eyes shifted down from mine and she said, "we're not getting along but that's not why I need to talk to you." I said, "what a shame. I was hoping you would ask me to kill him for you." Her hand was still on my shoulder and she began kneading my muscles with it. She went on "I live in the basement of my mother's house and every time it rains the walls have been leaking like a sieve. I had some guys from here look at it and one of them said the foundations cracked and the other one said I just have drainage problems. Can you take a look at it for me?" I said "if the foundations cracked there's not really much you can do about it and that's not my field of expertise. If it's the drainage I'll fix it, but you got to pay my costs and my labor. Believe it or not Geir actually does get paid." She laughed and I felt that old familiar feeling in my groin. She said "I don't expect you to work for free. I plan on paying you." I said "I don't want to be running into Vinnie while I'm there Dianne. If I do then I'm not responsible for what happens." She giggled uncertainly and said "I haven't even seen him in a week. When can you come over?" I said, "tomorrow afternoon." She told me where her house was. I had known where it was two days after I met her, but I played along writing down the directions.

    The next day I went over there. She lived in one of those Levitt house's behind the hospital in East Meadow. I had always figured the girl had never had a chance since the day she was born. But then who does? She looked really happy to see me when I got there and all I could think to myself was I had to be careful and not throw away my co-op in Lynbrook with the doorman who knew my name for a temporary home in a damp dingy basement in East Meadow. I would get her out of there and off that stage but when I was good and ready. That was the way she wanted it. Wasn't it?

    She had three big dogs and they were using the area directly in front of the foundation in the backyard as a run. The grade was lowest right by the house where the soil was hard packed by the incessant prancing of the dogs. I thought to myself; and I hate the parrots? I said "Dianne you can't just let the dogs run up by the house like this. The soils become hard packed and your gutters are draining right into it. Of course, waters coming into your basement. Where else is it gonna go? I have to till this soil and regrade it. Then we need to run those gutters out from the house. If you want I'll put some sod in." She asked me how much it was going to cost with the sod, and I said "six hundred dollars. But I have to do it in the afternoons after work." She said that would be fine. Yea for her. It was gonna cost me money to do the job and Geir and Andrew were not going to like their new hours. I couldn't run a full crew there. I was losing money as it was. I told her I would start it tomorrow. At the time I thought she really needed my help but in retrospect that foundation had probably been leaking like that for years. I don't know why this girl just couldn't speak her mind. All she had to do was state the obvious and say I'm sorry and I love you. I would have broken down in tears right on the spot. Why did I have to find out from Melissa Etheridge and Cher how she felt about things?

Those Who Would Arouse Leviathan

She was making her big play for me. The one I should have been ready for. The same one I had been telling myself would culminate with the redemption of the Gods. Now I thought I was on a landscaping job. It would have been better if I had been born with a little more understanding of woman and a little less Fire and Force. But who am I to second guess anything. I had my chance and I failed miserably.

I showed up early on the regular job and I worked like an animal to make enough time to do Dianne's job. I think I still had to take a separate day to lay some thousand square feet of sod. Cut sod doesn't keep well and it was already hot. I remember Andrew and I were working with our shirts off. I wasn't trying to impress Dianne. If there was one thing I knew I didn't have to do with her it was prove my virility just that I had a heart even a tiny one. Again, I failed miserably.

Her friends from East Meadow kept coming over. I guess she was showing me to them. I think I remarked to her how ugly they all were and didn't she have anything decent for my cousin. One guy asked me if I would be using lime. He looked like the town drunk. Him I told "I don't need any lime. I'm gonna go back to the yard and get the chipper. We can feed you into it. We'll just spray you all over the topsoil before we lay any grass. You're organic! We won't have to worry about the PH!" I'm sure I embarrassed the shit out of her. That was my intentions. It cost me more to do the job than she was paying for it and I was going to get my money's worth. Dianne had gotten me started long ago and unlike my hapless victims at the bars she had no one to drag me off of her. If only she had just went out with me after she broke up with Charlie. I still loved her just as much as I always did but I couldn't show her or tell her anymore. In fact, I had become afraid to.

She wanted me to come back after the first day and hang out with her and her friends in some parking lot on Hempstead Turnpike. I said, "Dianne I haven't hung out in a parking lot since I was seventeen years old." And really I hadn't since Tanner Park. She said "does it really matter where we hang out. I'm gonna be there! You'll have the best time of your life!" Then she scrunched up her face to a little girl war hoop. I told her I couldn't come because Michelle was expecting me home and she said, "Fuck Michelle!" I said "yes. I have over and over again. All night every night and I am already having the time of my life."

Dianne was wearing baggy grey sweat pants and dirty sneakers most of the time I was there. She explained to me without me asking "this is the way I dress when I'm not around the clubs. I know it's a little grungy, but this is the way I'm comfortable. You seem to think I wear that stuff I wear around the clubs all the time. I never wear it when I'm not in the clubs." I couldn't tell her. She already had me scared to say what was really on my mind. But without the leather and chains, in her baggy sweat pants and dirty sneakers, she was the most adorable thing I have ever seen.

I had to pick up the balance when I was done. She made me go into the bedroom and she shut the door on her friends who were sitting around the kitchen. We sat on her bed and looked at all her old photo albums. Really, it was the most romantic thing she could have done after making herself so inaccessible for almost two years, but something had hardened my heart. I had already determined that I was not going for this at least until the end of the summer. So, when she leaned in to kiss me and stuck her tongue in my mouth I pushed her away. I can still taste how sweet that tongue was, even though it was only a fraction of a second and I can still see the look of hurt in her eyes when I pushed her away. I had no right to do that. I had tried to kiss her some two dozen times. Not once did she ever even come close to pushing me away.

I still wasn't satisfied with the damage I had done so I made a little speech, easily the stupidest things that have ever come out of my mouth. I said "where's Vinnie Dianne? What am I gonna kiss you back? Then I'm gonna make love to you on the bed you grew up on. I'm gonna break up with Michelle. I'm gonna lose my co-op and my self-respect. Then Vinnie will show up at the backdoor." She said "well what do you want guarantees? I wasn't ready before and I told you that a million times." She was right. What was I, Richey examining his stock options?

I had been telling myself all along that it was so important that she should know that we were giving ourselves to each other for eternity, but she already knew that better than I did. She knew it in her subconscious where the Goddess dwelled. It was me who still didn't want to admit to myself that this was all real. Even if it was impossible that was inconsequential. There were those who believed it was possible, those with the power of Gods. Their rules were we had to die upon the consummation of our love. There is no turning back from death but sometimes you have to let nature take its course. Like the Rosarium philosophorum says when the Great Work begins at stage two, as it was about to do right then and there, "you should employ venerable nature, because from her through her and in her is our art born and in naught else: and so, our magisterium is the work of nature and not the worker."

I left without ever even apologizing for pushing her away. Now it was me who knew subconsciously just what I had done. It ate away at me for the rest of the summer like a malignant cancer. Now I hated myself more than I had ever hated anyone else, even God himself.

CHAPTER 62

Those Who Would Arouse Leviathan

Michelle had what looked to be a very heavy, very old, elongated oval door mirror propped up by a chair at the left foot of the queen-sized bed. It was framed in wood that was painted gold. I was told to never touch that mirror. Further back beyond the foot of the bed were the dresser and a large single piece mirror that hung above it on the wall. The walk-in closet on the right side of the bed also had mirrors on its sliding doors. There were polished brass lighting fixtures placed around the room randomly. The polished brass would reflect the images in the mirrors. The brass would sometimes show the wrinkles in the bed sheets reflected from the mirrors in the likenesses of Austin Osman Spare paintings. Hideously misshapen creatures engaged in orgiastic revelries and struck fantastic poses. If you messed the sheets up the polished brass would reveal different images. Many of the images were clear enough to have taken photographs of although I never did. There was nothing ambiguous about them. Some of the reflections in the brass were as detailed as Spare's paintings themselves.

Up to a quarter of Michelle's hair would at times rise straight up like something was gently lifting it. Sometimes a network of tiny blue sparks would appear in the hairs that were standing. Her hair would usually rise during intercourse particularly when she was on top facing and straddling me from a kneeling position. It usually occurred at night when we had ingested cocaine but not always. Whenever this phenomenon would occur Michelle exhibited praeterhuman intelligence. When it happened, sexual sensations were amplified and my ejaculation increased. It was as if something was draining me, prolonging my orgasm. These manifestations would last for hours and Michelle would say personnel things about me that no other human would know. She talked about having met my father and being sent to me by him. Some of what she was saying was outright bullshit but much of it was true. She seemed to know every sexual fantasy I had ever had, and she would talk about them in detail as she tried to reenact them in the bedroom. She did not know about Rosarium Philosophorum or any of the death and orgasm parts. Those seemed to be blocked from her and she knew she was missing information. She would become frustrated, frequently interrogating me while we were having sex. Sometimes she would get angry and conduct furious conversations to the mirrors complaining about having to be with me.

She had little memory of any of this during the light of the day except if we were still having sex from the night before. If the orgasmic succession remained unbroken the phenomena could occur at any time of the day or night. Sometimes I would try to trick her into revealing the origin and intention of the praeterhuman intelligence. She always maintained it was Lilith. When I tried to question her as to her childhood and her experiences with her mother her memories seemed jumbled and she was evasive. She talked about a staff engraved with some kind of letters that she said resembled Masonic ciphers that I had showed her from Manly Halls 'Big Book.' The staff made her mother very powerful within her coven. She also told me that when she was young she had been drowned to the point where she washed up on a Florida beach lifeless and had to be resuscitated by emergency personnel. After the incident, her mother had become furious with her and beat her.

One afternoon the sun was shining through the windows on a brilliant summer day, but the room appeared to grow ten times brighter than it already was. Michelle scrambled over me and jumped out of bed on the left side. She had a panicked look in her face. With her palms upturned and her arms slightly extended in front of her toward the mirror on the floor she said, "But I didn't tell him anything!" The light in the room grew even brighter and she fell to the floor naked. Her eyes rolled back showing only the white. She began to froth at the mouth. I jumped out of the bed to help her. All the while the light grew blindingly bright. I was suddenly overcome with overwhelming fear.

I ran out of the apartment and down a flight of stairs to another apartment door on the third floor. I banged on the door and a woman about my own age answered. I was still naked which did not at all seem to surprise her. She ushered me in. She opened the door to her bedroom and went in shutting the door behind her. She came out repeating the procedure of closing the door behind her in reverse and gave me a pair of sweat pants. She asked me what had happened. I told her my girlfriend was having a seizure. She went in her bedroom and closed the door. She came out a couple of minutes later, closing the door behind her again, and told me she had called the police and they were coming. She told me to just wait there. She then went back in her bedroom and shut the door again leaving me in the living room by myself. I knew the answers to all my questions were behind that door but also knew that I should not open it. The whole situation unnerved me all over again and I ran from her apartment too.

I ran down three flights of stairs and into the street and began running north on Peninsula Boulevard. I jumped on the roof of a car that was passing me and held on. The car accelerated up the road till it came to a light where it had to stop behind the other cars. I jumped off and kept running north. I repeated the procedure a few more times till I passed Southern State Parkway, about four miles north of where I started. Finally, a van style ambulance pulled up with a six man emergency crew. The guys convinced me to let them take me to Mercy Hospital right down Peninsula Boulevard. On the way there they complained of being interrupted from their weekend barbeques. They told me my condition was the same as they had seen in some Vietnam Vets. I said, "I'm too young to have ever been in Vietnam." One of the personnel said "let us just put this wet wash cloth over your eyes. We have found that light exposure will trigger the panic. It will relax you." They put a warm wet wash cloth over my eyes. Having the light shut down from my perception relaxed me a great deal. They took me from the ambulance by gurney into Mercy Hospital to a small emergency room where I was the only patient. They repeated the same procedure with the wet wash cloth. I heard a voice saying, "does anyone know who was with him when this happened." A frantic effort ensued in the seemingly make shift emergency room to locate my point of origin. In about a half hour Michelle arrived. She was dressed very sharply. She walked in like she owned the place and said "Lick. Oh, there's my Lickster. I've been looking all over for you." Then she turned to the couple of doctors that were there and coldly said "is he alright to go?" They answered in the affirmative and we just left. I never saw a cop. When I got in her car I said "I thought you were having a seizure. What just happened and why were there no police involved? You can't just do the kind of shit I just did without the police getting involved." She said "the police came but I was fine. I don't remember having any seizure. I might of. I used to get them when I was a little girl after I drowned in Florida. They left and I have been looking for you ever since." I said, "there were lines all over the dresser." She said, "I threw them away before they got there." I said, "how did you know they were getting there?" She said, "you were gone." I asked her the rest of the obvious questions. She had an answer for everything, none of them very plausible.

CHAPTER 63

A couple of nights later Bobby and Marlena came over. Michelle and Marlena started having a conversation about what had happened and all the flak from the board that Sal's family had been catching lately over our antics. There were guys and girls stopping in at all hours of the day and night, a few weeks before Geir and I had come up there past midnight. When I used my key, I found Michelle had chained the door. I was banging on that door for a half hour yelling her name into the darkened apartment. Everybody on the fourth floor came out of their apartments. I got no response from inside. Figuring somebody had to have called the police by now we threw our guns through the opening that the chain allowed in the door, locked it, and left. When I called her from my mother's Michelle said she had been sleeping.

Michelle and Marlena's conversation took on an unnervingly business-like tone. I had heard Michelle talk like this before, usually when she was Lilith, but never Marlena who almost always stuck to baby talk. The content of the conversation was innocuous enough but between the both of them they must have said Old Ones at least a half a dozen times. By now I more or less knew what was going on. I had read H.P. Lovecraft. In his famous Cthulhu mythos Lovecraft said 'the Old Ones were sleeping on the bottom of the oceans and biding their time till the right astral alignment when they can once again walk the earth in their terrible reign. They were a race of monsters from the far-off stars who had once ruled the earth as Gods feeding on human pain and depravity. They were served by a secret priesthood of Gods, humanoids, and magi, who awaited their return and worked tirelessly to bring it about.'

The Old Ones of HP Lovecraft, the Titans of the Greeks, and the Dragons whose heads are broken by the waters in the Zohar are one in the same. As Jung noted in Rosarium philosophorum the king and queen are sometimes depicted as dragons. In The Zohar's Book of Concealed Mystery Leviathan is the king dragon whom the God of Abraham has banished to the great sea. The Book of Concealed Mystery goes on to say that the king and queen dragons were two, but they have been reduced into one. Mathers pedantically explains that passage by saying 'God has slain the queen dragon lest they should mate and their judgments against man multiply.' But as Crowley knew all too well Mathers was a fool. He refused to accept that there were hidden masters that knew far more than his moldy old manuscripts. I was among them now, the witch's and sorcerers, the most ancient of the Magi.

In his boundless hubris the god of Abraham boasts in the Book of Job 41:10: "No one is so fierce that he dares to arouse Leviathan; who then is he that can stand before Me?" But he has already said In Job 3:8 that there are those who curse his days, "Those who are ready to arouse Leviathan." The Abrahamic God has contradicted himself once too often. It is he who is the real devil and as the Jesus says in John 8: 44 "a murderer from the beginning, and abode not in the truth, because there is no truth in him. When he speaks a lie, he speaks of his own: for he is a liar, and the father of it." We as men know that when faced by a tyrant there are those among us who are fierce enough to do whatever it is going to take to defeat him. I was one of them. In fact, to them I was Leviathan or at least one half of Leviathan. Nobody ever will say it better than Jim Morrison "I am the lizard king."

Those Who Would Arouse Leviathan

Michelle had been telling Marlena that the old ones didn't want us there anymore. I said "how come you both seem to need to use the words Old Ones with every other sentence? If the Old Ones don't want us here anymore we will move." I was feeling hostile and alone when I said "I don't need Sal's co-op just like I didn't need his Uzi. I don't need anything from them, and you can tell them that for me. He can have his hand carved dining room set back but I'm keeping the forty-four. You said it was yours. We're moving! Find us a new place." Michelle looked at me and then she looked at Bobby. She said "Bobby can you two take a walk outside for a while. I think he needs some fresh air." I said, "yea maybe I do need some fresh air."

When Bobby and I got in the elevator I said, "Marlena's one of them." He looked at me with his perplexed rat face and said, "one of who?" I grinned and said, "more like one of what." He said, "I'm not following you but I understand you're trying to say something important." I said "no Bobby I can't just say it. It's for you and the rest of the sub creatures to find out. Let me just say this. Have you ever wondered why the likes of John, Phil, and me, are in Richey's topless bars toying around with biker gangs and mobsters? It's like using a howitzer to shoot squirrels." He said, "yea to tell you the truth I wonder about that all the time." I said "I can't tell you why Bobby or I probably could but I don't want to ruin the surprise. All I can tell you is everything is not what it appears to be. Believe nothing that you're told and only half of what you see."

The panic attacks continued whenever I did cocaine. I did not run out of the co-op anymore naked, nor did Michelle have anymore 'seizures' but sexual arousal could turn to unrestrained terror within me in moments. Michelle, Lilith, and I, checked into the Sayonara Motel one night in Amityville and by 9AM I was running north up Route 110. For some reason it was always towards Dianne's house. This time I had put my clothes on before I ran out of the room. A paramedic van arrived once again this time in only a few minutes. They whisked me off to Brunswick Hospital where Michelle picked me up after a half hour, again like it was no big deal that I was running through traffic jumping on the tops of moving cars.

I told Michelle what had happened between Dianne and I. Lilith could not see what Dianne was doing. Lilith is an insect as compared to Hecate. Michelle was taken completely by surprise. She said "how come you weren't with her that's what you want isn't it? It's what everybody wants accept me." I said "I don't know what I want any more Michelle. That girl played head games with me for two years when she had no fucking reason to whatsoever. Now all of a sudden I'm with you and she wants me. Maybe I like being with you is that so impossible?" Michelle really didn't take it that badly only when I told her Dianne had went through her old photo albums with me. Then she began to cry.

CHAPTER 64

A few weeks later Whitehead and I went to Cypress Hills. When we came back we went to Geirs apartment. I needed some space from Michelle. I needed to think about all this but cocaine sure wasn't going to help me think. I had another panic attack in Geirs apartment. I was screaming and yelling, and I broke one of his windows. I grabbed a knife from the kitchen, and they wrestled it away from me. I accidently got stabbed through an artery in my bicep. Unless pressure was applied to the wound it spurted blood three feet out every time my heart pumped. We wrapped it up then I continued with my insanity. The fact that neither one of them ran out on me attests to a super human fortitude on their part. The police never came and the landlord that lived right downstairs never said anything to Geir that he had a crazy man up in his apartment. Every time they got me calmed down I would do another huge line and start all over again. Geir kept saying "did you ever think that all those things were really here and they're just waiting for you to die so they can get to you." I said "Geir on the day my soul leaves my body they will be running to the furthest reaches of hell to hide from me. You just don't get it. I want to die. This way I can get even with them and I don't have to deal with these two bitches anymore!"

There was a knock at the door, and somebody came up. I do not know why but for some reason I could not see who it was. They put a wet wash cloth over my eyes and whoever it was held me from behind. They were much stronger than Geir and Whitehead combined. They were stronger even than me. Sometime during the night, even though I was wired out of my mind on cocaine, I must have passed out. When I awoke that morning, sunlight was streaming through the window. Whitehead and Geir were both passed out sitting up on the sofa. I woke them both up and asked them who had come over to help them last night with me. Neither one of them would answer. Geir said "does it matter? That's the best friend your ever gonna have. He's the one who looks out for you. Always!" I said "Geir you have just become coherent this year after being a babbling idiot for seven years. Your now fucking one of Richey's best-looking dancers." He was; Lauren, she was an opera singer and she was hot. I would have been sleeping with her myself if I didn't have Michelle and he wasn't. I continued "that's because of me Geir. Don't make any mistakes about that. This is my world you are in. Please stop playing at being a hidden master. We have enough of them around here already. Now take me over Johns. Me and him have to talk."

When we got to his house in East Islip he was playing with his 'new' plasma cutter which he had set up in his garage. He said "it's one of the first ones ever made. I think I can even get it to work." I said "yea it's the coolest old piece of shit I have ever seen John. Aren't you tired from last night?" He didn't answer me and Geir just stood there with a stupid look on his face too. I said "John I've pretty much got it all figured out. Correct me if I'm wrong. I'm Aleister Crowley ain't I? And Dianne Rodney; Roddie Minor the Scarlet woman in the Amalantrah Working? Cute. Maybe I should just call her Rodney Major. The Amalantrah Working worked. He was able to incarnate the Sun into his own soul. That's what Ipsissimus means. He no longer needs the Sun God. He is the Sun God. Same thing with her, she was able to incarnate the Moon into her soul too, but they had trouble then and they're having trouble now. Did I really think we could just bring them both together and all would be forgiven? That was pretty stupid of me. Their trouble with each other started even before time began. If she left him she left him for a reason."

He just looked at me stone faced. I continued "There are far too many" I paused looking for a label but there were none "whatever they are; involved in this that are taking their directives from moldy old manuscripts. The Nazi's, the CIA, the Mafia, the Witch's, and let's not forget the Astrum Argentum and their Free Masons, and those are just the incarnated. By the way which one do you work for or is it all of them? You already told me that they told you their all the same thing. Remember? Jesus, or shouldn't I say that? How long have you known? At least since we were twelve and you took me to that island, and they used that tortoise to put Jim Morrison's soul in me. That's how it's done through changelings. I'm honored but when, exactly, did I acquire Crowley? My guess is when I had that dream when I was a kid. I guess Dianne had the same kind of dream or did she drown too? Or maybe she just died from the hepatitis. Was I just killing time when I was Morrison? Did I really need to spell it out for the sub creatures? Or was that all just for my own personal consumption?" He wouldn't answer me. He just kept saying "I don't know. Maybe. It sounds right." I said, "c'mon John Celebration of the Lizard "sun sun sun burn burn burn moon moon moon I will get you soon, soon, soon!" Yea soon, soon, soon. Meanwhile I've got a gaping hole in my heart, probably her too. I'm a Changeling John. See me change? When did Crowley first come into me? Was it when I had that dream or was it when I seen the Devil in my mother's kitchen, just like he did? No that couldn't have been it he was already in

Morrison. But that's right you said he could be in more than one place at the same time. In Celebration of the Lizard Morrison talked about playing strange games with the girls on the island. Crowley played his strange games on the island of Cefalù. I play mine on Long Island. And I'm gonna keep playing them John till you think of something else. This shits not gonna work. It's all fucked up and you know it! She's an unrepentant pig and that's just what I've become too." Suddenly the lights in the garage went out and we were in pitch black darkness. There were no windows in the garage. I figured maybe one of them was going to shoot me in the head and we were going to try all over again with the next incarnation. When nothing happened, I walked out into the sunlight followed by John and Geir. For the first time in his life John looked like he was afraid. I said "what's a matter John? Having trouble with the electricity?" He stammered "that's never happened before." I said "where gonna have to figure something else out."

Geir and I went to Gaslight after that and I was in the back room contemplating whether I should write my name in blood on the wall, for Dianne to see, with my severed artery. I decided against it so instead I had Geir take me back to Lynbrook. There I told the demons to heal the artery. There was a tingling sensation all around the wound and when I took the wrap off blood didn't spurt out anymore. A couple of days later I went to a hospital and had them put a stitch in it, but it was already healed.

CHAPTER 65

When I had told Geir I wanted to die I wasn't exaggerating. I just didn't care about anything anymore. I was walking death. I was drinking a couple of quarts of whisky and making two trips into Cypress Hills every day. I would start in the morning with one of Sal's collector's edition bottles then I would have someone take me to Cypress Hills in the afternoon. By evening I was repeating the procedure all over again. There was a liquor store right on the corner and after Sal's whiskey finally ran out I remember standing in front of it at 9AM in the rain wondering when it opened. I was still on probation. Somehow I never got a dirty urine, probably courtesy of the Astrum Argentum and the Free Masons. Every time I tried to sober up all I could see were Dianne's eyes staring into mine with that look of hurt I left her with.

We moved out of the co-op and into an upscale apartment complex in Deer Park on the outskirts of Babylon. I remember when Andrew and I moved all me and Michelle's stuff. It was a brilliant summer day not a cloud in the sky. No sooner did we pull up Peninsula with my International fully loaded than it started to rain from a clear blue sky. Andrew stuck his head out the window looking up and said "I never seen anything like this before. There's not a cloud in the sky and the sun is shining. Where is the rain coming from?" I didn't say anything. How could I tell my cousin the Goddess was crying?

I wasn't working for Richey anymore. I didn't want to be in the bars. I would never be able to bear seeing her face again without getting on my knees. I didn't work for myself either. I told my mother to keep all the money. I figured I had more than enough money to kill myself. Sometimes I would stop at Bogart's and Gaslight at four AM when I knew she wasn't going to be there. One time I went in the Gaslight and Doxie couldn't get this bachelor party out even though there were no more dancers left on stage. I went out to my car. When I came back in I had my three hundred Savage. I pointed it at the bachelor party chambered a round and yelled "the bars closed!" They trampled each other getting out of there. Another time Richey called me and asked me if I could beat up a drug dealer for him. I said as long as Dianne's not there. He told me she wasn't, so I went down to Gaslight. When I got there Richey was sitting by the bar with Doxie and some four-hundred-pound slob was stomping around claiming Doxie owed him money. Shocking. I knocked him out right in the bar, but he was too heavy for me to move by myself so Richey and Doxie helped me drag the whale out onto Horus's alter on the curb. When we got outside he regained consciousness and flopped to his knees. I nailed him with my Doc Martin, a kick Richey later told me looked like it was choreographed for the movies. It picked him up off the ground and blood and teeth went flying in all directions. He landed on his back with a resounding thud. His shirt had slipped above his huge belly as he hit the ground and his hairy stomach oscillated like a bowl of Jell-O in an aftershock. I left before the ambulance and police got there as was my custom.

CHAPTER 66

Our apartment in Deer Park became ground zero for the next twenty some odd years of perversion that the human race would defile itself with. There were times when I was blind folded, and my hands were tied in the darkness. I could actually feel Lilith's talons raking my ass. Later when I would ask Michelle "what was that you had on my ass?" She would say "my foot." It was no human foot.

I knew what I was doing, and I would have my war with God even if I could not win. I was going to go down just like Ahab stabbing at the brute with my harpoon even until my finale breath. Lilith would come into Michelle every night taunting me "why don't you just go to your little whore? You don't want to be here. You want to go look at more pictures of her when she was a little baby stripper. Go to your little whore. The two of you are meant for each other, a pair of losers!" Her sexual appetites grew more and more sadistic and frequently I would have black eyes for days. Michelle was nothing like this when she wasn't under the influence of Lilith. She was fun loving and wanted to please me to the point of being demure. It was me who was now conjuring up Lilith not her. All my friends loved Michelle even John. One-night Geir, who was sleeping over on the couch, snuck into our bedroom and sprinkled rose pedals all around the bed while we were sleeping.

    Geirs sentimental intentions aside I knew in my heart that Michelle was never supposed to have stayed with me. She was supposed to have backed way off when the time came, she probably even had a boyfriend stashed somewhere. I didn't believe her for one second about being asleep when that chain was on the door in Lynbrook. She had been fighting with her mother since the summer began about being with me. Michelle claimed it was because her mother didn't like me. I had never met her mother, nor had I ever spoken to her. They weren't speaking anymore, and they never would again. Michelle was falling in love with me. It was inevitable and they should have known. Fire and Force carry's over almost seamlessly from the battlefield to the bedroom. Every time we partied and engaged in marathon sex we would fight and either she would leave, or I would throw her out. But she would always come back in a day or two. All her stuff was there anyway.

    I began to really resent Lilith and her filthy habit of putting her hands on me. She was truly malevolent towards me and she had the ability to get inside my head when my resolve was weakened by cocaine. She is the God of Abrahams whore and the fact that she really wanted to kill me is what turned me on about her. One night when Michelle's hair was standing straight up I kicked some holes in the wall around her head and told Lilith to leave. She said, "you can't hurt me!" And I said "I can purge you from the face of the earth forever by using fire to burn this place to the ground. You think I care if you and I die? You think I care how many sub creatures I kill?" Michelle's hair collapsed in conformance to the laws of gravity and she made no more references to or by Lilith for the rest of that night.

    It was not long before Labor Day when Andrew threw an end of summer pool party over my aunt's house in Ronkonkoma. At the time I was the only one who had money in my family, so it was one of those above ground pools. Andrew, my sister, and all their friends were there. Ronkonkoma, just like East Meadow, is a solid White working-class town. There were no rich people at this party and no cocaine. We ran out of liquor and I was sending Michelle and my sister up to the store to get some when Andrew said, "I got booze." He opened up his bedroom closet door and he had commandeered the entire bar from Beefsteak Charlie's. He had been the night manger there before he worked for me. The chain had gone bankrupt, but Andrew certainly had gotten his 'golden parachute.' He had never said a word till we ran out of the booze I had brought to the party. Andrew would go on to become a very wealthy man.

    Maybe it was because I wasn't doing coke but all I could think of that night was Dianne. It was a crowd that was the same age as her and the same economic status. She would have loved the absence of hard drugs, the absence of airs of self-importance and the splashing around in the four foot deep swimming pool. She probably couldn't swim anyway. What was I thinking and why did I do this to her? After courting her like an obsessed troubadour for almost two years she had offered me her hand and I had bitten it and walked away. I was just a very tough guy with some very tough and strange friends. I was making far too much of it. She and I weren't Gods Nemesis. I was making UFO's out of swamp gas. We could have a long and happy life together. Richey had offered to sell me the busiest topless bar on the east end of Long Island; the Crazy Clown. My uncle was going to finance the deal with me. I would get her a strip club to run to satisfy her Napoleon complex and I would hold her close every night in the darkness of our bedroom. Neither of us would ever be lonely again. She would make me feel just like when I held her close in the clubs. 'Lilith' was right about one thing and one thing only Dianne and I were meant for each other.

    When I pulled up to Bogart's that day I thought everything was going to be alright and I'm never optimistic. She would be mad at me and she had every right to be. I hadn't even seen her in over two months. I knew she probably had gone back with Vinnie. I would compete with him for her affections like a gentleman. Why not? It was a foregone conclusion that I would win. I had kicked Michelle out and straightened up for a couple of days. If Dianne wanted me to quit doing cocaine I would. I liked cocaine. I loved her. She was up on stage when I walked in and she looked at me kind of funny like she had been waiting for me. She always looked like she had been waiting for me but this looked a little different. She looked like a gluttonous fat man whose diner had finally arrived. I spoke first almost breathless because I was so excited to see her. "How did the grass take? Have you been keeping water on it? I'm sorry I haven't seen you lately, but I've been really busy. I don't even work here no more. Is the water still coming in through the wall?" She said "there's still a little water coming in but it's much better. The grass is fine. I water it every day. Have you heard?" I said, "heard what?" She jutted her jaw out at me and said it like she was relishing it "I'm pregnant. It's Vinnie's. I'm gonna have it. I just found out a couple of days ago." Twenty guys who were sitting at the tables got up in unison, chairs clattering as they fell to the floor, and hastily left the bar. There was once again only me and her staring through eternity into each other's eyes. I just looked at her. I didn't say anything. I couldn't. I remembered Melody telling me she wanted to look in my eyes as I died. Dianne was.

    A day or two later I met Michelle down by Amity Harbor beach. She had been staying with my mother. I asked her why she had made no attempt to move on yet and she burst into tears saying that she needed me. I looked at her face with the morning sun shining on it and saw that she was still an extraordinarily beautiful women in spite of her presently semi hysterical condition. Her loyalty to me was now unquestionable and she was a lot of fun to have around. If I was going to have a companion for the rest of this charade she might as well be the one.

    Don Henley was playing Jones Beach for the Labor Day weekend. I could think of no better way to end the abased eighties than to hear Henley perform Building the Perfect Beast. It had been their anthem now it would be my eulogy. There were thousands of people at the concert, but I was probably the only one that knew what he was talking about when he boasted that they knew the secrets of eternity, they had found the lock and turned the key. As a sly aside he said Pandora's not going to like it. All I could think to myself was if you're going to open Pandora's Box you better know what's inside. Henley went on with his salutation; the day had come, soon he would be released, hallelujah they were building the Perfect Beast. I wondered where he was getting his information. He had better find a new source. I guessed those were heady days a few years ago when that song was written. Now that we had finished abasing the eighties we had finished ourselves in the process. The eighties were so abased that marriage vows before consummation was never even an option. If I had told Dianne we had to get married before we could have sex she would have thought me insane for real. Henley finished his tome by saying that they were going to take Olympus in an all or nothing attempt. No doubts the Titans would strike back but where did they think they were going without Hecate, nine out of ten times in chess when you lose your queen you've lost the game.

    When we got back from Jones Beach that night Andrew called the two Arab attendants in the Seven Eleven next door to my apartment complex Sand Niggers. One of the Arabs responded by pulling a pistol. I was outside the store, so I didn't see it but when I heard about it I went to go get my AR15. I figured shooting an Arab for no real reason had worked for Camus's character in The Stranger and it would work for me too. On the way back to the apartment a drunken Geir slipped on the wet grass and started trying to swim through it. The moment of levity diffused my homicidal intentions.

Late that night when everybody left Michelle and I went into Cypress Hills and got an 'eight ball.' When we got back we had an expensive bottle of vodka lying around and hours before the dawn. When daylight began to show through our window Lilith was with us and she seemed more powerful than she ever had before. Michelle was in a complete trance almost half her hair was standing up on end. Shadows appeared all over the walls, everywhere you looked. They began to move around the room with great rapidity independent of the wall. When I started feeling hands all over me I began to feel threatened and I was in no mood to run. I went into a red out. The next thing I remember is blasting away at them with the sounds of the gunshots ringing in my ears.

When I came too in the emergency room there was a cop there who looked a lot like some old pictures of a grandfather I had never met, my mother's father. He was a high-ranking Free Mason, the only mason in my family. In the operating room I was refusing the blood transfusions that the doctors told me were necessary for my survival. I kept saying "no just let me die. Why bother? I'll be going to jail for life. How many people did I hit?" The cop kept telling me in a soothing voice that I didn't hit anyone and that I would get off with a couple of years. There seemed to be this bright light behind him, and he was soaked in my blood. He finally convinced me to take the hospitals blood. I never saw that cop again. From recovery they wheeled me up to my room in a gurney accompanied by four cops. The elevator stopped on the way up and Dianne got on. She was dressed in a nurse's uniform. She asked the orderly how I was doing. He told her I was stabilized then she looked at me and said, "everything is going to be alright I'll be right on the next floor." She got off on the floor right below the one they were taking me. The lighting around her seemed unnaturally bright and I watched the elevator door close behind her. I tried to call out to her, but I was unable to speak. As Jimmy Carroll had said "my lips were chained they were filled with empty wonder."

Epilogue / אין סוף

From Stony Brook Hospital I would be transferred to Central Suffolk Hospital where 'inexplicably' enough I was given conjugal visits with Michelle even though we weren't married. When I got out a few weeks later I learned the Hebrew names of God. My uncle, as scared of me as everybody else by then, backed out of the deal for the Crazy Clown and bought a yogurt store with Andrew and became a Muslim because of a dream he had about me. Richey ended up letting Mark buy the Crazy Clown, but Mark would never get to enjoy it. He was shot dead in the parking lot before he was there a year. The yogurt store also went belly up in a year. I was in a wheel chair for months and Michelle moved me to a nice apartment complex in East Islip right around the block from Kenny's old place. John continued to terrorize Long Island's underworld, but I got the impression it was for the same reason he had hit that cop way back in Harlem. He ended up throwing his list of twenty-five dancers in the garbage because Richey bought him dinner. But that was only after a panicked Joey Massera called me hysterically ranting that Phil and John were stalking him. They had theatrically stuck a knife in a note on the bar of the Tender Trap demanding an audience with him. I told him there was nothing I could do since I was in a wheel chair and they were outside watching my front door. I said "if you want to find them you could just come over and knock on my door. The other day Bobby came over and knocked. By the time Michelle got to the door Bobby was already in Phil's trunk. Why don't you talk to him when he gets out of the hospital?" The grand total in unsolved homicides ended up around five. For anyone who thinks this wasn't real, think again. There are municipal records and witness's who can verify practically everything I said in this story.

  Ten years later Phil would remember he had forgotten to kill Richey who was by then one of the wealthiest men on Long Island. Richey employed me to be his 'bodyguard.' I was in the process of getting a divorce from Michelle and Wolf handled it pro bono. I was given free rein in the Café Royale, Richey's new mega strip club and for a while I ran the Café Royale in the same manner in which I had run Bogart's and Gaslight. I saw Dianne again when she jumped into the back of a car I was in at the Café Royale. She still looked good. She was no longer dancing and from what I heard was being passed around from strip club owner to strip club owner. She said she just wanted to see me. Then she abruptly got out of the car and left calling me a crazy bastard over her shoulder. I didn't care by then, or at least I thought I didn't. I was again, as Jimmy Carroll once said, "Worshipping devils and strangers in bed."

  But the strangest part of the whole thing was that when I had met my new Devil; Maria Davila (I shit you not), who was calling herself Julie at the time. She was sleeping with Richie. It was a rare excursion out of his fortified bay front mansion and Richie was locked in the VIP room of the Café Royale with her and her best friend Lisa V. I was standing outside the door of the VIP room with my pistol shoved into the waist band of my thousand-dollar suit. Richie kept coming in and out getting drinks from the main bar because he was too lazy to pour his own in the VIP room. He was sweatier each time he came out and about the third trip he had his shirt off, sweating profusely. I said, "Richey if you don't let me in there you're not going to have to worry about Phil killing you because I'm going to right now." It was an offer he couldn't refuse as they say. When I went in I met 'Julie' a Cuban Santeria princess of breathtaking beauty. Her friend Lisa V was a tall statuesque blond who worked as an entertainment director on a cruise ship when she wasn't striping. She wasn't far behind Julie in looks. Nobody was wearing very many cloths and from the way Julie was looking at my body and the way I was looking at hers I knew I was going to have a torrid affair with her. But at the time Richey wasn't sharing and he was telling everybody he was going to marry her. I took Lisa V back to her apartment down the block in West Babylon as a consolation prize and told Richey to stay in the bar till I got back. We got some coke and got kinky. I looked out the window a few times to make sure Phil wasn't dogging me and Lisa said "don't worry nobody ever comes around this place. Nobody knows where it is. I got it from another stripper named Dianne Rodney."

    At the time I didn't realize just how inevitable this thing between Dianne and me is. On an incoming tide a wave breaks on the beach and the water wash's back and breaks on the beach again with the next wave. Souls are the same way. Dianne isn't going anywhere, just like she said. And the tide is coming in now. Just like Milton said in Paradise Lost "I'll be back."

Citations
Forward Citations
1- "The Long Island Serial Killer – Uncaught Psychopath Terrorizing NY (Crime Documentary) (0:16)." https://www.cbsnews.com/news/48-hours-uncovers-missing-escort-shannan-gilberts-final-minutes/
2– Ibid: whole episode.
Body Citations
1 - C.G., Jung and R.F.C. Hull (translator). "The Mercurial Fountain." The Psychology of the Transference . Princeton, N.J.: Bollingen Series / Princeton University Press, 1966. 41. Print.
2 – Ibid, "King and Queen" 50.

3 – Ibid, "Immersion in the bath." 80.
4 – Ibid, "The Conjunction." 85.
5 - INXS. "INXS - Devil Inside." YouTube. INXS 12/26/2012, 1988. Web. https://www.youtube.com/watch?v=hv_zJrO_ptk
6 - Cannon, Joseph. "George W. Bush, Barbara Bush, and Aleister Crowley." CANNONFIRE. 1 Apr 2006. Web. https://cannonfire.blogspot.com/2006/04/george-w-bush-barbara-bush-and.html
7 - "Death." The Psychology of the Transference. 95.
8 - Ibid, "The ascent of the soul." 105.
9 – Ibid, "Purification." 111.
10 – Ibid, "Return of the Soul." 121.
11 – Ibid, "The New Birth." 144.
12 - Yeats, William Butler. "The Second Coming." Michael Robartes and The Dancer. 2001 Blackmask Online., 1921. Web. http://www.public-library.uk/ebooks/109/37.pdf
13 – Ibid.
14 – Ibid.
15 – Yeats, William Butler. The Wind Among the Reeds . Google Books, 1899. 45. Web.
16 - Yeats, William Butler. "Solomon and the Witch." Michael Robartes and The Dancer.
17 – Ibid.
18 – Ibid.
19 – Ibid.
20 - "George W. Bush, Barbara Bush, and Aleister Crowley."
21 – Ibid.
22 - "Return of the Soul." The Psychology of the Transference. 141.

www.ingramcontent.com/pod-product-compliance
Lightning Source LLC
LaVergne TN
LVHW020925090426
835512LV00020B/3212